Technology, Industrial Conflict and the Development of Technical Education in 19th-Century England

Modern Economic and Social History Series

General Editor: Derek H. Aldcroft

Titles in this series include:

Studies in the Interwar European Economy
Derek H. Aldcroft

Whatever Happened to Monetarism?
Economic Policy-Making and Social Learning in the United Kingdom since 1979
Michael J. Oliver

Disillusionment or New Opportunities?
The Changing Nature of Work in Offices, Glasgow 1880–1914
R. Guerriero Wilson

Raleigh and the British Bicycle Industry:
An Economic and Business History, 1870–1960
Roger Lloyd-Jones and M. J. Lewis

Battles for the Standard:
Bimetallism and the Spread of the Gold Standard, 1870–1914
Edward R. Wilson

The British Footwear Industry
Peter R. Mounfield

Trade Unions and the Economy, 1870–2000
Derek H. Aldcroft and Michael J. Oliver

The British Electronics Industry:
Innovation, Markets and Performance, 1930–97
John F. Wilson

The Seaside, Health and the Environment since 1850
John Hassan

Exchange Rate Regimes and Economic Policy in the Twentieth Century
edited by Ross Catterall and Derek H. Aldcroft

The Skilled Compositor, 1850–1914: An Aristocrat among Working Men
Patrick Duffy

Technology, Industrial Conflict, and the Development of Technical Education in 19th-Century England

B. P. CRONIN

Ashgate

Aldershot • Burlington USA • Singapore • Sydney

© Bernard Cronin, 2001

All rights reserved. No part of this publication may be reproduced, stored in a retrieval system, or transmitted in any form or by any means, electronic, mechanical, photocopying, recording or otherwise without the prior permission of the publisher.

Bernard Cronin has asserted his moral right under the Copyright, Designs and Patents Act, 1988, to be identified as the author of this work.

Published by
Ashgate Publishing Limited
Gower House
Croft Road
Aldershot
Hants GU11 3HR
England

Ashgate Publishing Company
131 Main Street
Burlington
Vermont, 05401–5600
USA

Ashgate website: http://www.ashgate.com

British Library Cataloguing in Publication Data

Cronin, B.P.
  Technology, Industrial Conflict and the Development of Technical Education in
  19th-Century England. – (Modern Economic and Social History Series)
  1. Technical institutes—England—History—19th century. 2. Technical
  education—England—History—19th century. I. Title.
  607.1'142

US Library of Congress Cataloging in Publication Data

Cronin, B.P. (Bernard P.)
  Technology, Industrial Conflict and the Development of Technical Education in
  19th-Century England / B.P. Cronin.
     p.   cm. – (Modern Economic and Social History Series)
  Includes bibliographical references.
  1. Technological innovations—Social aspects—England—19th century. 2.
  Technical education—England—19th century   I. Title. II. Series.
T173.8C75 2001
303.48'3'094209034–dc21

00–054340

ISBN 0 7546 0313 X

This book is printed on acid free paper.

Typeset by Manton Typesetters, Louth, Lincolnshire, UK.

**Printed and bound by Athenaeum Press, Ltd.,
Gateshead, Tyne & Wear.**

Contents

List of figures, boxes and tables	ix
Preface	xi
Abbreviations	xiv
Introduction	1
1 Nineteenth-century machine tools: the work of Maudslay, Nasmyth and Whitworth	11
2 The interaction of work and technology: the influence of F. W. Taylor and H. Braverman	40
3 Technology, changing definitions of skill and the use of child labour	72
4 Skill and the collapse of the craft apprentice system	98
5 Employers and the ideology of engineering management: the Great Strike of 1897–8 and its aftermath	124
6 Contradictions and struggle in ideas about a national system of technical education	162
7 Employers, the foundation of the City and Guilds of London Institute and government legislation	195
8 Industrial conflict and 19th-century technical and educational change	233
References and Bibliography	257
Index	291

Modern Economic and Social History Series
General Editor's Preface

Economic and social history has been a flourishing subject of scholarly study during recent decades. Not only has the volume of literature increased enormously but the range of interest in time, space and subject matter has broadened considerably so that today there are many sub-branches of the subject which have developed considerable status in their own right.

One of the aims of this new series is to encourage the publication of scholarly monographs on any aspect of modern economic and social history. The geographical coverage is world-wide and contributions on non-British themes will be especially welcome. While emphasis will be placed on works embodying original research, it is also intended that the series should provide the opportunity to publish studies of a more general and thematic nature which offer a reappraisal or critical analysis of major issues of debate.

Derek H. Aldcroft

Manchester Metropolitan University

List of figures, boxes and tables

Figures

1.1	A typical straight-edge lathe tool (left hand)	14
2.1	Two views of the standard ⅞" tool used in most of the cutting trials by F. W. Taylor	45

Boxes

1.1	Example of a calculation carried out by a machinist in setting up a machine for cutting a screw thread	16
1.2	The principle of 'idling time'	35
3.1	Comparisons of wages earned and production increases under the premium system	85

Tables

1.1	Common 19th-century steels	13
1.2	Machine handling time for a Betts horizontal boring mill	21
2.1	Chemical composition and tensile strength of materials used in cutting trials by F. W. Taylor, 1894–1906	44
2.2	Chemical composition and cutting speeds of tool steels showing inclusion of molybdenum and later vanadium, based on Taylor's experiments	49
2.3	The effect of high-speed steel on metal-removing performance	52
2.4	Experiments carried out with rapid-cutting tools in England, 1903	54
3.1	A typical workshop time schedule for three typical machining processes, using a premium system of payment	84
3.2	An example of earnings under the premium system, based on boring out a 10-inch cast iron pump	85
3.3	The differential piece-rate system: an example	89
6.1	Actual expenditure on education and science in Britain, 1871–1880	169
6.2	The Mechanical Engineer and Machinist: a three-year course (J. Scott-Russell)	173
7.1	Extent and distribution of institutes of technical education in Britain, 1878	202

7.2	Numbers of day and evening-class students in selected German and English towns in 1900	206
7.3	Membership of the Royal Commission on Technical Instruction, 1881–1884	211

Preface

My first contact with the kind of workers and machines mentioned in this book was as a young fitter-machinist apprentice. Squeaky-clean in my embarrassingly new overalls, I felt like a fish out of water as I waited at the machine shop entrance for the foreman to direct me to where I was to begin work. It seemed an awful, cacophonous place of clattering countershafts, with slapping leather belts driving the stepped cones of what I came to know as centre lathes. Apart from the unaccustomed din there was an all-pervading smell of oils, machine lubricants and coolants and an acrid taste of metals, steel and brass, mingling with the hazy dust of cast iron being machined.

It was here that I soon came to meet much older workers, some apprentices during the First World War, whose fathers had actually been part of the great engineering strike and lockout of 1897. I was to learn that over 25,000 engineering workers were involved in that crippling dispute. During breaks and lunchtimes, as we sat on boxes located near the machines, or, if one was privileged, in the smiths' forge during the winter, they often recalled the past. They spoke with evident pride of earlier days, characterised by order and discipline in the workshops, when one could identify the foreman as the man with the watch-chain stretched across a waistcoat, wearing a bowler hat.

Some were approaching retirement, having spent 40 years in what seemed to me at that time a grinding, relentless occupation working with unyielding materials which demanded high levels of manual skills, dexterity and stamina. They were proud of their ability to work with speed and, more importantly, precision. But the exhausted faces of some of them reflected the years of toil in an uncompromising industrial environment. I was struck by the regularity with which they referred to their lives as artisans, particularly the struggles to maintain their status and their insistence that they were not labourers – despite the fact that they were on obvious good terms with the unskilled helpers in the workshops. As I recall, they never referred to themselves as 'aristocrats of labour', as writers such as the Webbs had done. However, they clearly had a profound sense of being part of a community of skilled artisans, whose lives has been shaped by a common purpose, producing engineering products in which they could take pride, and maintaining solidarity in the struggle against skill dilution.

In time I came to recognise a more trenchant fact: that they were part of a class of men whose lives had been, more or less, completely dominated by work. Many, not all, had left school at 14 or even earlier, and had never been able to gain access to further education. It was not lack of interest or motivation, or ineptitude (they were producing machines of high precision, worth thousands of pounds, at times on antiquated tools). They were expected to, and could, with few exceptions, interpret and realise in the finished product, complex machine drawings in First and Third Angle projection. They understood and appreciated the skill required by those in management and the drawing offices. They harboured no grievance against management per se; neither did they embody anti-intellectualism or antagonism to theory. But I realised much later that they inherited an educational legacy from the previous century which had formalised the separation of what has been called mental and manual labour.

The opportunities for post-school education had been limited by a number of factors, not least of which were constraints of time; most men were working 47 to 50 hours a week. Courses at appropriate levels and at times compatible with their work commitments were simply not available to them. In the event, not a single man of the previous generation, in the five workshops of the company, had received any technical education.

My apprentice colleagues and I were more fortunate. One day per week we were allowed to attend the local technical college where, alongside apprentices from other companies, we attempted to get to grips with the National Certificate course in Mechanical Engineering. We were part of the post-Second World War kindling of educational and industrial ideals. Not that ideologies figured largely in our lives. But I had been influenced by my contact with that older generation of artisans and came, later in life, to attempt to understand why men of manifest intelligence and high practical skills had been so clearly disadvantaged. What is there about an industrial and economic system that allows work to be so pervasive as to relegate other aspects of men's lives to a second order? Were these machinists and fitters really unable to cope with the theories and models common in engineering practice? What patterns of technical education had been developed in the previous century that has such a profound effect upon the education of several generations of skilled engineering workers?

My own five-year apprenticeship completed, I became liable for National Service, after which I decided to train as a teacher. During a further course at the University of London my interest in technical education was reactivated and I decided to undertake research in this area. I had come to realise that some of the answers to the questions I had pondered regarding technical education, particularly for workers as opposed to management, were to be found in an analysis of provisions made in the previous century. Preliminary reading suggested that there was a link between the implementation of new technologies in the 19th century, such as self-acting machine tools and developments in metallurgy, and the response of engineering employers to pleas for support for technical education. This book is the result of the subsequent research.

My early attempts to structure ideas into a coherent form are due in no small measure to a number of helpful people who are not engineers, particularly

Michael F. D. Young, to whom I owe a special debt of gratitude, Rachel Parry, Alf Holt and Grenville Wall. Their sociological and philosophical insights heightened my awareness of the social implications of science and technology. I have drawn much from the advice and constructive criticism of Geoff Dench and Ian Jamieson, without whom many of my ideas would have lain dormant. Responsibility for what appears here remains solely mine.

Locating relevant texts is a perennial problem and I am grateful for the advice and guidance I received from the Librarian and staff at Middlesex University; they saved long hours of library investigation. The Institution of Mechanical Engineers has a veritable mine of material in its archives and I am particularly indebted to the chief Librarian, Mr Morrison, and his staff for allowing me access to it. Similarly, I would like to thank the Engineering Employers Federation (EEF) for granting me facilities to use their archives. Two libraries have proved invaluable, the TUC library and the library of the AEUW, both of which contain unique material without which much of this narrative would not have been possible. The Public Record Office (PRO) has been especially useful for references on 19th-century education. No research in this area could be complete without the advantages afforded by the British Library; and I have been considerably helped by having access to its newspaper and periodical archives.

My thanks are also due to Brenda Jamieson for her patience in typing my early manuscripts. A special word of thanks must go to Bernie for her constant encouragement and for spending hours trying to unravel the convoluted structure of the early scripts and assisting in preparing them for presentation in an acceptable form for typing; without her this project would have remained unwritten.

B. P. Cronin
2000

List of Abbreviations

ASE	Amalgamated Society of Engineers
ATTI	Association of Teachers in Technical Institutes
BSW	British Standard Whitworth
EEF	Engineering Employers Federation
EITB	Engineering Industry Training Board
CGLI	City and Guilds of London Institute
HSS	high-speed steel
ICE	Institute of Civil Engineers
I.Mech.E.	Institution of Mechanical Engineers
ITEA	Iron Trades Employers' Association
LCC	London County Council
NAPTSE	National Association for the Promotion of Technical and Secondary Education
RC	Royal Commission
WMC & IU	Working Men's Club and Institute Union
WMEU	Working Men's Educational Union
WTES	Workmen's Technical Education Society

Introduction

This book offers an account of the emergence of non-university technical education and its development in England from the middle of the 19th century. The particular concern is technical education for manual workers, as distinct from education for management in industry.

There are three main propositions. First, in order to offer an explanation of the origin and development of technical education it is necessary to look beyond changes in educational policy. Second, the social and technological changes emanating from industrial conflict, particularly within the mechanical engineering industry throughout the 19th century, crucially influenced the development of technical education in the period from 1850. Third, analysis of struggles over the organisation of work is central to an understanding of the sequence of events which led up to the formation of a national system of technical education in the last decades of the 19th century.

The questions addressed focus on the interpenetration of changing tactics of managerial control of work and labour, and new technologies, particularly the use of interchangeable manufacture.

Technical educational and technological developments

There is an attempt to move away from a reliance upon consensual models of 19th-century social and technological development. Much has been written on this, articulated principally in terms of educational policy and/or the significance of influential policy-makers. There is also a pervasive notion of technical education as an evolutionary growth out of the general education system. The objective here is to examine the nature of industrial employer–employee interaction with technical education. The development of technology has been characterised by analyses of the work and influence of the great Victorian engineers, in the mould of 'heroic biography'. Predominant in this work has been the contribution of the great engineers such Maudslay, Nasmyth, and Whitworth in advancing more sophisticated forms of technological hardware. Thus this tradition stresses the innovative and creative genius of 18th-century and Victorian engineer-entrepreneurs. Prominent also is analysis of the effects of introducing interchangeable manufacture, 'standards' and labour substitution. This approach may be found in work across a wide spectrum of perspectives, e.g. Clapham (1938), Cotgrove (1958, 1968), Ashworth (1963) Ashby (1965), Musgrave (1966, 1967), Chadwick (1965), Steeds (1970), Cardwell (1972a), Checkland (1972), Woodbury (1972), Ackrill (1987), Goss (1988)

In the present book, the focus is directed first to the conflictual nature of control over new technologies, particularly machine tools, from the mid-19th century, and second to the relation between technological innovations and social transformations such as radical changes in the control of labour, and the possible implications for the development of technical education. The attitudes and beliefs of powerful and influential groups outside education, with strong vested interests in the development of technical education, are recognised and examined.

Among these groups were employers, such as engineering employers, who controlled large numbers of young workers, towards whom 19th-century technical education was to be directed. Employers were clearly concerned with issues of labour control and work organisation. A different model of educational and technical change is put forward here which identifies and articulates a connection between the employers' concerns with work organisation and the way their views influenced the development of technical education.

Precision measurement and manufacturing: the key to employers' control of the labour process

A major focus of this book is therefore on the development of technical education in the context of the implementation of 19th-century machine tool technologies, central to which was the demise of craft skill characterised by control over methods of precision measurement. The implications for technical education from mid-century of radical changes in the recognition and definition of 'skill' form an essential part of the analysis. This also provides a model of technological development which highlights those elements of craft practice identified by writers such as Braverman as targets for deskilling, thus stressing the significance of employer–employee work interaction. As Piore and Sabel (1984) argued, 'the success of mass production (and *the concomitant decline of craft production*) ... lies in the *politically-defined interests of producers and consumers* – rather than in the logic of industrial efficiency ... ' (p. 21) (my emphasis). Nineteenth-century artisan skills were embedded in a specific set of production relations, and derived credibility from a particular structure of management and organisation. Definitions of skill therefore depended not on a priori categorisation of attributes of human performance or labelling, but more significantly on the interdependence of work and technology. The nature of the relations between the employers' ideology of production and the workers' perception of skill and work organisation is the key to an explanation of these events from mid-century.

The notion of 'scientific management'

Central to analyses of the decline of traditional craft skills has been the notion of 'scientific management'. Theories have emphasised control of the labour process as contingent upon an increasing division of labour, standardisation of work methods and 'enforced' workers' cooperation. These theories and the subsequent critiques are well documented, but they are often narrow in focus, barely penetrating the complex relation between definitive changes in technology and the deployment and control of labour. There are 'taken for granted' assumptions about the nature and deployment of technology and its relation to labour control. Innovatory technologies and changing production relations provided the social context of the unique quality of 19th-century manufacturing technologies, which, in effect, had changed little since the Middle Ages. The 19th-century technological revolution – for the work of Joseph Whitworth and the American engineer F. W. Taylor was revolutionary – was paralleled by a new ideology of production in which the idea of the manufacturing workshop as a source of technical learning became redundant. This ideology not only accelerated the demise of the craft apprenticeship system but further handicapped the faltering attempts at the formation of a technical education system.

The issues of labour control within the 19th-century productive process can be linked to control over incipient technical education, a common element in both being the influence of the employers. Consensual models of English technical education are thus challenged and the conflictual nature of social relations both in industry and education acknowledged.

The origin of technical education

The historiography of English technical education has been burdened with two common misconceptions: that it was a factor in the growth of 19th-century mass education in general; and that there was a discernible technical education 'movement'. Typically, much emphasis has been focused upon the movement after the 1870 Act, the formation of the City and Guilds of London Institute (CGLI) in 1878, the Royal Commission on Technical Instruction in 1884, followed by the Technical Instruction Act of 1889 (Clapham 1938, Argles 1964, Armytage 1964, Musgrave 1967, Bailey 1983).

These events were clearly significant, but much of this work implies that they were the only critical influences and developments in technical education operating at the time. This notion is paralleled by unqualified approval of the significance of 19th-century figures, such as Lyon Playfair, J. S. Russell and T. H. Huxley, who promoted the idea of technical education as a means of improving industrial 'efficiency' to counter foreign competition (Clapham 1938, Musgrave 1967, Ashworth 1963, Checkland 1972).

Craft apprenticeship as distinct from technical education

The industrial or craft apprenticeship system was a form of technical education in relation to which new forms of technical education were to be developed. Technical education, as perceived by those for whom it was intended, the workers, was not merely a system of theoretical training instituted as an adjunct to practical work carried on in the workshops. In the separation of theoretical and practical elements in a definition of technical education, unquestioned importance is given to the former.

The separation from the workplace of formal institutionalised education which came to supplement and virtually replace the apprenticeship system as the dominant form of technical education and training in the 19th century requires explanation. Examination of the relation between changes in work organisation and structure is therefore relevant to an analysis of the development of technical education.

Employers' influence in technical education

From the mid-19th century employers sought to widen their control of the labour process, often against the resistance of the skilled workers. The struggle for control, part of the gradual domination over all forms of labour, and the emergence of skilled workers' demands for technical education characterised industrial relations from the 1860s.

The 'efficient' operation of new machines, deployed from the 1860s, was premised upon the substitution of untrained workers for skilled artisans (Whitworth 1854, 1856, 1876; Nasmyth 1854, 1868). This process of substitution had two crucial effects. It lessened the employers' dependence upon skilled craft labour and encouraged the devaluation by employers of the traditional method of producing skilled tradesmen through the apprenticeship system. The first of these propositions accords with the conventional wisdom; the second challenges recent views, exemplified in writers such as Goss (1988), which argue that the managers' control over new technologies served to gain flexibility and increase productivity, not to decompose skilled labour: 'the exercise of managerial prerogatives was not used to deskill craft work ... [but] to raise productivity and this not only broadened the range of skills held by craft workers but also gave an increase in wage levels and shorter working hours ... ' (p. 419). Unofficial and official sources, such as the Children's Commission of 1864 and the Commission on the Depression of Trade in 1886, show this contention to be questionable.

Issues arising from the critical mid-century swing from artisan to management control of the process of production highlight the broader effects of the implementation of new kinds of technologies, such as precision measurement and gauging, and automatic machines. The related changes in the system of power relations in the industry centred on the decline of the apprenticeship system.

The apprenticeship and work organisation

Nineteenth-century engineering artisans consistently challenged the increasing use of substitution in the workshops. This resistance mainly took the form of demands for the retention of the apprenticeship system. These workers were virtually alone in also arguing, formally from 1868 when the first Trades Union Congress debated the issue, that artisan apprenticeship was central to a system of technical education. Many of the conflicts in 19th-century manufacturing industry directly concerned, or were related to, questions of what constituted skilled labour and the decline of the apprenticeship system. Employers' and workers' attitudes towards changes in the reorganisation of work patterns framed their respective perception of technical education.

The gradual and irreversible transfer of control of work from a predominantly artisan-controlled system to one involving employer-dominated technology marked a weakening of the artisans' traditional responsibility for the training of young workers. For most of the century the apprenticeship system was the only viable form of technical education. Thus the transfer of work control from workers to management from the middle of the century was related to changes in the mode of technical education; it symbolised a transfer of control of technical education.

What underlay changes in the system of power relations in the workshops as the structure of work control altered? In addressing this question the focus will be on the conflicts between employers and workers engendered by the struggle over the control of immediate productive processes and how they were expressed in the social and technical elements of the organisation of work. The forces underlying the development and implementation of new kinds of machine were also those at work in the demise of craft apprenticeship and the development of technical education.

The interaction between forms of technology, the organisation of work and the development of technical education highlights the significance of industrial employers, particularly engineering employers and skilled workers, in the origin and development of English technical education. The central thesis of the book therefore moves from further considerations of the ideas and influence of 19th-century educational policy-makers, and an acceptance of linear, evolutionary models of technological development. The critical importance of the mechanical engineering industry in the transformation of 19th-century industrial work and the reshaping of the concept of craft trade training is central and its significance cannot be overestimated.

The importance of the 19th-century mechanical engineering industry

The analysis of the transformation of 19th-century work is limited to the mechanical engineering industry for three reasons.

First, the mechanical engineering industry was the principal manufacturing industry throughout the 19th century and one of the leading industrial employers of skilled and unskilled labour. The first census of production shows evidence of this: the total gross value of goods produced in the UK recorded at the time of the census in 1907 was £1.76bn, of which over 21 per cent, was generated by mechanical engineering trades. Between 1851 and 1911 the engineering trades were in the top three single employers, second only to agriculture in 1851; by 1911 nearly 1.5m workers were employed in the industry (First Census of Production (1907); British Labour Statistics, 1868–1968 (1971)). It therefore seems appropriate to seek evidence within this major manufacturing industry regarding the attitude of leading employers towards the development of technical education from 1850.

Second, the industry was also the locus for the two most direct confrontations between unionised labour and employers in the 19th century, in 1852 and 1897. Particular emphasis in Chapter 8 below is on the strike and lockout of 1897.

The 1897 dispute was highly significant, for reasons other than the overtly economic and political. It threw into relief the attitudes of skilled workers and their employers towards technical education and the apprenticeship system. The strike also highlighted clear divergent interests on the part of government and employers regarding future provision of skilled labour. The government's putative aim for a national policy of technical education, implying long-term projections, contradicted its encouragement of individual employers seeking to satisfy short-term profits within a free-market policy. The successful outcome of the strike for employers served to reinforce their belief in economic 'short-termism'.

Third, the mechanical engineering industry in the 18th and 19th centuries was fragmented and characterised by the small firm. The structural position clearly had implications for work organisation and control; as Zeitlin (1987) says, 'British employers' labour strategies were also conditioned by the institutional organization of their firms ... most sectors of British industry were dominated by fragmented, family-owned firms ... (p. 174). Changing industrial relations, certainly from 1852, the year of the first major engineering industry strike, generated slow but substantive moves towards combination by employers. One of their main concerns was constraining the artisans' power in the workshops. As struggles over power relations between the engineering employers and the workers intensified from mid-century, the Engineering Employers Federation (EEF) concomitantly emerged. Thus by the time of the great strike of 1897, the largest engineering union, the Amalgamated Society of Engineers (ASE), was confronted by a forceful employers' combination which had not existed in strength before the strike.

Critical unintended consequences followed the engineering employer-employee conflicts leading up to and during the strike and lockout of 1897-8, not the least of which was the employers' lack of enthusiasm for the traditional apprenticeship system and its historical status a form of technical education. Evidence concerning the strike suggests that ideas about technical training and education often found expression in these employers' and workers' combinations and are an unexplored source of data on the principles underlying the early stages of the development of technical education.

Control of the labour process and technical education

Engineering employers, as principal buyers of labour power, were clearly concerned with the process by which it was reproduced. ('Labour power' is used in the sense of a capacity to work for a given period of time, and it was this potential for work that was 'bought' and 'sold'.) Throughout the period the maintenance of current production needs dominated employer strategies; planning future skilled labour requirements increasingly became a low priority. Production time was fundamental for employers and other considerations, among them education for young workers, were secondary (Nasmyth 1854, Robinson 1868, Royal Commission on Poor Laws and Relief of Distress (1909b). An explanation of the emergence of English technical education has to acknowledge the interests and purposes of those groups who controlled 'technical labour power' for a great part of the time.

The principle of part-time technical education became firmly established in the 19th century for ideological as well as pragmatic reasons. It reflected the employers' uncompromising insistence on young workers completing a full working week to meet the demands of production.

This proposition is at variance with a perception of part-time technical education as a means of vertical mobility for workers in Victorian Britain:

> an essential ingredient in the British approach to [technical education] ... which had to base its appeal on personal motivation ... of the employees who were anxious to improve themselves ... was that technical schools were a successful means ... of obtaining promotion ... (Floud 1985: 92).

Even from its inception the part-time system was subject to constant criticism because of its heavy demands on young workers. As late as 1935, the Association of Teachers in Technical Institutes (ATTI) was pressing the Board of Education to make even the part-time element of technical education compulsory, a policy that had still not been implemented by 1983 (Horn and Horn 1983). Firms were not interested in the education of their employees; a few conceded that the part-time system had some merit, but only insofar as it did not intrude into production time.

Changes in the organisation of work included the substitution of unskilled labour for skilled artisans. The skilled workers' resistance to dilution centred on the apprenticeship system, generating conflicts which encroached upon wider issues such as the place of technical education in an overall production system. Retention of the apprentice system became the centrepiece of the artisans' demands for a viable technical education system.

After the defeat in the first national engineering strike in 1852 artisans were confronted by the introduction of new technologies and new strategies of labour control, against which they were to prove to have little, if any, defence. Against this background the demise of the apprenticeship system was accelerating, with employers displaying a declining interest in projecting skilled labour requirements as long as the existing system was perceived as meeting current needs. The employers' interest, however, was maintained in changing the configuration of the labour process by radically modifying the conditions governing the pattern of craft-trade training and influencing the structure of incipient development in technical education. They strongly resisted demands made by the artisans for a retention of traditional craft training and any pattern of technical education directly related to it.

The precedence for working-class interest in education, other than as a 'provided' system, may be traced back to the Sunday school system in the previous century (Laqueur 1977, Joyce 1980). The artisans' first formal initiatives in technical education in the 19th century paralleled the work of the Artisans' Institutes, an offshoot of the Workingman's Club and Institute Union. The first TUC Congress in 1868 passed a motion calling for the inauguration of a system of technical education and for apprenticeship to be recognised as central to any such system (TUC Congress Minutes 1868).

These kinds of initiatives, however, embodied tensions and contradictions, the main source of which was the insistence of the skilled workers on negotiating with employers independently of unskilled workers. They also sought support from certain public figures from the employer class, such as Lord Elcho (Lord Wemyss), who, at best, was ambivalent concerning workers' combinations. Their relationship with leading scientists such as Lyon Playfair and Thomas Huxley was also to prove less enduring as their conflict with employers intensified towards the end of the century. The long-term interests of the skilled working class, the focus of which was the apprenticeship system as an essential feature of technical education, were undermined by the damaging conflicts generated by craft dilution.

In the manufacturing industry it was to the employers' short-term advantage to encourage unskilled workers to man new, 'foolproof' machines, which reflected the emerging ideology of production based on revolutionary innovations in technology and metallurgy. Nineteenth-century developments in mechanical engineering transformed the means of production, and irrevocably eroded the autonomy of the artisan class.

The mechanical engineering industry in the latter half of the 19th century

The combination movement in industrial enterprises in the final quarter of the 19th century affected a relatively small but significant part of the entire range of British industry (Payne 1967). One of the largest general engineering employers and a leading EEF spokesman, Sir Benjamin Browne, distinguishing the large and small firm, proposed as a criterion a company's ability to pay compensation: 'If you define the large and small employers a men who can or who cannot pay heavy compensation claims without feeling them, I think you might say that more than two-thirds of the working class work for small employers' (RC on Poor Laws, 1909b).

Two mechanical engineering companies were represented in the top 52 large companies by 1905, Vickers Maxim and Armstrong Whitworth which were ranked sixth and eleventh respectively (Payne 1967: 527, 539). (18 were in brewing and distilling and 10 in textiles – revealing an emphasis on the manufacture of consumer goods and British strength in textile production.) A different bias was evident in US manufacturing, where 37 companies of the top 52 were engaged in capital or producer goods as distinct from 13 engaged in consumer products.

Figures for the composition of the machine-tool industry at this time are not available from any official sources. One study using unofficial sources shows a relatively slow growth in the machine-tool industry in the period 1870–1913 in terms of the number of firms actually engaged in machine-tool production. Using commercially produced directories – *Kelly's Directory of Merchants, Manufacturers and Trades*, published annually from the 1890s – Floud (1976) catalogues this slow growth. Between 200 and 350 firms formed the industry in the 1870s and 1880s; the number grew to between 350 and 450 in the early 1900s, before a decline to around 250 between 1910 and 1913 (Floud: 32).

Statistics on the size of the firms are also fragmentary; different assumptions concerning the constitution of the 'firm' generate different figures. Generally, 19th-century machine-tool building was highly specialised and labour-intensive. Workforce size in industrial companies in the leading machine-tool companies appears from one authority's analysis to be atypical for the mechanical engineering industry as a whole (Saul 1967: 156). It was not uncommon for larger engineering companies to make their own machine tools. Sometimes these were also made to order for other engineering concerns.

Between 1842 and 1910 the average company workforce engaged in machine-tool construction in the UK was in the region of 650 persons. There were 19 principal companies engaged in this line of work of which 11 had 500 or fewer workers; and two with more than 1,500 employees (Greenwood & Batley, and Herbert of Coventry; see Saul 1967: 14). Economies of scale were becoming the norm in America in the early 1900s. The Allis Chalmers Company of Chicago employed 12,000 men in engineering in 1903. This figure was quoted by Barnes, the ASE secretary who visited this plant as a member of an Industrial Commission in October–December 1902. He noted the Armor School of Technology in Chicago, which at the time had 1,000 students engaged in engineering (Mosely Commission 1903: 58). The Westinghouse Company in Pittsbugh had a permanent workforce of 6,000 men; and the American Locomotive Company at Schenectady covered 62 acres and produced 35 locomotives a week, with a workforce of 10,000 (ibid., p. 14).

A more recent survey shows the predominance of the small engineering company in the sphere of general mechanical engineering in England, which would include machine-tool building. Of over 4,000 companies, 3,526 employed fewer than 25 persons; 44 employed between 400 and 999 persons; and 12 firms employed between 1,000 and 1,999 persons. There were 13 companies employing more than 2,000 persons by the 1960s (Digest of Statistical Information 1971: 47). The 19th-century trend of the small engineering firm has persisted well into the 20th century. The Engineering Industry Training Board (EITB), the coordinating body of technical training schemes in the engineering industry from 1964, covered 24,600 establishments. In 1981 it was reported that of these, 48.7 per cent employed fewer than 25 workers; only 2 per cent of firms had more than 1,000 employees; but over 40 per cent of the labour force worked in this 2 per cent of companies (Coombe Lodge Report 1981, 13, 14).

CHAPTER ONE

Nineteenth-century machine tools: the work of Maudslay, Nasmyth and Whitworth

The basis of the transformation of engineering processes

It is well documented that important changes in the technical mode of production were initiated in the 1850s, and earlier, by engineer-entrepreneurs such as Muir, Maudslay, Fairbairn, Nasmyth and Whitworth (Smiles 1876, Roe 1916, Clapham 1938, Chadwick 1958, Galloway 1958, Steeds 1970, Cardwell 1972, McGuffie 1986). Early technological innovations were also closely related to changing strategies of labour control, clearly illustrated by Whitworth's work on precision measurement and standards[1] in engineering and manufacturing production.

The deployment of innovatory machine tools and technological factors, exemplified by Whitworth's research into metrology, are conventionally perceived as evolutionary developments in new classes of machines and of new metrological precision. His technological innovations also entailed the reorganisation of technical and labour control in the workshops and may be realistically considered as significant factors in changing employer–employee relations and the reorganisation of work.

The standards of measurement and gauging, with which Whitworth was deeply engaged, were fundamental to the creation of new levels of workshop precision. An often neglected aspect of his pioneering work in this factor of production was his contribution to the decline of the apprenticeship system by encouraging the principle of substitution. This is not a denigration of his exemplary foresight in sponsoring the education of young engineers through the 'Whitworth Scholarships'. The decline of the apprenticeship system reflected the employers' increasing control over skilled labour and precision manufacture particularly, and a growing distrust of the craft apprenticeship form of training. There are important parallels to be drawn between the substitution of parts (interchangeability based on fixed standards of measurement) and the substitution of labour (part of the general process of 'de-skilling' of jobs and workers).

The specifics of engineering production, such as new techniques of precision measurement and control of rapid metal removal in cutting operations, were highly significant for employers in their attempts to control skilled labour. Any account of 19th-century technical change cannot be separated from analysis of the major employers' concern to transform the organisation of engineering work and extend their control over the planning and execution of the total labour process.

The machining of metals was a difficult and expensive process if accuracy was specified. Much depended upon the skill of the artisan and the basic design and structure of the machine tools. It was common up to the middle of the 19th century to view the self-activity of the skilled workers as autonomous, particularly in relation to the planning and execution of production processes. The artisan's traditional function of production control was increasingly curtailed by the employers' implementation and control of new technologies after the 1850s. There was thus enduring artisan resistance to management reorganisation of work.

Historically, skilled workers had demonstrated their 'indispensability' by working with speed and accuracy. In practice this meant that employers were forced to rely upon artisans to produce work to 'acceptable' tolerances in a manufacturing situation in which there were no universal standards governing levels of accuracy. The issue for management was to find strategies, and the technology, with which to replace essential artisan skills. Whitworth's insight was to recognise that employer dominance would always be undermined without control over machine-tool accuracy and production. His research into 'standards' clearly influenced subsequent technological developments, both in machine tools and metrology. Technical and social control of the workplace underwent fundamental changes, effecting changes beyond the workshop such as attitudes towards technical training, craft apprenticeships, and the employment of child labour generally, and the foundation of a formal and separate technical education system based predominantly on a part-time principle.

Apart from generalised workshop skills there were specific artisan attributes that extended beyond the banausic, the 'art' of engineering bridging the gap between science and the engineering product: 'The creative, constructive knowledge of the engineer is the knowledge needed to implement that "art"' (Vincenti 1990: 4). Two such skill elements were evident in the 19th-century workshop: a working knowledge of common metals used throughout the period; and a thorough understanding of the capabilities of a whole range of machine tools.

Common nineteenth-century materials used in engineering production

Maximum metal-cutting speeds depend mainly upon the material being cut and the metallurgical composition of the cutting tool. The principal material for cutting metals throughout the 19th century was plain carbon steel. The essential difference between cast iron, a common fabricating material of the period, and steel was the amount of carbon contained in the constituency of the metal. Pure iron, called ferrite, is a soft metal having a structure composed of crystals or grains. Cast iron contained approximately 92–4 per cent iron and about 3.5 per cent carbon, plus some small quantities of constituents such as silicon (2%), manganese (1%), sulphur (0.1%) and phosphorous (0.3–1.2%) (Chapman 1943: 12).

Steel is fundamentally an alloy of iron and carbon with the content of carbon varying from 0.1 up to a maximum of 2.5 per cent. If the carbon content is increased beyond this level, excess carbon is distributed throughout the material in the form of free graphite. Further increases would merge the metal into the group of metals termed the cast irons. Thus the crucial constituent in plain carbon steels was the presence of carbon up to about 1–2 per cent only. For a material to be classed as a steel there must be no free graphite (as in cast iron) in its composition. (*Spon's Dictionary* 1873: 2921). As a general guide the plain steels (as distinct from complex alloys, which were developed late in the nineteenth century) were classified according to their carbon content (see Table 1.1).

Table 1.1 Common 19th-century steels

Steel	% Carbon	Uses
dead mild	0.1–0.125	wire rod, sheets, tubes
mild	0.15–0.3	boiler plates, bridge work, drop forgings, general workshop use
medium carbon	0.3–0.5	axles, drop forgings, agricultural tools
	0.5–0.7	springs, locomotive tyres, hammers
high carbon	0.7–0.9	springs, shear blades, chisels
	0.9–1.1	press dies, punches, screwing dies, axes, picks
	1.1–1.4	razors, files, drills, gauges, metal-cutting tools

Source: Chapman (1943), p. 16.

Preparation and cutting sequence of metal-cutting tools

The geometry of metal-cutting tools and the cutting sequence of machine-tool operation would normally follow this pattern:

In order to remove surplus metal from the material being cut, the 'stock', the cutting tool was first forged by the machinist, that is, shaped from the raw metal in the blacksmith's fire. Then the basic tool shape was ground (shaped to size using a standard grinding or emery wheel) to produce the necessary

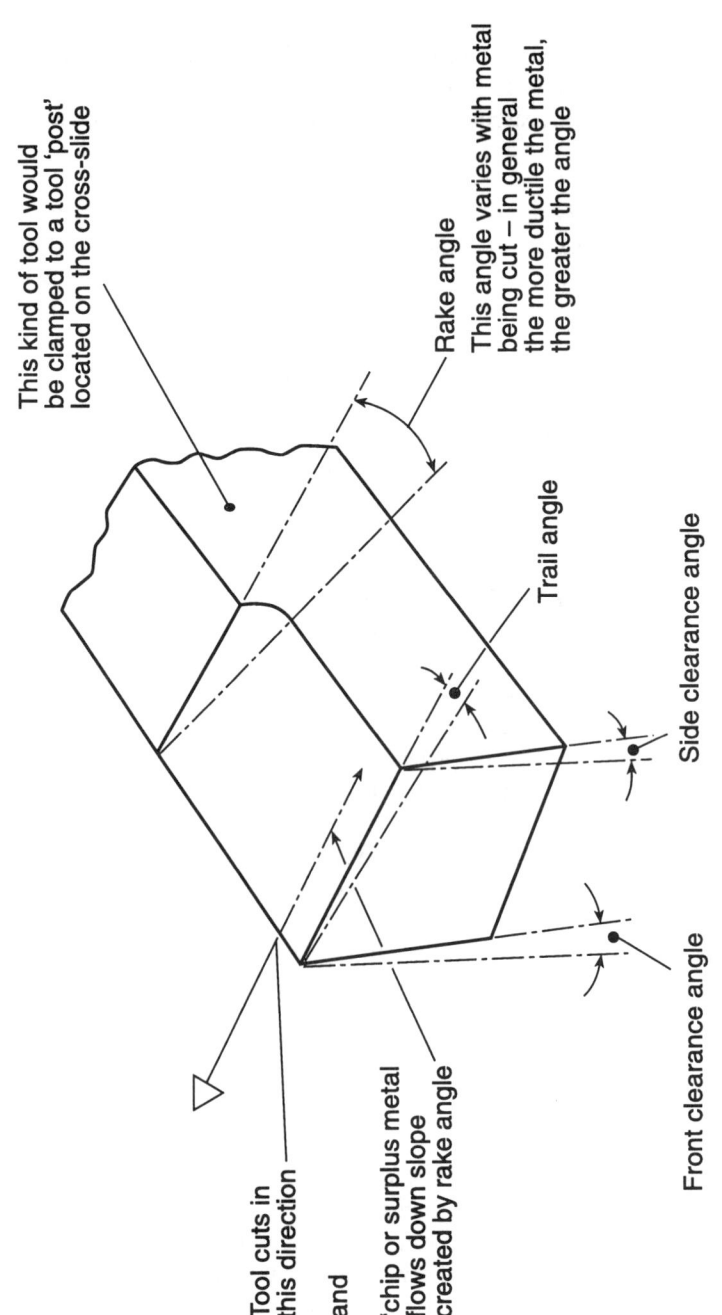

Fig. 1.1 A typical straight-edge lathe tool (left hand)

cutting angles (*Spon's dictionary* (1873), p. 2921). These angles vary according to the material being cut and the tool composition; in the period up to the late 1880s this tool material was known as plain carbon steel. The composition and metallurgical properties of this metal had a critical bearing on the rate at which various metals could be cut – the standard tool-preparation rule of the period was that the harder the material being machined, the greater the wedge angle and the smaller the clearance angle. The machinist was responsible for forming and maintaining the correct angles on the cutting tool; the main objective was to keep the tool edges sharp enough to slice through the metal, with a wedge angle sufficient to provide strength, and a minimum of clearance to prevent overheating from friction due to the cutting forces. Figure 1.1 shows the standard tool of the period.

It may be noted that, in general, the toughness, tenacity, and hardness of steel increase with the quantity of carbon it contains.

Apart from the cutting-tool angles, two other critical metal-cutting variables were determined by the machinist: the depth of cut (the amount of penetration into the workpiece by the cutting tool), and the feed rate (the amount the tool travels per revolution or 'pass'). Once these variables had been determined, the depth of cut (which depends upon material being cut and the cutting-tool material) was applied, often by use of a micrometer wheel, and an appropriate feed rate through the self-acting mechanism activated. This latter function employed the use of a lever to engage a nut housed in the saddle, carrying the slide rest, supporting the cutting tool, with the leadscrew driven by a gear train ('cogs' in mesh, i.e. driving and being driven).

Box 1.1 shows the arithmetic involved in calculating the gears required for thread-cutting, 'meshing', in order accurately to determine the correct ratio of turns of the work to linear movement of the tool. Referring to a lathe, the gear train was arranged so that the headstock, with a gripping mechanism, a 'chuck', carrying the material being cut, revolved in a constant ratio movement relative to the travel of the cutting tool. This means that, in the case of a centre lathe, the work revolves at a predetermined rate (revolutions per minute, r.p.m.) whilst the cutting tool advances a constant amount parallel or at right angles to the axis of the work (in inches per revolution).

Lathes were available with longitudinal and cross-feed motions driven by gears and the rack (a long 'screw', flat on one side and fixed to the bed of the machine), giving 16 changes of feed to each. The operator had only to secure a sliding arm to the proper figure on an index stud and the machine would cut the pitch indicated by the figure (Bement, Mills & Co. 1893: 29). As early as 1863 machines such as heavy-duty centre lathes were available with a capacity for taking work up to 20' diameter on a faceplate[2] 14' diameter with a bed 36' long.

It was in the development of heavy machine tools that the mechanisation of manufacturing processes found its most dynamic form.

> **Box 1.1** Example of a calculation carried out by a machinist in setting up a machine for cutting a screw thread
>
> A simple example will illustrate the kind of problem facing a centre-lathe turner (i.e. not a turret-lathe operator, who had automatic features which eliminated calculations). The turner had to calculate which gears (of a given number of teeth) would be required to connect 'in train' to cut a given pitch of thread. Assuming the lathe had a leadscrew of 6 t.p.i. (threads per inch) to calculate the gears required to cut a thread of 3/32 in. pitch:
>
> $$\frac{\text{pitch to be cut}}{\text{pitch of leadscrew}} = \frac{\text{number of teeth in driver}}{\text{number of teeth in driver}} = \frac{3/32}{1/6}$$
>
> (1/6 pitch means 6 t.p.i.)
>
> $$= \frac{3/32}{1/6} = \frac{3 \times 6}{32 \times 1} = \frac{18}{32} = \frac{9}{16} \text{ multiplying top and bottom by 5}$$
>
> $$= \frac{45}{80} = \text{45-tooth gear driving directly an 80-tooth wheel}$$
>
> A range of gears, known as 'slip' wheels or 'change gears', is available for each particular lathe as standard

Machine tool classification: basic machine tools in use in the 19th century

Machine tools may be classified according to the nature of the cutting action imparted to the work by the cutting tool. A simplified classification reduced the various cutting actions to shearing, paring and scraping (Rankine 1878; *Spon's Dictionary* 1874. The first designation implied a basic guillotine action; the second was based on the principle of a wedge; and the third literally the removal of excess material by a process of scraping by hand. A more elaborate classification from America introduced a fivefold typology in which machines for shaping and fitting metal acted by: (a) compressing (b) shearing, (c) paring, (d) milling, (e) abrading or grinding (Hutton 1883).

Those tools which act by paring (c) were the most common in the workshops and may be divided into two classes. The first includes those in which the relative motion of the tool and work is circular or spiral. These produce surfaces of revolution such as cylinders, and include lathes, drills and boring machines. There were two important classes of lathes: the plain centre lathe, a machine tool designed for the 'one-off' job capable of use with a wide range of fixtures and attachments, and semi- or fully automatic special lathes. The principal variants in semi-automatic lathes were capstan and turret lathes, which may be regarded as modified centre lathes embodying permanent fixtures suitable for batch- and mass-production work. By 1950 there were 120 lathe types, including ten kinds of turret lathe; 55 kinds of centre lathe; 10 toolroom lathes; 26 multi-tool and production lathes; 16 camshaft lathes; 13 specialist machines (relieving, wheel-turning, profiling, gun-boring); 25 screwing machines; plus 18 types of automatics ranging from Swiss types up to 5mm capacity; and eight different capstan or ram-type machines (Ministry of Supply 1950).

The group of machines which cut by paring includes those in which the relative motion of the tool and work is rectilinear. These will produce plain surfaces through the use of planers, shapers, and slotters, and also 'curved surfaces' (Hutton 1883: 75).

Milling machines (d) may be described as a class of machine tools in which metal was removed by causing the work to be moved against a revolving cutting tool, called a milling cutter, which could be mounted horizontally or vertically, and which had several cutting edges. 'The typical feature of the milling operation is the fact that the rotating tool (the milling cutter) has a number of cutting edges each of which works over only part of its rotary path and travels over the remainder without cutting' (Koenigsberger 1962: 116).

The first English application of the milling machine as a production tool, which tended to rival the longer-established shaping machine which worked in the horizontal plane, was at the remodelled Enfield Armoury in the late 1850s. One hundred of these early machines were ordered from an American company, Robbins & Lawrence of Vermont, to increase the production of gun locks at Enfield (Hollingum 1976: 190). The first 'universal' (or modern-type) milling machine was produced by the American company Brown & Sharpe in 1862. It did not figure as a standard production, or specialist tool, in England until some time later, and was not listed in the tool catalogues in the 1860s. The leading engineering journal, *The Engineer*, did not publish a detailed description of the milling machine until 1884 (Hollingum 1976: 192).

The grinding machine (e) comprises a wheel head or 'abrasive' wheel, and revolving wheel spindle on which the grinding wheel is mounted, and either a work head and revolving work spindle, or a reciprocating or revolving work table. The wheel and its spindle revolve independently of the work, and the wheel head may be controlled by a traverse feed, an infeed, or both. These machines could be used for grinding internally and externally, round section material or flat. Until the appearance of Brown & Sharpe's first commercial grinding machine in 1864, the technique was used entirely for correcting or 'truing up' steel parts which had been distorted by the hardening process. Hounshell (1985) has made the point that this function of 'truing up' was the only way that interchangeability in 19th-century mass production could be achieved. An article appeared in *The Engineer* of 25 April 1856 showing a machine for grinding or polishing circular saw plates (Hollingum 1976: 193). Parts used on the sewing machine, the bicycle (both new mass-produced high-consumption articles) and other devices requiring hardened steel parts of high precision were machined 'slightly over-size, hardened, and then ground to final size and finish with very light cuts taken on the simple grinding machine used in the period' (Woodbury 1967: 631).

Brown & Sharpe developed the grinding machine into a more general-purpose tool designed to increase production and cut costs. The new concept involved a departure from the grinding machine used for correcting operations on hardened components to an integrated production process based on 'roughing' (a machining technique developed and advanced by F. W. Taylor in his cutting-tool research and discussed in Chapter 2).

Rationalised integrated production techniques used by companies such as Brown & Sharpe with the development of new machine tools were also part of cutting-tool research carried out at the Bethlehem Steel Works, Midvale, and the Link Belt Company under F. W. Taylor:

> The only successful field which seems open to us ... is to use the lathe as a roughing tool, or machine to bring the work approximately to the desired size, then to finish by grinding with emery wheels on a suitably designed machine ... (and) in duplicating parts of small machinery on the interchangeable system, such as sewing machine shafts, needle bars etc. they are unexcelled. (Brown & Sharpe 1891: 9)

One of the most intractable problems for much of the early part of the century was the generation of screw threads by machine. It was a difficult task even for the most accomplished machining artisan. Although Maudslay had produced a leadscrew (a long screw of relatively large diameter, usually with a square thread, i.e. a thread of square section) of considerable accuracy in the early part of the century, the breakthrough in large-scale production came in the mid-nineteenth century.

Screw-thread production

The William Sellers Company of Philadelphia conducted research on screw-thread production and by the late 1850s had developed a screwing machine in which 'The screw thread (was) cut in a single operation and the finished bolt was released by the withdrawal of the dies, the machine being driven continuously in one direction without reversing or stopping' (Stewart 1861: 231). The originality of this development was that it embodied a semi-automatic principle in a complex machine-tool operation and enabled machine screw-cutting to be accomplished at speed, without the necessity of employing highly skilled labour:

> This ... machine has the advantage of rapidity of action, producing a perfect thread in one running up ... in the ordinary screwing machines the screw had to be run up three times to make a good thread, which with three times of with-drawing made six times altogether for a screw to pass through the machine; in addition the time of stopping and reversing the ordinary machines was entirely saved in the new one, the machine running constantly in the same direction. (Stewart 1861: 235)

The Sellers Company also advocated the adoption of a standardised screw-thread system for the United States, and eventually the American ('Sellers') threads incorporating a form angle of 60° became standard practice (Anderson 1867: 372). (The English system developed by Whitworth was 55° and is discussed below.)

Machines with American specifications were in use in the UK by 1858. One machine was producing nearly 1,000 bolts per day, ¾" diameter with 1⅜ inches of thread, as against 500 per day of 10 ½ hours, ¾" diameter, with 1¼ inches of thread when cut by a 'hand' machine, i.e. by the conventional method (Stewart 1861: 235). This level of production had nearly trebled by 1884 through the development of solid, collapsible dies (i.e. the thread-cutting element, the dies, collapsed or sprung open, releasing the work at the end of the cut); and further refinements, such as chip clearance (removing surplus metal from the component after being machined) and stock releasing through automatic 'jaws' (Sellers 1884: 6).

The machine in use before the Sellers research was a bolt-screwing machine capable of, more or less, continuous production 'arranged so that the machine need not be stopped to fix and loosen nuts ... ' (G. Buchanan & Co. 1864). A more sophisticated English machine was a self-acting stud (a 'headless bolt' threaded both ends) and screwing machine incorporating a semi-automatic principle, a capstan rest to carry six tools instead of the normal slide rest (Whitworth Catalogue 1882b: 2). (The capstan was a hexagonal 'head' mounted on a short slide on the lathe capable of carrying a variety of cutting and grinding tools on each of the six faces which could be automatically brought in to cutting position by the rotation of a wheel mounted on the front of the machine.)

American machines were capable of producing bolts of the above dimensions at the rate of nearly 3,000 per 10-hour day, with two inches of thread, using unskilled labour (Sellers 1884: 61). Tests carried out by the Niles Tool Works demonstrated that work requiring 30 hours on conventional lathe-screw cutting could be accomplished in 6½ hours on a specialised screw machine. 'It is enough to say that *one screw machine will do work which would require three or four small lathes,* and that the work is *uniform in excellence* ... these machines are *run by unskilled men*, the care and setting of the tools, of course, being confined to a skilled man' (Niles Tool Works 1891: 41, 55; my emphasis).

Increasing flexibility and productivity in machine tools

One of the most versatile machines of the period was the boring mill or vertical lathe, part of a range of machine tools developed for an increasingly complex configuration of engineering tasks: 'A lathe would be a tool when the work revolved while the tool has only linear motions, while a boring machine would be one in which the work was stationary and a cutting tool described the surface of revolution' (Hutton 1883: 73). It was an outstanding high-production machine, capable of taking large-diameter work located in the horizontal plane; and relatively high cutting speeds were attainable. By the 1900s locomotive tyres, 42" diameter, could be turned on such a machine at the rate of 25 pairs in less than eight hours. A detailed breakdown of this particular production process illustrates the revolutionary nature of machine-tool technology in the period spanning the centuries. A leading American machine-tool company, the Niles-Bement-Pond Co., recorded that 25 pairs of 3' 6" diameter wheels were machined in 7 hours 54 minutes with one operator and one helper; the average time for turning was 19 minutes. The operations were differentiated as follows:

average time putting wheels on lathe	2 mins. 53 secs.
average time roughing (i.e. taking rough, heavy cuts where finish is not critical)	9 mins. 26 secs.
average time finishing (light, smoothing cuts to size)	5 mins. 25 secs.
average time taking wheel out of lathe	1 min. 17 secs.
	total time 19 mins.

Cutting conditions: depth of cut 5/16" feed 13/32"; speed 16' per min. (Calder 1910: 959).

The vertical lathe featured largely in cutting trials conducted by F. W. Taylor, in the period from 1880 to 1903 (F. W. Taylor 1906). His work on machine-tool production techniques stands beside Maudslay's pivotal work on the slide rest.

The horizontal boring machine was another outstanding machine tool having a movable work table and a rotating boring head, the component carrying the cutting tool. The work table is mounted on cross-slide supports, 'ways', which are fixed to a 'saddle'. The saddle slides on the base or 'bed' of the machine. Capable of accepting heavy-sectioned work, the boring mill required high degrees of skill in 'setting up', the process of accurately locating and gripping the workpiece preparatory to machining, and also in tool maintenance and control. In the 'steam engine' period it was the machine used for boring out the large cylinders for these and similar kinds of engines. 'Boring is ... most difficult to do for the action of the tool cannot be watched as in turning ... ' (*Spon's Dictionary* 1873: 2322). By the early 1900s a systematised work sequence on this type of machine could look as shown in Table 1.2.

Table 1.2 Machine handling time for a Betts horizontal boring mill

Total handling time for turning table end for end	2.41 mins.
	minutes
Take off two bolts ⅝ × 4	0.38
Walk six feet	0.05
Take off other two bolts ⅝ × 4	0.38
Take out key	0.04
Turn table end for end	0.38
Put in key	0.04
Put on two ⅝ × bolts and tighten	0.52
Walk six feet	0.05
Put on other two bolts ⅝ × 4 and tighten	0.52
Walk six feet	0.05
Total handling time for:	
Moving spindle forward (2 in.)	0.08
Moving spindle back (2 in.)	0.08
This time includes going after helper	
Move end support back 2 ft	
Helper not at machine	2.35
Move end support forward and tighten (2 ft)	
Helper at machine	0.80
Move auxiliary table forward (2 in.)	0.26
Move auxiliary table back (2 in.)	0.29
Raise table, includes loosen four 4¾ × 4 bolts, start machine, raise and tighten	1.60
Lower table, includes loosen four 4¾ × 4 bolts, start machine, lower and tighten	1.60
Total time	7.06

Source: Hathaway (1914), Table A and Table 2 (p. 538)

Traditional workshop organisation, under which the workman was responsible for the method and pace of work, had clearly undergone radical changes by the early 1900s. The objectives in fast-working machines and accurate tools of the 'new' type were rapid production and the elimination of hand labour. The use of capital-intensive technology such as fixtures and jigs for developing the range of machines such as the universal mill, engine lathes (i.e. power-driven), shapers, boring machines, drills and grinding machines increased rapidly (Orcutt 1902: 36). These high-calibre machines were consistent in performance and accuracy, and formed the basis of what was termed the 'tool-room', where ' ... none but machines of the highest accuracy should be allowed' (ibid., p. 31). The 'tool-room' concept derived from work carried out by Taylor, Gilbreth and their associates in the 1880s.

The following range of machines was more or less standard in a mechanical engineering workshop in the period 1860–1910. Using a typology from Acherkan (1967: 14, 15) in addition to those already referred to, the common machines may be divided into nine main groups, depending upon the type of processing operations they perform or the tools they employ. Each main group is further subdivided into types 'characterizing the specific purpose of the machine tool, its construction arrangement, degree of automaticity or the type of cutting tool employed' (ibid., p. 14). The typology and its variants are based on modern machine-tool developments but provide a guide to the principal machine-tool forms developing in the period. The groups are as follows (items marked with an asterisk were available as standard production machine at least by 1864 (Descriptive List of General Machinery, G. Buchanan & Co.); items marked with a double asterisk were a development characteristic of the 1880s):

Group 1   Lathes, including semi-automatics; vertical turning and boring mills; turret lathes*.

Group 2   Drilling and boring machines, including upright drill presses (drilling machines); jig borers; radial drills (in which the drill can be moved over the work on a 'radial arm' to any desired position, so that a large number of holes may be drilled in the workpiece without moving it)*; boring machines; horizontal drilling machines.

Group 3   Grinding machines, including cylindrical grinders; internal grinders; tool and cutter grinders; surface grinders (all available from the 1860s).

Group 4   Combination machines, including general-purpose machines; semi-automatic machines; automatic machines.**

Group 5   Gear- and thread-cutting machines, including shapers and planers for spur gears (the conventional gear-tooth shape); gear and thread grinders.**

Group 6   Milling machines, including vertical knee-type milling machines (in which the spindle axis, the component carrying the cutter, is vertical and the table is movable longitudinally on a saddle and vertically together); horizontal knee-type milling machines; fixed-bed and planer miller machines (for work requiring heavy cuts).

Group 7   Planers, shapers, slotters, including open-side planers (machining through 'free-access' on side of the machine); shapers; slotters. 'The term planing is or may be applied to all tools with rectilinear movement, for producing planes or other work performed in straight lines. Shaping and slotting machines belong to the same class' (*Spon's Dictionary* 1873). (The last-named machine operates in a vertical plane vis-à-vis the other two, which are always horizontal in operation.)

Group 8   Cutting-off machines, including saw-cutting machines; power-hacksawing machines; cutting-off lathes (specially-tooled lathes for cutting bars to length).

By 1864 the London-based company G. Buchanan was manufacturing a range of the conventional tools, in addition to a specialised range, which included: (1) nut-shaping machines, capable of machining nuts, shaft ends up to 6 in. diameter, operating on two sides of the nut simultaneously, (2) plate-bending machines taking work up to 10 ft wide; plate planing machines, ' ... a very powerful machine for planing edges of iron plates for shipbuilding' (G. Buchanan, 1864; (3) hydraulic presses; bar-sawing machines, fitted with two circular saws 3' 6" dia. to cut bars 7 ft to 24 ft long; crank-axle lathes, to turn two wheels at once up to 4 ft dia.; slotting machines for locomotive frame plates, with bed (base) 24 ft long, stroke (length of cut, in this case, vertical 'stroke'), to admit articles 4 ft. wide; with two cross-slides and refinements, for example, a self-acting longitudinal rack motion (implying the cutting head (or ram) which was driven by gears, and self-feeding after each stroke).

Other special tools were in use, their nature reflecting the strong influence of railway engineering and shipbuilding in the development and marketing of machine tools. *Spon's*, the authoritative engineering reference of the period, also catalogued: multiple drilling machines (for drilling a number of holes simultaneously); compound planing machines for connecting rods (this machine incorporated four tools acting at once, quadrupling the work of an ordinary machine); axle lathes for turning the bearings and wheels fits on railway axles; hydrostatic wheel presses, for forcing on or off the wheels of railway cars.

Shipbuilding was deploying electro-magnetic tools in the late 1880s for riveting, drilling, tapping (generating internal threads), caulking (making joints water-tight). They afforded management further control over costs and production rates.

Until now the shipbuilding industry has been to a great extent controlled by the trades union of riveters, so that employers of labour have been unable always to regulate the cost of work as affected by the rate of wages or by the speed at which the work was completed ... it is of great importance that they should possess such a means of controlling both the cost of the work and the rate of construction ... as is furnished by these electro-magnetic machines. (Rowan: 330, 331)

The critical mechanical function of these new machine tools was their operating flexibility combined with accuracy and speed; they could be clamped to the side of iron and steel work in any position, offering a more flexible operation than the more traditional, static procedures. During the last decades of the century machine tools rapidly became more automated and were increasingly manned by unskilled labour. The discovery and implementation of metrological and technological innovations which preceded these developments were the indispensable conditions for the decisive break with traditional workshop practice which they represented. The origin of this critical change lies in the work of Henry Maudslay and Joseph Whitworth.

Machine tool accuracy: the slide rest principle and the work of H. Maudslay

Overall design and construction of the common machine tools had remained constant up to about the 1840s, but there had been recurring production problems. First, general-purpose machines, usually made of iron and wood, were often subject to errors of alignment, that is, parts of the machines were not always accurately fitted with other parts. Second, of particular concern to artisans and employers, was reliance upon manual control of the cutting tool. This involved rigidly holding and guiding the tool as it moved along the metal being cut, the workpiece, in a way which removed surplus metal according to the required size an 'finish'. The 'finish' is the condition of the surface of the metal after being cut; it may vary from 'rough' to 'very smooth'. It was standard practice for the machinist on the most common machine tool of the day, the lathe, to hold the cutting tool in his hands against a 'rest' in order to cut the metal (Spon's Dictionary 1874; Smiles; 1876; Musson & Robinson 1969). [1]

The setting of the tool relative to the metal being cut had always demanded high levels of skill, for example, consistency of pressure in hand-held tools. The mechanical efficiency of the slide-rest was far superior. It was the first mechanical invention of significance that literally removed the cutting tool from the craftsman's hands. As Evans (1986: 25) noted, ' ... the lathe (became) a new animal ... '. Designed by Maudslay to rigidly hold and guide the cutting tool, the more exact fitting of the slide-rest also refined the fitting of the saddle on the machine for precision machining. It was clamped to a sliding part of the machine, usually a lathe, which fitted over the bed, or base, of the machine; this was called the 'saddle'. The purpose of the slide-rest was to locate and grip the cutting tool as it cut into the metal being machined, as the slide-rest, on the saddle, moved precisely along the bed of the lathe, driven by a long screw (Galloway 1958; Woodbury 1967). The saddle was moved along the machine bed by the action of long screws, called 'leadscrews', bolted to the front of the machine. These screws were originally designed and made by Maudslay and were precisely hand manufactured. Improved leadscrews were later developed by Whitworth and incorporated into the cross-slide, an innovation which also greatly increased the accuracy of the cut and finish. Nasmyth said the slide rest was

> of great importance ... and consists in substitution of a mechanical contrivance in place of the human hand, for holding, applying, and directing the motions of a cutting tool to the surface of the work to be cut, by which we were enabled to constrain the tool to move along or across the surface of an object ... with absolute precision ... . (Nasmyth 1841: 395)

Originally conceived for use on the centre lathe, the innovatory development of the leadscrew was its application on machines designed for the replication of machined parts in large numbers. Production rates greatly increased and costs were more effectively controlled. Samuel Smiles (1876) writes of this development:

> The effect of the introduction of the slide rest were felt in all departments of mechanism ... all kind of work could now be turned out in quantity ... various modifications were introduced ... the result of which has been that extraordinary development of mechanical production and power ... (Smiles 1876: 214)

Machining practice was greatly simplified and regularised; control of the cutting tools and finish became features of the machine tool and not the worker. The introduction of the slide-rest and precision leadscrews mechanised machining skills, and routine machine operations henceforth required less manual skill:

> now that slide lathes and planing machines are becoming so very common in workshops ... and that *such machines, from their automatic power, no longer require regularly bred mechanics to attend them*, it becomes more than necessary to reduce the subject to those simple principles to which it is capable, so that the subject may be brought within the range of the supposed inferior capacity of a humbler grade of men, from whom we want no more than careful attention to secure the best results from these surprisingly productive machines. (Nasmyth 1841: 411; my emphasis)

It was thus the first major development in machine-tool construction which facilitated the transfer of control over the actual process of tool-cutting. From the 1880s and 1890s it was increasingly used in mass-produced products such as typewriters, sewing machines, bicycles, and to meet increased demand for firearms, particularly small arms. But controlling the standards to which the machine, and operator, worked required precise regulation; new concepts in metrology were needed.

Whitworth and the principles of workshop gauging and measurement and the standardisation of screws and screw threads

From the 1840s Whitworth made great advances in refining workshop practice and labour control. Precise control over dimensions and finish became the sine qua non for product accuracy in machine tools:

> Every consideration combines to enforce accuracy, ... when it is considered that the lathe and planing machine are used in the making of all other machines, and are continually reproducing surfaces similar to their own it will manifestly appear of the first importance that they themselves should be perfect models. (Whitworth 1840: 8)

Whitworth regarded two factors in machine-tool precision as fundamental: the 'true plane', and the 'power of measurement': 'the latter cannot be attained without the former' (Whitworth 1856).

Having joined Henry Maudslay in his works in London in 1825, he developed his system of 'true planes' during his time there. The crucial characteristic of the truly plane surface was that for all kinds of mechanisms which involved one surface sliding over another, as in many machine parts, frictional resistance could be reduced to a minimum. With this development, new standards of accuracy in mechanical construction and measurement became possible.

The introduction of the true plane was followed by his development of a system of measurement of 'ideal exactness', formalised between 1840 and 1850 with the conception and development of his measuring machine (*Dictionary of National Biography*: 167). Historically, artisans were allowed wide latitude over work processes, with imprecise limits: 'bare sixteenth' or 'full thirty-second'. That is, they worked to a given dimension within a sixteenth of an inch or a thirty-second of an inch of that size. The final precise measurement rested with the worker.

Whitworth held that no form of standardisation was possible with such imprecision in manufactured work; he said of the discretion allowed to workers regarding product sizes: 'What exact notion can any man have of such a size as "bare sixteenth" or a "full thirty-second" and what inconvenient results may ensue from the different notions of different workmen as to the value of these terms' (Whitworth 1857: 49). His datum was the true plane from which he derived much closer control over accuracy, that is, closer 'tolerances'. Expressions such as 'bare sixteenth' were replaced by a consistent set of specified 'close' tolerances relating to an acceptable margin of error within a given range of common sizes in engineering practice. Thus the larger common sizes in standard engineering practice would have a wider tolerance than smaller common sizes; but they would remain constant and thus, more or less, replicable (Nuttall 1956: 164).

This control was intended to remove the discretion over final component size from the worker. Working within 'limits' therefore presupposed acceptable levels of accuracy and finish, and was essential to what was to become known as interchangeability. The system of measurement was a priority for investigation.

Whitworth, convinced that no system depending on sight was adequate for precision measurement of engineering components, where exact size or good fitting was required, argued that a sense of touch was far more reliable (Whitworth 1857: 48). Drawing upon his metrological research, he concluded that central to 'exactness' was accuracy and uniformity in screw threads. The culmination of this research was a new measuring machine, with levels of accuracy never previously attainable in manufacture.

Whitworth's measuring machine

Prior to Whitworth's work in precision measurement, screws had been manufactured on an ad hoc basis with no recognised standards or system; each workshop manufactured a type of its own. Screw threads with individual variations resulted from artisan interpretations:

> There was an utter want of uniformity. No system was observed as to 'pitch' ... nor was any rule followed as to the form of ... threads. Every bolt and nut was a sort of speciality in itself ... to such an extent was irregularity carried, that all bolts and their corresponding nuts had to be marked as belonging to each other; and any mixing of them together led to endless trouble, hopeless confusion, and enormous expense. (Smiles 1876: 226)

The lack of uniformity generated a wide range of threads with varying pitch (the distance from a point on a thread to the corresponding point of the next thread), and thread angles (the slope of the thread relative to the axis of the bolt or screw). As early as the 1840s Whitworth observed that the 'economy and manifold advantage resulting from uniformity ... must be sufficiently obvious' (Whitworth 1841: 18).

He collected an extensive assortment of screw bolts from different English workshops, and deduced as a compromise an average pitch of thread, for different diameters; and also a mean thread angle of 55°, which he adopted all through the scale of sizes. By 1860 the Whitworth system was in general use (*Dictionary of National Biography*: 165). The system came down into modern workshop practice as the British Standard Whitworth system, threads incorporating his standard specifications being designated B.S.W.

Whitworth's contact with Maudslay had a marked influence on machine-tool developments. The value of the screw thread and its application as a means of transmitting linear motion for a given rotational movement was realised in machine-tool production. With Maudslay's 'beautiful screws' it was possible to devise instruments to measure with great precision: 'Our modern precision machining and measurements are descendants of their patriarchal Maudslay screw' (Evans 1986: 15). The use of screw-thread principles was early recognised in screw bolts to join certain parts of machinery. Accurately made screw bolts improved the location and fitting of machined components. The screw bolt had power, strength and durability: 'it is peculiarly adapted for (this) purpose by the compact form in which it possesses the necessary strength and mechanical power' (Whitworth 1841: 19). The micrometer wheel principle on Whitworth's measuring machine was therefore based on precision-made screws. It was also used on hand wheels of machine tools so that the machinist could determine precise movement of the sliding machine parts he was controlling.

Central to Whitworth's measuring machine was a system of parallel blocks of polished metal, so arranged that of two parallel surfaces one can be moved nearer or further from the other by means of a screw. The movements of the screw could be measured for each turn or part of a turn and hence the distance moved by the moving plane.

The screw thread on the machine had 20 threads to an inch; attached to the screw was a wheel, called a micrometer wheel, with 500 graduated divisions. With one division of movement of the wheel, the screw would advance or retract one 500th of a turn, that is by one 10,000th of an inch. Whitworth subsequently showed that the movement of a fourth part of a division, being one 40,000th of an inch, was 'distinctly felt and gauged'. By 1859 the measuring machine had been refined to the stage where 'movement of the micrometer wheel through one division, which is the millionth of an inch, is sufficient to cause the feeling piece to be suspended or to fall by its gravity' (Whitworth 1876: 66).

Deriving directly from his experience of the application of very precise measurements, Whitworth went on to design a system of gauges for checking rather than measuring. Whitworth's denomination of standard gauges was approved by the Privy Council in 1881, as standard under the Weights and Measures Act 1878.

The development of gauges for checking work sizes

Whitworth envisaged a system of standardised parts, made to high specification, as essential to interchangeability. In the production of close-fitting parts of machinery, precision was indispensable to accuracy. He therefore concluded that if a means of replacing artisan measuring skills could be found, the employers' dependence on the artisan could be reduced and a system of uniformity or 'standard' introduced. Using his own advanced measuring machine he developed a system of workshop gauges designed to check, rather than measure, specific components over a range of common workshop sizes (Whitworth 1876).

Whitworth had earlier demonstrated the importance of very small differences of size with gauges:

> I have ... an internal gauge having a cylindrical aperture .5770 inch diameter, and two external gauges or solid cylinders, one being .5769 and the other .5770 inch diameter. The latter is 1–10,000th of an inch larger than the former, and fits tightly in the internal gauge when both are clean and dry, while the smaller .5769 in gauge is so loose in it as to appear not to fit at all ... it is therefore obvious both to the eye and the touch, that the difference between these two cylinders of 1–10,000ths of an inch is an appreciable and important quantity. (Whitworth 1857: 44, 50)

The standardising of common engineering elements was thus based on the assumption that quantitative variations, within a given range of common components, could be realistically controlled within fine tolerances. The basic workshop structure of these standards was established with the development of ring and plug gauges available in standard sets of various dimensions.

The concept of standardisation had impressed Whitworth on his visit to America (as a member of an official delegation to report on the latest developments in arms manufacture, one of the results of which was the remodelling of the Enfield armoury). This took place two years before his later, definitive work on gauges. After a visit to the leading arms factory, the Springfield Armory, he noted that: '(The) complete musket is made (by putting together the separate parts) in three minutes. All these parts are exactly alike that any single part, will, in its place, fit any musket' (Whitworth 1854: 27). This is a clear, concrete definition of the principle of interchangeability.

A recent commentary on Whitworth's enthusiasm for the 'American System of Manufacture', essentially based on interchangeable manufacture, asserts that 'curiously', Whitworth made only one reference to interchangeability, and ' ... did not explain how it was achieved' (Hounshell 1985: 62). Clearly, Whitworth's protracted studies in metrology in England rendered unnecessary a detailed exegesis of interchangeability. Anderson, a colleague of

Whitworth, and chief engineer of the Royal Arsenal at Woolwich, on the American visit no longer doubted the complete interchangeability of parts of the Springfield musket (ibid.).

The ring gauge developed by Whitworth consisted of a heavy disc of metal with a hole very accurately bored and ground to close tolerances of size. A shaft could be machined until it just fitted into the ring gauge hole; slightly oversize the shaft would not enter, slightly undersize it would be slack. Corresponding to the ring gauge of a given size was a ground shaft which fitted the ring exactly; this was the plug gauge for that specific size with a 'pairing' function to determine hole sizes within prescribed limits of tolerance. It was possible with gauges such as these to produce work in the workshop to within 0.001 in. and with grinding, close tolerances of + or − 0.0001 in. Whitworth pressed for the official adoption of his standards, which he maintained enabled ' ... the workmen [to] measure to the 1–20,000th of an inch, and these measures are as familiar and appreciable as those of any larger dimensions ... ' (Whitworth: 48). The comprehensive nature of the gauges may be illustrated by an extract from the Denominations of Standard Gauges:

(1) Whitworth's External Cylindrical Gauges
External Diameters in terms of the inch.
Fifteen gauges from ⅛th to 1 inch, increasing by sixteenth of an inch.
Twenty-four gauges from 1⅛th to 4 inches, increasing by eighths of an inch.
Eight gauges from 4¼ inches to 6 inches, increasing by quarters of an inch.
Nineteen gauges from 0.1 to 1 inch, increasing by five one-hundredths of an inch.
Thirty gauges from 1.1 to 4 inches, increasing by tenths of an inch.
Ten gauges from 4.2 inches to 6 inches, increasing by a fifth of an inch.
(2) Whitworth's Internal Cylindrical Gauges: Internal Diameters in terms of an inch (see 1), etc. (Whitworth 1876: 71)

A range of 212 gauges was developed to cover a variety of sizes from 1/10 inch up to 6 inches for both internal and external measures. The importance for mass production processes of having stabilised standards for a given range of components was first realised, as suggested above, in firearm production.

Whitworth instituted a set of highly accurate, stable metrological data, or standards, over a specified range of engineering components such as shafts, bolts, screws. In this his contribution to 19th-century engineering production techniques was outstanding. A more or less universal range of standards was thus available for replication of components in large quantities. This underpinned mass production:

> It is of great importance to the manufacturer who makes parts of machines in large quantities to have a means of referring to an accurate fixed measure ... errors in standards are not only reproduced in the copies, but are superadded to the errors in workmanship, which will occur in the course of manufacture; and this is especially likely to occur in cases where one manufacturer supplies parts of machines for the use of another. (Whitworth 1857: 52)

Manufacturing according to a standardised system of parts encouraged the employment of unskilled 'assemblers' as opposed to skilled 'fitters', that is, artisans who worked on components by hand to make them fit. Anderson had confidence in the new system of substitution:

> Have you any doubts that the parts of a musket can be created by machinery so perfect that the assembler will take so short a time as 10 minutes in putting them together? – After a little experience ... there will be very little doubt on that point.
> Was it not the object with this improved machinery to reduce the amount of wages; to employ fewer persons, very few skilled labourers, but to employ a number of unskilled persons to manage under them the machinery? – Yes, I hope it will come to that. (Anderson 1854: Qs. 371, 794)

The introduction of a system of interchangeable manufacture was a revolutionary development. The substitution of parts implied a substitution of workers. In the period after the visit to America by the government commission, the small arms factory at Enfield was thoroughly reorganised, and production of rifles, requiring 700 separate operations, was 2,000 per week: 'The parts of each rifle being completely interchangeable' (Galloway 1958: 638).

By 1880 new machines embodied higher levels of precision and replication: 'one of the most suggestive characteristics was ... the growth of simple machines ... into a higher stage of development with almost human intelligence permanently embodied in the mechanism for its own self-preservation' (Anderson 1880: 38). The new machines referred to by Anderson were modified forms of the basic lathe, the principal tool used for producing round bars. The main development was the 'turret' lathe, which was an automatic, i.e. self-acting, machine developed from the significant work on the cross-slide by H. Maudslay. Automatic machines became a decisive factor in the intensification of labour.

Self-acting machines, interchangeable manufacture and the intensification of labour

The 1854 Select Committee revealed evidence of simplified machining practices highlighted by Nasmyth (1854: Q.1353). In that year Anderson had inspected the Colt factory in London with a view to appraising the level of machine automation in firearm production. Arms production was an exemplar of precision engineering processes in which components have to be replicated, in very large quantities, for easy assembly. Highly accurate, semi-automatic machines were necessary for long production runs of this kind. Anderson was impressed, and his conclusions suggest that as early as the 1850s advances in automatic machine-tool operations in small arms manufacture had reached a level where the requirement of skilled-machinist labour had been very much reduced. Skilled workers were engaged in setting the cutting tools in the machines, 'tool setting', for operation by unskilled workers. His observations were prescient and merit quoting in detail:

> The work in this manufactory is reduced to an almost perfect system; a pistol being composed of a certain number of distinct pieces, each piece is produced in proportionate quantity by machinery, and as each piece when finished is the result of a number of operations (some 20 or 30) ... and each operation being performed by a special machine made on purpose, many of these machines *requiring hardly any skill* from the attendant beyond knowing how to fasten and unfasten the article, the setting and adjusting of the machine being performed by skilled workmen; but when *once the machine is properly set it will produce thousands.* (Anderson 1854: Q.341; my emphasis)

Work which formerly took four days by hand was reduced to one hour:

> every part (of a musket) ... if made by machinery ... would be made with thorough accuracy, and very much more quickly ... a machine is used for planing canon between the trunnions; formerly this was chiselled by hand and then filed, and there was at least four days' work in it; now, by means of the machine ... it is put in and taken out again within an hour; the lad that watches this machine has to turn the trunnions of another cannon, so that it is produced for less than ten minutes of wages. (Anderson 1854: Qs. 343, 347)

As production became increasingly automated the range of skills tended to become less differentiated. The areas of work reserved for the highly skilled were increasingly circumscribed by what Braverman (1974) later referred to as a 'separating out of planning from execution'. Colt's London armoury gravitated towards a mass of undifferentiated labour, due to the introduction of automatic machine processes and new levels of precision measurement.

An arithmetic expression come from Anderson: for a production run of 150,000 firearms a recommended workforce of 1,000 would be envisaged of which about 150 would be men of considerable skill, and the remainder ... of moderate skill, labourers, boys and girls taken on without skill, but being trained to a simple operation become highly skilful at that particular process ... ' (Anderson 1854: Q.379). The wage differentials set out clearly the nature of the division of labour involved:

one man at 5 £ per week; two men at 3 £, five men at 50s; twenty men at 2.2.0.; twenty-five men at 36s; twenty-five at 30s; fifty at 24/6; seventy-two at 18s; one hundred at 15s; one hundred at 12s; one hundred and fifty at 10s; one hundred and fifty at 8s; one hundred and fifty at 6s; one hundred and fifty at 4s (*the latter would be of course, boys and girls*) ... amounting to 621 £ 11s or annually to 32,339 £. (Anderson 1854: Q.380; my emphasis)

Marx in his first volume of *Capital*, published at the time workshop transformations were increasing, put forward what he considered a threefold division of labour which parallels Anderson's. As Marx put it : there were those who were actually employed on the machines; attendants (almost exclusively children); and a third, numerically unimportant group, 'whose occupation it is to look after the whole of the machinery and repair it from time to time; such as engineers, mechanics, joiners etc. This is a superior class of workmen, some of them scientifically educated, others brought up to a trade ... ' (Marx 1977: 396). This division of labour Marx referred to as 'purely technical'.

Colonel Colt, an American from Connecticut, had opened his arms factory in London in January 1853 (Select Committee on Small Arms 1854: Q.1150). He had unequivocal views on the type of workers he wanted:

The more ignorant a man was the more brains he had for my purpose ... they first come as labourers at 2s per day ... in a little time ... if there be a machine vacant, I put them on it ... the best get 8s per day ... Do not bring me a man who knows anything if you want me to teach him anything. (Colt 1854: Q.1152)

The organisation and control of metal-machining exemplifies the way employers, using new technologies, had rationalised their resistance to the continuation of the traditional form of craft training, the apprenticeship. Colt's preference for unskilled workers for machine manning suggests that the level of technology was sufficiently developed by the 1850s and 1860s for employers to consider training for machinists to be redundant or at least minimal. Nasmyth held a similar view. He employed former agricultural labourers in the machine shops: 'the most trustworthy men I have were originally ... taken from the fields in my neighbourhood' (Nasmyth 1854: Q.1436).

Technological development was inseparable from social development and control in the reorganised workshop: control over technology was integral to control over the labour process. Job familiarisation replaced craft training; the emphasis was on the manning of repetitive machine operations: 'I select those that are the most intelligent, and in the course of one week I have them producing three or four times the amount ... of a legal hand ... ' (Colt 1854: Q.1437). Work reorganisation based on the new technologies lessened the employers' dependence on artisan machinists, and freed them from union prescriptions on machine manning. The Amalgamated Society of Engineers (ASE) was exclusive to skilled workers, and the employers' use of non-union men enabled both variable costs in the form of wages and rates (and methods) of production to be more effectively controlled:

> If labour is not raised in price, I know what a person can do in a day on all the details of operation done upon my arm [firearm], and I could tell you as to the very operation of boring that hole ... the cost of it per 1,000. There are hundreds of machine operations on that arm, and there is not one of them the detailed price of which is not upon my books, what it costs per 1,000. (Colt 1854: Q.12627)

The deployment of automated machine tools redefined the nature of the worker's skill. Often there was a redesignation from 'artisan machinist' to 'machine minder'. The assumption here was that having 'set' a machine fitted with a self-acting mechanism, machining could take place without further attendance on the part of the operator, beyond checking the progress of the cut – the notion of 'minding'.

The concept of 'machine minding' and the related concept 'idling time' provide clues in explaining how artisan machinists were downgraded and how the employers' equivocal attitude to trade training and technical education came to be institutionalised. 'Idling time' referred to the period during a cutting operation on a machine when the tool was automatically moving along the component being cut. The machinist was not actually 'working' while the cut was under way. Cutting mild steel of relatively large cross-section using plain carbon steel tools of the period could take many hours to complete. This time, it will have been noted, refers to actual cutting time when the machine is travelling (traversing) under self-acting principles. For employers, cutting time, particularly on large components, was 'idling' time in that the machinist was engaged in observing and checking the cutting action, not actually performing a specific technical task. Employers reasoned it was possible to use the machinist's 'non-productive' ('idling') time by increasing the number of machines supervised, that is, working more than one machine simultaneously (the intensification of labour). (For the principle of idling time see Box 1.2.)

A striking form of intensification of labour is provided by a boring machine, used for cutting large, accurate holes in heavy-sectioned or irregular shaped components:

> I have a machine for boring cylinders, a process that requires very great accuracy and care and found, after the cylinder was put in the machine and set to work by self-action, that here was a man at 32s a week *standing by for nearly a week looking at the machine*; ... and I thought the best way to keep him fully employed was to give him another machine to fill up his time, and he then said he would not do so ... the best thing you can do is walk out (I answered) ... I then took the very labourer who used to assist him in putting the cylinder into the machine

Box 1.2 The principle of idling time

An illustration of a machining operation shows the significance of the principles of 'idling' and cutting time on a centre lathe:

Given: a mild steel bar 5 in. diameter, 9 ft. long to be reduced to a diameter of average 3 in.

Speed of lathe = 150 revolutions per minute (r.p.m.) (workpiece speed)

Feed rate of tool = 0.062 in. (i.e. in. per revolution of the workpiece)

Depth of cut = 0.058 in. (i.e. 0.116 in. reduction of diameter)

In one minute tool advances 150 × 0.062 = 9.3 in.

$\therefore$ Time taken to travel 9 ft. $= \dfrac{9 \times 12}{9.3} = 11.6$ min.

Each complete traverse reduces diameter by 0.116 in.

$\therefore$ in order to reduce diameter by 2 in., $\dfrac{2}{0.116} = 17$ traverses need to be made

$\therefore$ Total time taken in actual cutting = 11.6 × 17 = 197 min. or 3.28 hrs.

---

and said, now you have charge of this machine and the other that this man refused to work; and for every additional machine that you manage I will give you an additional shilling a week. *That man now manages six machines, and he has plenty of time to spare.* (Nasmyth 1854: Q.1437; my emphasis)

Boring was used for cutting internally – 'bores', and might be called internal turning, the cutting operation being almost identical. But it was a difficult machining operation, requiring great care on the part of the machinist: 'for the action of the tool cannot be watched as in turning being as a rule out of sight, the dimensions are more difficult to gauge, while cored or interior surfaces are both harder and more irregular than outside surfaces' (*Spon's Dictionary* 1874: 2322). Machines of this calibre were capable of boring cylinders 90" diameter, 11 ft long (Buchanan & Co 1864: 81), indicating the magnitude of the machining task in this form of heavy engineering.

Self-acting mechanisms in machines were thus highly rated by employers such as Nasmyth, Whitworth and others, and constituted for them a 'great feature' by which 'brute force is completely set aside' (Nasmyth 1868b Q.19133). Whitworth's earlier expectations for automated machines were well justified, as the following extract from his testimony to the Parliamentary Select Committee reveals:

> Are you a manufacturer of machinery? – Yes.
> Is the class of work that your machine produce required to be accurate? – Yes, great accuracy is required.
> Do you make what are termed self-acting machines? – Yes.
> Is there much advantage in having machines self-acting? Very great.
> Is the work performed by them likely to be as accurate as it would be if the agency of an attendant were constantly employed? – Yes.
> Will you explain for what reason? – *Not requiring the attendance of a man, the work is often of a superior quality and more regular* than it would be if moved by hand.
> Do you consider the employment of self-acting machines as a general principle to be economical? – Undoubtedly. (Select Committee on Small Arms 1854: Qs.1920–1928; my emphasis)

Relatively precise work of large dimensions could be realised with new kinds of automatic machines using unskilled operators. By 1877 it was possible to report that 'in the automatic machines of modern times, tools have assumed a far higher relative position because in them, (the) mental faculties, the skill and craft are permanently embodied ... and many of them are qualified to transmit their virtues or vices without assistance' (Anderson 1877: 2127). Increasing employment of boys and other low-skill labour for machine manning was a direct consequence of the development of semi-automatic machines: 'All that the mechanic has to do now ... is to sharpen his tool, place it in the machine in connection with the work, and set on the self-acting motion, and then nine-tenths of his time is spent ... not in labouring, but in watching the delicate and beautiful functions of the machine ... ' (Nasmyth 1868b: Q.19133).

One of the leading automatic machines brought into limited service from the 1860s was the turret lathe: its principle features were special mechanisms, 'chucks' used for gripping the metal being cut, and facility for up to eight cutting tools to be brought into operation at speed.

The turret lathe: its influence in changing definitions of machine shop skills

The revolutionary properties of the new turret lathe were recognised in 1867. It featured in jurors' reports on the machine-tool section of the International Exhibition of that year: 'This class of tool is a great feature of the Enfield

Small-Arms factory, and it is much more used by engineers in America than it is in England' (Anderson 1867: 373–4). The first turret machines in production use were American, dating from the 1860s, made by Pratt & Whitney, and Brown & Sharpe, the latter firm becoming pre-eminent and in this field (Steeds 1969: 93). It was the first 'radical improvement on Maudslay's slide-rest' (Roe 1916a: 143). There was a clear reference to its use in England from 1851 for lock-making; the metal wire or bar passing through the centre of the revolving spindle, when 'tool after tool is successively brought into action, and screws of perfect identity are ... produced with facility' (Anderson 1867: 373).

The turret lathe used the basic principle of the cross-slide as in plain centre lathes. In addition to clamping one or two cutting tools to the slide-rest, this machine had a hexagon-shaped block fitted to a second 'saddle' mounted on the base. On each of the six sides of the hexagonal block one or more cutting tools could be fitted. The saddle and hexagon block, called a 'turret', could be moved back and forth by a large hand wheel placed on the front of the machine near the operator's right hand. As the hand wheel was turned clockwise the turret would automatically swivel one-sixth of a turn. It was possible therefore to bring at least six different cutting tools into action simply by turning the hand wheel one-sixth of a turn. Two further cutting tools could be mounted on the cross-slide itself.

The manufacturing advantage of this machine was that the six turret tools could be pre-set in the correct cutting position prior to machine cutting. Further adjustments as necessary after the setting were made by skilled workers retained after workshop reorganisation, known as 'tool-setters', the actual machine operation being left to unskilled machine operators. The machine-setting skills involved precisely locating the six tools in relation to the work being cut (data based on the Institution of Mechanical Engineers' Criteria for Turret Lathes, I.Mech.E. *Proceedings*, 1901).

The turret lathe was indispensable to the reorganisation of mass metal-machining using unskilled labour: in the turning and screwing of studs in large numbers with multiple manning, for example, five or six machines operated by a single man, there was an 'immense saving' (*The Engineer*, 1899).

Further potential of the turret was realised with the addition of a four-position front tool post and a single-tool rear tool post, both mounted on the cross-slide, and capable of movement 90° to the lathe centre line. This combination rendered possible a machine tool with eleven tool positions: six on the hexagonal turret, four on the front tool post, and one on the rear tool post. Provided the movements of the cutting tools were controlled with positive adjustable stops, the operator's time was focused on tending and loading and unloading the workpiece (I.Mech.E. *Proceedings*, 1901).

The introduction of the turret lathe led to the decline in the number of skilled artisans employed in machining. It was ideally suited to replication of large numbers of components and fitted the employers' strategy of promoting labourers to machine manning in conjunction with a new kind of wage-payment system, the piecework system. Furthermore, it justified the employers' virtual abandonment of craft apprenticeships.

By the 1890s the influences of a mass-market system, particularly the demand for products such as bicycles, were having effects on supply and on the use of high-production machines based on the turret principle. The dominating influence remained American in this sphere, for by the last decade of the century new machines imported from the United States demonstrated the operational effectiveness of manufacture using fully automatic principles. Further advances were made through the use of wire-feeding (automatic feeding of the material to be cut to the cutting position), and the automatic revolving turret (dispensing with the hand wheel) (Horner 1900: 121).

Production rates were also increased by the adoption of novel machining techniques such as multi-tool cutting:

> it becomes possible to use ... two turrets to be brought round in succession for the formation of a single piece of work ... some of these tools are operating on 2, 3 or 4 different faces and diameters at once ... the chief feature [in the production of 6,000 screws per day – BC] was the fact that four screws were being operated on at one time in revolving vertical turret. (Ibid.)

Before the end of the 19th century the generalisation of automatic machine-tool practice was widely acknowledged. The Northampton Institute in Clerkenwell was opened and classes were started for the training of 'engineers' in the use of automatic machine tools for making interchangeable parts (*American Machinist*, 9 Nov. 1899, p. 1071).

A contemporary English journal, *The Engineer*, argued the case for automatic machines:

> The English manufacturer is at length beginning to recognise that the restriction in the way of their use being now removed, automatic machine tools are of great importance ... the automatic tool has arrived at such a state of perfection that no longer need any hesitation be felt in adopting it. (*The Engineer*, 2 Dec. 1898)

This journal also recognised the mass-market potential of rapid production with automatic machines and 'stockpiling'. This was the production in very large quantities of a relatively small range of standardised parts, manufactured at speed, which were put into store. Potential customers were notified that high turnover of products might be possible if they restricted their demands to high-productivity components over this given limited range: 'Much of the (American) success is due to the fact that they do not wait for their customers to tell them what is wanted, but show how much more can be done than was deemed possible ... they lead and do not follow manufacture' (ibid.). Increasing automaticity, lower labour costs, faster production, diminishing training costs, increasing freedom from union-imposed restraints, all widened the appeal of the new mass-production machines such as the turret lathes. One feature was compelling: they could be successfully operated by unskilled operators:

> a large amount of work *now done by skilled men is to be shortly done on the turret machine by comparatively unskilled attendants*, who will eventually beat the trained turners to output, accuracy, and uniformity ... *the great advantage in the modern turret machine lies in the possibility of using operators, who*, in a few weeks *can turn out accurate uniform work in competition with lathe hands who have served several years' apprenticeship* ... (Orcutt 1902: 28; my emphasis)

The employers' control over technology was never entirely complete in the 19th century, despite the highly significant contributions of pioneers such as Maudslay, Whitworth and Nasmyth. Control was essentially limited by three factors: (1) the mechanical and metallurgical limitations of machine-cutting tools; (2) the organized resistance of skilled unionised labour against indiscriminate labour substitution on machines; (3) the limited craft capabilities and endurance of unskilled and child labour.

Central to the resolution of these problems were improvements in the metal-cutting properties of tool steels. The culmination of research in Britain and America was undoubtedly the discovery of High Speed Steel (HSS) by F. W. Taylor in America, which, together with the earlier work on machine-tool innovations and metrology, revolutionised metal-machining and brought engineering manufacture into the modern era. The effects were not confined to technical efficiency in cutting; they also dealt a hammer-blow to the aspirations of artisans striving to maintain their status in labour relations and the credibility of the traditional craft apprenticeship.

Notes

1. 'Standards' is the name given to a system of measurements which sets down limits within which certain component parts in engineering are to be manufactured; these limits are known as 'tolerances'. It was a characteristic of skilled workers to be able to work to 'close' tolerances, i.e. work within precise limits.
2. 'Faceplate': a plate-shaped iron device located on the 'headstock' for holding large or irregular-shaped work.

CHAPTER TWO

The interaction of work and technology: the influence of F. W. Taylor and H. Braverman

F. W. Taylor and the revolution in metal-cutting

The mechanical engineering industry in America in the late 19th century was characterised by the increasing professionalisation of engineering management, growth of banking facilities and entrepreneurial developments. These events generated a new dynamic in the American economy that dislodged Britain from the industrial pre-eminence it had commanded from the beginning of the century.

F. W. Taylor assumes a critical importance in the historiography of late 19th-century manufacturing engineering and is well established in the current orthodoxy of labour histories. His dominance in the field extended well into the next century. Three reasons for his undoubted influence may be distinguished. First, he was foremost in systematically researching the metallurgical properties of metal-cutting tools which had a profound effect upon manufacturing engineering both in America and Europe. Second, he consistently sought to relate changes in production technologies, such as machine-tool cutting and techniques, to new patterns of labour control based on the widespread deployment of unskilled labour. Third, he was one of the leading American production engineers of the century and a prominent and vociferous advocate of company-specific training, 'on-the-job' training, as opposed to the traditional apprenticeship system.

Combining metrological research of the 1840s and 1850s with modern engineering practice, his major achievement was not so much the institution of 'scientific management' as the introduction of radical new technologies. Embedded in these technologies were virtually unchallengeable elements of labour control, based on the deployment of raw labour. Technology for Taylor was not independent of control of labour.

New technologies and the notion of 'scientific management'

Taylor's metallurgical research beginning in the 1880s, the results of which were revealed in 1900 at the Universal Exhibition in Paris, was far more penetrating and influential than the stress on 'scientific management' would suggest. Within two years his new metal-cutting tool steels were undergoing trials in England. This was a major technical achievement; the new cutting techniques also had significant implications for the extension of management control over a wide range of production engineering practices. Analysis of Taylor's ideology of production, underlining social as well as technical parameters of basic workshop technologies, suggests further insights into our understanding of the dynamics of engineering developments outside America, particularly the engineering strike and lockout of 1897 in England.

Taylor's investigations enabled management, for the first time, to effectively dispense with the artisans who traditionally controlled the processes of machine metal-working and replace them with unskilled labour. A combination of new cutting materials and automatic machines, such as the turret lathes, radically altered the configuration of metal machining in addition to transforming the social relations of the workshops. This was accomplished by Taylor's introduction of new work schedules based on the following production principles: (1) the generation of consistent high cutting performance with a new class of highly effective tool steels; (2) replacing skilled machine operating by 'machine-tending'.

His 'scientific management' ideas thus interlocked with the original objectives of his metallurgical and machine-tool experiments, which lasted in all for 26 years. The objectives were clear from the outset, 'taking the control of the machine shop out of the hands of the workmen and placing it completely in the hands of the management, thus superseding "rule of thumb" by scientific control ... ' (Taylor 1906, in Thompson, p. 253).[1] The important issue for Taylor was to determine which elements of production were critical both in metal-cutting and in the decomposition of machine labour.

Cutting-tool technologies: their significance in the control of machines and labour

Writing on machinery and modern industry, Marx observed: 'fully developed machinery consists of three essentially different parts, the motor mechanism, the transmitting mechanism, and finally the tool or working machines ... ' (*Capital*, Vol. 1, 1977: 352). Of the last of these features he claimed that it was with the tool that the industrial revolution of the 18th century began (ibid.). This typology of machine functions was, more or less, constant throughout most of the 19th century, with this qualification: if control of manufacturing machines was a significant problem of the first half of the century, Taylor was one of the first to recognise that control over machine-cutting tools was the prime problem of the second half of the century.

Deployment of new machine-tool technologies entailed a transference of skill. Taylor expressed it in terms of workshop reorganisation and a changing ideology of production:

> The change from rule-of-thumb management to scientific management involves ... not only a study of what is the proper speed for doing the work and a remodelling of the tools and the implements in the shop, but also a complete change in the mental attitude of all the men toward their work and toward their employers' ... (Taylor 1911a: 53)

Taylor's concern was not just the substitution of one kind of mechanism of management for another, but rather the substitution of one set of underlying principles for a totally different set of principles. The rationale of this substitution was determined by management's grasp of the key variables of the processes of metal-cutting.

Metal-cutting processes

The object of machine tools was (is) the cutting or grinding away of surplus metal from raw stock (the metal being machined) so as to produce accurately machined components. Throughout most of the 19th century mechanical engineering employers faced two critical technological constraints when machining metals: the metallurgical properties of metal-cutting steels and their dependence upon highly skilled labour for sustained systematic and accurate production.

The rate at which different metals of the period could be machined was determined principally by the quality of the tools available at the time, known as plain carbon steel tools. Typically, cast iron, a widely used metal throughout the century, could be cut at 10–12 ft/min, steel at about 20 ft/min, brass at 50–100 ft/min (*Spon's Dictionary* 1874: 2322).[2]

Cutting above these speeds, that is, attempts to increase productivity or the intensity of labour by increasing machine speeds and/or feeds (the rate at which the tool advances along the workpiece being cut), led to frequent tool breakdown: 'The speed of the cutting tools in a machine is limited by the heat produced by their action, and the heat must never be so great as to affect the temper of the steel. Hence it is less, the harder the material of the work ... ' (ibid., 1874: 2324). Three main variables may therefore be distinguished in the cutting process: the cutting speed commensurate with the carbon content of the tool steel, the mechanical properties of the metal being cut, and the temperature attained during the cutting process.

Knowledge of the effects of these three variables had been traditionally part of the skilled machinist's expertise. Taylor understood that wresting control from skilled artisans was therefore contingent upon the discovery of new metal-cutting materials and techniques which would facilitate the process of labour substitution.

This was not an easy task, for the artisans had developed strategies to deflect skill transfer by the employers. Thus after Taylor's entry into the Midvale Steel Company in 1878 he observed that it was workers and not management who ran the shops, having 'carefully planned just how fast each job should be done, and they had set a pace for each machine throughout the shop, which was limited to about one-third of a good day's work ... ' (Taylor 1911a: 29). As a former machinist and shop foreman he knew that existing cutting-tool steels would need to be radically modified if the principles of metal-machining, essentially unchanged since the Middle Ages, were to be revolutionalised. Focusing his investigations on the exact determination and control of metal-cutting variables, he thus concentrated, not on the formulation of theories of metal-cutting, but on the daily routine practices of machine labour. 'The motive', said Taylor, 'was not abstract research after scientific knowledge, but was the very practical fact that we lacked the exact information, which was needed every day to help our machinists to do their work ... in the quickest time ... ' (1911a: 55).

He found in his initial attempts to increase production and to determine the fundamentals of cutting processes that his knowledge of what combination of depth of cut, feed and cutting speed would in each case do the work in the shortest time, was indeed much less refined and developed than that of the machinist (1906: 245). He recognised that this situation would need to change if artisans were to be more subordinate to management. This led him to seek ways of separating planning from practice in the workshop: 'There is no question that the cost of production is lowered by separating the work of planning and the brain work as much as possible from the manual labour ... ' (1911b: 121).

Sixty years later Braverman argued that the separation of conception from execution was at the heart of capitalist production: 'The breakup of craft skills and the reconstruction of production as a collective ... process opened up the only one way for mastery over labour processes to develop ... '(Braverman 1974: 443–4). A central problem for Braverman, and subsequent theorists, was precisely how management achieved the deconstruction of traditional craft skills. Taylor identified the core issues as first metallurgical – new cutting steels were required – and second the imposition of 'standards' within which to narrow the discretion allowed artisans. In other words, instituting a new concept of production based upon the intensification of labour through innovatory technologies.

Penetrating the 'craft mysteries' associated with metal-machining became a major priority for Taylor.

Variables associated with metal-cutting on machine tools

Taylor constantly stressed the interrelationship between his cutting trials and his management strategies, emphasizing the need for a unified approach to the problems of machine-tool production and labour control. By closely analysing the cutting variables, e.g. cutting tools, machines, machine drives (the way the work is held and rotated on the machine), belts and pulleys, the metallurgy of raw materials, 'scientific management' was more readily conceptualised as a means through which new patterns of labour control could be imposed.

Experiments were conducted under his direction in a number of companies from about 1878. He worked in the Midvale Steel Company until 1889, after which he continued in Cramp's Shipbuilding Company, followed by William Sellers & Co. The Sellers and Cramp's companies financed Taylor's research in 1894–5. Much of his final work was carried out in the Bethlehem Steel Company. His main concern here was to 'determine which make of self-hardening tool steel was ... the best to adopt as standard for all roughing tools of these ... shops (Taylor 1906: 247). The significance of 'self-hardening' tools and 'roughing' in the machining process is discussed below. Both concepts are critical to the understanding of the revolution in the workshops instigated by Taylor (see Table 2.1).

He succeeded in doubling output on his machines within three years, but his research revealed persistent critical defects in cutting-tool performance

Table 2.1 Chemical composition and tensile strength of materials used in cutting trials by F. W. Taylor, 1894–1906

Material being cut	Carbon C	Manganese M_N	Silicon SI	Phosphorus P	Sulphur S	Tensile strength lbs.
medium steel forging	0.34	0.54	1.76	0.037	0.026	70 280
hard steel forging	1.00	1.11	0.305	0.036	0.049	101 860
hard cast iron	total C 3.32 combined C^a 1.12		0.68	0.86	0.78	0.073

Note: [a] The hard constituent in the iron.

Source: Derived from table 138, folder 20, ASME (1906).

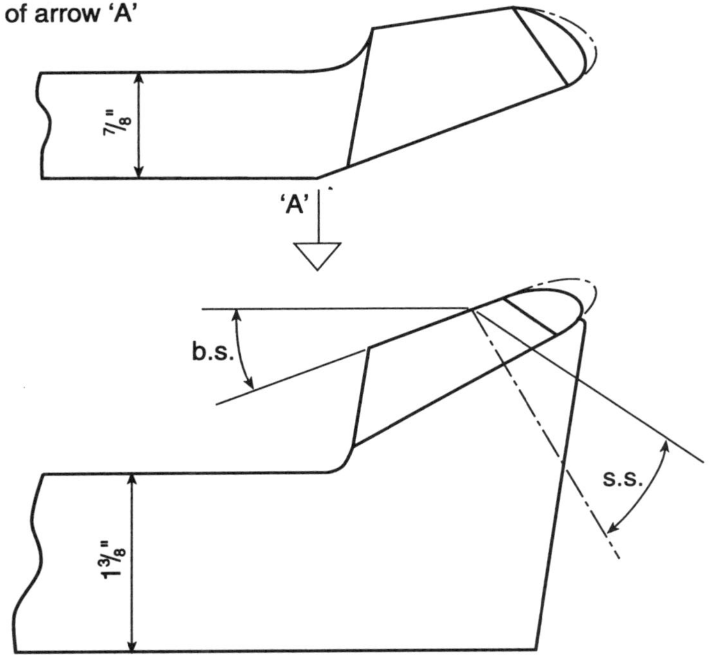

Material being cut	Tool angles	
	Side slope (s.s) 'rake'	Back slope (b.s)
Medium steel	14°	9°
Hard steel & cast iron	9°	5°

Standard 6° side clearance

Source: Derived from figs. 23 & 24, folder 5, ASME (1906), also ibid, table 138

Fig. 2.1 Two views of the standard $7/8$" tool used in most of the cutting trials by F. W. Taylor

and corresponding weaknesses in labour control (Taylor 1911a: 219). He had isolated, however, the two major problems associated with the mechanical properties of tool steels: (1) the inability to work at high speeds while retaining maximum tool hardness at elevated working temperatures due to increased friction, (2) the lack of durability which necessitated frequent regrinding, i.e. resharpening.

These were technological problems for Taylor; but their solution also clearly linked with his strategy of eliminating, as far as possible, skilled worker input. The process of tool sharpening or grinding, for example, presented special problems, for it was a complex task and required high levels of judgement and skill on the part of the machinist. The art entailed creating the correct angles on the tool profile in order to produce a defined quality of finish on the surface of the workpiece (see Fig. 2.1). The significance for machine-tool cutting of adding various alloying elements to basic carbon steels is outlined below.

The most common cause of cutting-tool failure was the considerable heat generated by friction in the cutting process; if the tool temperature at the point of contact with the work being cut exceeded critical levels, the structure of the tool broke up: 'steel which has been overheated ... suffers injury by the pores of the metal becoming open and expanded, the firmness of the texture destroyed, in which state it is quite incapable of sustaining a cutting edge ... ' (Weissenborn 1861: 20). The complexity of the elements of metal-cutting Taylor was investigating may be illustrated by the following observation by an American source as late as 1895: 'it is impossible to give any definite rule by which either the cutting speeds or rate of feed could be accurately calculated or even estimated ... ' (Usher 1895: 165).

Taylor's experiments in America were paralleled by similar developments in the metallurgy of cutting tools in England earlier in the century. He drew upon some of this work in his cutting investigations.

The composition of tool steels and metal-cutting

Much of the metallurgical data used in what follows is drawn from an Abstract of Selected Papers by the Cutting Tools Research Committee of the Institution of Mechanical Engineers. Between 1841 and 1921 these abstracts cited 369 articles on cutting tools research. After Taylor's published work in 1906 there were 145 articles up to 1921. In roughly the same period the American Society of Mechanical Engineers (ASME) cited 296 works, indicating a high level of interest in this aspect of production technology.

In 1868 an English engineer, Robert Mushet, in a series of experiments using a range of tool steels, added some new constituents to the basic composition of steel. As mentioned in Chapter 1 (see p. 13), steel is predominantly iron, with very small quantities of the principal alloy, carbon, usually not exceeding 2 per cent of the composition. Mushet succeeded in effectively producing an alloy composed of the basic constituents of steel with the addition of tungsten, chromium and manganese. These new elements were alloyed to 1.7 per cent carbon steel; the most important of which was tungsten, present at a level of about 6.0 per cent. The effect of this alloying was the dispersion throughout the structure of the steel of microscopic particles of tungsten carbide, an extremely hard element, enabling a tool of this composition to last longer without regrinding (C. S. Smith 1967: 597). This steel was known as 'air-hardening' or 'self-hardening' on account of the cooling procedure during the hardening process of the tool, which used a blast of air or was allowed simply to cool in air without quenching in oil or water.

Many grades of air-hardening steels based on the Mushet formula approximating in composition to those noted here, were developed and had been in use for several years before Taylor's intensive American studies. These new alloy steels largely replaced the plain carbon steels in the latter part of the 19th century and were capable of cutting efficiencies twice that of carbon steels, due principally to the property of retaining the cutting edge at much higher temperatures than carbon steels.

The wider research implications of the steels was that they constituted the basis for comparison for cutting performance in experiments conducted by Taylor.

The following details of alloying elements show how Taylor and his associates varied the constituents, which led to the discovery of High Speed Steel. The basic alloying elements being used in this research may be summarized as follows:

Tungsten. With from 4 per cent to 25 per cent addition to this constituent the brittleness of the steel is increased but the cutting capacity is greatly improved. Tungsten steels also possess a power of resistance to abrasion.

Chromium. The function of chromium is to form a double carbide with tungsten, which imparts a very high degree of hardness and excellent resistance to abrasion.

Carbon. As noted, too high a carbon content is undesirable, causing brittleness.

Manganese. This is present in all steels. Steels containing 1.5 per cent manganese and 0.3 per cent carbon are appreciably stronger and tougher than plain mild steel and were not considered expensive.

Silicon. Up to a maximum of 3 per cent, this element improves the hardness and cutting qualities for machining hard material. To a limited extent it counteracts the effects of tungsten, the durability of the tool increasing as the silicon content decreases.

Sulphur. Present as an impurity, it tends to form dangerous films of iron sulphide; in conjunction with manganese it forms manganese sulphide, which counteracts this tendency.

Nineteenth-century experiments with special metal-cutting steels

Taylor compared the performance of two steels, the English Mushet air-hardening steel and an alloy he had developed whilst at Midvale Steel Works (Taylor 1906). The compositions of these metals were as follows:

	Tungsten	*Chromium*	*Carbon*	*Manganese*	*Silicon*
Mushet	5.441	0.398	2.150	1.528	1.044
Midvale	7.723	1.830	1.143	0.180	0.246

Tests on metal-cutting properties were therefore made with tools of various chemical composition, and heated to different temperatures. It was during the course of this investigation that Taylor established a crucial empirical point that, although both carbon and air-hardening steel deteriorate rapidly when the temperature rises above a cherry red (the colour of the oxide film on the surface of the metal), some chemical compositions of the air-hardening class of steels rapidly pass through this condition. The efficiency rises slowly at first, and then rapidly as the temperature rises, reaching a maximum at the point when the tool begins to crumble ('burnt' steel). He noted that the Mushet steels were breaking down or were injured by overheating at between 1550 °F and 1700 °F:

> but to our surprise, tools heated up to or above the high heat of 1725 °F proved better than any of those heated to the previous best temperatures, namely cherry red; and from 1725 °F up to the incipient point of fusion of the tools, the higher they were heated, the higher the cutting speeds at which they could run. (Taylor 1906, in Thompson (ed.) 1914: 260)

The exploration of this phenomenon led Taylor and his colleague, metallurgist J. Maunsel White, to the inclusion of another constituent in the chromium-tungsten steels. This was molybdenum, used either in combination with or as a substitute for tungsten. The proportions of the Taylor–White metal varied but generally depended upon the work the steel was intended to do: 0.75 per cent chromium, with 4 per cent tungsten or molybdenum, or a mixture of the two latter with chromium would be suitable for machining mild steel at the highest speed. For working hard steel or chilled iron (iron usually with a very hard 'skin'), 3.0 per cent chromium, 5.0 per cent tungsten, 4.0 per cent molybdenum (see Table 2.2).

The heat treatments for the hardening of these steels was itself a radical departure from conventional hardening procedures (Gledhill 1904: 12): the

Table 2.2 Chemical composition and cutting speeds of tool steels showing inclusion of molybdenum and later vanadium, based on Taylor's experiments

Tool number (of 25)	Year of tool	Vanadium V$_A$	Molybdenum Mo	Tungsten W	Chromium CR	Carbon C	Manganese Mn	Silicon Si	Phosphorus P	Sulphur S	Medium steel forging	Hard steel forging (ft/min)	Hard cast iron
8	1903	—	0.48	17.79	2.84	0.65	0.12	0.087	0.013	0.112	70 ft	37 ft	45½ ft
12	1903	—	2.03	18.93	3.52	0.58	0.19	0.125	0.028	0.016		37 ft	45½ ft
13	—	—	4.21	13.44	3.04	0.76	0.09	0.052	—	—		37 ft	45½ ft
22	1903	—	0.75	14.91	2.80	0.45	0.10	0.090	0.018	0.008		34 ft	44 ft
17	1906	—	7.60	9.25	6.11	0.32	0.13	0.081	—	—	86 ft	37 ft	
18	1906	0.28	—	16.00	3.50	0.70	low	low	—	—		38 ft	

Source: Derived from table 138, folder 20, ASME (1906).

steel was heated to about 1000 °C, then rapidly cooled in a lead bath to about 800 °C, keeping it at that temperature for about ten minutes, followed by natural slow cooling in lime or some other inert non-conducting powder. When quite cold it was reheated to warm red, and allowed to cool in the open air (*Iron and Coal Trades Review* (1902): 1516).

A new class of revolutionary steels was emerging as the two fundamental problems in manufacturing engineering were being confronted: how to increase machine production with lower costs; and how effectively to substitute unskilled for skilled machine labour. These trials culminated in the cutting-tool demonstrations presented at the Paris Exhibition of 1900, where Taylor revealed his High Speed Steel (HSS).

Taylor and the development of high-speed steel (HSS)

Taylor's massive cutting trials, culminating in the first public demonstration in 1900, constituted a major contribution to machine tool-cutting techniques. The practical side of his research started on a 66 in. vertical boring mill, that is, a machine on which the workpiece is clamped to a circular, horizontal table and rotated against the cutting tool. During the whole period, between 30,000 and 50,000 experiments were recorded, on ten different experimental machine tools; 80,000 lb of iron and steel were used and the cost was estimated at $150,000–$200,000 (Taylor 1911a: 55).

In the period 1898 through January 1900, cutting and lathe dynamometer research at the Bethlehem Steel Works demonstrated the following changes in the configuration of machine-tool performance directly attributable to changes effected by Taylor: cutting speeds increased by 183 per cent; depth of cut, 30 per cent; feed rate, 24 per cent, rate of metal removal, 340 per cent increase (*American Machinist*, 16 Aug. 1900, p. 784).

These figures represent exceptional changes in the basic cutting dynamics. Even in the middle of the 19th century metal-cutting machines constructed of wood and iron were still in existence; and years after Maudslay's invention of the cross-slide in the latter part of the 18th century, artisans were still holding the cutting tool in the hand. After Taylor's discoveries machine tool-cutting was transformed: one commentator noted, 'the results are so extraordinary that they would not be believed if published … ' (*Iron and Coal Trades Review* (1902), p. 1576).

The cutting speed recorded by the new tools had increased by 600 per cent since earlier trials in 1894. When cutting cast iron these tools were removing metal at the rate of 7.325 lb/min, and in further trials in 1902 a metal-removing rate of 640 lb/hr was recorded. The exceptional technical properties of HSS were confirmed by findings which showed that power consumption decreased during cutting; the extra power required to remove metal at a higher speed with HSS was not proportional to the greater amount of work done by the higher cutting speed. Figures produced by another researcher, Gledhill, in 1904 indicated that with cutting speed increased by 250 per cent, the power absorbed fell by 19 per cent (Gledhill 1904: 14). In trials in England a cutting force of 30,600 lb at the tool face was recorded, with a metal-removing rate of 500 lb/hr (*Engineering*, 30 Oct. 1903, Table VIA, p. 595); Brackenbury, 1910: 934).

As Taylor had predicted, the durability of the new tools had considerable impact on machine production times, and generated a new machining technique not possible before HSS. This technique was called 'roughing', during which very rapid metal removal was possible, prior to subsequent 'fine' machining; the surface finish was relatively unimportant as the finish and final dimensions were established later. Taylor's prescription was ' ... to describe the fundamental laws and principles which will enable us to do "roughing work" in the shortest possible time' (Taylor 1906, in Thompson (ed.) 1914: 243). It was this technique that accelerated the decline of the skilled machinist and dramatically reduced employers' dependence upon artisans.

The use of HSS extended the time between tool regrinds, demanding less of the machinists' non-production time. It also compensated for errors in machining due to incompetence or operators' unfamiliarity, as these were less damaging to the workpiece and the tool with the roughing technique. The heat-resisting and high-strength properties of HSS reduced the risk of tool breakdown consequent upon overheating and heavy loading. For example, a Taylor–White tool when cutting dry, that is without a stream of coolant directed to the point of the tool, cut blue chips (the waste material cut from the workpiece), i.e. approaching red heat, continuously: 'It may be interesting to some to know that the point of the tool is frequently red hot when cutting dry; this fact showing conclusively the high temperatures at which the cutting edge is retained ... ' (*Iron and Coal Trades Review*, 22 June 1902, p. 1517).

Taylor was determined to push production rates as far as the machines would permit. This later prompted a machine shop superviser to observe:

> do you know I feel like advising the men to set the steel at full speed, start every machine at full speed, duck their heads and run for life. It would simply gut half the machine shops in the district and break 90 per cent of the machines, break belts, and blow fuses in every one of them. And yet when we try to protect our employers' property he tries to make the public believe we are restricting output (Evidence in US Commission on Labour, Eleventh Special Report, p. 115).

The figures in Table 2.3 show the effect of high-speed steel on metal-removing performance.

A practical illustration of the cutting performance of HSS, measured by the rate of removal of surplus metal, comes from a variant of HSS, called Novo

Table 2.3 The effect of high-speed steel on metal-removing performance (ft/min)

Name of tool	Year of trial	Vanadium V$_A$	Molybdenum Mo	Tungsten W	Chromium C$_R$	Carbon C	Manganese M$_N$	Silicon Si	Phosphorus P	Sulphur S	Medium steel forging	Hard steel forging	Hard cast iron
Jessop Carbon[a]	1894	—	—	—	—	1.047	1.189	0.206	0.017	0.017	16 ft	6 ft	15½ ft
Bethlehem Mesh	1896	—	—	8.40	1.86	1.43	0.23	0.126	—	—	61 ft	19 ft	39 ft
Bethlehem HSH[b]	1898	—	—	8.00	3.80	1.85	0.30	0.15	0.025	0.03	58 ft	30½ ft	43 ft
Tools used at Link-Belt Co.	1903	—	—	14.71	2.90	0.70	0.12	0.196	0.017	0.010	64 ft	34 ft	44 ft
The 'best' HSS used by Taylor	1906	0.32	—	17.79	5.95	0.68	0.07	0.049	—	—	99 ft	41½ ft	52 ft
		0.29	—	18.19	5.47	0.67	0.11	0.04	—	—			

Material being cut

Notes: [a] English tool.
        [b] Original Taylor–White steel.

Source: Derived from table 138, folder 20, ASME (1906).

steel, made in Sheffield. This new steel was used in a multiple-tool roughing operation as follows: a rope transmission sheave (a very large pulley), 23' 6" diameter, 6' long was roughed off simultaneously by five tools of 1" × 2" Novo steel. Using a cutting speed of 27' per minute the roughing operation removed metal at the rate of 500 lb per hour. These five tools ran continuously for a period of 36 hours without grinding, i.e. resharpening (*Iron and Coal Trades Review* (1902), p. 1516).

The Link-Belt Engineering Company in America, one of the first firms to introduce the new process into their machine shops, conducted tests on cast-iron rings of 6' 6" diameter bolted to the table of a 7' boring mill. A Mushet tool, under the test cut, removed 5½ lb of metal and broke down after one minute. A HSS tool, under the same conditions of cut, feed and cutting speed, removed 106 lb of metal in 10 minutes and when removed was in perfect condition (ibid., p. 15167).

The durable properties of these metals may be gauged by the level of cutting forces sustained during the trials. The force on the tool in each case exceeded 3½ t, while the pressure on one of the test tools (of larger cross-sectional area) was 143,000 lb per sq. in. (ibid.).

The machining stresses, whilst severe, were adequately accommodated by many grades of HSS, producing greatly increased rates of metal removal. Figures from trials on a 30-ton steel on a lathe (30-ton steel = steel with a tensile strength of 30 tons per sq. in.) make the point. Cutting conditions were: depth of cut of ⅞", i.e. 1¾" reduction in diameter in one cut, with a ¼" feed per revolution, at a cutting speed of 90' per minute. Metal was removed at the rate of 68.75 lb/min or 4,010 lb/hr. The stress on the tool was 78.5 t/sq. in. In a similar test with a 35-ton steel a pressure of 115 t/sq. in was recorded, suggesting that ' ... if proper care can be taken, tools of high speed steel are quite capable of withstanding any pressure likely to be met in workshop practice ... ' (Gledhill 1904: 15).

A series of tests were undertaken in Manchester in 1902–3. The extraordinary properties of HSS against the plain and Mushet steels are shown in Table 2.4. There were 300 serial trials, each requiring the making and recording of 50–100 observations, in all amounting to 15,000 to 30,000 readings in the course of the cutting trials. Submission of cutting tools was invited from the leading manufacturers of the time in England. Among these were Armstrong Whitworth, Vickers Son and Maxim, Samuel Buckley and John Browne & Co. Eight kinds of tools were tested, including high-speed steel, rapid self-hard, Mushet high-speed steel (*Engineering*, 30 Oct. 1903).

Significant advances in metal-removal rates are demonstrated in these English trials. One tool specimen recorded a cutting force of 30,600 lb at the tool face; and the metal-removal rate was equivalent to 500 lb per hour (Table VIA, p. 595). Similar findings were recorded in tests carried out by the leading English tool manufacturer, Alfred Herbert. Cutting speeds of 185 ft

Table 2.4 Experiments carried out with rapid-cutting tools in England, 1903

Material cut	Soft steel			Medium cast iron			Soft cast iron		
Cutting tool	Plain C	Mushet	HSS	Plain C	Mushet	HSS	Plain C	Mushet	HSS
Speed ft/min	31.2	63.0	132.5	24.6	23.6	60.0	22.5	31.6	52.25
Cut (in.)	0.058	0.058	0.058	0.062	0.062	0.053	0.191	0.186	0.364
Traverse (in.)	0.062	0.062	0.062	0.062	0.062	0.062	0.125	0.125	0.125
Cross-sectional area cut (in.²)	0.0036	0.0036	0.0036	—	—	0.0033	—	—	0.045
Duration (min.)	20	17	20	17	20.5	30	8.53	32.75	30
Area machined (ft²)	3.26	5.5	14.25	2.19	2.51	9.26	1.0	5.36	16.4
Area machined (ft²/min.)	0.163	0.326	0.712	0.128	0.122	0.308	0.117	0.163	0.547
Total weight removed (lb)	7¼	13¼	29	3¼	5¼	20¾	13¼	73½	219¾
Weight removed (lb/min)	0.362	0.794	1.45	0.191*	0.256*	0.69	1.55*	2.25*	7.325

Note: * tooled failed

Source: Extracted from Report on Experiments with Rapid Cutting Tools made at Manchester Municipal School of Technology under auspices of a joint committee of members of the Manchester Association of Engineers and of Members of the School of Technology Sub-Committee, October 1903. *Engineering* (30 Oct. 1903), 590–5, Tables I, IV, V, VIA.

per min. and a metal-removal rate of 8.8 lb per min. were returned (Brackenbury 1910: 934).

The next stage for Taylor was to integrate the new tool technologies with the imposition of pre-determined sizes and finish quality of machined components, through the use of 'Standards'. Machine workers were henceforth constrained by a new set of machining parameters.

The imposition of standards

Taylor's aim was to capitalise on the machining potential of the new tools by maintaining pressure on the workers to exploit their unprecedented production capabilities. He also recognised, as Whitworth had in England in the 1840s, that the key to this pressure in the engineering workshop was the imposition of Standards. These were not judgements of value, but predetermined technological limits laid down for a range of common sizes used in engineering practice. Each regular increment in size, e.g. 1", 2", 3", had an allowance for error, beyond which no deviation was permitted. A 1" shaft might be given an allowance of 0.010", i.e. + or − 0.005"; the finished size could therefore range from 0.995" to 1.005". This was the standard for all 1" shafts within that category of components. A corresponding set of standards was designated for all other common engineering sizes.

Whitworth devised a similar system in the 1840s and 1850s, which came down to modern practice as the British Standard Whitworth (BSW) (Whitworth, 1857). The crucial significance of Taylor's and Whitworth's work was that the whole edifice of interchangeability was built upon the principles of standardisation; it was also the key to the decomposition of skilled labour by substitution with raw labour. It was generalisable and reflected a new ideology of production gathering strength in England (Buckingham 1920; Clarke 1957; *Engineering* (Sept., Oct., Dec. 1897; Oct. 1903; 1905).

Taylor ensured that the discoveries which resulted in the revolutionary treatment of tool steels were not confined to the specifics of tool steels, but also 'in the adoption of standards ... It was through enforced standardisation of methods, enforced adoption of best implements and working conditions and enforced cooperation that faster work can be assured ... ' (Taylor 1911a: 480). Through the implementation of standards he sought to eliminate individual interpretation of methods and processes, making standards integral to his work organisation. It was not only desirable but 'absolutely indispensable' as a preliminary to ' ... specifying the time in which each operation shall be done within the time allowed ... ' (Ibid., p. 123).

Taylor granted few concessions to skilled workers, other than a small caucus of highly skilled artisans, usually employed in the 'toolroom'. The revolutionising of work practices, at the core of which was the decomposition of craft skills, was not, as has been asserted, on a trajectory of a deskilling cycle, within which deskilled workers were able to 'claw back' concessions from management on questions of 'skill and control' (P. Thompson 1983: 106). His penetration of the fundamentals of machine shop skills enabled him to systematically undermine the basis of artisan resistance and bargaining power, thereby increasing management control over the variables of machine cutting. These were henceforth located within management and operable through a number of devices, such as Slide Rules and the use of automatic machines, after the 1880s. The ability of skilled workers to negotiate on the basis of the retention of control over jobs, as opposed to control over craft status, was very limited.

Similar developments in England were highlighted by the engineering strike and lockout of 1897. Central to this damaging dispute was the 'Machine Question', which had been in contention from the 1850s until the resistance of machine artisans was finally broken by the employers' dogmatic refusal to negotiate on the issue of skilled status for machinists. They were confident that the introduction of new cutting tools and machines and the imposition of standards made substitution a non-negotiable proposition. The resistance of artisans in this period was more tightly circumscribed than in the previous national dispute of 1852 (*Engineering*, Sept. 1897; *Labour Leader*, 21 Aug. 1897; 11 Sept. 1897; *Engineering*, 15 Oct. 1897).

The reorganisation of both the American and English workshops generated new social relations. The ratio of unskilled to skilled labour had been greatly increased; machines being manned principally by raw labour. The presence of large numbers of unskilled workers operating machines at high speeds with high rates of metal removal required close supervision. New factors therefore were introduced under this regime. First, the traditional 'chargehand' or foreman was replaced by a new class of supervisers; tool setting (preparing machines to cut), formerly carried out as routine by skilled artisans, became their prerogative. Second, the notion of the engineering workshop as a source of technical learning, exemplified in the era of the traditional apprenticeship, became redundant.

Taylor recognised the core problems and advocated two strategies to overcome difficulties attendant upon the lack of training. He had long regarded the old type of chargehand, historically viewed as apprentice overseers, as too immersed in the old, independent artisan ways of working, and needing to be superseded. He thus introduced 'functional foremen' and implemented the Slide Rules to assert the authority of the employer at the machine.

The functional foreman

The imposition of the new principles of workshop practice forced Taylor to confront the issue of immediate control at the machine. He drew from the ranks of artisans, who had been virtually dispossessed, 'functional foremen', as 'suitable' men to enforce the new workshop regime. The commonly-held view that artisans had become exclusive or aristocratic was not borne out by events. Artisan exclusiveness failed to dissuade Taylor and other employers from substituting labourers for skilled machinists.

Taylor recruited artisan foremen according to their ability to accept without question management directives, and who had demonstrated the ability to force the pace of production. This inaugurated a system of labour control based on the recruitment of infinitely replaceable, cheap labour directed by conventionally skilled workers of unswerving loyalty to management: 'the full possibilities of functional foremanship will not be realised until almost all of the machines in the shop are *run by men who are of small calibre and attainments* ... cheaper than those required under the old system ... ' (Taylor 1911b: 105; my emphasis). He instituted a detailed division of labour within the supervisory ranks, arguing that 'functional management' should replace 'military' type organization: 'the work of each man in the management should be confined to the performance of a single leading function ... ' (ibid., p. 98). Two supervisory divisions were installed: 'Executive' Functional Bosses in the Workshops, and Functional Bosses in Planning. These were subdivided into Gang Bosses, Speed Bosses, Inspectors, Repair Bosses; Order of Work and Route Clerks, Instruction Card Clerks, Time and Cost Clerks, Shop Disciplinarian respectively (ibid., pp. 98–123).

The work of the Gang Boss exemplified the intensification of labour under the Taylor regime. He was in charge of all preparatory work up to the time that the workpiece was set in the machine. Every man under him should have had at least one piece ahead at his machine, with all the jigs (special devices for locating and holding the workpiece), templates, drawings, driving mechanism ready to go into the machine. He showed the quickest way to set up and was prepared to demonstrate when required (ibid., p. 100 ff). Taylor said, 'No Gang Boss is fit to direct his men until after he has learned to promptly obey instructions received from any proper source, whether he likes his instructions and the instructor or not, and even though he may be convinced that he knows a much better way of doing the work ... ' (ibid., p. 139). The authority relations in the workshop were clear and unequivocal: 'there must be men present in the organization who will not mistake the "form for the essence" and with nerve enough to make it unpleasant for (workers) who fail ... ' (ibid., p. 147). The ideology of production was equally forthright and premised upon the fundamental principle that production is ' ... first and last, and for all time, for the purpose of paying dividends to its owners ... ' (ibid., p. 143).

The implications for technical training were clear. The concept was redundant in such an ideology; as Taylor said, 'No worse mistake can be made than that of allowing an establishment to be looked upon as a training school to be used mainly for the education of its many employees ... ' (ibid.). Hence at Midvale, from 1881, there were no apprentices, but they took 'a great many boys, young men, and even older labourers ... There were no apprentices in the old-fashioned meaning of the term ... I would treat them as I would other men ... ' (Taylor 1895: 676).

The collapse of training based upon historically located skills hardened the distinction between artisan-controlled work processes and machine-dominated technology under coercive management. As Taylor graphically expressed it, 'I do not care who turns out my work. So much work is so much money, whether done by an apprentice or by a man just tottering to his grave ... ' (Taylor 1895: 676). Taylor's disregard for technical training in his workshops reflected the prevailing employer attitude to the apprenticeship system. In the period 1860 through 1910, the ratio of apprentices to the total employed in the manufacturing industry fell from 1:33 to 1:98. A study in Philadelphia, Taylor's hometown, showed a ratio of 1:25 in 1870 (Douglas 1921: 72–4). One explanation for the reluctance of employers to train young workers was that they were recruiting skilled workers from abroad and therefore had no need to train at home (ibid., p. 76).

Taylor recognised that with the introduction of Standards, interchangeability of parts and labour became a realistic production mode. The implications for future technological developments were not lost on him. Alert always to the need to reinforce control at every stage of production, and consolidating his tactics of rationalisation of work methods with new intakes of untried labour, he continued to refine the processes of skill transfer and labour control through another innovation, the introduction of the Slide Rules.

The Slide Rules and labour control

Slide Rules were sets of complex tables setting out the precise details of machining operations. Included were relevant cutting speeds, depth of cut and feed rate for each operation covering a range of metals. They covered all the common production engineering functions. Based on Taylor's research into the general laws on machine-tool and cutting-tool performance, these Rules theoretically enabled employers to exercise a level of control over skilled labour never before possible. With this instrument employers were thus, 'able completely to distance the skilled mechanic who had made the parts of this machine his speciality for years ... ' (Taylor 1911b: 96). The Slide Rules were developed between 1899 and 1902 by Taylor, the metallurgist Maunsell White and Carl Barth, a mathematician, the principal figure behind the Slide Rules, who joined in 1899 (Barth 1914: 406).

Incorporating twelve cutting variables, the Slide Rules were arguably the clearest evocation of the principle of the separation of planning and practical work in machine shops. The immediate effect of these instruments was to instil another management prerogative and add to the intensification of labour, whilst distancing the workers from the decision-making process. The Slide Rules transposed the complex set of variables associated with machine processes to an index form. Exclusively controlled by employers and specifically designed for use with raw labour, they could be interpreted and put into operation by managers or others. The significance was that they need not necessarily have the expertise or knowledge to execute the operation, further dismantling the historical pattern of technical training and education.

The American Federation of Labour (AFL), sensing continued decomposition of skilled labour, argued that skilled engineering workers' specialist tasks required systematic training, including some form of technical education. They held that the modern tendency towards specialisation within an increasingly complex division of labour was destructive of mechanical education and skill, and 'tended to gather up and transfer to management all the traditional knowledge, the judgment and the skill, and monopolizes the initiative of the worker in connection with the work' (The Trade Union Objection to Scientific Management: Hoxie 1914: 16; App. V, p. 170). The President of the American Federation of Labor, in his evidence to the Senate Commission of 1911, added that the 'Taylor' system was the 'very antithesis of industrial education, because it robs the man of initiatives ... ' (US Committee on Labor 1911: 24).

But the central problem for artisans in American workshops, and in England, was that oversight of two crucial elements of their work was passing irrevocably to management: substantive control over the method and pace of work processes, and the imposition of critical standards with guaranteed accuracy according to prescribed limits. The remnants of the traditional machine-shop artisan class had gradually become functionaries of management, supervising 'green' labour embodying none of the craft traditions and engaging a technology of which they had a decreasingly informed, and at times only peripheral, knowledge. The 'mysteries of the trade' had been significantly penetrated by management and made accessible to them in a form abstracted from practical expertise and rendered modifiable in the interests of the employers.

Resistance was not entirely dormant, for in 1911 unionized machinists at the Watertown Arsenal, where the 'Taylor System' was being introduced by Barth, struck. On being taken back they petitioned the Labor Committee of Congress to investigate the subject of 'Taylorism' and recommend legislation. Having been engaged in the intricacies of machine processes for such a long period, Taylor anticipated the lines of opposition, and his evidence, together with that of other engineering managers, to the 1911 Committee confirmed their uncompromising attitude on issues of machine and labour control.

Artisan resistance to work reorganisation

Taylor had realistically gauged the level of artisan resistance. He knew his adversaries and was used to confrontation. As early as 1878, on entering Midvale Steel, he was very soon put in charge of lathes and determined to raise production against the resistance of the machinists:

> 'Now Fred, we're very glad to see that you've been made Gang Boss. You know the game all right, and we're sure that you're not likely to be a damn piece-work hog. You come along with us and everything will be all right, but if you try breaking any of these rates you can be mighty sure that we will throw you over the fence.'

To which Taylor replied,

> 'I have accepted a job under the management of the company and ... I will tell you perfectly frankly that I am going to get a bigger output from these lathes.'
> 'Then you are going to be a damn hog!'
> 'Well, if you fellows put it that way, all right.'
> 'We warn you Fred, if you try to bust any of these rates, we will have you over the fence in six weeks.'
> (Testimony before the special House Committee, 1912, in Taylor 1964: 79)

He introduced the piece-rate system in an attempt to generate a more accommodating response from the machinists, but the ensuing fight with the men lasted three years (ibid.).

Taylor maintained this stance in all his dealings with his machinists and other workers, believing that no production increases would be possible unless the men were driven:

> as a class ... they are extremely conservative, and if left to themselves their progress from the older to the better methods will be exceedingly slow. And my experience is that *rapid improvement can only be brought about through constant and and heavy pressure from those who are over them* ... (Taylor 1906, in Thompson (ed.) 1914: 262; my emphasis)

He also knew that the workers' strategies for circumventing managerial authority had had a long history. This, he asserted, had demoralised them to the extent that, in some areas, '(they) are so lazy ... that no sufficient inducement can be offered to make (them) do a full day's work ... ' (Taylor 1895, in Thompson (ed.) 1914: 655). (His views here are at variance with the explicit faith he held when putting forward the Differential Piece Rate System as a means of doubling or trebling production rates whilst holding wage rates to a minimum. The Differential Piece Rate system consisted of offering two different rates for the same job: a high price per piece, in case the work is finished in the shortest possible time and in perfect condition; and a low price, if it takes a longer time, or if there are any imperfections in the work (Taylor 1895: 857, Table F).

The workers' traditional form of resistance operated in the workshops through control over the method and pace of production, that is, maintaining traditional craft practices, known as the 'stint' (In England the term was known as 'ca-canny'). Taylor's term for this kind of resistance was 'soldiering'. There were, he argued, two variants. The first arose out of the workers' natural instinct to take things easy; this he referred to as 'natural soldiering'. The second, developed from the social relations entered into by the men, and was a more reasoned and structured response to new working practices, which Taylor referred to as 'systematic soldiering' (American Society of Mechanical Engineers 1903: 1349).

The second variant interrelated with the first and was basically a reassertion of worker solidarity. Artisans exercised powerful constraints over other workers. Those who broke the stints were labelled one of a whole range of epithets: 'hog', 'hogger-in', 'bell-horse', 'horsing', 'chaser', 'rusher', 'runner', 'swift', 'rooter' (ibid., p. 18). Similar strategies were in use in England. Submissions to the 1868 Commission on Trades Unions revealed a system of workers' control through the use of 'silence' or 'sending to Coventry'. A prominent employer, Nasmyth, said that he had known instances of men who had ' ... been put into Coventry ... and their lives rendered as utterly miserable that they were obliged to give up ... ' (Royal Commission on Trade Unions 1868c, Q. 19127).

From his own machine-shop experience Taylor understood that the chief object of soldiering was to keep the foremen ignorant of how fast work could be done: 'I was on to the whole game of soldiering ... ' (testimony to the Special House Committee). In day-to-day operations in the workshops he used a number of expedients to counter artisan resistance directly and to make the men to 'a fair day's work'. He discharged or lowered the wages of men who refused to make any improvement. Another strategy was the hiring of 'green men', that is, raw labourers which Taylor trained against a promise to turn out increased rates of production. He also broke opposition through a system of fines whenever accidents occurred (Taylor 1964: 84). He was not concerned with principle of bargaining. Convinced of the indisputable correctness of his system, Taylor brooked no opposition, justified by his belief that a 'great part of the industrial world is deliberately soldiering and must be stopped before proper output can be reached ... ' (Taylor's evidence to the Senate Commission 1912)

Apart from government concerns such as the arsenals at Watertown and Rock Island, and the Brooklyn Naval Yard, by 1900 the ideology of production pursued by Taylor had been integrated by companies such as Midvale Steel, the first company to employ his principles. In his evidence to the Labor Commission of that year, the President, Harrap, arguing that Midvale Steel had no regard for machinery or men, said,

> the life of a hammer bar may be two years. If that hammer bar does not break inside two years I go for the forgemaster, because I know hat he is not getting the work he ought out of the forge. In the same way, in the machine shop ... if a lathe does not break before [two years] I would go for the engineer in charge ... We have absolutely no regard for machinery or men ... (US Committee on Labor 1911: 25).

The Chief of Ordnance at the Rock Island arsenal was clearly influenced by the advantages of decomposing skilled labour and the introduction of unskilled machine minders. In his evidence to the Labor Commission, arguing that he would employ skilled labour 'only when absolutely necessary', he recommended that stopwatches be used to determine 'unit times' and differential pay rates be used. He maintained that the rates of machine speeds be fixed so that 'only one in eight men could stand the pace' (ibid., p. 18) One of his machinists argued in the same inquiry that such a production ideology created a 'tremendous unemployment problem caused by the elimination of workmen who can not attain maximum efficiency ... ' (ibid., p. 22). He further added that the system was characterised by 'overworking and enslaving' (ibid.).

Management was undeterred: 'any machinist running his machine at less than the card speed is discharged on the spot ... we have had to discharge numerous employees for restricting their output ... and for attempting to interfere with the production of other employees ... ' (US Commission on Labour 1904: 137, 141). The system was thus established in government arsenals. In a reply to union officials criticising the implementation and further consolidation of Taylor's principles, it was stated, 'it would seem there could be no reasonable objection to extending the usefulness experienced along the lines indicated to other arsenals ... ' (Reply from War Department, 27 Apr. 1911, drawing on evidence from the Watertown arsenal, US Committee on Labor 1911).

The increasing use of the stopwatch highlighted in the objections by machinists, and an intrinsic part of new management controls was exemplified by Harrap:

> We had men with stop watches over the men working on an axle lathe ... and every time a man looked up they took his time; every time he stopped to breathe they took his time, and in that way they got absolutely the amount of time employed in doing a certain amount of work ... (Vol. 41, Congressional Hearings)

Intensification of labour at Midvale Steel determined by the stopwatch was replicated in other plants, despite the claim that the men were restricting output. In one company a 300 per cent increase in the production of wheel hubs was reported; and in the bolt department 22,000 ⅝-in. bolts were produced without once regrinding the tool. In one operation the HSS tool had worked for 90 days without resharpening (US Commission on Labor 1904: 110). The heat-resisting qualities and robustness of the new tools were demonstrated in a steel axle turning operation in Chicago. When the machine was cutting, the steel shavings as they fell from the point of the tool 'set the floor afire'. The machine shop superintendent stated that given such speed and feed, with the tool 'at an almost white heat, and the shavings hot enough to set the floor on fire, charges of restriction of output were hardly in order' (ibid.)

At the Rock Island arsenal in a demonstration, a machinist worked for three hours to fix a standard time at which machinists would be expected to work all the time. It was reported that he was working so fast that his clothes were dripping wet and the sweat was even oozing from the seams of his boots (US Congressional Hearings 1913–15: 14, Evidence of Congressman Taverner). This justified criticisms raised by Samuel Gompers, President of the American Federation of Labor (AFL), who in 1911 argued that the Taylor system 'was bad ... and under which ... the man at the lathe is robbed of all opportunity to think for himself, where he is not permitted to think out any problems in mechanics, but is driven to the fullest notch of his physical and mental endurances ... ' (US Committee on Labor 1911: 24).

The fact was that artisans were forced to come to terms with the new ideology of production as the employers consolidated their position. In the Link-Belt company of Pennsylvania a series of time studies had been conducted by management, as a result of which it was determined that a man should run three and one-half machines simultaneously. In effect this meant that in order to obtain his maximum wage a machinist was required to turn in three and one-half machine hours as the number of hours he worked (*American Machinist*, (1911): 18).

This exemplifies the transformation of factory work from the middle of the 19th century, emanating from changes in machine technologies implemented by forceful employers such as Taylor. Critiques of the Taylorist method of engineering production have been centred on his principles of 'scientific management', tending to underplay Taylor's immense contribution to metal-machining and the imposition of standards in production. Foremost among these analyses was the work of Braverman in 1974.

Braverman and the issue of deskilling

The transformation of factory work from the middle of the 19th century, based on machine technologies, is well recorded, often with a focus on industrial conflicts. The indispensable condition of these developments was the employers' deepening control of the labour process. In so far as it is possible to determine a clear picture of their basic elements, labour process theories have been mainly concerned with addressing issues surrounding management attempts to deploy new technologies in order to increase profits and subdue skilled labour (Braverman 1974; Marglin 1974; Friedman 1977; Berg (ed.) 1979; Lee 1979; Zimbalist 1979; P. Thompson 1983; Whalley 1986; Wood 1988; Warde 1992).

A major emphasis in this work has been on job fragmentation, homogenisation of labour, and the effects on labour of increasing mechanisation. The interpenetration of control within the labour process and 19th-century technical education is not usually investigated; unlike formalist histories of technical education and historical accounts of technology, there is a stress on analysis of the potential for conflict within the productive process and the relation between technological development and labour control. Much weight has been given to the nature of changes in the definition and use of skilled labour, the increasing domination of managerial control, and the transformation of work.

Of the labour process theorists, Braverman (1974) has been incisive, initiating debates on changing concepts of skill, job fragmentation, and work reorganisation. At the core of his analysis was a critique of F. W. Taylor.

The centrality of work in the labour process

The centrality of work in the labour process characterised much of Braverman's analysis, in common with a number of other studies which examine work reorganisation paralleling changing technological imperatives. As P. Thompson (1983) says, '(Braverman's) analysis played such a pivotal role in later debates because he combined a renewal of Marx's categories with an explanation of the dominant trends in the world of work... ' (p. 67). Braverman was particularly penetrating because he stressed that under a capitalist system of production there is a tendency for labour to be displaced in those occupations where technological progress is most rapid. Relating this to the mechanical engineering industry in England from the 1850s, there was rapid technical and social change, and labour substitution was a key feature of the conflicts between management and labour.

Braverman puts machinery at the centre of such a process: 'in addition to its technical function of increasing the productivity of labour ... machinery also has in the capitalist system the function of divesting the mass of workers of their control over their own labour ... ' (1974: 193). There is, nonetheless, a fundamental problem in Braverman in that it is not entirely clear how it was possible for employers to appropriate artisan skills and radically reorganise work. This hinges on the question, how could employers substitute unskilled labourers for skilled artisans when they were so dependent upon apprenticed journeymen who controlled both the pace and method of work? As Taylor demonstrated, the key was the imposition of standards through precision measurement. Taylor also knew that skill was not merely an issue of manual competence but embodied a critical mental attitude: 'The notion of tacit skill contains both technical and attitudinal elements ... practical skills ... which enable them to undertake jobs in an efficient manner ... and the ability to correct errors ... and guarantee continuity of production ... ' (Marchington 1992: 155). A crucial employer tactic was the deployment of new machines, instituted as part of an increasing division of labour, dependent upon the substitution of raw labour for artisans. This was highlighted in the 19th century by the employment of child labour, especially boys. The use of children illustrates the point as they were clearly not autonomous and had little, if any, control over their work. Two consequences stem from this.

First, child labour was suited to the subdivision or fragmentation of work, with an emphasis on the replication of many parts on automatic machines which could be pre-set. Groups of these machines could be set up and supervised by a single skilled worker overseeing up to six machines and unskilled operators (Nasmyth 1868b; Children's Employment Commission 1864; Robinson 1868). In a modern interpretation of this workshop organisation Friedman (1990) refers to a workshop division characterised by 'Responsible Autonomy' (workers with responsibility, status, light supervision), and 'Direct Control' (individual workers with greatly reduced responsibility, close supervision of work set out in advance and in great detail) (p. 178).

Second, employers accustomed to employing children as 'machine minders' were likely to be ill-disposed to both the apprenticeship system and technical education in any form which interfered with job specialisation or work fragmentation.

On the question of job fragmentation Braverman holds that 'labour power may be purchased more cheaply as dissociated elements than as a capacity integrated in a single worker ... ' (1974: 81). For post-1850 English artisans, a combination of innovative technologies and new means of labour control rendered it unnecessary for them to understand anything concerned with their work other than that required for their immediate tasks. As Braverman expressed it, 'Technical capacities are henceforth distributed on a strict 'need-to-know' basis ... ' (p. 82)

Significant changes in specific areas of work, for example metrology, the scientific control of measurement, and automatic machining, accelerated the rate of job fragmentation and labour substitution. These processes, largely structured upon increased use of unskilled and child labour, weakened the employers' interest in conventional training of young workers. There are two aspects of control at the point of production: a social dimension, emphasising the employers' need to overcome the artisans' traditional resistance to diminution of their workshop autonomy, and, in addition, control over technical knowledge, commonly referred to as Taylorism.

Control over technical knowledge and work reorganisation

The role of skilled labour substitution in the reorganisation of work figures largely in Braverman, with a strong focus on increasing employer dominance. For Braverman this dominance is so complete as to preclude any recognition of resistance on the part of the workers. He obscures the basic conflict of interest between employers and workers. The relations of production were (are) antagonistic. Littler (1990) observes: 'for Braverman, management was a two-stage process of the formal subsumption of labour succeeded by the real subsumption of labour as embodied in Taylorist principles ... ' (p. 57)

Braverman not so much overstated the case of employers as a dominant class developing a clear, unfettered ascendancy over a passive working class, but underestimated the nature and extent of skilled working-class reaction to new technologies and management ideologies. This was plainly the case in analyses of employer–skilled worker interaction in 19th-century England. This underestimation of the active resistance of workers to imposed changes obscures the fact that employers were motivated by factors other than increasing profits, and that reinforcing control had a significant influence on their organisational behaviour. Taylor's work clearly showed that the essence of control was breaking the resistance of the workers, skilled artisans in particular. Braverman, without highlighting the core of new technologies, presents the reshaping of the labour process as a format drawn up by the employers without consideration of possible reactions from those most actively involved with its outcome.

The three-year struggle Taylor encountered with his machinists at Midvale Steel in the late 1870s serves to illustrate that reorganisation was the outcome of a contested struggle rather than a 'blueprint' for action. It is clear that the decomposition of skilled labour and the deployment of new technologies took place within antagonist relations which were part of the dynamic of modern craft production.

As analysis of the Great Strike and Lockout in 1897–8 in England will show, the complexity of work and labour control engendered a new corporate apparatus (Federated Employers) specifically structured to challenge the militancy of skilled workers. A process of management organisation of such specificity finds no parallel in Braverman, with his assumption of worker acquiescence. During the 19th century, and particularly from 1897, coercive authority in manufacturing was clearly integral to capitalist organisation of work. To quote Thompson (1983) this was not a period during which employers 'found it necessary ... to use forms of limited autonomy, job enrichment and bureaucratic integration ... to maintain control ... ' (p. 215). More realistically, it conformed to Burawoy's characterisation of a despotic factory regime in which the search for profit led capital 'to intensify exploitation' (1985: 127)

Braverman's thesis is limited as far as the British industrial situation is concerned. His assumption of a homogeneous working class responding passively to a new, imposed work order is not recognisable in the aims of the artisans and the mass of unskilled workers and their respective relations with employers, in Britain. This point has been made by Burawoy (1979, 1985) in which he argues that the key strategy in confronting workers was 'manufacturing consent' inside the relations of production. This entailed encouraging 'horizontal forms of conflict'; workers directing conflict against other workers rather than management (p. 94). He writes: 'English workers are acutely aware of differentials ... conflict on the shop floor often arises from attempts by specific groups to maintain their position relative to other groups, rather than an implacable hostility to management' (1985: 134, 135). The deflection of struggles between employers and workers to inter-worker conflicts marked an important shift in power relations in the industry, significant in highlighting the employers' assertion of their 'right to manage'. This was most marked in the 19th century when they resorted increasingly to the use of unskilled labourers on new classes of machines, a critical outcome of which was aggravating antagonism between artisans and unskilled workers, particularly over the question of machine manning. (This was one of the main issues in the strike of 1897, and the subject of Chapter 5.) The English 19th-century context here does not fit well, however, with Burawoy's notion of artisans 'making out' under a system of hegemonic control (1979). Engineering employers systematically blocked attempts by skilled workers to 'play games to create space and time'.

After the middle of the century employers consolidated their control over artisans' creative knowledge, generating what Edwards (1979) refers to as a 'contested terrain' (p. 109). They encouraged unskilled workers to collaborate and to engage in substitution, indifferent to the accompanying demise of the artisan class and the internecine conflict this kind of 'consent' generated. A recent industrial management study testifies how this situation has endured and refers to the Japanization of work practices. It is suggested that adoption of Japanese methods is highly complex and made more so by 'the long-standing concern of British management to gain greater leverage over worker effort and initiative on the shop floor by recasting both formal and informal relations with work groups' (Elger and Smith (eds.) 1994: 50).

The technical and social aspects of production are inseparable, and are clearly illustrated in the work of F. W. Taylor, in the period from about 1880. His metallurgical discoveries are of major importance in any study of the transformation of work in the 20th century. The interpenetration of the technical and social elements of production was a basic principle of Taylor's notion of 'scientific management', which, Edwards (1979) also maintains, had as one of its most direct influences, 'the addressing of the issue of power relations in the workplace' (p. 104)

'Scientific management': Taylor's revolution?

Braverman's 1974 study not only presented a modern interpretation of Marx, but also stimulated a reconsideration of the critical importance of Taylor's work at the turn of the century and beyond. He relies heavily on the issue of 'scientific management' in Taylor's work. He says of the equation between Taylorism and work organisation: 'It is impossible to overestimate the importance of the scientific management movement in the shaping of the modern corporation and indeed all institutions of capitalist society which carry on labour processes' (Braverman 1974: 86). The emphasis on 'scientific management' has been exaggerated and has led to a distortion of Taylor's fundamental work, which found its principal focus in machine-tool and cutting-tool technology. He needs therefore to be re-evaluated against his metallurgical and machine-tool innovations. The application of 'Taylorism' was not universal, as implied in Braverman; in any event, it was controversial in America, based only in 200 firms at its peak (Littler 1980). 'Taylorism' became the subject of an official inquiry by a Senate Committee in the early 1900s, concerned with driving workers at the state Watertown Arsenal. It made little impression in England as a 'science of management' vis-à-vis his highly innovative work on cutting-tool steels, which had their first cutting trials in England in 1903. These had a profound effect on metal machining and, as was subsequently shown, in negotiations between employers and artisans in the great strike of 1897 (Institution of Mechanical Engineers 1903).

Thus 'Taylorism' was to be found in England in a modified version known as the 'Bedaux System' in the 1920s and 1930s (Littler 1980). One of the first 'science of management' texts in England suggested that 'Taylorism' failed to take hold in British industry because 'the industrial milieu presented an infertile soil ... (of) scepticism and apathy – an incapacity to understand that anything other than technology was of consequence ... and the opposition of organized British labour ... ' (Urwick and Brech 1946: 89, 92). Braverman, relying heavily on 'Taylorism' as a management strategy, assumes technological development to be autonomous. There is consequently an imprecision in his interpretation concerning the way Taylor methodically used technology, particularly metallurgical discoveries in cutting-tool steels, such as HSS. These innovations were implemented alongside new machining processes, to overcome skilled workers' resistance to work reorganisation and to cut costs.

For Braverman, technology and technological knowledge were readily appropriated by employers as an ineluctable part of a process of deskilling:

> The break up of craft skills and the reconstruction of production ... have destroyed the traditional concept of skill and opened up only one way for mastery over labour processes to develop; in and through scientific, technical and engineering knowledge. But the extreme concentration of this knowledge in the hands of management ... has closed this avenue to the working population ... (1974: 443).

The question as to how it was possible for management to appropriate artisans' skills within a 'science of management' in the way he suggested can only be answered within the context of Taylor's innovatory technologies and the advances in metrology and precision measurement. Taylor's major contribution to an employers' ideology of production lay not in 'scientific management' *per se*, but in bringing the pioneering work on workshop practices of engineer-entrepreneurs such as Maudslay, Whitworth and Nasmyth in the 18th and early 19th centuries into contemporary engineering practice.

The technologies developed and implemented by these British engineers in particular were designed to operate in a specific set of social relations within which the worker had minimal autonomy; the technologies were factors of labour control. This characterisation is not new, but serves to stress that the indispensable condition for the radical restructuring of control of work undertaken by Taylor was as much a technological as a management imperative. The machines were not technologies requiring new forms of skilled expertise but were designed, from the outset, for use of unskilled or raw labour (Nasmyth 1856; Whitworth 1854, 1856; Taylor 1911a; Hoxie 1918; Littler 1980, 1985). A recent study expresses a common perspective of this process as a 'zero-sum' situation: 'all work which management succeeded in bringing to the surface – that is brought under control – fell from the workers' control ... ' (Bonazzi 1994: 288). The common assumption here is that the technology originally had been under the control of workers. The pioneering work of Taylor and the earlier British engineers was premised upon the employment of raw labour for which no antecedent skills were assumed or expected.

Taylor's tool-steel developments embodied a virtually unchallengeable means of neutralising worker resistance by undermining the skilled workers' exclusivity regarding preparation of cutting tools and machine setting. He constantly refined the mechanism of labour control in order to subordinate skilled labour. Through the introduction of his high-speed steel tools that could 'tolerate' heavy loading, that is, were able to stand rough treatment during the cutting process, a characteristic well suited to use by unskilled workers, he denied skilled labour access to the new technologies (Taylor 1906, 1910). For Taylor there was no meaningful sense of 'reciprocal relationship of cooperation and mutual dependence ... ' (Sakolsky 1992: 244)

Taylor's metallurgical and cutting-tool research informed his management principles; they were inextricably linked, rather than technology being conceived as autonomous. Much of the technology introduced by employers from the 1880s was never 'in the hands' of the artisans, as argued in the deskilling theses. The rapid advances made in precision measurement control in England, for example, were from their inception a major part of an employer-dominated technology, and not appropriated later after years of artisan-dominated craftwork.

The chronology of technological innovation in this period from the 1880s has been overshadowed in Braverman and others by an insistence on seeing the process in terms of a gradual deskilling, in which the employers extracted pre-existing 'skills' from artisans. Domination over innovatory technologies, by definition excluding artisans, would have been impossible without Taylor's metallurgical discoveries and the earlier metrological advances which were so effectively exploited by him from the 1880s. His work both revolutionised the concept of manufacturing engineering and transformed engineering workshop processes. It was in the field of metal-cutting that Taylor all but destroyed the monopoly held by engineering artisans for centuries. His pivotal contribution to work reorganisation therefore directly derived from his revolutionary innovations in metal-cutting.

The broader effects of Taylor's technological innovations and his insight into the relation between technical developments and labour control were dynamic and have been underestimated. His major contribution to management and work organisation was to change irrevocably the way skill came to be defined and perceived by employers and artisans in America and Britain, particularly by artisans. For generations British engineering artisans had been regarded as the leading craftsmen, assuming the status of an 'aristocracy of labour'. By the end of the 19th century this was to change and the concept of skill lost the pre-eminence it had acquired throughout the century. Increasingly, skilled workers were replaced by raw labour, young workers especially.

Notes

1. This conceptualisation of engineering craft practice by Taylor displays some disingenousness, for of all system-management protagonists he was probably more conversant than most with the empirical quality of engineering skills in modern technology. If they were really 'banausic' i.e. 'rule of thumb', one

must question why their investigation under Taylor should occupy twenty-six years.
2. Speed of the metal moving in a machine while being cut, was usually expressed in this way. It denotes the amount of metal passing the tool point in a minute. With cylindrical work, as in a lathe, the length of material passing the tool point was expressed in revolutions per minute (RPM). For comparative purposes this common designation is used.

CHAPTER THREE

Technology, changing definitions of skill and the use of child labour

The introduction of new types of metal-cutting machines in England, based on automatic principles, had both technical and social purposes: the pre-setting of machines to ensure fast, accurate reproduction of work; and the substitution of unskilled labour for artisan machinists. This led to major disruptions in the engineering industry which culminated in the Great Strike of 1897 (*The Engineer* (1898); Clegg *et al.* 1964; Berg (ed.) 1979; Zeitlin 1979).

It has been suggested that the 'new machine' age induced investment in workers, a variant of human capital theory (Floud 1985: 83 ff.). The reality of life for most young workers in 19th-century workshops was an average 57 hours per week and, if available at all, education through evening classes. The employers' interest in systematic training declined as the new technologies were deployed (Nasmyth 1856; Children's Employment Commission 1864; Allen 1868b; Robinson 1868; Royal Commission on Secondary Education 1895).

It was an uneasy period for technological development, with increasing hostility between artisans and employers. The age was not, as one commentator noted, 'rather a dull one of assured progress, evolutionary improvement and with few startling innovations ... ' (Cardwell 1972b: 146). In addition to stimulating investment, the implementation of new technologies precipitated conflict. The engineering industry was involved in two national strikes in 1852 and 1897, both of which were connected with the introduction of new machine-manning principles by the employers (ASE Reports 1898; Royal Commission on Trade Unions 1867a; Shadwell 1906; Zeitlin 1979; Berg 1985). There were many localised strikes (in 1893 there were 615 disputes involving 634,301 workers). These disputes critically influenced the employers' perception of 'skill' within the context of rapidly changing technologies. Employers also radically modified their commitment to the traditional craft apprenticeship system and to incipient forms of technical education. Technological innovations were plainly part of a changing set of social relations and were not autonomous with respect to those changes.

Artisan reaction took two main forms: (1) resistance to the employers' imposition of new technologies, particularly automatic machines, which they perceived as a threat to their skilled-worker status; (2) the generation of an internecine conflict between skilled and unskilled workers. This derived from the employers' insistence that the latter could and should be deployed on the new automatic machines (Children's Employment Commission 1864; Robinson 1868; Nasmyth 1868a; Noble in Royal Commission on Labour 1893d; ASE 1897: reply to Col. Dyer).

The assumed autonomy of machine-tool developments

The idea of technology as autonomous assumes that tools were endowed with self-generating properties, detached from other social forces and governed only by the internal logic of the technology itself: '*Technical progress has a logic of its own*; one invention raises problems, intellectual and mechanical, which require time and effort for their solution' (Habakkuk 1962: 81; my emphasis). A similar concept of technology was advanced later: '[there is] an inner compulsion of technological development which is quite independent of social and economic forces ... '; my emphasis). (Woodbury 1972: 2). Technology according to such views is clearly autonomous with respect to social change. The abstraction of technology from its social context divests these perspectives of much of their precision. As Law (1987) states, 'if we wish to understand the growth of technologies, then we should treat them as an end-product of goal-oriented system building ... ' (p. 419).

'Technicism' obscures the wider implications of the implementation of new technologies, reflected in reorganisation of work and changing labour practices. Embedded in work reorganisation was a perception of technology as a means of diminishing worker power and increasing management control over the labour process. This was clearly expressed as early as the 1840s: 'Machines from their automation power, no longer need regularly bred mechanics to attend them ... it becomes necessary ... to reduce the subject ... [to] within the range of ... the ... inferior capacity of a humbler grade of men ... ' (Nasmyth 1841: 411).

Machine tools as a source of employer–employee conflict

The transforming technologies of the 19th century were not independent of the social and cultural context in which they found formulation. They also correlated with specific managerial strategies, which presupposed increasing worker subordination. Employers extended their knowledge over all the technical and material aspects of production, so amply demonstrated by Taylor in America from the 1880s. According to McGuffie (1986), this process engendered 'a more malleable workforce ... more subject to management-inspired planning, control, direction and diktat ... ' (1986: xvi).

Management-dominated technology was a necessary precondition of interchangeability, which was premised on accurate replication of parts (Anderson 1854; Nasmyth 1854; Buckingham 1920; Galloway 1958; Roe 1916b; Whitworth 1857; Wordworth 1905). Interchangeability is the process by which similar engineering components, which have been manufactured to precise measurements within prescribed limits of size, may be interchanged with each other with little or no modification.

The expansion of mass-production techniques interlocked with market forces, providing greater incentives for employers becoming more competitive and responding to consumer demand. The boom in bicycle and sewing machine manufacture after mid-century exemplified the accelerating process: 'As soon as public demand for the newly invented devices grew large, means had to be devised for producing great numbers of components accurately and economically ... ' (Galloway 1965: 640). The transformation of engineering work thus embodied changing strategies of labour control. Nasmyth and Whitworth, apart from being inventors of genius in the period, as employers sought to extend their control over skilled labour. Nasmyth 'was a pioneer of "scientific management". In his ideas of factory lay-out, work-flow, standardisation, and mass-production, he was one of the leading creators of the modern machine age ... ' (Musson and Robinson 1969: 509).

Human labour and machine production: workers' resistance to substitution

The growing use of transformed machinery after 1850 as a means of widening the extent of labour substitution went hand in hand with the growth of political economy. Its introduction met with variable but determined worker resistance, as the number of disputes has shown. The conflicts served to intensify the employers' control over labour: 'Faced with their resistance ... the industrial bourgeoisie and their associates adopted an attitude of increasingly aggressive ... determination and optimism' (Berg 1982: 2).

The radically changing social relations in production in England were similar to those associated with F. W. Taylor's innovations in machine tools from the 1880s. An American study of a national armoury, Harpers Ferry, in the 19th century revealed growing agitation among artisans similar to that experienced in England: 'Craft-trained artisans ... increasingly found themselves isolated from employers, irritated by the growing intensity of production, and threatened by the machine' (Smith 1977: 20). Focusing on Whitworth's visit to America as part of an official Parliamentary mission to engineering establishments in the 1850s, Smith highlighted the antagonistic relations which often accompanied technological innovations. Whitworth, he asserted, did not consider workshop relations in this way: 'Whitworth ... did not perceive the many difficulties that attended building the factory and adopting new techniques, [nor] ... the endless troubles encountered in getting workers to follow an industrial regime ... ' (ibid., p. 22).

With regard to imposed technological change, a parallel may be drawn between English artisans, who struck often throughout the 19th century, and recalcitrant American artisans, such as those at Harpers Ferry. As Smith puts it, 'Because so many ... had been reared according to the conventions of the craft ethos, they found it extremely difficult to adjust to increasingly specialized demands ... they considered themselves artisans, not machine tenders ... ' (ibid., p. 67).

The emergence of a reconstituted technology, skill redefinition and recomposition, and the English workers' reaction to them precipitated the growth of a number of competing groups in the engineering industry. There was a growing polarisation between employers and workers, with increasing tension, particularly between the artisans and employers. This emanated from the artisans' misplaced trust in their status in the skill hierarchy and their belief in the employers' dependence upon their traditional skills. The focus of the antagonism ranged around the various occupational groupings and the powerful Engineering Employers Federation (EEF): 'there is a sense of ... one group tend[ing] to form itself around the labour of superintendence and management and the other around direct production ... ' (McGuffie 1986: xxix). The conflicts accompanying technical change stemmed in large part from the artisans' self-conception as an elite or an 'aristocracy of labour' which fuelled their resistance to the employers' attempts to reduce labour to a factor of production, denying them, apart from other things, access to technical education and training.

An aristocracy of labour: merely a question of status?

The concept of 'aristocracy of labour' usually referred to a minority of workers, all of whom were skilled and constituted a literate caucus of workers intent on differentiating themselves from the unskilled. They were frequently known as 'artisans'.[1]

The idea of a 'labour aristocracy' may be found in a number of diverse sources, including Engels (1882), Webbs (1907), Hobsbawm (1984). Held by engineering craftsmen in the 19th century, the concept drew much of its legitimacy from the artisans' distinctive perception of craft skills, particularly in machine-tool work, and their attitude to the apprenticeship system.

There were two elements in this conceptualisation. The first was the artisans' belief in engineering skill as conferring status and social power. This has suggested to some writers that the skilled stratum of 19th-century workers was subject to an 'embourgeoisement' process, citing as evidence their assumed alignment with the Liberal party. Some leading figures in the Liberal party of the 19th century such as Mundella, Huxley and Playfair expressed active interest in working-class education, prompting the idea that there was a link between the exclusive, status-seeking skilled workers and the political ideology of the Liberal party.

Tradesman-writer Wright (1871), for example, feared the loss of status by skilled workers 'through democratisation of the labour force'. Artisans were men who 'by reason of the "push" and energy which have enabled them to accumulate money or property are amongst the most influential of their class and with their class' (p. 134). For Engels (1882) the skilled workers in Britain were a divisive element in working-class solidarity, dominated by the Liberal party and participating in industrial domination associated with England's monopoly of the world market: 'English workers are ... naturally the tail of the "Great Liberal Party" which for its part pays them small attentions, recognises trade unions and strikes as legitimate ... there is no workers' party here, there are only Conservatives and Liberal-Radicals' (p. 398).

Such ideas had had a fairly long history and give some credence to an embourgeoisement model of social development. Saville (1954), for example, points to the collapse of Chartism as a watershed in working-class political ideas. After the 1850s, he argues, 'there was an accommodation to bourgeois society by sections of the working class ... ' (p. 156). This view was echoed in Roberts (1958) and Tholfsen (1961) regarding 19th-century unions, the latter arguing that the most strikingly conservative characteristic of English democracy in the period from 1870 was the 'staunch loyalty of the working class elite to Liberalism and the Liberal Party' (p. 245). Hobsbawm (1968), the authoritative writer in this field, argues that the artisan group were 'an aristocracy of labour enjoying special privileges and therefore inclined to accept the views of the employers' (p. 273). A main focus is on the artisans' reliability and stability, often theorised within a structural functionalist framework in which dominant values were internalised (Tholfsen 1976). The mid-19th century was a significant period for working-class political change. According to the Webbs (1920), the early part of the century had been characterised by radical socialist ideology, later giving way to a more conciliatory approach.

A second element attaching to the notion of 'labour aristocracy' was the artisans' claim that the apprenticeship also constituted a form of technical education.

Modern research in this area puts much stress on the skilled workers' attempts to dissociate themselves from the unskilled, and less on the conflicts associated with machine-tool innovation and implementation. Strategies developed by the skilled workers in the course of their struggles with the employers were also part of their attempt to preserve the apprenticeship systems and elevate it to part of a formal technical education system, against the wishes of the employers. The antagonism generated by these conflicts of interest centred on the questions of innovation in machine technology and machine manning.

Artisan groups clearly attempted to distance themselves from unskilled labourers, sometimes referred to in the period as 'handymen'. This stress points up their claim to exclusivity in labour relations and a connection between the artisans' demands for a retention of the apprenticeship system and recurring conflict within the engineering industry.

Artisan exclusivity and inter-worker conflict

Labour histories of the period have thus focused on the artisans' concern with maintaining social and occupational distance from the unskilled.

Hobsbawm (1954) argued 'the artisan or craftsman was not under any circumstances to be confused with a "labourer"'. He quotes Wright (*Our New Masters*, 1873), 'labourers are an inferior class ... they should be made to know and keep their place' (p. 204). Hobsbawm focused on the power 'labour aristocrats' held vis-à-vis the unskilled, which enabled them to receive relatively high wages and to make their labour artificially scarce:

> Only certain types of workers were in a position to make or keep their labour scarce enough, or valuable enough, to strike a good bargain. But the relatively favourable terms they got were ... actually achieved at the expense of their less favoured colleagues ... (1968: 322).

A feature of histories of individual unions was 'the workers' overwhelming concern with their own sectional interests. As far as engineering workers were concerned, this ideology was evident in the policies of the 19th-century Amalgamated Society of Engineers (ASE). In his history of the Society, Jefferys (1945) points out that the union did not claim that it was its duty to secure the objects of a 'class', but rather to 'exercise ... control over that in which we have a vested interest' (p. 20).

Despite claims in recent scholarship that during the latter part of the century there was a transition from subordination to bargaining based on the skilled workers' exclusivity, it is doubtful after the 1850s whether the unions were ever realistically in a position of bargaining as opposed to subordination. A 'source of social tension', this transition was said to arise out of the transmission of middle-class values, based on the cultural exclusion of less-favoured working-class groups, the unskilled (Gray 1973: 450–51).

The assumed accommodation of the skilled working class was strengthened by qualified support from the middle classes through the press (and government). Artisans were portrayed as exemplars of what was possible through initiative and determination. Working-class values became circumscribed within an ethic of self-help; 'the "labour aristocrats" were no longer perceived as 'challenging existing inequalities' (Hearn 1978: 166).

Technological innovations: some implications for skilled workers, with special reference to the 'Junta'

Great importance was therefore attached by artisans to the maintenance of their power over workshop relations, particularly regarding control of apprentices and unskilled labour. This control characterised artisan autonomy, and derived from their strength as organised, unionised labour. The mass of the unskilled was non-unionised for much of the 19th century. Being part of a highly structured organisation, the artisans believed themselves – erroneously as it transpired in 1898 – equipped to protect their interests against expanding employer authority. Therefore decisions reached at TU Congresses reflected only the concerns of the skilled workers, without reference to the unskilled.

This configuration of industrial labour was the framework of a hierarchy of labour, whose upper echelon of administration, up to about 1871, was later referred to as the 'Junta'. This group generated particular resentment within unskilled workers due to its persistence in distancing itself from the unskilled in order to maintain status and privilege. For a time unskilled worker reaction was articulated through a journal, the *Bee-Hive*, and particularly through the personal antagonism of the editor, Potter, towards the Junta.

The Junta: an inner cabinet

The Junta was a name coined by the Webbs in referring to a small group of leading trade unionists of the period who constituted an 'inner caucus' of the movement. They were the general secretaries of the principal unions, and were bitterly opposed by George Potter, the leader of a much smaller, relatively insignificant union, the London Carpenters. The Webbs' account of this rivalry points up the nature of the distinction between workers of high status and labourers.

The Webbs argued:

> It is difficult to convey any adequate idea of the extraordinary personal influence exercised by [the Junta], not only on their immediate associates, but also as interpreters of the trade union movement, upon the public and governing classes ... for the first time in the century the working class movement came under the direction, not of middle class

sympathisers like Place, Owen, Roberts, O'Connor or Duncombe, but of genuine working men trained for the position ... (S. and B. Webb 1907: 221)

The unionists for whom the Webbs had such high regard were Allen (Engineers), Applegarth (Carpenters), Guile (Ironfounders), Coulson (London Bricklayers), Odger (Shoemakers). They aligned themselves with the newly-established Trade Councils (local branches of the leading unions) to make them the political organs of the trade union movement.

The Webbs held that between 1867 and 1871 this small elite, 'the effective cabinet of trade movement' (ibid., p. 240), dominated trade affairs through meetings under the auspices of the 'Conference of Amalgamated Trades'. They exercised a distinctive combination of extreme caution in trade matters and 'energetic' agitation for political reforms (ibid., p. 223).

It was this tendency, caution, which precipitated a major rift with Potter earlier in 1865. Potter, through the *Bee-Hive*, advocated active support for striking North Staffordshire ironworkers, a policy which directly opposed the Junta's restrained control from the centre. The issue exemplified the conflicts over the question of trade union militancy (Kynaston 1976: 26).

Potter represented the London Workingmen's Association, held by the Webbs to be 'an unimportant society of nondescript persons' (S. and B. Webb 1907: 238). Through his journal he maintained his personal and political opposition to the Junta, though at pains to make a name for himself as a 'good Gladstonian Liberal' (Coltham 1965: 53).

The mutual antagonism displayed by Potter and the Junta came to symbolise the underlying contradictions in working-class relations throughout the latter half of the century. It was significant, for example, that Burnett (ASE secretary later in the century), in his denunciation of the unskilled as 'a threat to social order', emphasised the growing fracture in working-class solidarity by suggesting that technical education was the preserve of the skilled worker.

The weakness of the non-aligned unionists in confronting employers was highlighted in the rivalry between Potter and the Junta. This was brought out in the submissions made to the Royal Commission of 1867 on Trade Unions. Giving his evidence, Potter was 'edgy and defensive in manner, leaving a poor impression', whereas members of the Junta, Allen and Applegarth, 'shone almost continually' (Kynaston 1976: 27).

In the wider context of industrial relations Potter was less well placed to confront any anti-union tendencies on the part of employers. His attempts to challenge the power and influence of the Junta serve to underline the point that the employers, with widening control over new technologies, were able to exploit working-class rivalries to weaken the historical status and privileges of the artisans by encouraging the unskilled to press for recognition as union members. By the 1880s and 1890s this was to have a critical effect on the ability of the craft unions to constrain the widening hegemony of the employers.

As part of a self-centred political structure, the craft engineers, as represented by the ASE, sought to maintain power and status vis-à-vis other workers. Central to this organisation was the artisans' relatively privileged position of exclusivity and conservatism. Membership of a craft union reinforced the artisans' belief in their indispensability and emphasized that they were not in the business of promoting class solidarity. Conference resolutions represented a minority working-class view only. Hobsbawm (1961) has suggested, for example, that at no time in the Victorian period did this group exceed more than 15 per cent of the working class.

From the 1850s the ASE had been regarded as the archetypal craft union: it was highly structured and wide-ranging after amalgamation, well-administered and financed; dominated by the skilled artisans, particularly the fitters. Artisan exclusivity was exemplified by the ASE. Allen, ASE secretary, in his evidence to the 1867 Royal Commission on Trades Unions, made clear the position of craft unions. Referring to a 'non-union' Trade Conference held in London, he said, '[those] that convened the meeting do not belong to any trade society at all ... we refused to connect ourselves with them in any shape or form ... ' (RC on TU 1867b). Burnett, was to re-present this view in stronger terms much later. There was a need, he argued, 'to impress upon the minds of the employers that unionists are indeed the pick of British artisans ... '. This judgement was extended by the observation that 'unorganized labour was dangerous to social order ... ' (Burnett 1886: 36).

The differentials existing between the skilled and non-unionised workers points up the contradictory elements active in the trade union movement about this time. They constituted a significant backdrop for a crucial development, the alignment of the unskilled engineering workers and the employers, in the period preceding the Great Strike and Lockout in 1897–8.

The struggles between workers and employers and within workers' groups were as much about control of the labour process as issues of economic or technical management innovation, and practical questions of wages or skilled workers status. They are therefore central to explanations of the nature of the conflicts arising out of changes in the mode of production and reorganisation of the workplace.

There is a strong parallel between deterministic notions of machine-tool technology and orthodox, evolutionary accounts of technical education. Technical training and education have to be recognised within the context of other social forces and as social phenomena other than an evolution out of mass general education. An undue emphasis on changes in the artefacts of new technologies, focusing on their significance for economic growth, deflects attention from the social context in which these developments were being implemented.

A concept such as 'labour aristocrats' has increased explanatory power if it extends to forces outside the production process, for example to the system of trade training and education. It was this system that produced a highly skilled minority of workers. There is no question that, in terms of wages and lifestyle, there was a privileged stratum of skilled workers. They had traditionally determined the method and pace of production and were responsible for the supervision and training of apprentices. This labour 'elite' combined high levels of skill with direct supervisory tasks, often incorporated into a 'piecemaster' system. This was a system in which 'the skilled top one-third of the labour force acted as pacemakers and taskmasters over the rest ... ' (Foster 1977: 228 ff.). It is misjudged, however, to assert that 'the technological demands of the industry ... identified firmly the skilled worker with management ... ' (ibid.). This claim is not supported by the evidence of contradictions and conflicts within the mechanical engineering industry. It also underestimates the effects of the transition of the traditional form of training of young workers to an ad hoc system of on-the-job training, often under a piecework system premised upon wider implementation of reconstituted machines. The concept of the apprentice form of training was gradually eroded and replaced by greater exploitation of child labour.

The piece-work system and child labour

Rapid manufacture according to principles of interchangeability was a major advantage for employers, achieved principally through the expansion of automatic tools. Large numbers of components could be replicated, each within specified limits of tolerance and interchangeable as required. The small arms industry typified this method of engineering production.

This method implied that the rate at which specific detail components could be manufactured came under stricter employer control than had previously been possible, before standardisation of parts. The sequence in which various machining and assembly operations were carried out was also more systematically developed, with less dependence upon skilled labour.

Data for production rates based on the extension of automatic principles support these assumptions. In the last quarter of the 19th century the demand for mass-production consumer goods such as bicycles and sewing machines stimulated research in techniques for accelerating production rates. For example, by 1913 Britain exported 150,000 cycles, Germany 89,000; and the rest of the world none. The Singer Sewing Machine Company was producing 8,000 machines a week by 1885, reaching 13,000 per week at the turn of the century, with a UK workforce of 7,000 (Saul 1970: 125, 160).

The combination of automatic machines and the introduction of a piece-work system of wage payment was a product of the employers' overall strategy in extending their control over the labour process based on the new technologies. Because of its attraction for employers in the employment of children as cheap labour, piecework particularly influenced employers' attitudes to technical training and education, which was given low priority, at best being 'tolerated' as a part-time system only.

The remodelling and reorganisation of significant centres of production engineering such as the Armstrong Whitworth Works, the Rowan Company, and the Enfield Armoury were instrumental in the adoption by English workshops of new high-production methods (Jefferys 1945). These methods, employing semi-automatic and automatic machine tools, had their English origins in the mid-1850s. The developments in machine technologies and new methods of measurement control also made it easier for employers to extend the system of payment 'by the piece', that is, wages paid according to the number of components produced to a predetermined schedule. It served to justify increased child employment, in capacities other than as apprentices. The American influence in the new wage system was marked and was clearly evident in a House of Commons report as early as 1855: 'In the government and private enterprises of the United States, piecework when applicable is universally preferred to day-work, as this arrangement yields the greater amount of work at the least possible cost to the employer ... ' (Report of the Committee on the Machinery of the United States of America 1855). This report strongly recommended acceptance of a piecework system in arms production, citing three reasons:

1. Payment by the piece stimulated the economic interests of the workers and encouraged the development of labour-saving devices 'that may occur to them as likely to increase the production of the machines they attend' (ibid.).
2. Fewer supervisors were necessary, as 'time-wasting' or inefficient work on the part of workers entailed loss of wages and 'no loss upon his employers'.
3. Men paid by the piece could be held financially responsible for any work they might spoil through carelessness, which was particularly important with the manufacture of replicated parts: 'any workman who may be employed in some trifling operation on an article that is almost finished, by carelessness in looking after his machine may spoil and render useless a large number of parts on which a great deal of careful labour has been already bestowed' (ibid.).

The recommendation by the 1853 Mission to America supporting the adoption and extension of a kind of premium system of payment of wages was related to the introduction of automatic tools. As the 1853 evidence suggested, variants of schemes for paying by the piece reputedly encouraged the economic interests of the workers. It protected employer interests through the relatively simple expedient of sanctions and penalties attaching to the worker for components incorrectly manufactured or exceeding production times.

Payment for work by the piece was generally by 'time' or by 'money'. In the former, work was allocated on a 'floor-to-floor' time, in hours or days; the latter implied a set sum of money accredited for the job. In both 'time' and 'money' systems the incentive for the worker was to cut machining and assembly times in order to increase bonus rates.

These schemes embodied a self-correcting principle which ensured that faulty components manufactured in any part of a production sequence would be passed back by a 'receiving' worker to the preceding stage for correction. This procedure incurred a loss of bonus for the worker responsible and was a common feature in piecework systems throughout the latter half of the century. One employer, Robinson, in 1868 maintained that quality production was assured:

> Q. 'You are satisfied with the quality of work which is produced under the piece work system?'
> 'Yes, and there is a check in this way. A smith, for instance, does his work by piece work, a turner or fitter comes after him, and if the piece of work is bad, it is sent back to the smith to be replaced without cost. The man in the after process is always ready enough to find fault with the man in the previous process if he has not done his work well.' (RC on TU 1868a, Q. 19090)

The piecework system in action (1): the premium system

By the turn of the century the piecework system had gained much ground. One prominent engineering employer and leading proponent of the system, R. J. Rowan, was satisfied that following its introduction into his works in 1898, his control over the labour process was not only simplified but the overall effect was 'revolutionary' in terms of work reorganisation:

> It has resulted in a largely increased output from the machines for the same labour cost ... To prevent any chance of scamping or bad work, a strict rule is enforced that if any part of work, however small, done under contract, is not right, the man loses his whole premium under the contract (Rowan 1901: 898)

The advantages to the employer were cumulative. In the period 1898 to 1903, the time taken by machinists on standard machining jobs had, on average, been reduced in the succeeding years by 20, 23, 31 and 37 per cent respectively (Rowan 1903: 218). The method was generalised to fitting and assembly with equally satisfactory results:

Up to this point the system has been treated as applied to the machine shop, but it is equally applicable to the erecting and other departments ... if erectors are to actually lose money by the carelessness of a machine man, as they would on premium, they rebel, with the result that great care is taken by the men and foreman that work when it leaves the machine is correct. (Ibid., pp. 219, 220)

The reorganisation of labour using Rowan's 'premium system' produced 'a complete revolution in [the] shop' (Rowan 1901: 884). It was found, for example, that its introduction revealed discrepancies in the performance of certain machine tools; investigation led to the replacement of under-powered machines with heavier, more powerful tools, 'all along the line' (ibid., p. 887).

Rowan's production schedules show how these new working principles affected the rate at which work was produced. Table 3.1 shows the three most common types of machine processes: turning (lathe work); slotting (for making square or rectangular slots in metal); hole production (drilling and boring). In the application of this particular form of piecework the practical considerations were such that in no case were the operations carried under a premium contract of longer duration than 50 hours (Rowan 1901: 897). The system paid a premium of 50 per cent on the time saved. This principle is shown in Table 3.2.

There was a tendency for advantages to accrue to employers at a faster rate than wage increases earned by the piece worker. It will be noted in the first case shown in Table 3.2 that under the premium system there was a 33.3 per cent saving in machining time, and 25 per cent increase in workman's earn-

Table 3.1 A typical workshop time schedule for three typical machining processes, using a premium system of payment

Description of work	Time taken under old time system (hours)	Time taken on introduction of premium bonus	Record time taken (hours)
Turning connecting rod 1 off	43½	36	29
Slotting connecting rods 3 off	31	24½	20
Crank webs (finishing holes) 1 off	7⅔	5½	3½

Source: Extracted from Rowan (1901), Table 1, p. 886.

Table 3.2 An example of earnings under the premium system, based on boring out a 10-inch cast iron pump

Time in hours			Rate of wages per hour	Workman's earnings
allowed	taken	saved		
40	24	16	8d.	24 hrs. at 8d. + 16/2 at 8d. = 21s. 4d.

Source: Rowan (1901): 898.

Box 3.1 Comparisons of wages earned and production increases under the premium system

Taking the first machining operation from Table 3.1, turning a connecting rod; assuming time allowed was 43½ hours, and machining completed in record time of 29 hours, at rate of 8d. per hour, the rates become:

(i) $\dfrac{\text{time saved (hr)}}{\text{time allowed (hr)}} = \dfrac{14½}{43½} = 33.3\%$ saving of production time

(ii) $\dfrac{\text{premium wages}}{\text{normal wages}} = \dfrac{½ \times 14½ \times 8}{29 \times 8} = \dfrac{57}{234} = 25\%$ increase in wages

The second operation, slotting connecting rods, produces the following figures:

(i) $\dfrac{\text{time saved (hr)}}{\text{time allowed (hr)}} = \dfrac{11}{31} = 35\%$ saving on machine time

(ii) $\dfrac{\text{premium wages}}{\text{normal wages}} = \dfrac{½ \times 11 \times 8}{248} = \dfrac{44}{248} = 17\%$ increase in wages

Source: Rowan (1901): 898.

---

ings. Box 3.1 illustrates this regressive tendency. The advantages of the system for management may be summarised thus:

1. Largely increased output from the machines 'for the same labour cost'.

2. Increase in workmen's average wages of from 10 to 40 per cent.
3. The practically compulsory maintenance of machines in 'the highest state of efficiency'.
4. Greatly increased interest of the men in their work, machines, and equipment, and a 'fair amount of co-operation in all the schemes for improving the factory'.
5. A wider choice of men than previously, resulting 'in the employment of only the best class of steady workmen'.
6. A change in the foremen's function from task-masters to providers of work and inspectors of that work. (Rowan 1901: 899)

Piecework in action (2): the use of the contract note as a form of labour control

On completion of a contract, that is, a specific job to be wholly or partially completed a 'contract note' (a standardised document detailing operations to be carried out, with appropriate times, issued from a 'premium office') was checked-punched by the inspector. Either the inspector or the foreman of the department thus certified that the job was done correctly and the full operation denoted on the card had been carried out (ibid., p. 898).

Time allowed for any job was fixed by management, curtailing the autonomy of skilled labour. This time allowance included all the time necessary to procure tools, set up the machine and obtain material for doing the job, and was not restricted to actual machining of the work. This was a critical condition, for setting up or locating the work in a machine was an essential precondition for accurate machining. It was also time-consuming if the workpiece was irregular or heavy (Rowan 1903: 211).

Another employer (Wigram, of John Fowler, Engineers, Leeds 1893), estimated in 1893 that in his works 'probably one-quarter to a fifth of the time of a machine is occupied in setting the work up on it' (RC on Labour 1893b). The imposition of tight time schedules thus directly influenced premium earnings in cases where the work to be machined was in any way irregular. This particular factor became more regulatory and exploitative when considering the condition that 'the time taken on a job will include all working hours between the starting time of the job, and the starting time of the next job' (Rowan 1903: 212). The rate at which the work was set up and the accuracy and speed with which it was machined plainly determined bonus payments. Under the principles of the system adopted by Rowan, articles that turned out to be defective while being machined and were condemned due to a flaw in the material resulted in loss of premium (ibid.).

If completed components did not pass inspection, premium would be paid only if the work was made good within the time allowed. Considering the 'total-time' schedules referred to above, this imposed a significant restraint, for time used in correction would have had an effect on the time allowance for the next job.

A type of gang system also operated with a time allowance fixed for the complete job. If the total time taken by the squad was less than the time allowed, a premium was paid to each man in the squad. This premium had the same relation to the time wages (ordinary rate) for the job as the time saved by the squad had to the time allowed (Rowan 1903: 213).

The operation of the system showed a significant increase in the employers' control over the implementation of new technologies and highlights their widening control of work.

The practice of 'rate fixing': a variation on job control

Central to the system was 'rate fixing', the establishment of job time comparisons by management using existing production data. When sufficient data had been gathered for a particular manufacturing process, a card bearing 'lines' was prepared and given to each man working a machine (Rowan 1903: 215). These were drawn up by the rate-fixing department and issued to the foreman, who gave them to the men. They were card devices for keeping checks on work progress, the card being designed to show, as a quick reference, the daily progress of each man, workpiece and hours allowed and taken. The relevant data, arranged in columns, indicated machine number, time allowed for each number of articles on 'line' or in the batch, the times the workman had been working on the job to 10.30 a.m. on the date on the card, and finally the record time, that is, the shortest time in which each job had been done previously (ibid., p. 214).

On completion of the job the worker handed his 'lines' to the foreman, who noted the time the work was completed and indicated if he was satisfied with the quality of the work. The card was then handed to the rate-fixing department and the cost of the work and wages, including premium if earned, was calculated.

With this system, oversight of individual workers was simplified and more efficient for management. The use of gauges and similar instruments was significant in controlling finished sizes. A new principle of 'work control' was available to employers with the introduction of the system of gauges developed by Whitworth, who earlier in the century had stated: 'If the operative has a standard article beside him, from time to time, he can apply his gauges, and see what the progress of the work going on is, and he may detect anything is wrong at a very early period' (Select Committee on Small Arms 1854, Q. 1569).

Deriving directly from these new production principles, penalising 'inefficient' workers increased managerial control. As early as the 1860s employers recognised and generally welcomed the control elements associated with the piecework system:

> ... piece work is the fairest mode of securing the payment of a workman, in proportion to his skill and industry, since in our business it is easier to watch the quality of work produced than to watch the efforts of every workman in the establishment ... the profitable result ... depends upon the amount of exertion used in executing the work. (Robinson 1868: 55)

The economic and labour-management strategies of some leading engineering employers in the second half of the century were a product of the innovation and control of new production technologies. The use of a wage system involving payment by the piece marked a further decline in the autonomy of skilled labour and broadened the range of work supervision. It was a major source of contention in engineering employer–employee relations from the 1850s and 1860s (Allen 1867b: Q. 841)

Employers' and unions' views on the piecework system

ASE secretary W. Allen argued that as a general rule, piecework was inferior, it degraded skilled labour and 'injured the trade'. He noted also that work rates essential to the piecework mode were determined by employers using the work patterns of an expert workman. This technique of setting production norms based upon the rates of the fastest workers had characterised F. W. Taylor's Differential Piece-Rate System in America. This procedure proved less beneficial to the ordinary machine worker because the rates were commensurate with high levels of skill:

> The wages of piece work are generally settled by an expert workman; so that if he gets what may be considered a fair wage, those who are not such good hands come down to almost a starvation price ... there have been instances in which a workman has been obliged to go with less than his ordinary wages would be ... so we endeavour to destroy the system wherever we possibly can. (RC on TU 1867b, Qs. 674, 675, 698)

An illustration of Taylor's system serves to reinforce the point that payment by the piece tended to favour the employers, an unsurprising finding.

Under the Differential Piece-Rate System of payment Taylor proposed a mechanism of paying 'men' not 'positions' and sought to isolate the worker in terms of personal skill, energy, punctuality and rapidity with which he performed his work. Two different rates were offered for the same job: a high price per piece, in case the work was finished in the shortest possible time and in perfect condition; and a low price if the job took a longer time, or if there were any imperfections in the work. The avowed intention was an enhanced daily wage rate; a numerical example shows how the system worked

Table 3.3 The differential piecerate system: an example

	Ordinary system of piecework	Differential rate system
Man's wages	$2.50	$3.50
Machine cost	$3.37	$3.37
Total cost/day	$5.87	$6.87
Pieces produced	5	10
Cost per piece	$1.174	$0.69

Source: F. W. Taylor (1894–5), 879.

in practice (see Table 3.3). The real incentive was the offer of a permanent $3.35 per day, with increased output. The arithmetic shows that wages increased in this instance 40 per cent while production was doubled and per-unit costs were reduced by 41 per cent. It was estimated that as a result of 'efficiency' measures at Bethlehem Steel, output increased from 300 to 500 per cent; costs were reduced by over 60 per cent, making a saving strictly on the level of labour costs of $126,000 over a two-year period (Palmer 1975: 39).

The ASE resisted piecework principally on account of its exploitative character and the divisive nature of its operation in the workshops:

> ... piece work (even in its best features) is without doubt the worst evil we have to contend against, for under the most favourable conditions it is utterly selfish in its operation, and is calculated to set man against man, by tending to benefit those most opposed to our Society ... we recommend the members generally to use their utmost influence in putting an end to piece work... (Allen 1872: 15) [Extract from Resolution (passed unanimously) at the Manchester Conference of the ASE, 24 July 1872]

The unions regarded the system as a crucial part of an overall management strategy to dilute craft skills in engineering workshops. The employers favoured it because of its 'normalising' effects in providing work opportunities for what they perceived as different grades of skill. A leading employer, responding to union criticisms, said:

> ... the abolition of piece work I look upon as another mode of keeping down the skilled and industrious workman to the level of the idle, incompetent, and careless one, since a good man working by the piece simply earns a higher amount of wage in a week than an indifferent man, and in exact proportion to his ability and industry, but if hindered from doing so his employer as well as himself is prevented from reaping the advantage of his superior skill, and so from producing the work a the lowest possible price. (Robinson 1868: 56)

The advantages of employing undifferentiated labour in a rigorously supervised system of production were manifest, particularly with respect to former skilled artisan labour. Towards the end of the century Captain A. Noble, vice-chairman and managing director of Sir Wm. Armstrong & Co. (Newcastle-upon-Tyne), maintained that piecework generated higher rates of pay and assisted in categorising workers according to ability. He also asserted, 'If you have a large piece of work put in a large machine, the foreman knows the rate at which the machine should go, and ... he can ascertain without much trouble whether the proper amount of work is done or not ... ' (Royal Commission on Labour 1893f). He also held that where precise labour control was not possible, piecework still remained viable, as a means of: 'knowing that you are getting a proper amount of work out of the men employed' (ibid., Q. 25207).

The direction of the manufacturing process centred on the foreman or leading hand, not the machinist; this was similar to the 'functional foreman' instituted by Taylor: 'it is clear that Victorian foremen were pivotal figures in many of the staple industries. Their status often depended upon the degree of technical knowledge required' (Melling 1983: 91). The rate and quality of production was therefore, to a large extent, determined by the foreman's expertise in calculating and determining the method of production and fixing cutting and feed rates.

This clearly affected 'floor-to-floor' times, that is, complete machining practice, including setting-up and the subsequent machine work. Direct technical input from foremen in this way reduced the machinists' function to machine tending, as F. W. Taylor had done in his American workshops. The piecework system was realisable only under certain conditions of technological development and machine/labour control. Rigorous management and operation of reliable machine tools of predictable performance was fundamental, also, standardised quality-control methods.

The piecework system did not meet with universal approval by employers. One employer regarded it as limiting and contradictory. This is brought out in reference to a group system of working:

> ... individual piece work I think is very bad. Dick has a piece of work set him, and he does not care a bit what Tom and Harry are doing, and he will break his tools to get his piece through. There is ... constant fighting ... whereas if you make the whole responsible, each one produces more than if he had not been working himself alone. (Royal Commission on Labour (1893a).

A strategy designed to overcome this kind of objection was the encouragement of the Piecemaster or 'Butty System'.

The piecemaster system or 'butty system'

The tactic of group or 'gang' working provided an important variant of the piecework model, the 'butty' or piecemaster system, and illustrates how young workers became closely integrated into dominant work norms.

The piecemaster system entailed a specific job organisation in which a gang of skilled men, labourers and boys worked under the direct control of a skilled artisan foreman, the 'piecemaster'. In a large factory there might be up to five such gangs, each under their respective piecemaster.

Three features may be noted about this system. The first was the control of the wage bill. Within the gang boys or labourers replaced skilled men, with a division of labour under the direct control of the piecemaster (Jefferys and Jefferys 1947: 45). Whilst in the majority of cases the piecemaster had no right of hiring and firing or responsibility for payment of his gang, he did use his influence with employers to keep wages down (ibid.). The Children's Employment Commission (1864) revealed that a system approximating to the Butty method did, in fact, operate covertly in some instances, and in others with employer connivance.

Second, there was a tendency for piecemasters to 'drive on' the men; bonuses were gained for working within prescribed limits.

The third feature concerned the payment of such bonuses. This process, known as 'settling', concerned the sharing out of bonuses and inevitably involved decisions by the piecemaster as to the relative worth of the contribution of different members of the gang.

Considerable criticism was mounted against the piecemaster system. The ASE criticised the unfair distribution of accrued bonuses; workers were frequently in debt to their employers as a result of not meeting production schedules; wages generally were brought down by the process, to the lowest possible point (Allen 1867: Q. 675).

This view was supported much later by one employer who considered the gang system very undesirable. The comments in this particular critique crystallise the more generalised criticisms of the system:

> I found that the men were grinding each other; sweating each other ... when the balance was paid (over and above the flat rate) we paid it to the leading hand of the gang, and we left him to divide amongst his mates; we found he did not divide amongst his mates ... (RC on Labour 1893b: Q. 25740)

The incidence of the Butty system tended to be disguised by its generally uneven distribution throughout the industry. But it was prominent in two sections of the industry, railway workshops specialising in wheel and axle turning jobs; and arms manufacture, particularly in the arsenals at Woolwich, Enfield and the W. G. Armstrong's workshops in Newcastle. These government establishments employed relatively high levels of piecework; the former at 60 per cent and the latter 'a very high proportion' (Jefferys and Jefferys 1947: 39).

In Coventry, working by the piece was practically unknown in 1861; by 1891 83 per cent of ASE members were working by the piece. During the same period in the West Midlands and the eastern counties there were 30 per cent and 36 per cent increases in the practice, respectively (ibid., p. 43).

Although sporadic, the piecemaster system was increasingly used throughout the century and the evidence shows there was systematic use of children within it. The employment of children highlights how new social mechanisms of control were reflected in the employers' attitudes to children as a form of cheap labour rather than as young workers under training. The Children's Employment Commission of 1864 provided illustrations of the situation in the period.

The use of child labour in the workshops

A screw-bolt works in Darlaston employed 35 women and girls and 26 boys. The boys were from nine years of age upwards and were principally employed at 6*d.* to 10*d.* a day from 6 a.m. to 6 p.m. as 'blowers' (operating heating systems for making metal red hot). The lowest earnings the girls received was 3/– per week and it was suggested that any amendment to the existing Factory Act would seriously affect their earnings as 'They work piece-work, and one girl can earn twice as much as another in the same time' (Children's Employment Commission 1864(1), p. 24).

A machine-maker of relatively larger capacity employing 563 workers included 13 boys under 13 years of age, 110 boys between 13 and 18 years of age, and three girls under 13. The large number of children present in the works was accounted for by the owner as a consequence of a strike in the foundry, which entailed the sacking of men and the employment of boys as substitute labour. They were paid by the piece, through the men, 'in all cases in fact, where we can get a fair measurement of the work produced' (ibid., p. 182, Evidence of John Hetherington).

Another screw-bolt works ran machinery non-stop from 6.30 a.m. to 6.30 p.m. All the men and women were on piecework; the youngest girls received 2/6 per week, the others 3/– and 4/–. It is clear some of the children were at risk on the machines: 'In one case ... a girl had her arm broken ... [she] let it throw the bolt out before she ought to have done, and the bolt hit her arm. Another girl had her wrist put out in the same way' (ibid., p. 24, Evidence of George Norton, Manager of Horton's Screw Bolt Manufactory, Darlaston).

Responsibility for hiring and firing sometimes rested with adult workers rather than management; this required the building up of a team or gang, usually children, often workers' own children: 'Three-quarters of the feeders are girls and young women. They were hired and paid by the fitter' (ibid., p. 24, Evidence of W. Elkington, Manager of The Crown Nail Company, Wolverhampton). Some firms set limits to child employment but tolerated informal hiring procedures, a strategy that enabled management to benefit from their labour:

> ... no boy under 14 had any business there at all; all that were below that age had been 'smuggled in' by the parents or overlookers. Whatever their age and length of service, they were not recognised as having any position in the place, and were put on the footing of an apprentice till they were 15, that is, would receive only 3/– a week, the wages of an apprentice at 14 ... (ibid., p. 87, foreman at Messrs. Walker & Hackney, Bury)

The children were evidently conscious at time of the effect of this type of employment on their own, and others', health:

> Am 14 years old, have been here 17 months working at grinding iron; began that work at 10 years old ... the dust makes my chest bad at times. Father used to grind here too; he died of it; he was 35 when he died ... (Ibid., p. 183, Nathaniel Shaw, of John Hetherington & Sons, Machine-Makers, Manchester)

Children employed in work teams

A common work practice known as 'integrated work processes', in which boys worked as a member of a team with adult workers, placed further constraints on some children. Release before completion of a 12-hour shift for education or training was discouraged and likely to be a hindrance to employers:

> It was thought that a limitation of the labour of the young persons under 18 to 10½ hours a day would not work well, for the men would be at a standstill, when, as was very common, they worked on for 12 hours, if the boys did not work equally long to keep them supplied with the articles they wanted. Such a restriction would involve an increase of tools, of room and of young persons to one-fifth beyond the present state of things, and would thereby be extremely distasteful to the adults ... (Ibid., p. 187, Mr. Walker of Walker & Hackney, Bury)

Wage incentives encouraged children to remain in repetitive, low-status jobs. A machine manufacturer in Lancashire employed 44 boys under 13 years, and 354 between 13 and 18 years. Some of the 15-year-olds were employed in the glazing and grinding shed:

> ... that is unhealthy work, but not nearly so bad as the cutlery grinding in Sheffield; still for the reason of its unhealthiness, they are the best paid of any Superintended by one man to six boys; their wages 6/– per

week on average. All paid by the piece, and we settle every seven weeks with them. Others were machine minders. (Ibid., p. 184, W. Madeley, Partner in Messrs Parr, Curtis & Madeley)

Any form of 'part-time' release, that is, being allowed off early, was subordinated to work schedules. A concession to 'education' was granted by certain firms, one of which allowed half of its under 13-year-olds to leave in time to go to night school. But this could have been a problem for the children, for the hours worked normally were 57½ hours in the week, from 6 a.m. to 6 p.m. on four days, and on Mondays from 7 a.m. to 5.30 p.m., with occasional overtime of two hours four days in the week. Any suggestion of limitation of work to 10½ hours in the day was perceived by the foremen and adult workers as fragmenting, for 'men and youths work in sets, and the work of one is dependent on that of the other' (ibid.).

It is clear that the concept of machine-tending by unskilled workers and boys was well established by the 1860s and became generalised practice in a wide range of engineering and engineering-related firms. Among the largest, substitution of juvenile labour for artisans' work was related to machine-tending and piecework.

> ... by far the greatest part of what may be called the preparing work, – drilling, planing, slotting, and turning, and the like, – is done by lads under 18. (Ibid., p. 156, Evidence of Mr Palmer, partner in Messrs Platt Brothers & Co., Oldham, employing a total of 4,471, including 115 under 13 years, and 778 13 years to 18 years)

Boys were paid about 3/6 per week at 11 years, but the preferred age at the Platt Works was 12 years, after which they were put to drilling and turning; '*none are apprenticed*' (ibid.; my emphasis). The need for overtime working was obviated by two factors at Platt's: a recent completion of the extension of factory space, for which extra hands were always available 'for a pressure'; and piecework, which provided sufficient incentive for children to make 'as much in 10½ hours, as they do when they know they have two hours longer' (ibid.).

Breaks in a production run precluded payment by the piece and other work strategies were used. For example, in a firm such as Messrs Iver & Hall in Bury, if a particular job was difficult to cost under a piecerate system, they favoured overtime work. Normal hours were 6 a.m. to 6 p.m., extended to 8 p.m. 'when times are good', and occasionally till 9 p.m. or 10 p.m.; and at times 'all night'.

This firm was not concerned to investigate the age of children employed: 'if a boy looks from his appearance up to the work the foreman lets him come on' (ibid., p. 187). It employed 40 children under 18 years, 13 under 13 years, one between 10 and 11, and one under ten. Starting at 2/3 a week, those that were 'at all sharp get promoted to the machine room, and become screwers, drillers, turners, and so on' (ibid.).

The largest railway carriage makers in the country, the Ashbury Railway Carriage & Iron Company, employed 1,367 workers, 23 under 13 years of age, and 149 between 13 and 18 years of age. The youngest boys were employed as errand boys and the 'brightest were promoted' to drilling machines at about 13 at a wage of 6/– per week, paid by the piece in common with 'nearly all [the] hands' (ibid., pp. 191, 192, Johnson of the Ashbury Railway Carriage & Iron Company, Openshaw, Lancs.). Some of those aged 12 assisted in the foundry at 4/6 per week, whilst in the trimming department girls were employed at about 4/– per week. About 45 boys were operating machines such as lathes and screw-bolt making:

> Am 12. What I am at is 'tapping' [putting the screw in an iron nut with this machine]. Have been here three years; was 'pulling out' for one year at a furnace on the other side there. Went to day-school for a year, before I came to work here. Go to Sunday-school now. Can't read ... (Ibid., p. 192, Evidence of John MacEwen, to investigator H. W. Lord)

Pressure for orders often meant working long hours, particularly in the wheel and axle department: 'we are celebrated for wheels and axles; sometimes involving day and night turns of 12 hours for as much as ... 10 months out of the last 12' (Johnson, ibid.). Boys of ten were not exempt:

> Am 13. Have been here two years in the smithy; before that was working at rope walk. Went to that at 10 years old; used to work there from 6 a.m. till dark, that was till 8 and nearly 9 sometimes in summer. Have never been to day-school. Go to Sunday-school, but don't read; they read to us there; I don't know what it's about'. (Ibid., Evidence of James Alcock)

The generalised employment practice using child labour, particularly on machine-tending, was not a singular focus of attention for the ASE; as a component of the piecework system it was clearly perceived as an element of exploitation. There was a resistance to payment by the piece, and systems based on pre-scheduled production times.

ASE secretary Allen referred to a differentiating grade of machine-tool operator that marked off the traditionally trained machine artisan from unskilled operatives, who were known as 'machine men' ('machine minders'). They were regarded by the Society as labourers because they 'were not in receipt of what we call ordinary rates of wages ... and members must be in receipt of the ordinary rate of wages' (Royal Commission on Trades Unions 1867b: Q. 895). The employers reasoned that rigid demarcation in job practices based on union definitions of skill differentials hampered production efficiency. The employment of 'unskilled' workers, such as children as machine-minders, dovetailed with the piecework system of payment. In deploying self-acting machines, employers stressed the simplicity of operation, and the logic of employing marginally skilled labour to man them. The unions challenged these assumptions.

Allen argued that machine shops and tool-making establishments were particularly vulnerable to the effects of employment of unskilled labour vis-à-vis skilled machinists: 'there are a large number of boys employed, and in some instances they [employers] have introduced boys to what we think an alarming extent, and result is that the men have objected to it' (ibid., Q. 846).

The substitution of skilled machinists by unskilled workers in machine-manning became a particularly contentious area of dispute between engineering employers and skilled labour during the period from the 1850s (ibid., Q. 841). It aggravated employer/union discussions throughout the period and became a major factor in the 1897 strike and lockout.

The piecework system was relatively widespread, although its incidence throughout the industry was uncoordinated and piecemeal. The employers who used the system in well-organized structures clearly gained both in terms of productivity and the marginal cost of labour.

New mechanisms of labour control were available to employers; one was built into the system of piecework itself. The self-correcting checks on workers in serial production was significant not only for quality control, but it also clearly simplified labour control. Variations on the basic principle of piecework, such as the piecemaster or Butty system, consolidated the exploitative aspects of work control, particularly for children working within 'integrated working processes'.

The introduction of accurate, automated tools with sophisticated means of measurement control simplified many production processes to the extent that children were more easily integrated and exploited. The unions' objection to this was not necessarily motivated by humanitarian concerns for factory children, but revolved around two factors: the intensification of existing labour with increasing use of child labour, and the accompanying decomposition of machinists' skills.

Other than a slight increase in wages, the piecework system militated against young workers gaining any realistic advantages either in terms of progression in work or education. Tied in to a 'production by the piece' system, individual workers found it increasingly difficult to break the pattern of production by seeking access to education requiring time off work. Young workers' access to technical education, based on what was to become a predominantly part-time principle, was critically influenced by the employers' pursuit of short-term profits using, among other strategies, the piecework system. Employers were reluctant to forgo the contribution of young workers integrated into work patterns designed to depress costs.

Labour control under the piecemaster system, although not universal, was significant. Foremen generally in the engineering industry and those controlling piecework schedules were emerging as an influential group within the changing social relations of production. Later in the century, for example, foremen were to become key figures in deciding whether boys could be released early from work in order to attend evening classes. The ASE's claim that its members were responsible for training workmen was rejected outright by the employers on the grounds that this function was 'the responsibility of foremen'. The part-time day-release system was a tediously slow feature in the development of technical education and then only after the turn of the century. The structure of a 19th-century technical education system became increasingly tied in with prevailing work patterns. The majority of students attended evening classes and were heavily dependent upon the goodwill of their immediate supervisors, the foremen, for release from work.

Underlying production control processes, such as the piecework system, was the continuing conflict generated by the employers' attempts radically to redefine engineering craft skills against the resistance of the artisans' union. The unions were intent on revitalising the apprenticeship system, not solely to protect their skilled status, but also as a means of retaining craft instruction as an integral part of a technical education system.

Note

1. The term 'artisan' appears in the literature as synonymous with skilled craftsman. This seems to be its use in generalised accounts of the history of technology and labour history, or as part of a hierarchy of authority relations in the division of labour in sociological accounts. The point here is that the term can have a more precise connotation, namely, 'instructor in the arts'. In this sense artisans in the 19th century were craftsmen responsible for instruction in the art of engineering craftsmanship, usually in relation to young workers. The term also implied a kind of 'sub-managerial' function, a view put forward by Foster (1977), Brecher et al. (1978) and Stark (1980). This function entailed the supervision of other, mostly unskilled, workers. The employer could not necessarily tell artisans how a job should be done; the artisan thus generally took responsibility for the instruction and supervision of unskilled worker and apprentices. There was often no other source of instruction available.

    For the purposes of this book the term' artisan' is used to suggest the dual aspect of skilled engineering workers' tasks: the manufacture of engineering products by hand and machine to relatively high levels of accuracy, and the supervision and instruction of young workers, apprentices. This was a historical form of craft development and training adopted by most trades and embodied in the articles of the Amalgamated Society of Engineers (ASE), the principal trade union of metal workers in the 19th century. The artisan–apprentice model of trade training was the only form of such training for skilled trades through most of the century.

CHAPTER FOUR

Skill and the collapse of the craft apprentice system

Employer tactics to overcome skilled workers' resistance to the implementation of new technologies were part of their search for more efficient means of work and labour control. Engineering employers instigated the substitution of skilled labour as a managerial imperative. The first official enquiry into trade unions in the 19th century clearly shows that some engineering employers insisted upon employing non-union labour wherever possible: 'After the strike of 1851–2 we required every man who came into the works to sign a declaration that he did not and would not belong to a union ... ' (Robinson 1868: Q. 9005). The history of the last hundred years has been characterised by successive attempts by employers to abolish the need for skilled craftsmen (Penn 1983). A precedent had also been established by other employers with the publication of a 'black list' of Society (ASE) members after they had struck in 1855 (Allen 1867: Q. 876). In justification it was argued on behalf of the employers at the Royal Commission that there were few formal associations of employers, and those which had been formed were instituted 'for the ordinary regulation of their respective trades, for the purposes of obtaining labour upon the most favourable terms, and for self-defence against the proceedings of the trade unions' (RC on TU 1868–9, p. xvi, para. 43). But this emphasis on a defensive position by employers tends to obscure more aggressive policies. From the 1880s there were hundreds of lockouts, the most feared and devastating of the employers' strike-breaking tactics (McIvor 1984). On the question of whether the employers' federating tendencies were merely contingent upon union activity, a minority report by three members of the Royal Commission, Lichfield, Hughes, Harrison, acknowledged that the employers' views, as represented by testimony to the Commission, were 'entirely similar to the rules of the unions' (RC on TU 1869b, p. x).

In the event, ASE rules of the time did not categorically preclude unskilled men being employed on machines, although there was a tacit understanding that Society men would generally be employed in that capacity (RC on TU 1867a: Q. 641). Although machine-minders were recognised as 'society men' in some provincial towns, they were differentiated on grounds of skill and length of service, that is, they were not regarded by ASE members as being 'legal hands' (ibid., Q. 643). The union was conscious of the legality attaching to the exercise of restraints over the introduction of what it regarded as unskilled labour. The union constitution reiterated the need for a protective association concerned with the maintenance of the boundaries between 'skill' and 'non-skill', but operating within discrete and legal parameters:

> Our object is not to do anything either indiscreet or illegal; but if constrained to make restrictions against the admission into our trade of those who have not earned a right by a probationary servitude, we do so knowing that such encroachments are productive of evil, and, when persevered in unchecked, result in reducing the condition of the artisan to that of the unskilled labourer, and confer no permanent advantage on those admitted. It is our duty, then to exercise the same care and watchfulness over that in which we have a vested interest as the physician does who hold a diploma, or the author who is protected by a copyright. (Rules of the Amalgamated Society of Engineers, Machinists, Millwrights, Smiths and Pattern Makers (revised 16 May 1864), as submitted to RC on TU, 1869a: 246).

However, the criterion of skill used by Society members seems to have been less rigid than the term connoted, for it referred to 'a man who has been five years in the trade, whether apprenticed or not, is capable of earning his livelihood at it and has become a competent workman' (RC on TU 1867a: Q. 631)

Plainly there was a link between the introduction of new tool technologies, based on the slide-rest and innovations in metrology, and the increase in the employers' power to reorganise work patterns and control strategies. Through standardisation and interchangeability of parts and labour, the interaction between the skilled worker and the object of his labour changed. No longer requiring a process of traditional craft training, the skilled workers' job, formerly characterised by precision, speed and manipulative skills, was reorganised and redefined. The craft of fitting exemplifies this process.

The importance of 'assembly' as distinct from fitting

The construction of machinery was transformed by mechanisation, radically affecting the process of fitting. By producing components of improved accuracy and finish, the need for subsequent work by 'fitters' diminished, but it was not entirely eliminated. The craft of fitting was, and remains, a highly regarded practical hand-skill in engineering practice because it was difficult completely to mechanise the process of building machines, that is, the actual process of fitting components together.

With more generalised use of standardisation employer sought to reduce their dependence upon individual fitting skills, which were used to rectify minor errors and facilitate construction. 'Assembly' of accurately dimensioned and finished machined components, using less skilled or unskilled 'assemblers', became increasingly the norm. It was argued that standardisation of parts made the employment of girls on assembly in fitting shops a viable proposition. The bulk of the work in the engineering trade could be carried on by boys, but 'the day will come in which steam engines will be made by girls. There is as much mechanical skill required in superintending a power loom or a spinning jenny with its thousands of spindles as a steam engine' (Nasmyth 1868b: Qs. 19190, 19194).

Whitworth, also, envisaged a wider application of 'fool-proof' standard components as regards size and finish, enabling assembly to be accomplished with little or no skill:

> Fifty years ago thousands of spindles in a cotton factory had each to be separately fitted into a bolster in which it had to work. At the present time *all these spindles are made to gauge, and are interchangeable* ... it cannot be imposed too forcibly ... that *accuracy of measurement is essential for good and efficient workmanship, and that it tends to economy* in all branches of manufacture, so as to have the parts interchangeable. (Whitworth 1876: 68; my emphasis)

The processes of fitting explained

Fitters were skilled engineering workers employed in the construction of machine tools, and the fitting and maintenance of general-purpose and specialised machinery. Fitting was (is) a primary engineering craft skill in the engineering industry embodying not a single, but a number of generally recognised mechanical skills.

Fitting usually began with 'marking out' (the translation of dimensions of engineering components from technical drawings, 'blueprints'). These were laid out in what was termed first-angle or 'English' projection, that is, drawings, to scale, representing a component viewed in three directions, 'views', to encompass the complete article. This process required geometric precision, and facility for working to close tolerances (within specified, close limits of dimension).

The preparation and execution of a variety of smaller machining processes was a fitter's main task and this entailed the use of general machine-shop tools, drilling, shaping, milling, turning, and grinding, together with the fabrication (putting together) – 'fitting' – of components previously prepared. The preliminary work was carried out by the fitters or executed on machines.

The complex and varied nature of fitting commanded high status within the ASE and also with engineering employers; fitters thus constituted a pre-eminent group among society members, and remained so despite the increase in the use of machines. ASE admissions indicate that fitters outnumbered turners (lathe workers, the other principal artisan group) in the period up to 1889. Up to 1869 there were 54 per cent fitters and 24 per cent turners, in the period 1875–9, 57 per cent and 25 per cent respectively, and in 1885–9, 58 per cent and 27 per cent respectively (ASE Annual Reports).

Fitting skills were of such an eclectic quality, embodying both fabrication and machining abilities, that realistically they would not have been easily replaced by less skilled workers. The important assumption here is that it was very difficult to manufacture components in the forge or machine shop preparatory to fitting to a level of precision and finish that would completely rule out further work by fitters. Whitworth concluded that, despite advances in machine-tool processes, the skilled fitters' work remained crucial:

> Would the application of these inventions [gauges invented by Whitworth for checking components] render the parts of a musket more nearly alike in diameter than at present they are? – Yes, it enables a person to make them of the exact size, whereas he has not exact means of ascertaining whether they are so or not.
>
> Then it is your opinion that it is possible to produce the several parts of a military gun with sufficient accuracy by machining, so that they shall fit together, and require comparatively little finishing by hand labour? – It is hardly possible to do that; they do require hand labour.
>
> What amount? – That would depend upon the care that was taken in attending to the machines, and in their quality.
>
> You think that it is not possible to make them with sufficient accuracy, but that some hand labour would be required? – Quite impossible. (Select Committee on Small Arms 1854: Q. 1943–6)

Absolute interchangeability was a very difficult goal to achieve in mid-century mainly because it was expensive and contingent upon complete mechanisation of the work process. Whitworth acknowledged this factor in production. Rather than absolute interchangeability, uniformity in production was probably more realistic – as an effect, not an absolute goal of mechanisation (Hounshell 1985: 49). The combination of precision machine-tool work based on nationally agreed standards, and assembly of components using unskilled labour, was therefore well established by 1878. It was reported that

> Where the machine tool system of construction has been introduced in its entirety ... the several parts of [the] structural skeleton are so planed or otherwise shaped by accurate machine tools that, when the several parts are brought face to face for the first time, they fit each other exactly without adjustment ... (Anderson 1880, Vol. 2, p. 296)

From the early 1900s interchangeable manufacture in the machine-tool section had achieved almost universal acceptance among production engineers. Evidence from America confirms its incidence there:

> Thus the advantage to be gained ... by the use of up-to-date machines and special tools and fixtures are obvious, as the cost of the machines and the amount expended in the designing and constructing of special tools will be quickly balanced on the profit side when the increased output and the efficiency of the parts produced through their use are compared with the results under the old methods. Another advantage ... is the almost total elimination of the obtainable results depending upon

the degree of skill and intelligence possessed by the workman; thus allowing of employing less expensive help in the manufacture of the required parts. (Wordworth 1905: 513)

By 1913, in America, it was possible to turn out 'large amounts of consistently accurate work' (Hounshell 1985).

The development of 'assembly' in England, as distinct from 'fitting', was characterised by contrasts between the old and the new technology:

> In the new [technology], accuracy and interchangeability of dimensions are maintained by a suitable equipment of gauges and the establishment of limits; in the old, there is a variety of sizes depending upon the skill and judgement of individuals ... In the new method, machining is done accurately to dimensions; in the old, machine and tools are mainly used ... (Orcutt 1902: 10).

English 19th-century engineering practice was reorganised using a combination of highly developed automatic machine tools and controls over precision measurement through the metrological and machine-tool innovations of entrepreneurs such as Whitworth (and F. W. Taylor in America). Direct workshop supervision of unskilled labour, assemblers, was undertaken by a small number of highly trained skilled workers.

Overall workshop management also changed; the new concept of the 'toolroom' marked a crucial division between manufacturing production and quality control. This ensured centralisation of control. An English engineer noted:

> ... (the) practice is to construct machines so automatic in their nature that it has become possible to employ practically unskilled labour to a large extent, engaging at the same time highly skilled and thoroughly educated foremen and managers to superintend the setting and keeping in order of the automatic machines which can then be left in the hands of unskilled men, who can only command a low wage ... (Amos 1898–9: 274)

Additional refinements, such as multiplication of cutting tools with automatic feeding of the work, made it possible for machines such as the turret lathe rapidly to increase production, maintaining quality despite the fall in the number of skilled workers (Horner 1900; Benjamin 1906; Woodbury 1967: 628).

Organised artisan resistance to work reorganisation was weakened by dilution of craft skills, including fitting, which had hitherto been difficult to rationalise to employers' satisfaction because of the varied nature of fitting skills. The implementation of new levels of precision manufacture was not exclusively an economic issue; it also influenced the employers' attitude to the craft apprenticeship and training. It fostered a growing reluctance by employers to continue the apprenticeship scheme in its historic form.

The traditional craft apprenticeship system

The craft apprenticeship system that Nasmyth (1867) had referred to as the 'fag end of the old feudal system' dated from the Elizabethan Statute of 1563. As originally conceived, the apprenticeship system was carefully regulated, defining the social classes from which apprentices might be taken, and stipulating that seven years was the qualifying period to practise any trade. In this way the skilled were bracketed out from the unskilled and there was a clear demarcation between the various skilled trades and with the unskilled (RC on Labour 1894).

The concept of the 'company' or 'fraternity' was important in the earlier period, for the apprentice was committed to a period of 'servitude' to a specific company from whom 'freedom' had to be acquired after fulfilling the obligations of the statutory period. Those responsible for apprentices were 'masters', and conditions imposed on both parties were strict and obligatory. Such conditions emanating from the 'Statute of Apprentices' of 1557 remained in force for two and a half centuries (A. Evans 1890: 7). This was a system characterised by a strictly delineated teaching and learning situation for clearly defined and discrete skills.

The watershed in the dissolution of the master–apprentice relation may be put at 1814, in which year the provisions relating to apprenticeships in the Elizabethan Statutes were finally repealed. From that period there ceased to be any legal guarantee for the restriction of the number of workmen in any trade (A. Evans 1890). The legal requirements and obligations under the old system constituted a formal contract between the relevant parties. With the repeal, it seemed only a matter of time before the methodical exploitation of young workers would be unprotected by any form of legislative enactment. There were various legal instruments extant, for example, the Employers and Workmen Act of 1875, which laid down conditions of employment and procedures governing disputes between master and apprentices (39 and 39 Vic. Cap. 90 1875, p. 1020).

Statutory obligations notwithstanding, what was clearly present in the old system and conspicuously absent by the end of the 19th and the beginning of the 20th century was the expectation and reciprocal basis of the relationship between the apprentice-learner and the master. In the main, the concept of 'master' in the old meaning of the term had been rejected by the employers.

Forms of craft apprenticeship

During most of the period under discussion three forms of apprenticeship may be distinguished: apprenticeship under indenture, apprenticeship under written agreement and apprenticeship under oral agreement.

In the first case the agreement is expressed in a form which sets out in detail and with solemnity the various conditions to which the employer and the apprentice agreed to be bound (the concept of the 'bound apprentice'). There was a clear set of expectations formalised by a designated transmission of specific skills, accompanied by a cluster of norms and values associated with those particular skills. As originally conceived, the agreements were a recognition of the autonomous character of skilled artisans' work: 'the apprentice shall and will diligently, faithfully, soberly, and honestly, according to the best of his knowledge, skill and ability, serve the masters ... during the said term, and obey, observe, and fulfil all instructions, orders, and lawful commands of the masters and those put in authority under them' (Indenture of 1904, quoted in HMSO 1928b, pt. VI, App. E, pp. 192–6).

The employers' obligations were clear: 'The masters will accept the apprentice as an apprentice during the said term, and by the best means that they can, will instruct him, or cause him to be instructed in the branches of the business of a manufacturing engineer ... ' (Indenture ibid. (a)).

The term 'apprentice' presupposed a defined specificity in relation to a branch of the engineering industry and implied an obligation to engage in the practice of teaching a trade. The 'mysteries of the trade' were part of a cultural as well as a technological transmission in the engineering workshops. Formal adherence to this particular form operated under highly structured agreements, embodying legal sanctions: 'the apprentice ... signing this indenture [doth] bind himself for the whole term of his apprenticeship to serve his masters ... and do all he can to further his masters' interest their secrets to keep and their lawful commands to obey' (ibid.).

Written agreements were usually simpler in form than indentures and were required where an apprenticeship was entered into for a period of more than one year but less than the traditional period of four to six years. This was necessary in order to make the contract enforceable. There was a commitment laid upon the employer to teach the apprentice, commonly through the use of skilled journeymen, and upon the apprentice to serve for the stipulated time.

Both the indenture and written agreement patterns embodied simple but necessary features. The employer undertook to teach the apprentice under the various conditions laid out, and the apprentice to serve the employer. In addition it was usual to provide for the terms of apprenticeship, the wages to be paid in each year of the apprenticeship, the trade(s) or branches of trade which the apprentice is to be taught and the binding of the boy's parent or guardian as a third party to the agreement (Board of Trade Report 1915: 15).

Apprenticeship under oral agreement was used when an employer orally agreed to take a boy as apprentice for the purpose of being taught a skilled trade. The terms of such a contract seldom went beyond fixing the length of the apprenticeship, the hours of work and the wages to be paid. The terms and conditions might be explicitly advertised conditions of apprenticeship obtaining at a particular establishment. An oral agreement was valid, but unless it was to be performed within the space of one year it was unenforceable (ibid., p. 18).

The essential features of the traditional methods of trade training were thus being radically changed from the 1850s. Apprentice relations were based essentially on paternalism. By this is meant such relations were characterised by a master being 'an authority' (in a traditional craft); the apprentice was in a learning situation and adopted the role of 'pupil'. This was at the centre of the historical English craft system of technical education and the only form for much of the 19th century.

The retention of the craft apprenticeship, or some model based on it, was central to the skilled workers' resistance to work reorganisation and underlay many employer–employee disputes from mid-century. For the craft unions skilled status was crucial to their self-conception as 'respectable' engineering artisans, superior workmen. The notion of 'skill' was also perceived as a form of investment in human capital.

The concept of skill

Existing literature reveals little in the way of clear definitions of skill. The debate since Braverman's (1974) analysis of the labour process and his articulation of the process of deskilling has tended to focus on the negative aspects of skill in the sense that it is a quality in human work performance which is diminished or eliminated as a result of increased mechanisation. But few explicit definitions exist of what it is that is actually affected in the process of deskilling. As Thompson (1983) says, 'in most cases skill is measured less by formal definition than by historical context and comparison ... ' (p. 92). Many disputes between 19th-century employers and workers frequently related to the credibility afforded definitions of skill and the implications it had for the struggle over workshop control and the experience of young workers learning a trade. Artisans argued that many classes of work required a generalised expertise which could only be acquired through systematic training and instilling 'flexibility' (Rainbird 1988). Employers regarded the artisans' rationalisation as exaggeration and held that skills were often no more than mere 'defensive' categories used by the workers to maintain status (Nasmyth 1868b; Robinson 1868).

The nature of skill may be distinguished thus: First, there is the notion of skill as learned attributes, abilities, and knowledge developed over a period of time by training and experience.

Skill is a multi-purpose concept inasmuch as the worker is able to demonstrate the degree to which he has a mastery over certain manual operations. It could involve planning and decision-making, flexibility and dexterity in performance, competence and manipulative sophistication in various aspects of work, and the ability to work at reasonable speeds within prescribed limits of size with minimum supervision.

Second, there is the approach to skill which rests primarily on labelling, an approach which emphasises the social construction of skill as opposed to explicitly defined technological categories of human performance (More 1980).

Clearly, a specific skill which embodies learned characteristics of expertise and methodology, under normal circumstances, is inviolable in the sense that it is embedded in the personality structure of the individual. Polyani (1964) writes of 'tacit knowing' in an apprenticeship, 'By watching the master and emulating his efforts in the presence of his example, the apprentice unconsciously picks up the rules of the art, *including those which are not explicitly known to the master himself...* ' (p. 53; my emphasis). An important implication of the conception of tacit skills is that the exercise of skill should not necessarily be seen as a 'conscious activity' (Mainwaring and Wood 1985: 179).

A critical characteristic of skill is the skilled workers' capacity for accuracy, adding to a firm's productivity. Skill characteristics may of course fall into disuse, be 'unlearned' or forgotten, but in the context of deskilling it seems more likely that the skill requirements for particular jobs would be changed, or redefined. Nineteenth-century engineering developments indicated how jobs could be, and were, technically redefined, as analysis of the issue of precision measurement developed by Whitworth (1854, 1856, 1876, 1882a) demonstrates.

Hobsbawm (1984) stressed that skill required a formal structure for its realisation, a process he referred to as the 'professionalization of craftsmanship'. He maintained that the division of workers into 'artisans' and 'labourers' represented, from the men's point of view, 'a qualitative superiority of skill so learned ... ' (p. 358). This model fits with his notion of 'labour aristocracy', the structure of which reinforced the status differences between the skilled and the unskilled.

The separation of the objective 'technical' content of a particular job and the social dimension of skilled status presents difficulties. It is not clear what the 'objective technical content' of a job implies. A technicist view of technology disregards the human input and social purpose underlying all technological developments. Craftsman were capable of working from start to finish on a job without employer interference: 'in practice it proves difficult to find an objective basis for the labour quality of jobs ... Changes in skill levels are linked to the modes of work control. This means ... it is not possible to define skill independently of organizational and control processes ... ' (Littler 1982: 9).

Employers seeking alternatives to artisan skills, upon which they had been so reliant, realised them through the work of entrepreneurs such as Maudslay,

Whitworth and Nasmyth in the late 18th and early 19th centuries. Their contribution to the transformation of workshop practice was outstanding in that they introduced new classes of machines and tools in which 'skills were embedded'.

The key concept in an explanation of the changing character of 19th-century skills was interchangeability; and accuracy was a prime factor in the drive for increasing mechanisation. Accuracy was the essential precondition of interchangeability. As Colt said, of his arms (musketry) 'In my own arms one part corresponds with another very nearly.' (quoted by Hounshell 1985: 23). There was little chance of interchangeability without precision and a recognised set of standards. This was ably demonstrated by Whitworth. It was clear that perfect interchangeability was unattainable in the early stages of advanced machinery, as Whitworth himself conceded in his evidence to the Small Arms Commission.[1]

The number of strikes and conflicts over machine manning and skill redefinition show that employers did not entirely satisfactorily transform the division of labour in the 'direction of standardization' (Zeitlin 1987: 173). There was no breakthrough in Britain into a new 'Taylorist' mode, based on the notion of 'scientific management', until much later in the century. Taylor's metallurgical research and development into new cutting tools and techniques of metal machining were essential preconditions of innovatory workshop processes and were concomitants of standardisation (Taylor 1906, 1911b). The new technologies embodied direct control over both the production process and labour.

Increasingly the development and use of company-specific skills vis-à-vis recognised and generalisable skills became an issue for unions. The practices of the ASE in the 19th century illustrate the case. 'Tramping' was common in the period, whereby artisans (journeymen) would tramp for work from place to place. The local union office supplied details of work available in the area on arrival, and the 'skill credentials' of the worker were attested by local union members (Hobsbawm 1974). In this way general engineering craft skills were identified and accredited. To quote Zeitlin (1987):

> The very notion of craft control implied the formulation of a set of rules which reached beyond the individual workplace ... craft unions sought to protect the market value of their members' skills ... standardizing ... working conditions ... to ensure that they encountered similar conditions in each workshop ... ' (p. 172).

Trade union sources in the 1860s point to a general concept of skill regarded as an investment, and as a means of differentiating the journeyman from the labourer. An assumption frequently associated with skill formation was that it was an investment by both employers and workers. In terms of human capital theory the most efficient training system will be that which allows each participant to capture the value of his investment (More 1980;

Floud 1985). Another assumption in human capital theory is that the employee would receive training from the employer in the detailed processes of the trade, and would become manually proficient.

The nature of skill and 'human capital as investment'

The craft unions first put forward a conception of skill as investment in 1868. During the Congress of that year it was argued that 'skill and labour' in the working man was his 'capital' over which the 'employer had no right of interference' (TUC 1868). It held that its membership was limited to men who were 'possessed of good ability as a workman, of steady habits, good moral character ... ' (RC on TU 1868b).

In 1867 Allen, the ASE secretary, outlined the social effects of amalgamated unionism on the skilled worker. The salient points revolved around the use of the skilled worker:

> I think it [the Union] has been a means of decided improvement to them in the position and character generally; for we have a controlling power over them ... we have the opportunity of dealing with them, and we do our best to keep them up to the mark so far as regards their position. (RC on TU 1867a, Q. 644)

Another view was given by ASE member, later general secretary, John Burnett. The engineering craftsman was characterised by skill and intelligence:

> ... their work [engineers] requires both skill and intelligence, and the best workmen are really scientific artisans, working under conditions which require the exercise and very highest faculties of brain and hand. (*Newcastle Weekly Chronicle*, 3 July 1875 – John Burnett, 'A Model Trade Society').

He later formulated his ideas on artisan exclusiveness in terms of 'skill as property' and stressed the need to distance the artisan from the unskilled labourer. For him the skilled man was a bearer of economically valued capabilities:

> Skill is the only property of the artisan ... [it] is in perpetual danger from competitive struggles of society ... the union is his only hope of security ... [non-union men] to the common cause contribute nothing; on the contrary they hand like a millstone round the neck of their more thoughtful and courageous fellows who have to make the fight and find the means for all. (Burnett 1886: 18)

The qualifying time for membership of the ASE was five years in order that the Society 'may be satisfied that the candidate is a competent workman' (RC on TU 1868b: Q. 985). The notion of the 'aristocracy of labour' held by 19th-century artisans had a broad connotation. Not only did it imply high occupational status ('good ability'), but also qualities of moral rectitude ('steady habits'), and 'influence' as members of a respectable stratum of the working class. The differentiation from the unskilled was an imperative. George Howell, well known as secretary of the Operative Bricklayers Society and Secretary of the London Trades Council (1861-2), emphasised the exclusiveness of the artisan groups. He despised and feared the onset of the new unionism, which encouraged the inclusion of unskilled workers; he gave 'sincere assurances that he wanted to have nothing to do with the dictatorship of the proletariat' (quoted in J. F. C. Harrison 1974: 98). A later, more centralist ASE secretary, Barnes, urged the union to accept 'specialization and open the union to the less skilled' (Zeitlin 1983: 43).

Artisans were thus separated from the unskilled both in terms of identifiable workshop skills and the most pervasive of Victorian social concepts, respectability. The lifestyle of artisans derived from their ability to bargain for a minimum level and regularity of earnings, and the facility to live outside the slums (Hobsbawn 1954). Wright (1871) said artisans were thrifty, sober and had drive. They were 'men who, by reason of the "push" and energy which have, as a rule, enabled them to accumulate money or property, are among the most influential of their class and with their class' (p. 66). He condemned aspiring labourers: 'any clever or ambitious labourer who shows a desire to get out of his place ... by attempting to creep into a "trade" ... is guilty of a deadly sin, and deserving of the abhorrence of all right-thinking members of the craft ... ' (ibid.). 'Respectability' was thus highly regarded by artisans and held to be a kind of moral attribute, one which also provided a common link between the various skilled trades. Artisan leaders such as Howell (Bricklayers), Allen, Burnett (Engineers) and Applegarth of the Carpenters' amalgamated union agreed that craftsmen embodied norms and values which emerged from their respectable position in the workplace and society.

They had most to lose as a result of substitution. Allen in his evidence to the Royal Commission on Trades Unions (1867) clearly intended to dissociate his members from the ranks of the unskilled. He reaffirmed union opposition to any amalgamation with the unskilled when recalling his union's refusal to attend the Trades' Conference in London in March 1867, on the grounds that 'a large number of what is called the Working Men's Association, which convened the meeting, do not belong to any trade society at all, and we were determined not to identify ourselves with parties who do not belong to unions' (RC on TU 1867b, Q. 998). Historically there had been a marked distinction between skilled and unskilled workers, in terms of wage differentials, autonomy over work procedures, control of labour, including apprentices and living standards (British Labour Statistics 1978; Hobsbawm 1974, 1984); Census of Production 1906.

Problems with the notion of craft exclusivity

Criticism of union attitudes to employer–employee relations centred on the wider political effects of skilled workers' exclusivity. Engels (1889) argued that working-class zeal had been sapped by artisan quasi-alliances with the Liberal party. They promoted a lethargic and undemonstrative substratum, intent on extending and consolidating those attributes of respectability that marked them off from the unskilled: 'The most repulsive thing here is the bourgeois "respectability" which has grown deep into the bones of the workers' (Engels 1889). Marx held that the accommodation and deradicalisation of the working class had been continuing since 1848. He spoke of the demoralisation of the English working class which had 'got to the point when they were nothing more than the tail of the great Liberal party, i.e. the henchmen of the capitalists' (Marx 1878). He also maintained that artisans were a privileged group, and 'an aristocratic minority, excluding the unskilled and enrolling in the East End of London one worker in ten' (quoted in Collins and Abramsky 1965: 51). This discounts much of what was happening among skilled workers within the manufacturing industry who consistently challenged the employers from the 1850s. The criticism does add weight to the view that skilled workers were not overconcerned with notions of a 'working-class' solidarity at this time: 'The archetypal independent-minded radical working man of the 1860s owed allegiance to a personal, not a collective, morality ... [they] aspired to an individual ideal in order to show that they were not as other men' (Shepherd 1978: 61).

The fact that unionised, i.e. skilled, workers constituted a small proportion of the workforce lent credence to the idea of exclusivity. The first TUC meeting of 1868 was unrepresentative, for it did not include representatives from all 'eligible' unions. It has been argued that the Trades Union Congress up to the 1890s were representative of little more than half a million skilled workers (Cole 1937; Roberts 1958).

Parliamentary Committees rarely took into account the concerns of the mass of the unskilled who had no apprenticeship system and demarcation rules to control the flow of applicants for their jobs (Roberts 1958).

The apprenticeship viewed as a source of conflict

From mid-century engineering employers increasingly recognised the potential for resistance embodied in artisan exclusivity. After the first national engineering strike in 1852 they insisted that on their return all workers sign a declaration that they would not belong to a union (RC on TU 1868a). They perceived artisan autonomy as a block on efficiency and productivity. The union's ability to exercise sanctions over the members was regarded as 'an impediment to trade' (ibid.).

Artisan exclusivity had wider-ranging political consequences for worker solidarity later in the century. The skilled/unskilled friction was exploited by the employers in the 1890s when they actively encouraged the unskilled, i.e. the non-unionised, workers to take up jobs formerly held by skilled workers and press for union recognition. The employers' case against the ASE was that its restricted membership increased production costs and 'weakened the competitive capacity of the industry' (RC on TU 1868a: 56). Did union strength constitute a genuine threat?

Exclusivity and autonomy in the workplace, based on the formal apprenticeship, were, for the most part, illusory. Artisan notions of 'skill as an investment' were clearly undermined by the employers' widening hegemony in the industry.

Self-acting machines were specifically designed for operation with a minimum of skilled labour, not new kinds of machines requiring more advanced skills. Technologically deterministic notions suggest that 'the technology of the industry demanded the skilled, all-round worker, and the all-purpose lathe which could be switched about to different types of production ... ' (More 1980: 154). The implementation of new technologies precluded serious consideration of systematic craft training and education. Conflicts were generated by unionised workers seeking to retain autonomy and thus relevant technical education through the craft apprenticeship, being blocked by employers intent on witnessing its demise.

The employers' challenge to artisan control over trade training

The ASE sought to enforce an informal ratio of apprentices to journeymen of 1:4, but in parts of the country it reached 6:1. There was a 'subversion of apprenticeship into a form of cheap labour' (Zeitlin in Harrison and Zeitlin (eds) 1985: 202).

The Children's Employment Commission in 1864 revealed a well-established routine of child labour operating in the factories. This precipitated a decline in indentured and premium apprenticeships which was to last into the next century. One of the largest companies in England, Messrs Platt Bros of Oldham, with 430 workers under 18 years of age, and 95 under 13, told the Commission, 'we like them to be 12 years old ... but many are brought at 11 ... they earn 3/6d per week ... *none are apprenticed* ... ' (p. 23; my emphasis).

The employers officially challenged unionised labour at the Inquiry into Trades Unions in 1867–8. The apprenticeship system was a prime focus of contention. Nasmyth, a leading employer and engineer, in his evidence to the Inquiry derided the apprenticeship system. At this time he employed 1,500 workers and could be regarded as a representative of the substantial engineering employers of the period (RC on TU 1868c: Q. 19137). For Nasmyth, current developments in machine technologies made many artisan skills redundant: 'When I began to introduce these mechanical contrivances that facilitated the production of work, independently of dexterity, enabling me to do the work with boys and labourers, I reduced the numbers fully one-half' (RC on TU 1868c, Q. 19138). The use of the term 'independent of dexterity' in this context is significant. It pointed to a central feature of the new tools, accuracy.

Another leading engineering employer, Beyer of Beyer, Peacock & Co. of Manchester, in his evidence argued that the ASE ruling on apprenticeship and the five-year rule was 'degrading'. He stated that employers would resist the 'implementation of such rules in the workshops' (RC on TU 1868c, Q. 18887).

This attitude prevailed throughout the period from the 1860s. Robinson, of the Atlas Engineering Company, provides a further illustration. At the 1868 inquiry he confronted the ASE over the apprenticeship mode of training as a means of promoting work autonomy for the skilled. (Robinson's company employed about 1,600 workers at the time.) Limitations on apprenticeship conditions, he maintained, 'were an intrusion by union upon management prerogatives'. Thus in his company the question of apprenticeship was 'resolved' by debarring the union from discussions between the company and the men. On this crucial issue he stated, 'we have fought a battle with them [the ASE] and beat them' (RC on TU 1868c, Q. 19058). His company used an informal method of company training, the operation of which even to management seemed to be unclear. In reply to the question: '[And] you have retained the privilege of educating apprentices to any extent you think right?' Robinson replied, 'So far as we know that is so, but the foremen sometimes do things that we are not cognisant of ... ' (RC on TU 1868c, Q. 19059).

Increasing mechanisation and changing conception of skill

The increasing dequalification and 'downgrading' of skilled workers continued throughout the century. This took two forms. The first was explicit: displacement and even loss of employment: As Noble, the managing director of the Sir W.G. Armstrong Mitchell Company, stated: 'In times of depression the journeymen are generally the first to lose their employment as the employer fancies ... ' (RC on Labour 1893c, Q. 26149). The second implied a gradual loss of status for the skilled worker:

> When a man gets to a certain age he is not able to do quite the same amount or perhaps class of work. There is a great deal of work that he may do, and usefully, but it becomes the interest of the employer to get rid of that man altogether, whereas in former years he would have been

kept on at some class of work, although possibly at a reduced wage. (RC on Labour 1893d, Q. 25248)

The concept of skill was being redefined both in terms of quality of individual performance and skill content of the job. New levels of metrology, instituted by Whitworth, were highly significant factors in rationalising production based on redefined skill requirements. Management had access to a system of 'quality control' hitherto unavailable, until the research on metrology was brought into practice. The employers' perception of skill altered as technology made substitution of skilled labour by the unskilled more viable; thus the apprenticeship lost much of its purpose for employers and its decline encouraged the use of boy labour.

Before the end of the century boy labour was used to ameliorate the effects of strike action by skilled men and as a lever to gain more purchase in the longer-term aim of expanding labour substitution in machine manning: Noble said 'I have known at one time, while all the machines were occupied at one particular factory ... at least 300 or 400 boys were on the books waiting for their turn to get in, and when we were on strike they took these boys in all at once' (RC on Labour 1893, Q. 23235). The scale of this enterprise may be gauged by the fact that his company had 15,000 workers on its books, including an Italian subsidiary at Pozzuoli, and at the time of the 1893 Royal Commission had a UK workforce of 12–13,000 (RC on Labour 1893, Q. 25229).

Boys and apprentices were traditionally exempt from strike call. Thus Noble stated:

> During the last strike we caused our boys to carry on such of our machines as could be carried on by moving the apprentices, and these apprentices were advanced a little sooner than they would have been under ordinary circumstances ... when the strike terminated I refused to put back those lads who had advanced and distinguished themselves, by putting them back to their old machines, or to their old work. In fact their old places had been filled by new lads ... unfortunately ... an immense number of men were left without employment ... in our works we have somewhere between 1500 and 2000 men less than we had before the strike. (RC on Labour, 1893d, Q. 25217)

Clearly, the enforced unemployment of between 1,500 and 2,000 workers demonstrated the weak position of skilled workers, contrary to their belief in exclusivity.

Another employer distinguished between 'apprentices' who were sons of farmers, 'or people of that class', who were taught a trade 'as well as we can'; and those who were 'ordinary workmens' sons, what we call boys' (RC on Labour 1893, Q. 25777). The boys were moved into different departments, and provided they showed themselves anxious to learn, they were moved forward in two or more shops (ibid.). The concept of boy labour, as distinct from bound apprentice, characteristic of the traditional master–pupil relationship, gained more currency with employers as new machines came into production.

Noble's reference to the Wm. Armstrong Company illustrates the decline, under which most of the apprentices were not bound: 'We take boys as boys, first they go to small machines, if they are found competent they are advanced to be apprentices ... if you put them to the proper class of work *they are unquestionably cheaper*' (RC on Labour 1893d Qs. 25217, 25218; my emphasis).

The employers' consistent rebuttal of the ASE defence of the apprenticeship system encouraged the influx of untrained workers. They had no tradition of militancy in the industry and the division of labour was effectively changed, disrupting the system of power relations: 'The division of labour which prevailed in most engineering workshops during the second half of the 19th century ... might result in the eventual elimination of skilled craftsmen as a significant component of the engineering workforce' (Zeitlin 1985: 198, 199). The implementation of new machines became a significant factor in the transformation of work, paralleling redefinitions of traditional skills. It specialised the workshop tasks of young workers:

> Apprentices ... are very frequently on classes of work which they are not fully qualified to perform ... in many instances they are kept upon particular classes of work, and they do not become generally acquainted with all the details of the trade ... as a result these apprentices turn out rather inferior workmen ... (RC on Depression of Trade 1885–6).

By 1894 it was reported that the old system of apprenticeship had 'almost died out', and that in certain industries such as some branches of engineering,

> ... lads, though not indentured are still 'for all practical purposes', apprentices, but it is a very loose system at present ... and there is no guarantee either that the lads shall serve for a proper period, or that, during that period, they shall be properly instructed. (Evidence submitted to the RC on Labour 1894)

Thus in trades where boys' labour was found to be relatively more expensive than men's, due to their lack of familiarity with machines and inexperience in certain processes, there was a tendency to do without apprentices altogether, or to confine their training to certain specialised areas of work. Other sectors of industry revealed the over-recruitment and exploitation of boy labour. In either case a constant factor may be distinguished, the abrogation of responsibility by employers to educate and train apprentices and young workers in various trades. This was highlighted by the 1894 and subsequent inquiries, and referred to

> This absence of responsibility on the part of employers as to the instruction of the lads in their employ, combined with the fact of the excessive

numbers of apprentices (in some cases 'the very foremen do not know how many apprentices there are'), results in a lowering of the standard of efficiency. (RC on Labour 1894; RC on Poor Laws 1909c; HMSO 1915)

A product of the many disputes over trade training was the almost total abandonment of a training period of 'apprenticeship'. No longer controlled by statute, the situation in engineering was formalised as a result of the Terms of Settlement which concluded the Great Strike of 1897–8 and which were ratified in 1907. These Terms imposed conditions which clearly diluted any attempt by the unions to restrict the number of 'apprentices' that might be employed as a proportion of journeymen in mechanical engineering.

It is clear that the unions had underestimated the effects of the employers' intention to expand the use of cheap child labour. By the first decades of the 20th century the ranks of journeymen were being constantly recruited from those who received an irregular training (RC on Poor Laws 1909c: 241; (HMSO 1928b: 12).

A submission by an engineering firm on the north-east coast in 1915 showed that some employers used the non-binding agreement as a disciplinary measure: 'The unbound apprentice is more amenable to discipline'. The employer was able to discharge the young worker without fear of redress through the breaking of a covenant: 'We may explain ... that the apprentices are not indentured and no written agreement is come to ... ' (HMSO 1915: 55). Unapprenticed learners obtained by promotion from adult unskilled labour were found in greater numbers in large machine shops with highly specialised or self-acting machinery (ibid., p. 57). Some of the leading engineering employers, confident in their strength in combination through the Engineering Employers' Federation (EEF), simply imposed the new production ideology on the workers, disregarding what remained of legal restraints.

Repeal of the statute of apprentices: some general implications

The law of apprenticeship in England reflected its traditional character. It was based, in the main, on the paternal or fiduciary character of the relationship existing between employer and apprentice, and also on the apprentice's status as a minor (HMSO 1928a: 19). This paternal character was revealed in the written indenture, common in the traditional pattern of apprenticeship, under which the 'master' exercised a wide responsibility, beyond trade training: 'The said (company) will at all times during the said term provide for the apprentice board, lodging, clothing, and all other necessaries ... ' (Indenture in Ministry of Labour 1928c). What remained of legal sanctions failed to deter employers intent on circumventing statutory obligations relating to apprenticeship. The 1880 TUC Congress had concluded that some form of statutory obligation, approximating to the old statutes, might be reintroduced.

A motion was passed proposing that 'parents should be able to sustain an action in a court of law for the non-performance of the covenants of an indenture, the failure to instruct the apprentice in the mysteries of his trade being a breach of the covenants (TUC Congress Minutes 1880).

In 1882 the TUC reiterated the view that there was both a local and more general need for the reorganisation of a conventional apprenticeship model of craft training. They argued 'it is to be deeply regretted that a growing tendency exists in many trades to discourage the employment of indentured apprentices, thereby deteriorating the quality of skilled labour and inflicting serious damage upon our industrial progress' (TUC Congress Minutes 1882).

A motion put in the House of Common highlighted the problems of the increasing employment of children as cheap labour. It called for legal sanctions covering the employer–apprentice relationship:

> The law of apprenticeship must be amended and employers must be made responsible for the fulfilment of the contracts entered into by them when they took apprentices into their firms ... Apprentices, not uncommonly, were employed in unskilled labour in order to save grown up labour. (Hansard 1881b: col. 546)

The increasing specialisation of craft skills in production was emerging in the drive for cheaper production, with new technology using unskilled labour and increasing use of a premium system of wage payment. The debate in 1881 also pointed up the relationship between a decline in skilled craftsmanship and the seeking of more profits: 'We have gone in too much for cheapness at the cost of quality, and that had tended very much to degrade our handicraft skill ... the apprenticeship has broken down here ... [and] cannot much longer be maintained' (Hansard 1881b: cols. 527, 537). The interest shown by the House of Commons on this occasion served to highlight the inertia associated with attempts to challenge the prevailing economic short-termism of the Victorian period. Parliamentary reports show that the debates on this subject were initiated in 1869 but were fragmentary; between 1884 and the passing of the Technical Instruction Act of 1889 there were seven attempts to pass a Bill on the subject of 'technical education'.

However, the apprenticeship system was virtually inoperative by the last two decades of the nineteenth century. The repeal of the Act controlling the training of craft apprentices in 1814 underpinned the engineering employers' deprecatory attitudes concerning the definition and implementation of skills. They increasingly adopted a more laissez-faire attitude to the conditions governing the employment and training of young workers.

The concept of the free contract in apprenticeships and the politicisation of apprentices

The notion of being 'bound' as an apprentice entailed a legal and moral obligation on the part of an employer to teach a young person a specific trade for a set number of years, formerly on payment of a premium. Boy labour carried no such obligation for employers. Accelerated changes in the character of the apprenticeship model of training were a product of the constraints imposed upon engineering artisans after the 1852 and 1898 settlements. It became a 'free contract', differing in essential features from the traditional mode of apprenticeship agreements: 'the relationship was one of 'mutual agreement' ... it signalled the emergence of the proletarian apprentice by removing his social-legal status ... ' (Knox 1986: 172).

As a consequence of the 'free' contract, young workers were engaged under a variety of labels, one of which was loosely termed 'apprentice'. It did not necessarily imply a regulated period of systematic training. As early as 1864 the Children's Employment Commission showed, for example, that none of the machine makers in its inquiry had formal apprenticeship agreements. One employer summed up the situation thus:

> ... apprentices ... (are not) legally bound to us, that practice is now rare in the trade, but the name is still maintained whenever the lads are being taught any process that involves using their hands, except as common labourers, and results in skilled labour as opposed to working with a self-acting machine ... ' (Thomas Heatherington of the Heatherington Machine Company; Children's Employment Commission 1864)

Engineering employers such as Nasmyth, Robinson and Noble, whose evidence to the public inquiries recorded their determination to dequalify skilled labour, used the 'free contract' to draw non-unionised labourers into machine manning. Labourers were no longer perceived by the employers solely as 'helpers' but as potential machine-tenders.

The labourers were increasingly identified by artisans as a threat to their status, whose continued existence depended so crucially on the apprenticeship system. Union fears expressed early in the century by officials such as Allen and Burnett of the ASE seem to have been justified by the course of events.

The new concept of the 'free contract' was more than a label of convenience; it constituted an important structural device for engineering employers. The traditional master–pupil relationship was substantially broken. The employers regarded the deregulation of the apprenticeship system as the key to their struggles with the artisans. The employers' refusal to permit union regulation of the skilled labour supply through the operation of a fixed apprentice–journeyman ratio was 'an integral element of the managerial prerogatives they defended in the Lock-outs of 1852 and 1897 ... [and 1922]' (McKinley 1986:1).

'Apprentices' acquired a political role in the social relations of production. They became an important bargaining factor in disputes: 'Changing technologies not only specialized the labour of the apprentice ... but they also enhanced his strategic importance in the occupational structure of the industry ... ' (Knox 1986: 179). Employers were by-passing the traditional agreements on apprenticeship, and employing young workers both as substitute labour and as a counter to artisan workshop power. The politicisation of apprentices, accelerating under the impetus of the new production ideology, radicalised the relation between work and technology. The strike and lockout of 1897 will show that the basis of power relations in the industry had graduated to a new level beyond economic considerations. The changing political character of the relations of production concerning trade training was a clear break with tradition.

Unlike the semi-skilled, with no tradition of resistance to work reorganisation by employers – primarily because they were non-unionised – the fulcrum of the skilled workers' long-standing struggle, from 1852, was the defence of the apprenticeship. The history of the apprenticeship from mid-century is also the history of the skilled workers' struggle to maintain traditional power relations in the workshops; it thus had a significant political dimension: 'unlike the semi-skilled, the key problem for the skilled was the challenge to the traditions of resistance they had erected since the 1850s ... ' (Price 1983: 68).

From the repeal of the Statute of Apprentices it was clear that the employers' control over the labour process grew in inverse relation to the strength of the craft-apprenticeship mode of training. Despite more recent claims that the 19th-century apprenticeship survived (More 1980; Hobsbawm 1984; Buchanan 1985), much of what was designated as 'skill' after the 1890s was a species of labelling. There is little evidence of 'en-skilling' (More); nor is it possible to sustain the view that by 1914 60 per cent of the workforce of the EEF was regarded as skilled and retained 'privileged positions' (Hobsbawm 1984: 356). Much of the 'mystery' of the artisan's trade had been stripped away by the inventions of engineers such as Whitworth and Nasmyth. The first major study by a metropolitan authority, London, reveals the extent and effects of apprenticeship decline.

The London employers: Sidney Webb and the London County Council

Sidney Webb, chairman of the London County Council Technical Education Committee, commissioned the first major study of the provision of technical education in London. A report was published in 1897 after extensive research by a Committee member, Llewellyn Smith. It has been widely quoted as the first comprehensive study of technical education carried out by a metropolitan area.

The general conclusions of this first survey were confirmed by the findings of a further London County Council report in 1906: employers had abrogated their responsibility with respect to the training of young workers in skilled trades. It was reported that the old system of indentured apprenticeship had for many years been falling into decay; 'In the majority of the industries it has almost entirely disappeared' (LCC Report 1906). From this report Webb was to argue that many London employers not only refused to teach apprentices, even for premiums – they often refused to have boys on those parts of their establishments in which anything could be learnt. This practice, according to Webb, was coincident with the increasing scale of engineering enterprises which discouraged the master–apprentice relationship. As Webb expressed it, 'the village blacksmith can take an apprentice, but a large engineering firm does not take anything like a proportionate number of apprentices' (RC on Poor Laws 1909d: Q. 93031, 93035).

The LCC reports considered the subdivision of labour, the introduction of 'machinery' and the development of mammoth factories as contributory factors in apprenticeship decline. It is not clear in the report what kind or species of machinery is referred to; it seems reasonable to assume that the reference is to automatic machines. The Reports said these factors rendered the old practices of apprenticeship either undesirable or impracticable: 'The large employer does not care to be troubled with boys if he is compelled to teach them the whole trade. He prefers to divide his processes into men's work and boys' work, and to keep each grade to its allotted routine' (LCC Report 1906: 1). The routinisation of the labour process based primarily on advanced machinery in the engineering and allied trades had proved a disincentive to employers regarding apprenticeships. The advantages of using boy labour rather than apprentices outweighed the incentives to be derived in the form of grants from outside agencies. The aggregate of endowed charities' funds that might be employed in apprenticing children was nearly £24,000, of which not more than one-third had been used for that purpose. The trustees of the charities had considerable difficulties in reviving the apprenticeship system in London (LCC Report 1906).

The case of the London employers was significant. Statistical returns of children, young persons and adults working in factories and workshops in 1904, indicate that of the total industrial population of England and Wales, thus employed, London contained one-seventh. The proportion of children entering any form of skilled training at this time was about one-third. The remainder drifted into unskilled occupations (LCC Report 1909b: 415; London Statistics, Vol. 18, quoted in *The Economic Journal*, Sept. 1909, p. 408).

The number of boys covered by LCC returns was 8,756, of which 27.1 per cent entered occupations categorised as skilled; 64.2 per cent entered unskilled occupations. Just under 3.8 per cent were reported as having 'higher education' (LCC Report 1909a). A further 2,028 boys included in the census were returned under 'non-provided'. Of these 34.7 per cent entered skilled jobs, 63 per cent unskilled, while 2.3 per cent were returned as entering higher education. The total for this survey of boys shows that of 10,784 boys, 28.5 per cent and 67.9 per cent entered skilled and unskilled jobs respectively. Those entering higher education averaged 3.6 per cent.

Findings based on more general research for the same period in the UK confirm that there was a regular drift by young workers into the low-skilled labour market. In the case of London the trend was attributed to the enormous growth of the city as a distributive centre. A Royal Commission put the level of drift at between 70 per cent and 80 per cent of boys leaving elementary schools who entered unskilled occupation (RC on Poor Laws 1909c, para. 136).

London presented innumerable 'dead-end' openings for errand boys, milk boys, office and shop boys, bookstall boys, van, lorry boys, street sellers:

> In nearly all these occupations the training received leads to nothing; and the occupations themselves are ... destructive to healthy development, owing to long hours, long period of standing, walking, or mere waiting, and, morally, are wholly demoralising. (RC on Poor Laws 1909c, para. 137)

The majority report of the Royal Commission on the Poor Laws noted that in addition to the 'blind alley' labour of boys in the streets as messengers and errand boys, there was systematic exploitation within the factories where they were taken on as 'process workers': They were 'put to machinery, and, while becoming expert in one operation, learn nothing of the fundamental principles of the trades in which they are engaged' (RC on Poor Laws, para. 590). The Poor Laws Commission of 1909 concluded that some employers of child labour were exploitative in character and 'get more than they ought of the physical and moral capital of the rising generation' (ibid., para. 545).

The adverse effects of modified productive processes were reiterated in a minority report of the Poor Laws Commission. This commented that a mass of unemployment was continually being sustained by 'a stream of young men from industries which rely upon unskilled boy labour, and turn it adrift at manhood without any general or special industrial qualification ... ' (RC on Poor Laws 1909c). There were many unskilled sectors of the economy to which many young workers were drawn, particularly in metropolitan areas. Clear disadvantages for the young were discernible. Without apprenticeship into trades, but attracted by relatively high wages, boys often remained as unskilled labour until they were too old to enter any other regular occupation. If this trend is put against the work-life expectancy of the time it becomes highly significant: in 1894 the average age at death for manual workers was 45 years. According to union sources, the number which continued at work after that age was so trifling that it was disregarded statistically; for practical purposes there were no men available after age 45 (Inglis 1894: 7). Taking 22 as the age at which a journeyman's life began, the duration of his working life would therefore be taken as 23 years. The availability of a mass of undifferentiated young labour, unprotected by bound agreement, precipitated an almost total collapse of the apprenticeship system in the capital, and signalled a corresponding disregard for technical education.

Employer attitudes to apprenticeship

General criticism of employers regarding their indifferent, and at times hostile, attitude to the apprenticeship system was persistent: official sources such as the Children's Employment Commission of 1864, Inquiry into Trades Unions in 1867, the 1886 Inquiry into the Depression of Trade, the 1893 Poor Laws Commission, and the 1894 Royal Commission all added weight to criticisms from specific unions such as the ASE.

In the case of engineering there was a clear conflict of interest between the ASE and engineering employers regarding the training and education of young workers. On the question of the apprentice–journeymen ratio Inglis (1894) deduced a ratio in the order of 3–4 per cent. Figures from EEF sources for the turn of the century for the Federation as a whole show a variation between trades. The proportion of apprentices to journeymen has: Fitters 12 to 100; turners 6 to 100; planers, borers and slotters fewer than 1 to 100; smiths 46 to 100 (EEF Minutes 1906, circular letter to Local Associations Jan. 1901–Dec. 1906).

The conflicts between engineering employers and workers on the subject of apprenticeships turned chiefly on the issue of the manning of new machines, but also on more general concerns over limiting the number of apprentices in the trade. The 1881–4 Inquiry had been specifically instituted to examine provision for a national system of technical education with the apprenticeship system as an integral feature.

The decline in apprenticeship was clearly uneven, and the Charity Commissioners' annual report of 1897 showed that vestiges of the old system remained in 27 engineering trades (PRO files 1897). As a general concept, however, the apprenticeship system was in rapid decline, particularly in London; craft training was no longer perceived in terms of a historical master–pupil relationship.

Throughout the century, and more particularly from the 1890s when they acted as a federated body, the employers continued to modify the conditions governing the apprenticeship, a strategy used to consolidate their control of the labour process. They became more adept at devising new methods of labour control: 'the employers' side took the initiative in evolving new forms of organization with which to prosecute their aims ... engineering employers gave the lead in organized strike breaking ... ' (Cronin 1987: 162). Thus

Noble, director of one of the largest engineering concerns of the country, was able to argue in 1906 that due to their policy of employing cheap, 'defranchised' boy labour, it was possible to maintain production at his Elswick works even throughout the damaging 1897–8 strike and lockout. This was carried through with no fewer than 10,000 men: 'while nearly all the engineering works in Newcastle were stopped ... we had ... hundreds of machines at work ... and at *not one of these machines was there a turner or a high class machine-man employed*' (RC on Trade Disputes 1906: Q. 2415; my emphasis).

Some major employers therefore were able to minimise the effects of strike action by militant artisans, the politicisation of apprentices being highly significant in this regard. The implementation of late 19th-century changes in technology and management worsened relations between the skilled and the unskilled workers. Traditional legal restraints governing apprentice–employer relations were so diluted as to be meaningless, strengthening employer controls over skill definitions and the employment of boy labour and machine manning.

Machines were increasingly manned with unapprenticed labour; skilled labour resistance was circumvented. The concept of 'apprenticeship' had been redefined. This was reflected in three of the clauses of the 1898 Terms of Settlement, following the 1897–8 conflict, directly confronting the principle regarding apprenticeship as understood by the Amalgamated Society of Engineers. The ASE argued that tradesmen maintained areas of autonomy over methods and pace of work through a structured craft-apprenticeship system, or a system approximating to it. Large employers such as Noble and Armstrong had successfully challenged the unions over this issue. The traditional mode of craft training, the apprenticeship system, was allowed to languish.

The decline of the apprenticeship symbolised the employers' increasing dominance over the total labour process: any ideology or traditional craft practice perceived by them as challenging their hegemonic control over the disposition of labour power and machines was vigorously confronted. The 19th-century collapse of the apprenticeship system therefore took place against a background of long-term struggles over industrial power relations. The culmination of these struggles was the Great Strike and Lockout of 1897–8.

Note

1. F. W. Taylor's research at the Bethlehem steel plant in the 1880s took the development of precision in manufacture a stage further. He concentrated the areas of work requiring close accuracy into a small department within the workshops, the 'toolroom' (Taylor 1906, 1911b, 1912). It was here that non-production components were made, such as jigs, fixtures, dies, templates, models. These and other aids were specifically designed to determine and monitor accuracy in mass production in the general workshops. Oversight of the critical factor of accuracy

was thus removed from general practice and strictly controlled by supervisors and management rather than remaining within the discretion of the artisans (Taylor 1906, 1911b; Zeitlin 1983).

CHAPTER FIVE

Employers and the ideology of engineering management: the Great Strike of 1897–8 and its aftermath

Engineering management and the ideology of engineering production

New technologies such as screw-cutting, milling machines and the turret lathe represented a crucial part of the essential technical preconditions for the dequalification of skilled engineering labour.

The process of dequalification was characterised by skill substitution and dependent upon a pool or reserve of unskilled labour. This reserve comprised largely unskilled adult labour and children, particularly boys, and increasingly displaced skilled labour. This surplus of labour underpinned employer management strategies from the 1860s, and from this period the ideology of engineering labour control centred particularly on the exploitation of these groups. The increasing use of unskilled workers, in time, radicalised the political nature of machine production and machinery assembly. The unskilled workers came to be aligned with employers' attempts to weaken the solidarity and resistance of the amalgamated unions.

Artisan exclusivity and its historical near-monopoly over certain trade practices were necessary points of pressure as the employers pursued their attempts to extend and exploit the advantages derived from 19th-century expanded machine-tool technology. Employers also perceived technical developments as a means of displacing the traditional functions of skilled craftsmen, which enabled them to deploy unskilled labour more effectively and further increase the pressure on skilled labour autonomy. The demise of the apprenticeship system paralleled these developments.

This chapter examines one of the key events of the period: the 1897 strike and lockout as the culmination of a series of struggles throughout the century. This became a conflict over power relations centring on employer and artisan interests regarding control over certain workshop practices such as machine manning and the training of young workers. The nature of the strike and lockout is a necessary background to charting the development of technical education. The strike points up the specificity of industrial conflict in four areas: first, as the first major conflict in the engineering industry between employers and skilled artisans, after the engineering strike of 1852, it represented a major challenge to employers' dominance in a principal manufacturing industry. Second, it was the first major industrial strike to be primarily concerned with principles of labour substitution. Third, the 1897–8 conflict was concerned with the changes in the system of power relations that developed as the structure of work control altered. And finally, the strike and the Terms of Settlement which concluded it highlighted the way engineering employers perceived technical training, and thus influenced the development of technical education.

The challenge to skilled workers' workshop autonomy

Employers, in defining certain areas of engineering practice as independent of craft skills and artisan direction, for example, with machine-tool operations using automatic principles, rejected the historical patterns of training skilled craftsmen, and promoted the widespread use of non-artisan labour. As Cole (1937), in his discussion of trade unionism in the latter part of the nineteenth century, argued, there was a clear division between the skilled and unskilled workers, a division that employers were always seeking to break down, 'at particular points, by employing cheaper men to do work claimed by the craftsmen as their monopoly' (p. 5). Marx said:

> ... the less the period of training, therefore, that any work requires, the smaller is the cost of production of the worker and the lower is the price of his labour, his wages. In those branches of industry in which hardly any period of apprenticeship is required, and where the mere bodily existence of the worker suffices, the cost necessary for his production is almost confined to the commodities necessary for keeping him alive and capable of working. The price of his labour will, therefore, be determined by the price of the necessary means of subsistence. (Marx 1976: 26)

The aims of 19th-century unskilled engineering workers came to be increasingly allied with the employers' by their cooperation in the process of substitution, and by taking up some skilled workers' functions in machine-tool operations. As early as the 1860s an important objective of employers was to break skilled artisan monopoly, and promote the cause of non-unionised workers:

> The interests of the operatives, in their ultimate development, are identical with those of the employers, inasmuch as if the restrictions on labour sought to be imposed by the unions result in increasing the cost of the products of their labour to such an extent as to allow foreign competitors to obtain orders ... [and] the country loses the trade, and the workman his share of the wages which might otherwise have been his. (RC on TU 1868a: 56)

The employment of non-union workers in jobs formerly the exclusive property of ASE artisans advanced the cause of both the unskilled workers and their employers. By the 1890s engineering employers were arguing that the skilled workers' claim to autonomy within the labour process extended beyond the exercise of traditional practices. They maintained it constituted interference with output, restriction on overtime working, control over access to certain machine tools, and unwarranted intrusion into the management of the shops (*The Times*, 6 Nov. 1897).

Employer hostility towards traditional workshop practices may be illustrated by the case of the London firm of Daniel Smith & Co. The firm had been challenged by the ASE over the placement of labourers on mechanics' work, and for employing a driller to operate a boring machine. The reaction was unequivocal:

> In consequence of the inconsiderate, selfish, uncharitable, and uncalled-for interference of a small section of our employees endeavouring to enforce us to inflict an injustice and deprive other men of their liberty or right to progress in a higher branch of our trade, we consider it necessary to make the following announcement:
>
> It is our firm intention from this date to have whomsoever we choose, put them to whatever kind of work we think fit, and pay such wages as are initially agreed, without any dictation or interferences on the part of our workmen.
>
> No discussion or interview relating to Society's rules will be allowed during working hours. (Quoted in *Engineering*, 12 Nov. 1897)

Another large company provides further illustration. Two copying lathes were rated by the ASE at 35/– per week, or 70/– for the two. As a result of a strike a labourer was put in charge of both machines, and received 24/– per week, which was 'a large increase on his former wage' (*The Times*, 6 Nov. 1897). The firm maintained that output was increased and, in this single machine function, 46/– per week was saved, arguing that interference by ASE men was manifest in this case by insisting on a one-man-one-machine operation. They refuted this ASE claim and stipulated that both machines 'can be easily and capably worked by a single "handy" man' (ibid.).

Labour substitution was a critical factor in the case of a northern firm which reported a marked reduction in the amount of wages paid on individual machines, compared with similar machines before the strike. On one special lathe an ASE man had 35/– per week for turning a certain class of pulley taking 26½ hours. On the same lathe a 'machine man', at 24/– per week, was turning slightly large pulleys in 22¼ hours, after being 'advanced': 'There has been a much better turn out by the non-union men since the strike than there was before it' (ibid.).

A promoted labourer in a Manchester firm was producing work on a large planing machine in 135 hours; an ASE man took 190 hours for the same class of work. The firm took the view that increased production rates were possible as a result of supervision being carried out by a non-union shop foreman. Disputes over work control by non-Society foreman were common; it was significant in the employers' tactics of substitution. This was clear in the particular case of a firm on the Clyde.

The firm concluded that in the period from 1895 to 1897, production times for engines had increased by 20 per cent, due, it was contended, to ASE shop steward interference, which had become 'simply intolerable' (ibid.). The firm offered 'low-class' mechanics a 5/– per week increase if they would work any machine to which they might be put; the alternative to this was that of 'leaving the works'. Ten immediately left, refusing to work machines vacated by ASE men. The relations of production were unsettled: 'Even non-society men who have tried to work in our place since the commencement of the strike have been persecuted out of it by the pickets during meal hours and at night ... driving away even our new foremen over the machines.' (ibid.)

In the period following the strike of 1852, employers were increasingly prepared to challenge the skilled workers over historical work practices. They responded to skilled-worker resistance to work reorganisation by questioning the basis of traditional artisan autonomy and particularly ASE influence with respect to machine-tool operations. By the 1890s they were prepared to confront the unions directly. A mechanical engineering journal argued that 'capitalists are absolutely justified in trying to smash Trade Unions as they exist' (*Engineering*, Sept. 1897). ASE reaction was regarded as a direct challenge to management prerogatives: 'It has ... come to this: Trade Unionism as now practised in the British Engineering trade has to go ... it is the duty of the employers to smash the union' (ibid.). The issue for skilled engineering labour had revolved around the critical question of how and to what extent employers were to develop the potential of the new classes of machine tools, and the use of undifferentiated labour.

As distinct from previous employer–employee disputes, from the 1890s the employers were gaining political confidence, emanating from two sources. First was their control over important new classes of tools, which stiffened their reaction to ASE demands for exclusivity regarding certain classes of work. Second, ASE and EEF sources show that more employers were rejecting individualism and veering towards a form of federation. This combination was crucial in the changing political and ideological structure of union–employer relations from the 1880s. As the *Spectator* put it: 'The owners of capital have for the moment control of the markets in their hands, and if they learn to combine and make common cause they will be as powerful as ever the feudal barons were ... ' (25 Sept. 1897). This injunction was supported by the claim that a reduction in the numbers of skilled workers in the factories was possible because of 'the use of machines still more nearly self-acting or "alive" ... ' (ibid.).

Trade unions and federating employers: early developments

Movement towards a national engineering employers' federation was fitful and had started about the mid-1880s, with Colonel Dyer, Chairman of the Sir William Armstrong Mitchell Company, Newcastle, as a prominent figure. This development was the outcome of engineering employers' continued awareness of the unions' potential for national collective action, which, despite trade rivalries, was showing signs of increasing solidarity.

This is not to imply a solidarity in class terms, but referred to a narrow stratum of the working class, skilled artisans. At one level, combinations of tradesmen such as the London Trades Council alone constituted a federation of organised trades consisting of 49 societies, 35 districts and 15,480 subscribing members (RC on Technical Instruction 1884b: Q. 3584).

At another level, the ASE itself had evolved by the 1890s into a highly eclectic but relatively cohesive organisation, the diverse number of engineering trades eligible for membership indicating its comprehensive character.

The society consisted of craftsmen in the following trades or branches: smiths, fitters, turners, pattern-makers (highly skilled machine woodworkers who manufactured precision patterns for use in moulds for the casting of metals), millwrights, skilled fitters and machinists responsible for machine installation and factory lay-out; planers, borers, slotters, mechanical draughtsmen; brass finishers for manufacturing non-corrosive metal products; coppersmiths employed in the engineering trade; machine-joiners (erectors) employed in the construction of machinery for cotton, silk and woollen production, and ships' smiths (RC on Labour 1893f: Q. 22655). The overall membership of the Society increased continuously from 43,150 in 1874 to 71,221 in 1891, with an increase in the number of branches from 377 to 509; by 1898 the total membership was 91,000 (Jefferys 1945: 93, 138).

The growth in the size of the ASE membership coincided with the high point of organised trade unionism in 19th-century England. It occurred in the period 1896–8 when there were between 1,326 and 1,358 trade unions, with a total membership in 1898 of 1,752,000 members, including 144,000 woman members (British Labour Statistics 1978, table 196, p. 395).

An important measure of the political and financial strength of a union was its ability to withstand protracted disputes. The longest strike in the mechanical engineering industry began in Sunderland in June 1883. It was also notable in that it provided the background for a tactical realignment of employers. The strike arose over a claim by the ASE local executive for an increase in wages and a restriction in the number of apprentices. There was also a demand for the withdrawal of the Inquiry Note (*Record* (1883–4), pp. 71, 76). This seems to have been a limited but bitterly contested dispute and lasted until 1885. The employers took out writs against the men to force them to return to work; and with assistance from the Iron Trades Employers'

Association (ITEA), non-union labour was imported in an attempt to break the strike (*Record* (1883–4)).

During the course of this dispute there began a loose federation of engineering employers in the Tees and Hartlepool and Tyne and Wear areas, and a joint committee was set up to coordinate policy action. Subsequently, the ASE were forced to withdraw on all points in December 1885; the employers conceded no issue and recorded 'a decisive victory' (*Record* (1884–5). This employer combination gave rise to what became known as the North-East Coast Association (Wigham 1973a: 22). In the following year came a link-up between the Clyde and Belfast employers. But a more comprehensive federating attempt came about in 1895.

The first meeting of the incipient national federation was held on 20 November 1895, when it was proposed that the Clyde and Belfast, Barrow and N.E. Coast Engineering Employers should combine. The immediate issues addressed by the combined employers were significant in so far as they related to the definition and deployment of craft skills. They concerned: (a) apprenticeship, (b) overtime, (c) minimum rates, (d) limitation of hours, (e) demarcation of work (EEF Minute Book 1895–1899).

The initial confrontation between the ASE and the newly formed federation came in the following year, 1896, and clearly displayed signs of employer recalcitrance over questions of substitution. The Society had put forward a number of claims in different geographical areas concerning the employment of non-union men on work traditionally reserved for artisans, and restructuring of overtime. The claim employers considered most contentious was 'only members [of the Society] should work machines at rates fixed by the Society, and that one man should work only one machine' (*Record* (1896–7), p. 134). The conflict gradually intensified and in relation to the strike of Society members at Dunsmuir and Jackson's at Govan, a special meeting of the executive of the Federation was convened at Carlisle in August 1896. The chairman, Dyer (Sir Wm. Armstrong & Co.), reiterated the employers' position regarding machine manning, and advocated that the Board should give the widest possible publicity to the machine question and to their determination to 'exercise their rights'.

The employers argued that they 'have always exercised their right to appoint any man whom they might choose to man the machine in their shops ... whether the man is a skilled or unskilled workman or whether, he belongs to any Society or not ... ' (EEF Minute Book 1896b). This particular dispute concluded with a central figure in the Govan dispute, a non-union man, leaving the workshop (to take up a 'better appointment'), and another non-unionist being taken on in his place (*Record* (1896–7), p. 135).

The principle of substitution was reasserted during the next strike involving Messrs Earle's at Hull. In contention was the insistence by the ASE that their fitters or turners only should be allowed to work milling machines. The employers' executive meeting resolved that 'the Federation should strenuously resist all demands, and the Associations should agree and resolve to support such action' (EEF Minute Book (1896(b)). This was an appeal for the local associations of engineering employers in other parts of the country to demonstrate their solidarity. The Belfast Employers Association, the North Western Association, the N.E. Association and Barrow all agreed to support the Federation. The combination had strengthened the resolve to resist ASE claims, particularly concerning machine manning. The EEF executive wrote to the Glasgow district committee of the Glasgow ASE, where a machine-manning dispute had also arisen. The letter made it clear that as far as engineering employers were concerned, ownership of property constituted the right to its disposition, and they rejected the right of the Society to control of machine tools: 'the Federation distinctly decline to admit the right of your Society to claim for your members exclusive rights to work any particular class of machines' (EEF Minute Book 1896b). The message was unequivocal: the machines and their manning were under direct managerial control: 'The machines are the property of the employers and they are solely responsible for the work turned out by them; they therefore will continue to exercise the discretion they have hitherto possessed of appointing the men they consider suitable to work them' (ibid.).

The machine question and the Great Strike

Agitation on the part of the ASE therefore continued, generally revolving around the substitution question, until a crisis was reached in February 1897. There were strikes at the works of the Sunderland Forge and Engineering Company, and at Barrow. An ASE claim regarding the former workshops was that two boring, milling and horizontal drilling machines should be worked by Society men. At Barrow the issue concerned the employment of unskilled workers at reduced rates and fixing of rates governing payment to men on machines (*Record* (1897–8), p. 135). These issues were discussed at a specially convened meeting of the Federated Association in London, where the significance of the ASE's actions was spelled out by the Federation Chairman: the ASE men at Pallion, Sunderland, attempted to restrain non-Society men from working some new boring machines introduced into the Sunderland Forge and Engineering Company. Three turners at the Naval Construction and Armaments Company, Barrow simultaneously lodged a claim to enforce a rate of wages, being the amounts the Society had rated the machines they were working. The third major issue was at the Armstrong Ordnance Works at Elswick, where there was a Society claim over the manning of a new automatic gauge-grinding machine (EEF Minute Book 1897).

A special meeting of the executive Board of the Employers' Federation took place in London on 26 February and resolved that a letter be sent to ASE secretary Barnes specifying instances of the aggressive action on the part of the ASE, causing 'considerable trouble to the employers who are members of the above Federation' (ibid.). The letter clearly stated that the call for the displacement of unskilled machinists at Sunderland was unacceptable, as the men 'have been and still are working [the machines] to the satisfaction of the employers' (ibid.). The meeting resolved to resist 'encroachments' upon the rights of the employers, and pledged to assist the three companies directly involved in the dispute. As a practical measure the executive also agreed to subsidise the Sunderland Forge and Engineering Co. to the rate of 15/– per man on strike. The ASE executive was informed of two principal conditions attaching to the employers' directive: unless (1) work was resumed at Sunderland and Barrow on or before Friday 12 March, and (2) the Society agreed to meet with the Federation to discuss the settling of all questions at issue, the Federation would issue notices to end the employment of ASE members in their employ. The Federation resolved, as a result of the negative reply on both counts from the Society, 'that on the 27th March and on each of the three succeeding Saturdays, the services of 25 per cent of the members of the ASE in their employment will be dispensed with' (ibid.).

The scale of the lockout threat was considerable. If the employers carried out their threat, notices of a lockout would have been posted at Barrow, Belfast, the Clyde, Liverpool, N.E. Coast and London, at all shops owned by members of the Employers' Federation. This would affect between 20,000 and 30,000 engineering workers, besides many thousands of unskilled workers indirectly (*The Times*, 10 Marc. 1897). It was agreed on 23 March that a meeting between the parties be arranged, the disputed machines at the works of the Sunderland Forge and Engineering Company to remain idle during the negotiations.

On 2 April, the Manchester District Engineering Employers Association was formed: 'Twenty important northern and Midland firms have announced their adhesion and they are desirous of federating with the Employers Federation of Engineering Association' (*The Times*, 3 Apr. 1897). This group of employers, many of whom were already members of the ITEA, were admitted to the Federation.

The machine conference and the 48-hour issue

Conferences were held in London on 1, 2, 13, 14 and 15 April 1897. The machine question was most exhaustively discussed, 'indeed it being the most important matter under discussion, it took up the greater portion of the time of the Conference' (*Record* 1897–8, p. 136). Despite the protracted discussions both sides remained adamant and held to their position. The Conference has since been known as 'The Abortive Machine Conference'. The men at Sunderland and Barrow had remained at work, but the ASE was evidently anxious to test the popularity of its cause in pressing for a resolution of its claims. The ASE Secretary, Barnes, expressed the inevitable confrontation as a 'trial of strength', outlining the Society's strategy in terms of its appropriateness in relation to trade and the popularity of its cause. In a letter to the *Dundee Weekly News* he wrote, 'a trial of strength with this Federation is inevitable, and the present is as favourable an opportunity as was likely to be presented to us. Trade is brisk, the weather good, and the issue a popular one' (22 May 1897).

Anxiety over the impending major confrontation stimulated a more rapid growth of companies seeking federation. They assumed that employers' combinations were crucial in opposing what was financially and numerically the strongest amalgamated union at the time. The evidence suggests that they were realistic in this. Indeed, Mann, a prominent ASE member, who stood for the General Secretaryship of the ASE in 1891, seemed to personify the militancy and politically growing awareness in the ASE, when he wrote 'let them have it. Everything favours the men; the state of trade, the prospects for the next year, the unions' finances and the opinions of the members' (Mann 1897: 144).

London provided the location for a tactical turn of events, although it seems initially to have been in an ambiguous position vis-à-vis the other major centres of employer interests. There was no Engineering Employers' Association there. The ASE, making a rational assessment of the prevailing situation in this area, extracted important concessions from a number of the smaller firms. Prominent among these was the granting of an eight-hour day, the culmination of society pressure, due principally to the circular sent on 30 April to firms from a Joint Committee of Trades. This body seems to have been an ad hoc strategic Committee composed of members from the ASE, Boilermakers, Steam Engine Makers, United Society of Smiths and Hammermen, London and Provincial Society of Coppersmiths, London Society of Drillers, United Machine Workers Association (*Record* 1897–8: 137).

Up to 5 August the ASE claimed to have had concessions regarding the eight-hour day from 204 firms in London. This, however, was disputed by the Federation, who argued that their investigations revealed that only 66 of these could have been classed as engineering firms, the remainder being public bodies, brewers, contractors and similar bodies (*Record* 1897–8: 138). The Federation also maintained that it had persuaded many of the firms who conceded the eight-hour day to rescind and to join the Federation. The ostensible cause of the dispute was the eight hours' question, but the more substantive issue was that of labour substitution.

The 48-hour issue originating in July 1897, for practical purposes, may be regarded as peripheral to the central issue, machine manning. A leader in the journal *Engineering* argued: 'The length of the working day is only part of the question in dispute; a more important matter is the control of machines' (1 Oct. 1897). *Engineering* held that labour control was the central issue. There was, it was suggested, no objection to trade unionism 'in the abstract', but the dispute was to be resolved by ousting 'sundry trade unions from privileges of which they ... gained possession in the past ... the 48-hour question is as nothing' (ibid.). According to *The Times* of 4 December, the eight-hour day issue was not discussed seriously at all at the Conference.

Iron Trades Employers' Association (ITEA) reports suggest that employers were confronting the ASE behind the eight-hour issue, but were clearly determined to press for the extension of unskilled machine manning: 'employers were determined not to agree to any settlement that did not include all the points that had previously been at issue, and which were discussed at the abortive Machine Conference in April 1897' (*Record* 1897-8: 139). Those London firms who were members of the ITEA brought the matter before that body, who asked for the cooperation of the Federation. As a result the largest London employers formed themselves into an Association which was admitted to the Federation (ibid.).

An ultimatum was sent by the Joint Committee of Trades to a number of firms in the London region that had refused to concede the eight-hour day. Failure to concede was threatened with a strike on 3 July at 1 p.m. On 1 July an employers' meeting was held in Manchester with representatives from the three leading engineering employer Associations, the Engineering Employers Federation, the Shipbuilders Association, and the Iron Trades Employers' Association. It was clear from the nature of the resolution passed at that meeting that confrontation was inevitable. A telegram was sent to the Joint Committee intimating that in the event of a strike as indicated, notices would be immediately given by the members of the Associations affiliated to the Federation that a 25 per cent reduction of workers would take place of the members of each union in their employment. Each society represented on the Joint Committee received a copy of the lockout threat.

On 7 July, it had been reported that in London, on the N.E. Coast, at Glasgow and Greenock and elsewhere employers had posted notices for the discharge of 25 per cent of their men, and it was further reported that 'it has become clear that notices will be necessary for the remaining 75 per cent' (*The Times*, 7 July 1897). Simultaneously the Leicester Iron Trades Employers' Association passed a unanimous decision to lock out 25 per cent of union men employed in their shops. It was estimated that in all 80,000 would be affected (ibid.).

The Boilermakers Society and Pattern Makers withdrew from the negotiations at this stage, arguing that they would not take part in the stoppage of work in the London district. The remaining union members struck and the employers discharged members of these unions. The notices to the 25 per cent of members of the unions connected with the Joint Committee terminated on 13 July, on which date the remaining 75 per cent withdrew their labour on instructions from their Societies; 16,944 members of the ASE left work in this way, the total number of men of all trades on strike being over 25,000 (*Engineering*, Oct. 1897, p. 136).

At the beginning of the action about 180 firms were involved; by the middle of July 250 firms had aligned against the workers (*Record*, p. 139). Throughout August, September and October further accessions were recorded. On 8 October the Board of Trade estimated that 579 firms were directly concerned in the dispute and that the total number of men on strike, or locked out, was 45,000. Employers at Sheffield, Oldham, Keighley, Ipswich, Heywood, Edinburgh, Leith, Aberdeen, Nottingham, Dundee, Bristol, Hanley, Preston, Blackburn, Burnley, Rochdale, Wigan, Ashton, Leicester, Huddersfield, Bradford, Carlisle and Otley joined during this period. The cost to the ASE from their contingency fund was put at £127,000 (*Engineering*, Oct. 1897).

The percentage of enforced unemployment among members of trade unions rose from 2.5 in July 1897 to 5.1 in December. Total membership of unions at this time was 1,731,000. The number of skilled and unskilled workers, unemployed and unionised workers, that is, constituting a reserve of relatively experienced labour, was 43,275 in July and in December 88,281, figures from which persons locked out or on strike have been excluded. If the latter were included to take into account the engineers, the total would have doubled to approximately 168,200 in December 1897. The published figures for the engineers were: men idle, engineers 25,000; allied workers 10,500; non-unionists, 10,000; labourers, 33,000 – total 78,500 (British Labour Statistics 1971; *The Times*, 20 Dec. 1897).

From the outset of the dispute the employers claimed that a combination of factors instigated by unions rendered economic production impossible:

> Their opposition to piece-work, their insistence on uniform rates of wages, their restriction of the number of machines a man may look after, and their hampering regulations in regard to demarcation of work, are alone sufficient to put British producers at a disadvantage, which must bar them from the markets of the world. (*Engineering*, Sept. 1897)

This claim was vigorously contested by the ASE secretary, Barnes; although at first confidently predicting a successful outcome to a dispute of not more than six weeks, he was forced to concede that the 'fight is going to be one of the biggest things we have ever had in this country' (*Labour Leader*, 21 Aug. 1897). Keir Hardy, editor of the *Labour Leader*, argued that the employers were in fact using the dispute to seize the opportunity to smash the ASE, a result of which, he contended, would be more substitution of skilled by unskilled workers: 'They will in future recoup for themselves for any present losses by being free to run their machines with low-paid labour, run their shops with apprentices and youths at half a journeyman's pay, and even reduce wages all round' (*Labour Leader*, 11 Sept. 1897).

Barnes was convinced that 'a war against Trade Unionism has been started' and that there was collusion between certain members of the aristocracy (e.g. Lord Wemyss, later Lord Elcho), Dyer and his associates, and members of the Free Labour Protection Association (report in *Labour Leader*, 18 Sept. 1897). This latter body had some 182,000 members; having been formed in 1893, it seems to have been a source of 'blackleg' labour of the kind called up by the ITEA. Its main function was to supply strike-breaking labour. Ideologically it counterposed the assumed threat posed by 'Socialistic agitators' and provided the common ground that was purported to exist between the 'cause of Labour' and that of Capital: 'The free labourers and the employers are on the same side ... ' (*Engineering*, 15 Oct. 1897). According to Jefferys the Association was in fact composed entirely of 'riff raff [who] broke and damaged in a few weeks more tools and machines through inexperience than a skilled engineer damaged in a life-time' (Jefferys 1945: 416).

The interaction of political and technological aspects of the conflict

The financial aspect of the dispute was proving serious for the ASE. It was reported by Barnes that £30,000 had been distributed in early September as part of the fifth distribution of strike pay since the onset of the dispute. Resources were being depleted at the rate of £10,000 per week (*Labour Leader*, 16 Oct. 1897). John Burns, ASE official, writing to *The Times* in September, argued that the dispute was particularly destructive to working-class aims despite an upturn in the economy. He cited, among other things, the economic background against which the strike and lockout took place. For example, in the 20 years from 1876, engineering trade exports increased tenfold (to £70,000,000); up to 1895 there had been a diminution in the number of strikes, for example, from 1,211 strikes in 1889 to 876 strikes in 1895, while lockouts by masters increased: 'This unfortunate dispute has for its object, on the masters' side, the crippling and annihilation of working class combinations ... that is the impelling motive and the real object of the Employers Federation' (27 Sept. 1897). Burns, a member of the ASE since 1859, was also well known as a member of the Social Democratic Federation, and prominent in advancing the cause of the unskilled as well as his own Society Members. He was to figure largely in the 1897 dispute, together with ASE Secretary Barnes, in writing pamphlets and letters to the press such as *The Times*, where he attempted to counter the bias evident in them, and muster support for the men (Jefferys 1948; Kynaston 1976).

Hardy, also conscious of the deleterious effects of a protracted dispute both on the morale and financial resources of the union, proposed a strategy to force the issue: (1) Pool all the unions' funds as a fighting fund for those locked out; (2) proclaim a general strike and 'bring the trade of the nation to a standstill' (*Labour Leader*, 16 Oct. 1897).

However, confidence in their ability to exploit the new technology seems to have pre-empted any possible concessions on the employers' side regarding machine-operating with unskilled labour. In response to an initiative by the President of the Board of Trade (Sir Courtenay Boyle) on 20 October to bring the two sides together, the EEF executive drafted what might be termed an Engineering Employers' manifesto (see the Appendix for a version drawn up at the conclusion of the strike and ratified in 1907). It was prefaced by two clauses drawn up by the President of the Board of Trade to the effect that both sides were to acknowledge the right of combination of each other. The Board of Trade proposed:

> The Federated Employers, while disavowing any intention of interfering with the legitimate action of trade unions, will admit no interference with the management of their business [1st Clause]. The Trades Unions, for their part, while maintaining the right of combination, disavow any intention of interfering with the management of the employers [2nd Clause]. (Quoted in *Engineering*, 2 Nov. 1897)

Three basic principles of employer control were reasserted in this document and clearly reiterated the employers' views, which had increasingly hardened during the course of the dispute: the inability of employers to reduce working hours, due, it was argued, to increasing foreign competition; that Britain had no monopoly of labour-saving machines; and new machines in use could be more profitably used with inexperienced hands.

Press reaction

As might be expected, Press reaction varied according to affiliation. One source suggested that the EEF proposals were characterised by the rhetoric of employers 'defending common rights' and 'staving off revolution': 'The employers have revolted against the encroachments by way of tyranny of certain trade unions, and that their proposals may be taken to represent the charter of freedom ... ' (*The Times*, 4 Dec. 1897). *The Times* further suggested that the confrontation had evolved beyond the boundaries of a single trade dispute to embody more universal principles. The engineers' dispute was perceived as a cause célèbre of wider employer–labour relations at a particularly crucial period. Thus the proposals, it was argued, 'have the support of a strong body of employers unconnected with the federation and having nothing to do with the engineering trade' (ibid.). This newspaper consistently encouraged the employers' side, and countenanced their actions throughout the strike and lockout: 'the employers' ... proposals ... may be taken to *represent the charter of freedom*' (ibid.; my emphasis).

Other sections of the Press favoured the workers' side. The *Birmingham Trades Journal* had referred to the ASE with evident pride, as 'the boast and pride of trade unionism in this country' (July 1897). Early in the dispute, critical of the employers' refusal to accede to a conference or to accept mediation, one view was that 'There is the overmastering feeling that the refusal of mediation by the Masters implies a determination to smash the Engineers' union irrespective of the merits of the Controversy' (*Daily Record*, 12 Oct. 1897). The position of the Masters was argued to be untenable, according to another source, because of their intransigence over the question of a full representative conference (*The Saturday Review*, 20 Oct. 1897). Public opinion, it was asserted, 'is all on the side of the men' (ibid.).

There seems to be substance in the assertion that the Federation was attempting to break the unions, if the views of Siemens, as President of the London Employers' Association, corresponded to any consensus of employers' views: 'The fact is ... we want to get rid of Trade Unions altogether, for their interference in the working of our business has been intolerable in the past' (reported in *Labour Leader*, 16 Oct. 1897). Union opinion was sceptical of this kind of rhetoric, believing that profit margins had been maintained at reasonable levels. The Armstrong Whitworth Company's results, for example, showed a profit of £446,871 16s. 11d. for the year ending 30 June 1897 (published in *Labour Leader*, 2 Oct. 1897). Col. Dyer, the Federated Employers' principal negotiator, was a director of that particular company.

The Unions initially refused to accept the proposed 'Conditions of Management' and the decision of the employers not to reduce hours in any way. The management proposals were, however, seriously discussed by the union representatives despite the overt hostility displayed in statements of some of the management representatives. Sir Benjamin Dobson, for example, head of the largest machine and engineering firm in Bolton and employer representative, contended that 'employers have made up their minds not to lend their establishments to the furtherance of a system of tyranny which insists that, willy nilly, every employer must bow down to the local union panjandrum' (quoted in *The Times*, 14 Dec. 1897).

The engineering employers' manifesto: preliminary considerations

The employers were determined to extend the reorganisation of work and widen control of labour by eliminating constraints imposed by skilled workers, particularly in the operating of machine tools: '*The machine is still the most important feature of the dispute*. We have heard of no offer of compromise in this matter, and we do not see how the employers can entertain any' (*Engineering*, 1 Oct. 1897; my emphasis). The emphasis on labour-substitution was evident in the employers' policy document. As an EEF letter to the President of the Board of Trade said:

> ... during the past three months ... in many cases from 20 per cent to 50 per cent more work of equal quality has been produced from machines by comparatively inexperienced hands compared with that produced by the men who previously worked the machines. (EEF Minute Book, no. 1, 26 Oct. 1897)

There were two significant factors in this declaration. The first was that EEF employers no longer regarded skilled artisan labour as indispensable labour; it could be replaced by unskilled labour using the new technology.

Second, it seems to bracket out the areas in which engineering employers had consolidated their widening control over skilled labour power, and thus over the means of production. For this reason it is important to explain these in detail in order to explore some of the forces which strengthened employer power.

The dilemma facing the union representatives was evident in their reports to their members. Burns issued a statement to the effect that only two courses of action were open to the men: (1) to summon a national convention of trade unions for the purpose of organising a fund of not less than £15,000 a week to enable the men to continue to strike; (2) to declare the strike at an end, accept the Masters' proposals, and resume work as soon as possible (*The Times*, 9 Dec. 1897).

Neither Hardy's nor Burns' strategies was adopted, and in early December, management proposals were put to union officials who reluctantly reported to their members:

> ... only a consciousness of the serious position in which our members are placed, and the length of time over which the stoppage has extended, with all that such involves, induces us to put before you such proposals, which to our mind, are diametrically opposed to the first principles of trade unionism. (Quoted in *Engineering*, 10 Dec. 1897)

The EEF stance in general was severely criticised on 13 December by an Oxford group,[1] who argued that 'it cannot be held that, prima facie at least, the ultimatum is anything but a deliberate attempt to overthrow the principle of collective bargaining – that is, in a word, an absolute denial of the legitimate action of trade unionism as such' (quoted in *The Times*, 14 Dec. 1897). The use of the term 'ultimatum' in this context provides an illuminating commentary on what were purported to be areas of discussion and negotiation.

The inflexible nature of the EEF proposals was restated in the same issue of *The Times*, in which there was a threat of further lockouts: 'An official of the Employers' Federation last night stated that, in the event of the conference breaking up today 30 additional firms will lock-out their men at the end of the present week. He expressed the opinion that the fight was only now commencing.'

On 17 December the clauses of the management proposals were considered by the ASE executive as a whole and, in general, approved. The 48-hour question was again raised as a separate issue and on the refusal of the employers to negotiate on this point, the official conference deliberations were adjourned, and the union memberships balloted on the whole of the matters in dispute (*The Times*, 18 Dec. 1897).

The 24th distribution of strike pay took place the day after the adjournment and £35,000 was paid out to the 80,000 engineering workers locked out and on strike. The skilled workers received strike pay at the rate of 15/– per week; the allied workers, 12/– to 15/–; non-unionists, 8/–; and labourers, 5/– (*The Times*, 20 Dec. 1897).

The vote taken by the ASE demonstrated a high degree of unanimity in rejecting the EEF proposals, despite apparent hardship. Of 40,000 votes recorded, 39,850 rejected the proposals; 150 voted for acceptance. A ballot among non-unionists throughout the metropolitan area showed 370 against acceptance, and 0 for acceptance (ibid.).

Thus by December no form of settlement had been reached, and Barnes in a speech at Enfield was pessimistic about the outcome. He argued that proposals resubmitted by management, put forward as a result of the ASE ballot, showed some gains in that the status of the union had been recognised; and the right of unions to take the initiative in case of grievances was conceded by employers (*The Times*, 19 Dec. 1897). On other more substantive issues he admitted that the crucial factor was the employers' strong position regarding the deployment of unskilled workers. Their production policies would radically change workshop organisation. The influx of partially trained or untrained labour into the industry would, he argued, clearly accelerate the division of labour and increase narrow specialisation:

> ... on other points there was considerable risk, and they really amounted to the bringing into the workshop of a new body of workmen, which would answer the purpose of the employers, leading to the specialisation and subdivision of the trade. The unions would have to be extremely careful in adapting themselves to the new conditions ... (ibid.)

His analysis was perceptive, for on 31 December a leading engineering employer, Sebastian de Ferranti, put the case regarding the employment of unskilled workers. In a speech to the Manchester District Engineering Trades Association he argued that employers were now part of a political struggle and were engaged in a conflict with Socialism: 'It is not the ASE simply, it is absolutely Socialism, and that Socialism would ruin the country ... ' (quoted in Wigham 1973a: 282). Employing fresh men irrespective of the level of skill in order to train them in narrow, company-specific skills was a tactic designed to break ASE control. He reasserted, 'one of the strongest things we can do today is to show the ASE that they are not masters ... ' (ibid. 283).

What was the source of the employers' confidence as demonstrated by De Ferranti? For him it was the increasing use of standardised tools and instruments, such as gauges (deriving from Whitworth's research earlier in the century). Through this technology unskilled labour could be more effectively deployed: 'Most of them appreciate what it is to use a gauge within three weeks or a month. They turn out work much better and several times over more quickly than our experienced mechanics did before ... ' (ibid., p. 283). Thus the existence of a large reserve of labour and simplified machining operations considerably strengthened the employers' structural position, less dependent than it had been on skilled artisan labour. De Ferranti argued, 'I think it is very important that you should get your works going and push on without the ASE ... ' (ibid.).

Employer control of technology was clearly vital to management's conduct of the strike. As a leader in *Engineering* said:

> 'If there had been no improvements in methods of production ready to hand it is quite possible that Mr. Barnes would have won the 8-hour day ... the employers would have trusted to quicker speeds, heavier feeds, and more energy on the part of the men to compensate for the loss of the hour in the dispute'. (28 Jan. 1898)

The increasingly conciliatory nature of the ASE secretary seemed to be a retraction of the union defiance in the early part of the dispute and a tacit acceptance of the reorganisation of engineering workshops. But ideological and political pressure by the employers intensified during the closing stages of the dispute. The denigration of the political stance of the union side was paralleled by a sustained and more general criticism of socialist principles. The focus of this strategy was the unfortunate Barnes, ASE secretary, who was also subject to increasing criticism from his own side. The pro-Federation journal, *Engineering*, remarked, 'Socialism, as preached by Mr. George Barnes ... and others of the same school, means social disintegration and the destruction of industry' (31 Dec. 1897). Simultaneously, it was argued that management was the cohering factor in engineering production, 'without [whom] every factory would be a mass of useless machinery, and its workmen an undisciplined and dangerous mob' (ibid, p. 803).

Hardy, in his journal leader, refuted a claim that it was the socialists on the ASE executive that were responsible for the union collapse. He contended that it was an 'open-secret' that the pressure exerted by the smaller societies had a good deal to do in weakening the engineers' case (*Labour Leader*, 5 Feb. 1898). In this connection the refusal of two of the most important craft unions in the industry, the Boilermakers and the Patternmakers, to join the stoppages in London may be noted.

Sellicks, the ASE President, tried to compromise on the 48-hour question, a move which stimulated further criticism of the way he and Barnes conducted the union case against the employers. He argued his case to the employers: 'Give us fifty-one all round ... you have given wages equal to it when trade has been good; and if you give us that the men will return to work on Monday' (quoted in *The Engineer*, 14 Jan. 1898). Hardy contended that this gambit was construed as dissension among the union representatives, and gave the employers 'a necessary impetus ... [and] the rank and file learned with dismay of the withdrawal of the eight-hour day' (*Labour Leader*, 22 Jan. 1898).

Reynolds Newspaper was also highly critical of Sellicks and Barnes and attributed the engineers 'gigantic collapse', to the ASE leadership executive under these two officials: 'We expected the failure of the engineers ... we cannot say that we are surprised at what has been for some weeks a potent fact, and which is now an acknowledged fact' (Reynolds Newspaper, 30 Jan. 1898).

Formal EEF proposals of November 1897: an analysis

The EEF November proposals linked the reorganisation of work with the use of new types of machines manned by unskilled labour. With increasing skill dequalification and decomposition, the implementation of auto-machine production, the reserve pool of labour expanded to include displaced skilled labour as well as the mass of the unskilled labourers. Hence employers could argue: 'Every employer shall be free to employ any man, whether he belong or not to a trade union' (*The Times*, 4 Dec. 1897) (Proposal). Two fundamental principles may be distinguished. First, there was a direct challenge to the principle of collective bargaining and a stress on individual negotiation; second was a reassertion of employers' management prerogatives and extension of integrated production processes based on labour substitution.

The proposals in the Settlement covered: I – Freedom of Employment; II – Piecework; III – Overtime; IV – Rating of workmen according to ability; V – Apprentices; VI – Selection, Training, and Employment of Operatives; VII – Proposals for avoiding Further Disputes. (The full text is reproduced in the Appendix.)

The Federated employers conceded few points throughout the dispute; they particularly rejected any union proposal that challenged the authority structure of factory organisation. Under the first head, Freedom of Employment, the union delegates had requested as a quid pro quo a guarantee that the employers would distinguish unionists and non-unionists, and would show no preferences for the latter. The employers' response was to guarantee only the 'harmonious working together of unionists and non-unionists' (4

Dec. 1897). It was not made clear how this equilibrium was to be maintained – any sanctions were not stated.

The piecework principle (Proposal II), which was a major source of contention in previous disputes, was to be extended under the employers' proposals. The framing of this proposal was an attempt to strengthen the principle of individual negotiation. This was evident in the clause which related piece price to the individual workman and not to collectively agreed rates: 'The prices to be paid for piecework shall be fixed by mutual agreement between the employer and the workman who is to perform the work' (*The Times*, 4 Dec. 1897; See the appendix below).

Notwithstanding the long-standing resistance of engineering workers to the practice, it was to be extended further. Burnett, former ASE Secretary, had written in 1876 that piecework tended 'materially to impoverish men employed by the day ... and increases the probable element of disagreement between employers and employed' (*The Times*, 12 Jan. 1876). Burns put the same view 20 years later, in a letter to *The Times*, condemning the practice as exploitation: 'in a word, piecework in the engineering industry is but a transient method of stimulating a workman to greater intensity of toil, often to inefficient work thereby' (27 Sept. 1897). Thus the first two proposals, embodying the notions of employers' rights to employ any form of labour, and to negotiate conditions and wages outside the area of collective bargaining, were substantially supported by the 'Rating of Workmen' proposal (IV). Together they proposed a framework of work organisation through which employers substantially strengthened their control of the labour process.

Under Proposal IV, the rating of workmen was formulated to facilitate a workshop organisation based on undifferentiated labour. The reserve of available labour could be drawn upon and paid according to terms and conditions determined by employers, independently of recognised skills: 'No employer shall be restricted in employing *any* workman at *any* rate of wages mutually satisfactory to them' (*The Times*, 4 Dec. 1897; my emphasis). The inference here was twofold. First, the framing of conditions of employment and settlement of wages were solely management prerogatives and were negotiable only on an individual basis. In addition, under this proposal existing arrangements of collective bargaining could be more easily abrogated as the traditional craft skills constituting artisan status became more fragmented.

The journal *Engineer* rationalised the proposals first by arguing that there had been a revolution in the methods of engineering. Barnes, ASE Secretary, for example, was criticised as 'he attempted to establish a corner in skilled labour at the very time when skilled labour was becoming a drug on the market' (*The Engineer*, 28 Jan. 1898). The development of new forms of technology rendered skilled labour more or less redundant: 'The heads of the leading firms of mechanical engineers ... had begun to see that skilled labour was by no means so essential to the conduct of their business as it had been' (ibid.). Second, the *Engineer* argued, wages should be calculated according to the laws of supply and demand, the element of 'skill' being discounted. This ideology seems to have been inspired by developments in the United States:

> Let the individual take care of himself; what is he that he should be considered? This spirit extends through society generally; and it resulted ... in getting all that was possible out of the workman; then it was found that the better the man was paid the more could be got out of him ... the United States have supplied an object lesson to the English Engineers. (ibid.)

Underlying the issues of collective bargaining and machine manning was the provision and deployment of labour. Two proposals relate to these issues. On apprentices (Proposal V), there was an unequivocal statement: 'There shall be no limitation of the number of apprentices' (Wigham 1973a: 285–9). The ASE had recommended that the ratio of apprentices to journeymen should be one to three, and that the average number of men employed in the previous five years should be taken as a basis of calculation. The employers were intransigent on this issue, and stuck by Proposal V on unlimited 'apprentices'.

Implementation of machine tools was also a critical factor in this proposal. Ownership of the machines, it was argued, entailed control over their disposition and responsibility for the work turned out. It was further contended that a feature of that responsibility was the employers' discretionary power to appoint 'the men they consider suitable to work them and determine the conditions under which such machine tools shall be worked' (Wigham 1973b). The kind of labour envisaged was to be adaptable and cooperative rather than quasi-independent skilled workers: 'The employers consider it their duty ... to employ those whom they consider best adapted to the various operations carried on in their workshops, and will pay them according to their ability as workmen' (ibid.).

Underwriting this principle was the availability and accessibility of alternative labour together with highly developed machine tools. It was argued, for example, that 'men of superior quality' were less in demand, because 'apprentices and labourers have been doing work ... which has been supposed to be only within the compass of men who have been trained for years in the trade' (*Engineering*, 4 Feb. 1898). Clearly, the employers' concept of new workshop organisation depended upon a mass of undifferentiated labour, with a small echelon of skilled supervisors: 'Some employers ... only wanted one or two special men in a department, and were perfectly content in other respects to go on with the labour they had' (ibid., p. 116). Employers thus asserted that the control of the relationship of the number of apprentices to skilled journeymen was part of the inexorable laws of political economy over which they had little control. This represented a crucial change in manufacturing ideology from one based on *labour* to one based on *system and tools*.

The termination of the strike and lockout

The Joint Committee of Trades formally withdrew their demand for an eight-hour day on 15 January 1898; this action was endorsed by the ASE. The retraction was evidently sudden; even Hardy was writing optimistically on 8 January that 'the year opens well, and the prospects of a settlement by the end of the month are more rosy than ever ... ' (*Labour Leader*, 8 Jan. 1898).

An important political element was introduced with the setting up of negotiating machinery to deal with future disputes. Here, the advantage to employers of federation was manifest: 'The formation of the Employers Federation will render impossible the occurences of the troublesome little district and local strikes which have in the past done so much mischief ... ' (*The Engineer*, 21 Jan. 1898).

Extension of reliable supervisory control in the workshops through a less militant middle echelon was anticipated in a proposal to withdraw foremen from union influence as much as possible: 'we are happy to see a determined effort in that direction being made ... ' (ibid.).

On the practical issues of the resumption of work, the concerted efforts of the EEF and the significant contribution of associated institutions such as the ITEA were demonstrated by the uncompromising conditions laid upon returning engineering workers.

Barnes, in the withdrawal of the strike notice of 15 January, assumed that as a consequence the lockout notices would similarly be withdrawn, and the resumption of work would proceed on conditions negotiated during the dispute. The reply from the joint secretaries of the Engineering Employers' Associations Executive Committee, Biggar and Robinson, to the Joint Committee of the Allied Unions made it clear that there could be no such guarantees (EEF Minute Book, no. 1, 21 Jan. 1898: 'In the first instance, the employers can only restart a portion of the men ... ' (quoted in the *Engineer*, 21 Jan. 1898). Federated employers were at liberty to re-engage workmen who had belonged to the unions, but subject to satisfying employers 'that they have definitely left their respective societies ... [and] shops will remain closed to trade union members until the Terms of Settlement have been accepted by the representative trade union societies ... ' (*Engineer*, 14 Jan. 1898).

The radical shift in power relations to the employers' advantage was consolidated in the post-strike situation, particularly regarding the autonomy of craft workers, the issue of machine manning, and the use of unskilled labour.

The employers extended the use of labourers of the Free Labour Association. Clearly these were gains by non-unionised labour, as the craft unions' exclusivity was challenged as result of the lockout and later by the Terms of Settlement:

> During the thirty weeks the dispute has lasted, many of the smarter labourers have been able to seize the opportunity of rising to the ranks of skilled workers ... so far as these men are concerned ... they will take the place of those who managed the machines before the trouble ... (*Engineer*, 4 Feb. 1898)

Biggar was unequivocal in his determination that the EEF would strictly control work resumption. Accordingly, only 25 per cent of unionists were to be taken on. Employers were, he maintained, also morally obliged, and in practice, pledged to support the 'free labourers [who] have helped them in their need ... ' (quoted in *The Engineer*, 4 Feb. 1898). One outcome of this policy was that workers, instead of being allowed to resume work in body, were forced to apply individually:

> These works will be opened on and after Monday 31st January to the members of the Allied Unions ... it will not be possible to start all the machinery at once. It will therefore be convenient if workmen desirous of employment will send in a written application, giving name and address to the manager of the department where they previously worked. The managers will, from day to day, inform men whose services are desired when work can be resumed ... (Quoted in the *Labour Leader*, 5 Feb. 1898)

The strike and lockout had lasted from 13 July 1897 to 31 January 1898, and 702 firms were involved. It was estimated that over 47,500 men had been implicated directly; and in the period up to December 1897, allied trades such as shipbuilding showed a marked increase in unemployment, from 4.4 per cent to 14.1 per cent.

Following the strike the traditional function of the craft unions of confirming skilled status through union membership was considerably weakened.

The presence of a reserve pool of experienced skilled labour, supplementing the reserves of unskilled workers, constituted a situation after the strike which had not previously existed. Employers were in an unassailable position. This may be illustrated in the case of an incident at a machine-tool company where about 70 members of the Society had struck. When the dispute terminated, 30 of these men 'presented themselves at 6 o'clock on Monday morning last ... in the hope of getting back their work. One solitary applicant was engaged ... ' (*Engineer*, 4 Feb. 1898).

Ratification of employer control

Judgements about the immediate practical effects of the dispute are tempered by the fact that there was no census of production until 1907. Figures for overall engineering production at the time of the first census give an approximate evaluation of the 'state of the market' against which the dispute had taken place. The value of gross output of engineering factories in the United Kingdom in 1907 was £87,817,000 (Census of Production 1906, Cd 5005). This figure applies to the group of enterprises concerned with 'General Engineering', which included such areas of machine tools, hydraulic machines, boilers, mining industry, textile machinery, agricultural machinery. For the engineering industry as a whole (including electrical engineering), figures were not available until the final report of the census of production in 1913. These indicate that for the iron and steel, engineering, and shipbuilding trades the gross value of work done was £375,196,000; total UK production was valued at £1,765,366,000; the generated value of engineering industries thus amounted to 21.2 per cent of the total output, and the average number of persons employed in those industries was 1,539,415 (Census of Production 1913a, Cd 6320).

These figures are arguably close enough to the actual period of the dispute to indicate a highly productive market during the period of the strike and lockout. The specific area of concern of this analysis, covered in the census by 'machinery', generated gross values of £34,955,000 (Census of Production 1906), the largest single contribution under General Engineering, constituting nearly 40 per cent of total production in this area. The machine-tool sector, a relatively small part of the industry as a whole, alone constituted 7.7 per cent of the gross value.

The data outlined here suggest that the prevailing market ensured economic returns were secure during the dispute. In addition to preserving profit rates, the employers widened even further the areas of control over the organisation of work, the implementation of new technologies, and the redesignation of skilled work in the industry.

Trade union support for the engineers: a question of solidarity

Of the social aspects of the dispute, on the union side, moral and financial support came from a variety of sources. In early December 1897, MacDonald, the Secretary of the London Trades Council, issued invitations to a general conference of trade unionists of the country to consider the best means of affording support to the organisations engaged in the dispute. He received 112 replies, all to the effect that the unions were prepared to take part in the proposed conference. Solidarity was expressed by the following: the Amalgamated Society of Railway Servants, the Durham Miners' Association, the Gasworkers and General Labourers' Union, the Ironfounders' Society of Great Britain and Ireland, the London Society of Compositors, the Operative Bricklayers' Society, the Cigarmakers' Society, and the British Smelters' Association (*The Times*, 23 Dec. 1897). In one day, officials of the Engineers' Society received £3,500 towards the lockout fund. Included in this amount were the following donations: £225 from the members of the Engineers' Society in Johannesburg; £100 from the Boiler Firemens' Society of Great Britain; £50 from the Penrhyn quarrymen; £50 from the Mill Sawyers' Association; £50 from the United Kingdom Coachmakers' Society; £50 from the Card Machine Tenders' Society (ibid.).

At the termination of the dispute it had been estimated that a total of £140,000 had been subscribed from outside sources to the workers in contention. To this was added £65,000 from the capital account of the different societies included in allied trades and £230,00 subscribed in levies by men working (*Labour Leader*, 5 Feb. 1898). The capital account of the ASE had been subvented by £65,000, which, taken with loss of wages estimated at £1,200,000 for engineers and £1,800,000 for allied workers, made a specific loss of £3,000,000 and a general total of £3,700,000 (ibid.).

The financial position of the Engineers' Society was parlous after such an enormous outflow of funds. Some practical measure of the extent of the loss may be gauged from the evidence relating to the social labour costs during and preceding the dispute. In 1880 a fitter in London earned 36/– for a 54-hour week (32/– in Birmingham); at the end of the 1890s this had risen to 38/– (36/–) (British Labour Statistics, Table 1). Taking the industry as a whole, in 1886 nearly 60 per cent (59.4) of all engineering workers earned between 20/– to 35/– per week; less than 9 per cent (3.8) earned between 34/– and 40/–; and 3.8 per cent earned above 40/– (ibid, Table 35). Some retail food price fluctuations in London provide an illustration of the cost of living obtaining during the same period. For example, potato prices showed a 4 per cent drop in the period 1886–98; the cost of bread rose by 12 per cent; bacon rose 4 per cent; tea fell 30 per cent, while flour rose 21 per cent (ibid., Table 87). In the period 1892–8 alone, rent increases were nearly 7 per cent (ibid., Table 88). These figures show some of the cost, in social and financial terms, for an amalgamated union, albeit of much-vaunted strength, incurring a loss of nearly £3¾m. against a background of increases in staple food prices and rents while skilled worker wage rates had increased, in the 18-year period 1880–98, 5.5 per cent.

The accumulation of substantial funds for contingencies such as benefit and death schemes had been carried out by the ASE in the period since 1851 and represented a demonstrable stability and astuteness on the part of the ASE executive. The weekly levy for ASE members was 1/– per week, with an entrance fee ranging from 15/– for 25-year-old men to £2.10.0 for workers at age 40, after which membership admittance was not possible (RC on TU 1867a, 1869c).

This business acumen, aligned with the confidence engendered by a belief in their indispensability in key sectors of manufacturing, had generated a groundswell of resistance which culminated in the challenge to the engineering employers. The employers reacted by establishing a closer network of cooperation and confronted the ASE over key issues which had been sources of contention since the onset of machine-tool automation: 'the vital character of the issues brought daily accessions to the Federation ... 702 firms successfully resisted the attempt to enforce a reduction of the working hours ... and vindicated the Employers' right to Freedom of Management' (EEF 1898).

The significance of the engineering employers' combination was not confined to regularising the implementation of new technologies, accelerating the decomposition of artisan skills and reaffirming their hegemony. As the proposals in the Terms of Settlement show, it reinforced their predominantly negative attitudes to trade training and education, the future of the apprenticeship and the status of skilled workers.

These factors interacted with emerging ideas on technical education which were overshadowed by part-time, evening-class principles.

The issue of machine manning after the settlement of 1898

Although it is clear that the engineering employers were determined to consolidate the advantages gained through the 1898 Terms of Settlement and their ratification in 1907 (see the Appendix), the question of machine manning was repeatedly in contention from 1898. Between 3 February and 25 October 1898 six major disputes were recorded concerning unskilled manning of machine tools (EEF Case Register 1895–1906: 1901, 15 Jan.). The Armstrong Whitworth Company was challenged in February over the use of labourers on a grinding machine. The General Electric Company in Manchester insisted on the employment of labourers on 36" vertical boring mills in July; while in August a Scottish firm (Clyde Mitchell) was confronted by Society men over the use of labourers on lathes. A strike occurred again in August against unskilled labourers being used on two rolling mills in Manchester. In October, men at the J. Bertram Company in East Scotland refused to man more than one machine (Ibid., extracts from months stated.)

The following year saw a similar situation, with employers using unskilled labour on machine tools as the Terms of Settlement prescribed. Skill substitution generated resistance from Society men, despite the conditions laid upon them by the 1898 settlement. On three occasions the manning of turret lathes was contested. At Hull, Blackburn and Burnley the employment of labourers, or 'handymen', on automatic machines was challenged by the union. The attitude of one company towards 'self-improvement' was demonstrated by the sacking of a worker and the confiscation of machine-part drawings done by him in a firm in Sheffield (ibid., extract for 29 Nov. 1899 – Crooke Bros., Sheffield). Multiple-machine manning was again challenged at a firm in Blackburn where the working of two lathes by one man was pressed by the management, the 'employers right [being] admitted' (ibid., 13 June 1899). Similarly, two adjoining planing machines in a plant in East Scotland were assumed by management to be capable of operation by one man, a position that was also contested.

Throughout the 1900s the process of challenge and counter-challenge over machine manning therefore continued unabated. Automatic machines such as turrets and capstan lathes were particularly in contention. In none of the recorded cases in the EEF minutes was there evidence of any concession granted by employers. In March 1906 a circular letter was issued to Local Associations of the Federation on the specific management problems associated with turret lathes. A case was developed over the manning of a no. 16 combination turret lathe at the Manchester firm of Wm. Muir. A handyman was put to work on the machine under a chargehand (an ASE member). Two members of the ASE refused to handle work, turned off the machine and consequently 'discharged themselves'. The firm replaced the turners with non-society men and continued to work the turret lathe with handymen. The ASE men and apprentices struck in protest. The Federation decided to make a test case and took up the strike with the London Council of the ASE (EEF 1906).

Some implications of the Great Strike and Lockout for employers and workers

Engineering employers in the latter part of the century exercised the considerable advantages gained from their domination of new machines and different labour forms. The effect on the apprentice–journeyman ratio, for example, was evident. The ratio tended to increase as the perceived need by employers for any systematic training receded.

Even before the strike there was an inclination to dismiss apprentices when they became expensive: in some cases, 'there [was] a tendency to do without apprentices altogether' (RC on Labour 1894: 115). There was considerable use of boys as a form of cheap labour in this period. An illustration from Belfast shows this apprentice decline in practice. A small engineering concern in Belfast employed five journeymen and 33 apprentices. The recommended ratio at the time was 1:3 (ibid.). In a report of 1893 Whittaker of the ASE produced evidence which showed that it was not uncommon to find a ratio of 12 apprentices to two journeymen (RC on Labour 1893f: Q. 22762).

The ITEA had previously advocated a 'flexible' non-binding system of training for young workers, canvassing the view that such a system would allow freedom 'on both sides', and permit a change of occupation 'where a lad is found on trial to be unfitted for the one at first chosen' (ibid., p. 116).

The confrontation between engineering employers and workers in the late 1890s was not simply about the economics of production. It was also concerned with the reproduction as well as the deployment of labour power. The ability of ASE members to confront employers turned largely on their claim to superior skills in the various engineering functions within the trade. In the view of the ASE especially, the chief guarantee of such skill lay in the apprenticeship system.

The perception of engineering skill held by employers had changed. For some it was characterised by an increasing separation between basic craft skills and the underlying technical and scientific basis of those skills: 'The part played by manual labour in the creation of wealth is exaggerated. The part played by administration, by the genius which invents and the brain which controls, is persistently minimised' (*Saturday Review*, 2 Sept. 1897). In other words, control over the labour process in engineering was seen in terms of regulation of new technologies in which the contribution of skilled workers was marginalised. Control over machines had become central to the dispute, reinforcing a closer direction of artisans whose skills, shedding their transferable qualities, had become increasingly company-specific: 'The masters are indisputably in the right in claiming full control of their machines, for if intellect is not left as free as industry in the entire labour region there is no hope for the country which consents to see its brain-power laid in fetters' (*Spectator*, 22 Jan. 1898). Sections of the Press reflected the changing emphasis on labour-control through technology:

> It is, in short, a fight for supremacy between a Union which regards itself as 'the aristocracy of labour' and the employers who feel that the power of directing their own works is rapidly slipping out of their hands ... they ... want to lessen the power or the disposition of the Union to impose exasperating terms upon the conduct of industry. (*Saturday Review*, 4 Sept. 1897)

Conflict over power relations: job demarcation

The post-strike disputes, viewed as part of the ongoing struggle over power relations in the workshops, highlight the ideology of control which rested on the contentious issue of job demarcation.

Faced with a prospect of gradual and persistent downgrading of their skills by employers, a number of strategies were open to engineering artisans. Among these was the maintenance of clear skill boundaries, i.e. the demarcation of jobs. This attempted to counter employer tactics to diminish the social and technical currency of any particular engineering craft skill by increasing job differentiation.

Employers, such as Robinson, Beyer, and Noble, argued for (a) the 'democratisation' of all skills, i.e. the breaking down of skill boundaries; (b) a rejection of the claim by a skilled minority that their skills demanded systematic training: 'If ... our conception of the "skill" which we might have worked for and desired is what might be called "craftsmanship", we must conclude that the demand for skill is, on the whole, declining' (RC on Poor Laws 1909a: 346). The employers' belief in the new technologies encouraged increased specialisation in the workshops, undermining the generalised skills of the traditional metal tradesmen: 'The all-round ability, which used honourably to mark out the mechanic, is no longer in demand, so much as the work of the highly specialised machine minder' (ibid.).

The essence of the demarcation issue was the claim by craftsmen to control delineated areas of craft knowledge and expertise. As Barnes argued, 'the skilled men require even more skill than they did because of the finer work and more intricate machinery ... side by side with automatic machinery there has come about more intricate and highly complicated machinery' (ibid., Minutes of Evidence, Vol. VIII, Q. 82943). But the employers had been consistent and saw it in terms of an ideology of production, as an issue of control of work and labour. As they claimed during the dispute: 'trade unionism ... [as] the inviolable restriction of certain work to the members of the union, and demarcation of work is the necessary result of such a policy ... a new unionism which must therefore disappear ... ' (*Engineering*, 15 Oct. and 5 Nov. 1897).

Later evidence submitted to official inquiries such as the Poor Law Commission (1909) confirmed these hostile views on the part of employers regarding the demarcation policies of the unions: 'There is ... pretty general agreement that at present Trade Union ideas and regulations are very inimical, if not hostile, to trade mobility – the many bitter and prolonged disputes about "demarcation" being cited in proof' (RC on Poor Laws 1909a: 348). The Commission held that trade mobility could be facilitated through 'technical training': 'If, at school, young people were taught, first of all to be intelligent – to "think", in fact – and if technical training were general, and teaching principles rather than practice – mobility would have a better chance' (ibid.). According to this view, the relation between engineering production and 'technical training' was unproblematic – it promoted trade mobility, the breaking down of barriers between trades, and 'democratised' the labour process: 'There would be no difficulty in providing for trained machine labour at least' (Ibid., para. 239).

The concept of trade mobility was clearly used to promote the idea of fluidity of labour across skill boundaries. Ramsay Macdonald, in his submission to the same 1909 Commission, put forward the view that, with respect to trade mobility, there was an integral link between the organisation of labour and the organisation of capital (ibid., Minutes of Evidence, Ans. V).

Trade union rivalries: employers' initiatives

Developments after the turn of the century show that employers continued to capitalise on their extended control over the labour process. Noble, EEF spokesman at the 1906 Royal Commission on Trade Disputes, adopting a new tactic, argued that inter-union rivalries had generated a new function for employers; they were now occupying objective roles as mediators, a conception of management as 'innocent bystander' (RC on Trade Disputes 1906: 161). Another commented earlier that they were compelled to stand 'helplessly by' as demarcation disputes took place: 'Employers need more power ... to say what men shall perform certain work ... ' (*Saturday Review*, 25 Sept. 1897).

But between 1890 and 1903 there were 24 serious strikes recorded by the Employers' Association. These principally concerned the issues of demarcation and the expressed right of certain trades to exercise some kind of authority over methods and pace of their work. Of these, ten were directly concerned with the question of machine manning and related issues, and the assertion by the Society that its members were the competent workers for employment on machine tools.

In a particular case in 1901, the ASE claimed that turret lathes should be worked by turners or at least apprentice turners. This claim brought them into dispute with unskilled workers, 'machinemen'. Management's response in this case was to reassert their own claim that these machines had always been worked by 'machine boys' and 'machinemen' (on account of the Factory Act now allowing boys to work through the night) (Synopsis of Demarcation Cases, EEF, Marc. 1901). The point at issue was recorded as a demarcation dispute between the members of the 'A.S.E. and Machinemen'. Noble's evidence to the 1904 Royal Commission shows that in this, as in the other recorded cases, the employers' view was enforced by the Federation (RC on TD & TC 1906: Q. 2411).

Noble implied that the terrain of dispute had shifted from the confrontational arena of capital and labour to internecine rivalry within and between unions: 'In comparatively recent years a far larger number of strikes in the north eastern district were due, not to disputes between employers and the employed, but between different trades among themselves ... ' (ibid., p. 163).

The employers' belief in the durability and consistency of their triumph over the unions in 1898 underpinned the continuing struggles with the ASE; the watershed in labour policies was clearly located in that year.

Federating employers: the pattern set for the future?

It is evident that from the inception of the EEF as an entity there was an increasing inflexibility characterising negotiations concerning labour substitution: 'In the engineering industry the epoch of change dates from the agreement effected between the Federated Engineering Employers and certain Allied Trade Unions in January, 1898, and to this the attention of the Commission is specially directed' (RC on TD & TC 1906: Q. 2410). The Engineering Employers Federation by this time had expanded to a membership of 865 employing 500,000 workers with an annual wage bill of £25,000,000 (ibid.)

The employers reaffirmed their control which had been gradually expanding since the 1890s. W. Glennies, the ASE secretary, highlighted the long-term effects of an earlier dispute: 'During our last dispute, while we were out for thirteen weeks, the employers filled the machines, and other places, where the men had been working, with apprentices, to the extent that when the strike closed, 24 per cent of our members could not get started again ... ' (RC on Labour 1893e: Q. 22795). Other than the direct, profound consequences of unemployment, this was an issue that had other serious implications for skilled adult workers. With a substantial reserve of unskilled and boy labour to call upon there was added pressure on them. One of the effects was the restriction of the majority of skilled adult workmen engaged in the engineering trade to a working life of about 20 years (RC on Labour 1893f, 3rd Report, Whittaker (ASE) Q. 22762): 'the majority of shops will not set a man to work who is over 40 years of age. That is the limit at which they will engage them ... if he gets out of a shop where he has had continuous employment as a permanent hand, he finds great difficulty ever getting into this trade again' (ibid., Q. 22704). A restriction on the length of working life acted as a disincentive for employers regarding both technical education and their response for appeals for a more radical reactivation of the moribund apprenticeship system.

The process of labour substitution by 19th-century employers took a number of forms; the most common was 'upgrading' labourers to machine work. Particularly noticeable was the employment of unskilled operators on repetition work, using automatic-type machines. This was a tactic favoured by Noble, in his 1893 Royal Commission evidence:

> In the particular works where I am engaged we have a great deal of repetition work. We have, for instance, a machine that does one particu-

lar thing and nothing else, and we have found that labourers who have been gradually trained and advanced do their work better than skilled mechanics. They devote themselves to one thing and they do it very well ... (RC on Labour 1893d, Q. 25220)

Clearly there was a marked decrease in employer reliance on skilled machinists. Employers had access to a reserve of labour, providing alternatives to artisan labour on a scale which had not existed in previous disputes.

Issues concerning the survival of the apprenticeship system and the question of machine manning interpenetrated and underlay many engineering employer–labour disputes of this period.

The 1897–8 strike and lockout was more than a conflict over economic issues, but had wider ideological and political implications. It plainly strengthened the engineering employers' resolve to replace skilled labour and in the process confirmed their declining interest in the historic form of trade training, the apprenticeship system. New technologies implemented by them were specifically designed to ensure as far as possible the accommodation and integration of low-level skills. Concerns over skill differentials therefore assumed a central position in the dispute, and in any explanation of the critical importance attached by both sides to the question of machine manning and skill substitution.

From the 1860s the employers had focused on what they perceived to be the main impediments to the extension of their power and control in the factory system, of which the ideology and solidarity of the amalgamated union were the most significant. The employers carried their suspicion and hostility regarding the trade unions, which they had demonstrated in the Inquiry of 1868, throughout the century. Thus by the 1890s they were 'absolutely resolved' to defeat the unions on significant issues, and believed that the 'engineering trade of this country cannot be carried on unless they carry their point' (*The Times*, 4 Dec. 1897). Employers at the 1897 conference expressed views that serve to highlight the significance of these basic issues: 'The question of management is paramount ... , the mere fact that the men entered in early summer upon a conflict which they had not the slightest chance of winning has brought the question of management to the fore ... '. The strength of this conviction was drawn from the belief that 'the skilled man grows less and less and the machine grows more and more' (ibid.).

The dispute demonstrated the power and effectiveness of the employers' combination; it also highlighted their capacity to extend control over the total labour process, especially over the organisation of work. They insisted on the capitulation of the combined unions, despite what would seem to have been a weakness in their case, by spreading the dispute from London to the provinces. In effect, this move made the cause of the metropolitan employers the cause of the whole trade. The struggle of power relations in the industry entered a new phase. For the first time the amalgamated union, the ASE, was confronted by a 'national' combination of engineering employers.

What of the effects of the strike on the issue of trade training and education?

Although obscured by the intensity of the conflicts over machine manning, more profound ideas about the apprenticeship system and technical training were incorporated indirectly into a national engineering employers' policy.

The successful outcome of the conflict confirmed for employers that the historic method of trade training for young workers under apprenticeship schemes was clearly inappropriate for management needs. By consolidating their decisive control over workshop training, according to their own prescriptions, they rendered ineffectual government aspirations for a national system of technical education.

EEF deliberations in the period from 1898 through 1907 (the year the 1898 Settlement was ratified) and beyond were consistent in that they perceived management control of the labour process as characterised by employer dominance of new technologies manned by mainly unskilled workers. Operational imperatives clearly took priority over training and education for young workers; 'the continuous evolution of the engineering industry has made it incumbent on the employers continually to be adjusting their processes and methods to meet the demands of the industry ... ' (Engineering and Allied Employers Federation 1927: 20). The insistence upon full discretionary and exclusive powers in the area of training labour to meet their own limited specialised needs enabled employers to circumvent the traditional resistance of artisans and the craft unions to labour and work reorganisation.

The unions' claim to be beneficiaries of traditional craft skills turned largely on what they perceived to be a rational (and legal) basis for their authority over engineering skills, the apprenticeship system. In contrast, the employers diluted the relationship between young workers, 'apprentices', and journeymen, thus weakening the exclusiveness of skilled workers. The 'bound' apprentice was replaced by an ad hoc 'trainee' system contingent upon the needs of individual companies and 'the iron law of the market system'.

Economic short-termism underpinned the employers' argument that the apprenticeship issue was in any event made more complex by the machine-manning issue: 'the latter is in a transition stage and how far the work of the skilled man will be ultimately modified or restricted by the introduction of machines is impossible accurately to appreciate ... ' (EEF 1927: 19).

Satisfying the needs of the internal labour market became the basis of the highly modified 'training' to be afforded under the Terms of Settlement at the end of the strike. This had already been gradually implemented during the years preceding the 1897 Conference. Col. Dyer, of the Elswick Works, Newcastle, and Chairman of the Employers' Federation, principal spokesman on the employers' side, wrote in September 1897 that learning a trade was contingent upon the needs of production: 'The majority of the men employed had to go to the works during the strike as unskilled men and had been trained to perform the duties required of them, with the result that the output had been increased two-thirds ... ' (*The Times*, 5 Sept. 1897). The position was reaffirmed in the subsequent agreement of 1907 under which management formalised the tentative proposal of 1898 concerning selection and training. Under this article control over two critical areas of craft training – the apprenticeship system and the general principles governing access to traditional engineering skills, for example, young apprentices working alongside tradesmen – were forfeited by the unions: 'Employers in view of the necessity of obtaining the most economical production whether by skilled or unskilled workmen, have full discretion to appoint the men they consider suitable to work all their machine tools and to determine the conditions under which they shall be worked ... ' (EEF 1907).

The collapse of coordinated engineering union resistance marked a decisive turning point for both unions and employers; the unions were forced to reassess their position vis-à-vis the employers and the unskilled workers in the engineering trades. One source suggested that a political outcome of the strike was the conversion of the trade union movement to the Independent Labour Party: 'Thoroughly disillusioned the unionists sought to supplement their inadequate industrial power by recourse to more determined political action' (Crowley 1956: 662).

The 1897–8 conflict in the engineering industry consolidated the interpenetration of work and technology, and the power of the employers over their organisation and implementation. It also vindicated the analysis by Marx of the interaction between labour power, machinery and modern industry. He argued that with substitution of human skill and labour by machine, the exchange-value of the workman's labour power vanishes. This put the worker at considerable risk:

> The workman becomes unsaleable, like paper money thrown out of currency by legal enactment. The portion of the working class, thus by machinery rendered superfluous, either goes to the wall in the unequal contest of the old handicrafts and manufacturers with machinery ... or swamps the labour market, and sinks the price of labour power below its value (Marx 1867; 1961:431)

The dynamics of the 1897–8 confrontation were not confined to the engineering industry, where skilled workers were 'rendered superfluous'. They also profoundly affected the ideological and political nature of the whole of manufacturing industry, the manifestations of which extended beyond the confines of the factory. The concept of trade training had been gradually transformed throughout the second half of the century; undermining the central artisan case for the retention of the apprenticeship system and appeals for a system of technical education. The Technical Instruction Act of 1889, the first piece of legislation specifically designed to promote some form of technical education, made little impact on employers in the engineering industry. They unquestionably influenced the gradual and ill-defined development of technical education, which was further impeded by contradictions and ambiguities associated with developing educational strategies.

APPENDIX: Agreement between the EEF and the ASE, March 1907

AGREEMENT
made this Twenty-second day of March, 1907.
between
THE ENGINEERING EMPLOYERS' FEDERATION (hereinafter called 'The Federation') of the one part,
and
THE AMALGAMATED SOCIETY OF ENGINEERS, THE STEAM ENGINE MAKERS' SOCIETY, AND THE UNITED MACHINE WORKERS' ASSOCIATION
(hereinafter called 'The Trade Unions') on the other part

The Representatives of the Engineering Employers' Federation on the one hand and of the Engineering Trade Unions on the other being met in joint Conference, and being convinced that the interests of each will be best served and the rights of each best maintained by a mutual agreement, hereby decide to adopt Measures to avoid friction and stoppage of work.
IT IS THEREFORE AGREED as follows:–

1. *General Principles of Employment*

The Federated Employers shall not interfere with the proper functions of the Trade Unions and the Trade Unions shall not interfere with the Employers in the management of their business.

2. *Employment of Workmen*

Every Employer may belong to the Federation and every workman may belong to a Trade Union or not as either of them may think fit.

Every Employer may employ any man, and every workman may take employment with any employer the workman or the Employer belonging or not to a Trade Union or to the Federation respectively.

The Trade Unions recommend all their Members not to object to work with Non-Union workmen, and the Federation recommend all their Members not to object to employ Union workmen on the ground that they are Members of a Trade Union.

No workman shall be required as a condition of employment to make a declaration as to whether he belongs to a Trade Union or not.

3. *Piecework*

Employers and their workmen are entitled to work piecework, provided:–
  (a) The prices to be paid shall be fixed by mutual arrangement, between the employer and the workman or workmen who perform the work.
  (b) Each workman's day rate to be guaranteed irrespectively of his Piecework earnings.
  (c) Overtime and Nightshift allowances to be paid in addition to piecework prices on the same conditions as already prevail in each workshop for time work. All balances and wages to be paid through the office.

4. Overtime

The Federation and the Trade Unions are agreed that systematic overtime is to be deprecated as a method of production and that when overtime is necessary the following is mutually recommended as a basis, viz:–

That no Union workmen shall be required to work more than 32 hours overtime in any four weeks after full shop hours have been worked: allowance being made for time lost through sickness, absence with leave, or enforced idleness.

In the following cases overtime is not to be restricted:–

Breakdown work, repairs, replacements or alterations for the Employers or their customers.

Trial trips and repairs to ships.

Urgency and emergency.

5. Rating of Skilled Workmen

Employers have the right to employ workmen at rates of wages mutually satisfactory to the employer and the workman or workmen concerned.

In fixing the rates of skilled workmen, the employer shall have regard to the rates prevailing in the District for fully trained and skilled men.

Unions, while disclaiming any right to interfere with the wages of workmen other than their own Members have the right in their collective capacity to arrange the rate of wages at which their Members may accept work.

General alterations in the rates of wages in any district shall be negotiated between the Employers' Local Association and the local representatives of the Trade Union or Unions concerned.

6. Apprentices

There shall be no recognised proportion of apprentices to journeymen, but it shall be open to the Unions to bring forward for discussion the proportion of apprentices generally employed in the whole Federated area.

An apprentice shall be afforded facilities for acquiring a practical knowledge of the branch of trade he adopts, and shall be encouraged to obtain a theoretical knowledge thereof as far as circumstances permit.

7. Selection, Training and Employment of Operative and Manning of Machine Tools

Employers have the right to select, train and employ those whom they consider best adapted to the various operations carried on in their workshops and to pay them accordingly to their ability as workmen.

Employers in view of the necessity of obtaining the most economical production whether by skilled or unskilled workmen, have full discretion to appoint the men they consider suitable to work all their machine tools and to determine the conditions under which they shall be worked.

The Federation recommend their Members that, when they are carrying out changes in their workshops which will result in displacement of labour, consideration should be given to the case of the workmen who may be displaced, with a view, if possible, of retaining their services on the work affected or finding other employment for them.

8. *Provisions for Avoiding Disputes*

With a view to avoid disputes, deputations of workmen shall be received by their employers, by appointment, for mutual discussion, of any question in the settlement of which both parties are directly concerned: or it shall be competent for an official of the Trade Union to approach the Local Secretary of the Employers' Association with regard to any such question: or it shall be competent for either party to bring the question before a Local Conference to be held between the Local Association of Employers and the Local Representatives of the Trade Unions.

In the event of either party desiring to raise any question a Local Conference for this purpose may be arranged by application to the Secretary of the Employers' Association or of the Trade Union concerned as the case may be.

Local Conference shall be held within twelve working days from the receipt of the application by the Secretary of the Employers' Association or of the Trade Union or Trade Union concerned.

Failing settlement at a Local Conference of any question brought before it, it shall be competent for either party to refer the latter to the Executive Board of the Federation and the Central Authority of the Trade Union or Trade Unions concerned.

Central Conferences shall be held at the earliest date which can be conveniently arranged by the Secretaries of the Federation and of the Trade Union or Trade Unions concerned.

There shall be no stoppage of work, either of a partial or of a general character, but work shall proceed under the current conditions until the procedure provided for above has been carried through.

9. *Constitution of Conferences*

An Organising Delegate of the Amalgamated Society of Engineers shall be recognised as a Local Official entitled to take part in any Local Conference, but only in his own division. In case of sickness, his place shall be taken by a Substitute appointed by the Executive Council.

Any Member of the Executive Council or the General Secretary of the Amalgamated Society of Engineers may attend Local Conference, provided that the Member of the Executive Council shall attend only such Conferences as are held within the division represented by him.

A Member of the Executive Council or the General Secretary of the Steam Engine Makers' Society and of the United Machine Workers' Association respectively may attend any Local Conference in which the Societies or either of them are directly concerned.

Central Conferences shall be composed of Members of the Executive Board of the Federation and Members of the Central Authority of the Trade Union or Trade Unions concerned.

An Employer who refuses to employ Trade Unionists will not be eligible to sit in Conference.

Signed on behalf of:–
The Engineering Employers' Federation:–
'A. P. HENDERSON', Chairman.
'ALLAN M. SMITH', for Secretary
The Amalgamated Society of Engineers

'DAVID GARDNER', Chairman.
'GEORGE N. BARNES', Secretary.
The Steam Engine Makers' Society:–
'HENRY DAVIES', Chairman.
'WM. F. DAWTRY', Secretary.
The United Machine Workers' Association:–
'WILLIAM KEMBLE', Chairman.
'MATTHEW ARRANDALE', Secretary.

SOURCE: Engineering Employers' Federation, Minute Book, No. 3, 1907.

Note

1. The Master of Balliol, the President of Trinity, the Principal of Jesus, Professor Esson, Dr Fairbairn, Mr Arthur Sidgwick, Mr T. C. Snow, Professor Markby, the Revd H. Rachdall and other members of the University.

CHAPTER SIX

Contradictions and struggle in ideas about a national system of technical education

It has long been argued in economic-efficiency models of 19th-century technical development in Britain that foreign competition was adequately met without a structured technical education system. Typical of this perspective is Ashworth (1963): 'With all its technical shortcomings and its retention of many practices that were not the last word in modernity, British industry seems to have been fairly well adapted to current needs and practices' (p. 107). 'Objective economic factors' were clearly crucial in Britain's industrial decline, but it is equally clear that industrialists were unwilling to make a commitment to technical training and education; they 'wanted neither to pay rates nor dip into their own pockets ... to pay for technical education' (Gowing 1978: 6).

British employers, economically rational in seeking profit maximisation, had achieved so much in the early 19th century with such little education that an reformed educational infrastructure seemed unnecessary, choosing to ignore the fact that foreign competitors were doing just that (Gowing 1978). This rationalisation provides a partial explanation for a loss of impetus in the technical education 'movement'; more common is the judgement that it was a lack of direction. After its initial boost the movement began to waver, due to the lack of clear directives on the part of the leaders. There was 'a curious vagueness surrounding the ideas of the leaders of the movement that makes it difficult to specify ... ' (Cardwell 1972a: 187).

An explanation of imprecision on the part of the leaders was linked therefore to the problem of the definition of technical education: 'It seems to have been the case that many enthusiastic advocates [of technical education] reduced themselves to proclaiming "we cannot say what technical education is, but we must have it"' (ibid.$_1$ p. 158). This begs a number of questions: if the maximisation of profits represented rational economic behaviour, how can the apparent irrationality accompanying the decline of the skilled artisan class be explained other than in terms of employer complacency and suspicion? Was it possible to articulate clear objectives for technical education if the context of technical education was unclear and unformulated? How critical was government thinking in all this?

The problem of definition and lack of direction for technical education was still evident well into the 20th century. According to Lord Eustace Percy, the

President of the Board of Education, in response to a report of the Emmott Committee, '"technical education" was an instance of the artificial language which tends to confuse all educational discussions ... ' (1928 PRO ED/24/1869). Coming 40 years after the passing of the Technical Instruction Act in the previous century, it was being argued that 'a good deal of the money we spend on so-called "technical" education has no apparent effect ... ' (ibid.). This suggests government was less than fully committed to the idea of a technical education system despite the recommendations of the first Inquiry set up in 1881 under Samuelson.

In manufacturing industries the decomposition of skills underscored the contraction of skilled artisans accompanying the process of expanding technologies. This production ideology was pre-eminent in the organisation of work from the 1850s (Whitworth 1854, 1868; Nasmyth 1868a; Anderson 1884b; Donnelly 1868; 1884). The early development of technical education therefore took place against the background of an accelerating decline in the skilled work base and also in relation to the government's equivocal position on mass general education from the 1870s. Speaking in the House of Lords, the Lord President of the Council, Viscount Cranbrook, reiterated the point that the Technical Instruction Act 'was never meant to teach trades ... '. Along with others he clearly assumed that craft training was taking place in the workshops: 'a young man learning dexterity in the use of materials [in the workshops] ... no less important for him that he should attend evening classes as is done in certain parts of the kingdom ... ' (Hansard 1892, col 428).

Twenty-five years after the establishment of compulsory education in 1870 and in 1880, government was still debating whether it had any significant role, even in mass general education. The Bryce Commission of 1895 reported a lack of clear objectives, administrative fragmentation, disorganisation and frequent overlapping of educational resources. Despite the assumption that it was an extension of general schooling; there was an unmerited belief that technical educational development was more adequately provided for through market forces. Government was also confident that employers embodied laissez-faire policies congruent with its own. A leading engineering employer, Wiliam Mather, commenting on the 1892 Act, argued that 'it must be worked in the mode of a rate in aid of voluntary action and not superseding voluntary action ... ' (ibid., col. 424). The uncertainty associated with the government's position lay in the belief that short-term rational economic behaviour by individual employers was somehow consistent with a *national* policy for technical education. The rationale behind this ambiguity is not difficult to discern.

Commitment to laissez-faire doctrines was a prominent feature of Victorian Britain's economic affairs and was reflected in attitudes to technical education. A key figure in this general philosophy was John Stuart Mill, who said: 'the great majority of things are worse done by the intervention of government than the individuals most interested in the matter would do them, or cause them to be done ... ' (1848, 1994: 331). The Commissions of the 1850s and 1860s (Small Arms Commission 1854; RC on TU 1868; and the later RC on Technical Instruction 1884) revealed the government's reliance upon the workings of the market with respect to technical education. According to market principles, demand for technical education would call forth appropriate supply; if demand was not forthcoming supply would respond accordingly (*The Times* 1868; Playfair 1869b; Forster 1870; Lord Armstrong 1878, 1888; *The Times* 1896–7). The relation between market forces and educational development is further articulated in the various pieces of legislation relevant to technical education up to the turn of the century and in the first decades of the 20th century, discussed below.

These views parallel the Royal Commission in 1884 in advocating that further public funds should not be allocated to technical education: 'It will be necessary to look ... to local sources for any large additions to the funds' (Report of RC on TI, Parliamentary Papers, Vol. XXIX, 1884a, col. 515). Wholehearted state intervention in technical education developments was discouraged under a liberal ideology, with its stress on individualism and market forces. This casts doubts on the strength or even the existence of the so-called technical education 'movement'.

Consensualist accounts of technical education development underrate the economic and wider social implications of work reorganisation. Laissez-faire economic behaviour, with which technical education was assumed by government to correlate, was essentially short term. But the government's putative aim for technical education was premised upon long-term projections for skilled labour (RC 1884b; Bryce 1895). Thus from the 1850s, well into the next century, there was no recognition that the disjunction between government's assumptions regarding technical education and the working of the free market relating to it led to the neglect of technical education development, and that this was one of the major consequences of 'short-termism'. This situation prevailed despite the intervention of well-known public figures.

The influence of prominent public figures on the origins of technical education

Technical education literature has been largely dominated by a stress on the way the force of foreign competition stimulated the interest of key public figures in England, 'who have spoken for technical education ... [providing] ... stimuli towards technical education throughout the 19th century' (Musgrave

1966: 177). The influence of prominent people associated with the rise of technical education pervades most of the literature, permeating accounts which emphasize an evolutionary model of technical education, and perpetuate the idea of an unambiguous development. From this point of view, technical education evolved steadily throughout the century; by 1851 'many important features of the system had already emerged'. By 1882 the broad outlines of the development were 'largely determined' (Cotgrove 1958: 15). The main stimulus was direct and came from scientists and philanthropists (ibid., p. 22). Such was their assumed prescience, their pronouncements on scientific and technical education reached elevated status: they were a 'handful of prophets', Lyon Playfair, T. H. Huxley, Bernhard Samuelson, who 'campaigned ceaselessly [for technical education] ... against the tide of the time ... ' (Argles 1964: 136; Simon 1965: 165). Matthew Arnold was said to have stimulated the technical education movement by, 'ceaselessly pointing ... to the growing demand for technical training for the lower classes' (Armytage 1964: 63).

Continental countries' educational developments were different in that they paralleled technological developments. The poor quality of English education 'worsened the country's industrial position' vis-à-vis Europe. It is clear that in Britain technical education was hampered throughout the century by the equivocation of the government and the suspicion and obduracy of the employers over access it.

Despite opposition, the interest of key figures such as Playfair, Huxley, Roscoe and Samuelson continued and was central to any technical education initiative, keeping it before the public eye, when, but for them, 'it might have been forgotten ... ' (Musgrave 1966: 177). The passing of the 1889 Technical Instruction Act set the seal on the movement's development; it also confirmed its bias towards a part-time pattern.

Pressure from influential public figures had a broader function than advocating the provision of extra classes for technical education; it also generated political support for the movement, such that 'the Liberal identification with cause of technical education was complete in 1881' (Ward 1973: 34). The strength of the contribution of scientists, the link with the Liberals and their imputed support for a 'movement' lay in the value of extended science education as a means of improving economic efficiency. Their influence was significantly affected by the vagueness surrounding the so-called 'movement' for technical education and the baneful effects of an ill-coordinated system of general education which prevailed.

The idea of a technical education 'movement': South Kensington

The government department responsible for education in schools was located in South Kensington. After 1878 the City and Guilds of London Institute was also centred there in the form of the Central Institute, which began operations in 1880. Thus it is accepted that a technical education movement had its origins in this source.

1851 is presumed to have marked the beginning of this 'movement', symbolised by the Great Industrial Exhibitions. Two exhibitions in particular figure in accounts of the development of technical education, those of 1851 and 1867.

Cotgrove (1958) cites the 1851 Exhibition in London as a main stimulus for a technical education movement, and argues: 'the threat to Britain's industrial pre-eminence [was] first apparent at the 1851 Exhibition ... [and] provided one of the strongest arguments in support of technical instruction ... ' (p. 19). The Department of Science and Art at South Kensington was the 'cradle of technical education'; the 'spirit of South Kensington has shone over technical education for over one hundred years' (Argles 1964: 12).

After the Great Exhibition of 1851 a technical education 'cause' evolved and gathered momentum in the second half of the century. The 1867 Exhibition in Paris pointed the way forward for technical education in Britain through the foundation of provincial institutes, adding further impetus to the movement. The fear of economic competition from Europe forced industrialists to 'raise their voices in advocacy of technical education ... ', becoming in the process the mainspring of educational reform in England (Ashby 1965: 784–5). German economic competition had a part to play, providing a further impetus to the foundation of institutions of 'technology and education' in England.

The movement thus expanded and the stage between 1881 and 1884 was heralded by the 'trumpet blast' of the appointment of a Royal Commission in 1881 to inquire into the provision of technical education in England (Argles 1965). There was also a ripple effect with the formation of the Central Institute of the CGLI. Birmingham, Manchester, Bristol and other industrial cities vied for prestige in establishing foundations as part of the surging Victorian entrepreneurism. But was all this no more than window-dressing?

This exaggerated focus on a technical education movement attributes the rise of technical education as a response to the political pressures of economic decline. One of the main sources of these pressures was the Exhibition jurors' reports covering the various industrial categories exhibited by the competing nations and published a short while afterwards.

A technical education movement in England therefore evolved in part as a response to criticisms from English jurors, the main thrust of which was that by the 1860s Continental countries were technologically 'superior', as shown by the exhibits at London and Paris: 'the Great Industrial Exhibition of Paris in 1867 ... revealed a state of affairs highly discreditable to England ... as a result there was ... *near panic and a movement was initiated ... this was the technical education movement*' (Cardwell 1972a: 111; my emphasis). Impelled by the lack of economic competitiveness on the part of British industry during the second half of the century, the Department at South Kensington has come to be represented as one of the most far-reaching developments following the Great Exhibition of 1851. Underpinned by a clear and unquestioned relation between science, economic performance and technical training, the stress on economic competitiveness embodied a consensual notion of technical education primarily structured to meet the needs of industry through the improvement of labour efficiency. A concept of technical education positively contributing to a national culture was non-existent; technical education was purely instrumental. More significantly, the general educational infrastructure was not sufficiently developed or adequately administered to support a technical education movement.

General education provision

Growth in educational provision in England and Wales from mid-century was not continuous or coherent. Often, agencies responsible for various aspects of education appeared to be not only independent of others, but also operated with little regard to their existence. For example, there was a Committee of Council with two departments running side by side: the Elementary School Department which was independent of, and received no aid from, the Science and Art Department, both under the President of the Council. In the 1860s administration of these two principal agencies of state-provided education was imperfect (RC on Secondary Education 1895: 9). The teaching profession in 1868 was principally concerned with servicing both elements controlled by the Committee of Council and was almost entirely unorganised, its members isolated, with few common aims (ibid., p. 14).

There was also a third body involved in state education, the Charity Commissioners. This institution had little to do with the Education Department at Whitehall, and hardly had any contact with the Science and Art Department at South Kensington. The Charity Commission, had an important relation to certain aspects of the apprenticeship system. It was responsible for the administration of various charities' funds, including the financing of apprentice schemes, for example, those concerned with children 'under care', such as paupers.

Another agency, the Endowed School Commissioners, was loosely aligned to the administrative structure of the others, but also seemed to act independently. In 1874 this Commission was merged with the Board of Charity Commissioners. Subsequent Acts modified the function of this body, giving it wider powers regarding endowed schools. But later, the Bryce Report considered its significance weak and powers inadequate (ibid., p. 9).

Other Government schools existed outside the Education Department. There were union and workhouse schools under the Poor Law Board; military and regimental schools under the War Office; naval and ship schools under the Admiralty; factory and 'industrial schools' under the Home Office. The administration of this disparate group of educational agencies was poor, one view being that it was in 'a state of chaotic confusion' (Playfair 1871: 61).

During the period from the 1860s through the 1890s the organisation and development of provided education and its administration was neither logical nor consistent (RC on Secondary Education 1895: 17). The lack of coherence and organisation in general education was reflected in the early attempts to develop a national system of technical education. Both suffered similar problems with funding. After the 1889 Act, technical 'instruction' grants (the 1889 Act referred to technical 'instruction', not technical 'education') were being made with little regard to parallel grants made by the Science and Art Department. The overall effect generated needless competition and overlapping of effort.

As early as the 1860s and 1870s artisans advocated the need for technical education provision, based on the apprenticeship system. They concluded that such a model would require state funding. But the government departments were ill-equipped both in administration and funding to control and oversee a universal system of technical education. This could account for the prevailing tendency of educational administrators at the time to consider technical education narrowly as an extension of 'science education'. The agency responsible for science in schools in the 1860s and 1870s was the Science and Art Department.

The Science and Art Department at South Kensington

The Department of Science and Art was formed in 1853 under the direction of Henry Cole. He was joined in 1856 by the chemist Lyon Playfair, who was Professor of Chemistry at the School of Mines from its inception and had played a leading role in organising the Great Exhibition of 1851. He represented the Universities of Edinburgh and St Andrews as a Liberal from 1868 to 1885. Despite the overwhelming success of Britain in the 1851 Exhibition, Playfair was among the few critics who seemed to realise that it was to mark the end of industrial pre-eminence for Britain, not the beginning (Williams (ed.) 1969: 421).

Playfair assumed responsibility for the 'science' aspects of the Department. One of the primary objectives of the Department was the administration of a system of grants for the provision of science teaching in schools. This provision was limited in the period from the 1850s. In 1860 there were nine 'science' schools, with 500 pupils, in 1867 212 schools with 560 classes and 10,230 pupils (Privy Council 1867b). Official data for the period 1855–78 demonstrate that government expenditure on elementary education, science and art increased from 1.26 per cent to 4.88 per cent in absolute terms. But the relative disposition of funds specifically for science and art fell 14 per cent in the same period (British Association 1879: 466). Other official data for the period 1871–2 to 1878–9 confirm the decline in expenditure on science and art: total expenditure for education in Great Britain, £1,107,430; expenditure on science and art, £211,083 (19%) (1871); with figures of £2,732,534 and £305,324 (11%) respectively for 1878–9 (PRO ED 23/71, Appendix A, 1889); Table 6.1

Table 6.1 Actual expenditure on education and science in Britain 1871–1880

Year	For education (£)	For science and art (£)
1871–2	1 107 430	211 083 (19)[a]
1972–3	1 313 078	230 420
1873–4	1 424 877	257 788
1874–5	1 566 275	262 637
1875–6	1 881 630	285 234 (15)
1876–7	2 127 522	301 620
1877–8	2 463 287	299 494
1878–9	2 732 534	305 324 (11)
1879–80	2 854 067	317 086

Note: [a] Figures in brackets represent percentage of total expenditure spent on science and art.

Source: Actual expenditure as per appropriation accounts, Board Memorandum, App. A (PRO Document ED 23/71).

In this early period, science education was equated with technical education, partly explaining the government's reluctance to distinguish and take responsibility for technical education. The Directory's policy on technical education, as an extension of science teaching, was flawed, underfunded and provision generally inadequate.

That the Directory at South Kensington considered science and technical education to be more or less synonymous may be inferred from a Science and Art minute of 1867: 'In order to assist the artisan classes who may show an aptitude for scientific instruction, My Lords resolve to aid local efforts ... '. And later the rule covering the award of exhibitions for Science in Schools/

Colleges stated ' ... The exhibitioner must be of the artisan class or a poor student, as defined by the Science Directory' (Privy Council 1867a). Pressure for 'technical education', from whatever source, was perceived by the Directory as proposals for the extension of existing provision rather than demands for a new form of education. But even existing provision for science teaching in schools was not meeting the needs as perceived by certain groups of workers, such as skilled workers. There was no change in structure or content in the Directory's scheme for at least 30 years.

In terms of administration and funding, science and art education was a relatively low government priority over this period. The reluctance of the state to extend its financial and administrative responsibility in this area of education was paralleled by the static nature of the curriculum in the same period, through to the 1890s. Apart from the issues of government priorities regarding funding and administrative responsibility, there was the issue of what was taught under the heading 'science' and to whom it was directed. A Select Committee set up in 1868 provided an initial focus for these issues.

The Paris Exhibition of 1867, and the Select Committee on Science Instruction

The Select Committee on Science Instruction was appointed following critical reports from observers at the Paris International Exhibition of 1867. Among them were submissions by Lyon Playfair and another well-known scientist of the period, John Scott-Russell, who were jurors at the Exhibition. They focused attention on the relatively poor placing of British industrial contributions. Playfair suggested that the 'failure' of British manufacturers vis-à-vis Continental countries was primarily due to a lack of technical education. Writing to the Chairman of the Select Committee, Lord Taunton, in 1867, he emphasised that continental countries 'possess good systems of industrial education for the workers and managers of factories and workshops, and that English possesses none ... ' (Playfair to Taunton, 1867). Playfair thus initiated the first public discussion of this issue by criticising the lack of technical education provision in England through the columns of *The Times*. Fellow Exhibition jurors, and others, supported his arguments.

Frankland, scientist and fellow-juror, argued that the lack of science education was a defect in school and college education which 'affects the masters and managers of our factories even more deeply than the workman themselves ... ' (*Engineering*, 19 July 1867, p. 48) Frankland's contention was that lack of scientific training, in physics and chemistry especially, prevented them from 'originating inventions and improvements'.

In the machine-tool section another Paris juror maintained that the lack of technical education would lead to increasing costs and a lowering of quality of work turned out by artisans (McConnell 1867). Scott-Russell added to his previous comments in the official Exhibition reports by advocating some form of 'technical training' for 'all youth destined to skilled trades and occupations' (*Engineering*, ibid., p. 49).

The evidence taken by the Select Committee was used to evaluate the system of science instruction in schools and other institutions and of the aid granted to it. This evidence fell under two headings, giving some indication what 'science' was held to be, and to whom it was presumed to be of value. Science teaching was thus reviewed under (i) the state of scientific instruction of (a) the foremen and workmen engaged in manufacture, (b) the smaller manufacturers and managers, (c) the proprietors and managers-in-chief of large industrial undertakings; (ii) the relation of industrial education to industrial progress. The division between the groups was clearly identified in the Report and its distinctive structure reflected the relation between science and industry held by scientists. The influence of Continental systems, although treated with circumspection, was found in an appeal from an engineer juror for the setting up of an institution like the Arts et Métiers of Paris (ibid., p. 48). This, it was argued, would be valuable not only to working men and their 'superiors' but to engineers.

Technical education as an extension of science teaching

Playfair and the Select Committee focused on factors which they assumed were inhibiting productive efficiency. The lack of science education was perceived as having a critical bearing on the competence of those engaged in the manufacturing industries. The assumption was that by defining science education as technical education, technical requirements and also the social needs of industry could be satisfied. On this latter point, Playfair was to note in his letter to Taunton that industry 'suffered from the want of cordiality between the employers of labour and workmen ... ' (Playfair to Taunton 1867). The Select Committee supported this view and outlined an educational scheme in its proposals, emphasising the need for efficient elementary schools (for foremen and workmen) and the reorganisation of secondary schools (for the smaller manufacturers and managers). The proprietors and managers-in-chief were considered the group to benefit from the other principal recommendation that 'there was a claim upon national funds for grants in aid of the provision of superior colleges of science and superior schools for technical instruction requiring costly buildings and laboratories' (Select Committee on Scientific Instruction 1868). It also accepted that the range of sciences offered under the Directory suited the various grades of industrial worker and management in the manufacturing industry, provided elementary and secondary education were greatly improved: 'foremen ... for example were unable except rarely, to take advantage of scientific instruction ... ' (SC on SI, p. iii). The Inquiry also noted that second only to the defective elementary instruction of the student was the scarcity of science teachers: 'science teaching is scarcely followed as a profession ... ' (ibid., p. v).

The clear implication was that a scarcity of science teachers and the depressed state of general education were linked to the inadequacies in industrial 'efficiency', as suggested by Playfair, Scott-Russell and other Exhibition jurors. It was Playfair who raised the issue of the parlous state of science teaching in the House of Commons when he revealed that at the time of the Select Committee of Inquiry, there were no science teachers under training anywhere in England (Hansard 1869b).

The Directory's science scheme, however, reaffirmed the theoretical emphasis of the sciences and a narrow interpretation of their function: 'The object of the grant is to promote instruction in Science especially among the industrial classes by affording a limited and partial aid or stimulus towards the funding and maintenance of Science schools and classes' (Privy Council 1868, Appendix D). These provisions were subject to market forces and not intended to encourage gratuitous provision. Local funds were to be used for providing suitable premises. If these were not found, it was inferred 'that there is no [such] demand as the government is justified in aiding for instruction in the locality ... ' (ibid., p. 43).

At the time the Directory at South Kensington coordinated and organised a mainly theoretically-based examination structure of 23 subjects. Included under this structure were some subject areas that might be termed 'technological': mechanical drawing; mechanical, plane and solid geometry; mechanical and machine drawing; theoretical mechanics; applied mechanics; magnetism and electricity; elementary and higher mathematics (Privy Council 1867b: 18).

Thus the limited aid and theoretical bias of the Directory's scheme continued, the structure and content remaining intact with the approved list and examination procedure unchanged until 1898, when two further subjects were added, hygiene and agriculture.

Few engineering courses existed, but a proposal was put at a Society of Arts meeting in 1868 by Scott-Russell for a course for 'the mechanical engineer and machinist' (*Journal Society of Arts* (July 1868), p. 628). In content it was similar to the subject elements contained in the Directory's approved 'science' list. The course outlined is shown in Table 6.2. The concept of a six-month 'sandwich' was innovatory, as was the 'course of travel'. Neither seems to have become the norm in the late 19th or early 20th century.

The theoretical bias of the sciences offered by the Directory and Scott-Russell suggested a high level of expectation, despite prevailing criticism

Table 6.2 The mechanical engineer and machinist: a three-year course (J. Scott-Russell)

THE MECHANICAL ENGINEER AND MACHINIST

A THREE YEARS' COURSE

[Proposed by J. Scott-Russell]

First Year

Pure Science	Mathematics Physics Chemistry Descriptive geometry
Applications of Science	Elements of mechanism Strength of materials of construction

Practical work in laboratories and drawing offices and museums to accompany each study.

Second Year

Pure Science	Mathematics Physics Natural history Constructive geometry
Applications of Science	Prime movers and steam engines Nature of raw materials History of inventions Elements of mechanism

Practical work in laboratories and drawing offices and museums to accompany each study.

Third Year

Pure Science	Mathematics Ultimate mathematical physics Political economy Statics of machinery Hydraulic machinery

Table 6.2 continued

Applications of Science	Prime movers Electro-magnetic mechanism Engine tools Metallurgy Design of factories

Practical work to be carried on in laboratories, drawing office and museums, and collections of machinery during the Session.

Practical work in factories and workshop should, if possible, alternate with study in periods of six months.

At the end of apprenticeship a course of travel, with work and study, should be recommended.

Source: *Journal of the Society of Arts*, 24 July 1868, p. 628.

that elementary education was at a poor level. It also embodied a degree of over-optimism, given that in 1867 any person wishing to be recognised as a science teacher was free to do so provided he 'offers himself for examination once a year' (Privy Council 1867a). A science 'school' or class was quite simply any place where one or more of the Directory's sciences was taught, and teachers in such a situation received payment according to results (ibid.).

However, arguments put forward for technical education by Playfair, T. H. Huxley, and, to a lesser extent, Scott-Russell in the main were clearly proposals for an extension of existing science education provision. For example, Huxley argued, 'the great thing wanted [in technical education] was scientific instruction to artisans ... ' (Huxley 1868: 199). His view stemmed from his close connection with the Mechanics' Institute at the time. As external examiner in the sciences to the various institutes, he was receiving an annual average of 2,000 sets of papers, mainly from artisans. Other examiners in these fields could expect three or four times that number of papers (Hansard 1869a). As principal of the School of Mines, he was also aware of the practical interest shown by artisans in the series of science lectures put on by that institute. The 600 tickets issued for artisans in connection with the series were regularly over-subscribed (Privy Council 1868, col. 160).

Scott-Russell's research into Continental technical education on behalf of the Samuelson Commission of 1868 led him to a similar conclusion: 'the teaching of science was indispensable for youths intended to be craftsmen ... '. He was convinced that the reported advantages in European industrial efficiency were due to systematic scientific education (*JSOA* 1867, 7 June).

Playfair had long been an active supporter of state-provided education. His earlier comments to the 1868 Select Committee have been noted. In 1888, he could still argue that 'the object of technical education is to give an intelligent knowledge of the sciences and arts which lie at the basis of all industries … ' (Playfair 1888: 327). He asserted that because industry had become more scientific, its management had become more 'professional': 'Industrial occupations are acquiring the dignity of a profession, because they are now based on a knowledge of science' (ibid. p. 332).

There is an interesting parallel here with Marx's views. Writing with reference to the revolutionary technical basis of industry, Marx argued, 'by means of machinery, chemical processes and other methods, it is continually causing changes not only in the technical basis of production, but also in the functions of the labourer, and in the social combinations of the labour-process' (Marx 1887, 1977: 457). The point is not to reveal assumed congruities between the theories of Playfair and Marx but to suggest that the emphasis on 'science' characterised in the work of these commentators of the early period concealed an ambiguity in their contribution to educational thinking at the time.

Notwithstanding his approval of the idea of technology as applied science, Scott-Russell had reservations about the separation of science and technology in contemporary thinking and expressed concern about the removal of theory from practice. He argued, 'the divorce of practice from science has been the great misfortune of our generation … ' (Scott-Russell 1869: 349). 'Students', he said, 'should be exposed to the best examples of craftsmanship' (ibid.).

He maintained that the separation created a division between management and labour. The former, lacking skill, abrogated responsibility to a 'middleman' and became 'a buyer and seller of other men's work'. Skill, he asserted, disappeared under the 'reigning maxim of "cheap work" to be sold dear' (ibid., pp. 119, 126).

Writing in the *Journal of the Society of Arts*, he also introduced the first use of the concept of 'further education'. He described it as follows:

> … a schooling midway between the elementary day school and the workshop, which the youth should enter after he knows his reading, writing and counting, in order to learn to apply his reading, writing and calculation to his purpose of requiring such knowledge of mathematics, mechanics, numerology, chemistry, drawing etc., … '. (*Journal SoA* 7 June 1867)

The implications of Scott-Russell's notion of 'further education' for the long-term development of English technical education have been underestimated. His proposition gave credence to the views of employers concerned with piecework and the apprenticeship system, that demands for technical education were best met, if at all, on a part-time pattern. If 'further education' implied evening classes, then such a system suited a conception of technical education which made few demands on production time. Other models, such as 'day-release' or full-time periods of education of short duration, were not seriously considered as alternatives. A possible reason for this was the lack of understanding of the changing patterns of technological and organisational innovation being implemented at the time.

Scott-Russell retained his conviction that science education was a means of improving technical efficiency and later broadened his views on further education in his definition of the technical college as an institution of continuing education: 'Technical Colleges have a special duty to those who leave education at 18. They are to be shown how all the abstract science they have learnt leads up to the work they are about to do' (Scott-Russell 1869: 347). However, with Playfair, Huxley and Frankland, he misjudged the crucial influence of strong industrial employers. Almost by definition, the institutional context of technical education was conceived in a way which abstracted it from the organisation of work and actual industrial work practices. Their limited recognition of the interaction between work, technology and technical education precluded consideration of technical education other than on a part-time basis.

The rationale underlying the part-time principle in technical education

The redefinition and regulation of artisan skills were contingent upon management strategies, particularly those aiming to replace skilled labour through a policy of substitution. The implementation of 19th-century technology was as much a political as a technical phenomenon; the relation between technology and technical education coalesced within the framework of skilled labour reproduction.

Technical education, not perceived as a top priority, was 'tolerated' by employers so long as it remained peripheral to workshop procedures. The location of technical education in evening classes was an extension of the condition that low-cost production should remain uninterrupted, as exemplified in the 'Butty' system; the logic of technical production was clear. Immediate production concerns were paramount. Limited technical education was to be a part of the continuation school which functioned to meet the needs of the wider social system. A pattern of technical education based on a part-time principle equated with the structural needs of employers seeking to minimise possible loss of labour time through absence of young workers at classes. The figures for part-time day and evening classes indicate the scale: a 1911 survey showed there were just over 14,000 day students in technical institutes, and 765,000 evening students (cited by Cotgrove 1958: 68).

There was an assumed cohesion and interlocking of reorganised work, technical education and the social system which is often stressed in accounts postulating integrated developments in technical education. This representation obscures the reality that technical education was conceived and developed in an ambiguous and limited way, as the late 19th-century legislation and the formation of the City and Guilds of London Institute will show.

Employers, resisting government appeals to demonstrate a positive attitude to the development of a national technical education system, insisted upon a part-time model: 'They were unwilling to believe that there were any benefits to be gained by making any significant adjustments in established patterns of work organisation' (Robertson 1974: 23, 24).

By 1902 the part-time, evening pattern of technical education had become institutionalised. It was dominated by the idea that it was the only viable means of any form of further education, including remedial education, available to the mass of young workers. Technical education had been consolidated into a part-time, evening pattern premised upon the assumption of its abstraction from the workplace and the apprenticeship system. The apprenticeship system was not regarded as embodying any educational character, technical or otherwise. Technical education was perceived as theoretical and examinable, and, by definition, exclusive from work.

Technical education as separate from the workplace

Huxley, a leading member of the inaugural committee members of the CGLI, advocated a part-time pattern for technical education. He maintained, however, that the demands of industrial work took precedence over theoretical classes: '[if they were not] to tap the reservoir of labour needed in the great manufactories ... the only way was to augment the apprenticeship with evening classes, but these would have to be local' (quoted in Lang 1978: 17).

An early 20th-century version of this thinking equated evening classes with 'continuation schools'. These schools were favoured as a means of technical education, particularly in towns where small workshops prevailed: (Sadler 1907), 'The main impulse to the [technical education] *movement* for the increase of technical continuation schools, has come from towns in which the small workshop has held its own against the advance of the factory system ... ' (Sadler (ed.) 1907: 532; my emphasis) Confirmation of this dual aspect of technical education came in a Board of Education report: 'The usual combination of workshop and school in the preparation for industrial work assigns the evening only to school and requires the young worker during the day to give full-time attendance in the workshop ... evening classes have provided an open avenue for talent ... ' (1908, para. 98, p. 83). This has reinforced the view that the part-time evening class model was inevitable: 'it is difficult to see how, under the circumstances ... technical education could have developed other than as an extension of night school' (Cotgrove 1958: 66). The 'circumstances' in question were the 'apathy' of the leaders of manufacturing industry and the 'indifference of' the workers towards technical education, and a lack of technical qualifications among managers (ibid., pp. 93, 94).

Other factors, were equally crucial to the 'circumstances' governing technical education provision. The introduction of new machine technologies, increasingly based on automatic principles, and the employers' widening control over the labour process, were highly significant developments, representing radical changes in labour control and training. The employers were extraordinarily well placed, for the first time in the history of metal working, to perform complex operations, with accuracy, on machines using unskilled labour. The rationale for perpetuating the traditional craft apprenticeship was therefore successfully challenged by them. They gained further purchase over the artisans by meeting current production demands without employing the same level of skilled artisans, or entertaining any pressing need for a technical education system.

The corporate strength of employers and their grip on the development of advanced technologies radicalised their attitudes towards the whole issue of technical training and instruction. Their dogmatism grew as artisan resistance to labour substitution diminished, especially after the 1897–8 strike and lockout. Technical training and education became irrelevancies in the drive to improve production and thus, a small minority of employers excepted, technical education was marginalised.

Only a very limited number of companies displayed more than a passing interest in technical education. These were highly concerned with company-specific skills, not with reproduction of generalised work skills. This represented, not so much interest in training skilled labour, as actively seeking ways to replace it with automated machines and cheaper labour, and strengthening the culture of new working practices.

Artisans, on the other hand, could claim a long-standing, respectable history in the attempts to establish technical education.

Early technical education: an alternative perspective

In the 1860s and 1870s the Directory's science provision and the Society of Arts's technical examination scheme were the only available sources of what could be loosely called 'technical education'.

Artisans held a different conception of science, alongside the prevailing orthodoxy. The first TUC conference, sensing the need for adequate primary education as a precondition of technical education, proposed: 'this

Congress, recognising the immense value of education, primary and technical, recommends the trades of the U.K. to aid by all means of their power, in every effort to advance national education' (TUC Minutes 1868). Apart from their own independent sources, such as the Artizans' Institute, the Workingmen's School Union, and the Trades Guild of Learning (discussed below), the TU Congresses focused upon the traditional system of craft apprenticeship, regarding it as a central feature of technical education: 'the genuineness, and the superiority of British manufacture was built up under the old system of apprenticeship, which, though rude, and often tyrannical *was a sort of technical education*' (ibid.; my emphasis). The relationship between primary education and technical education was clearly reaffirmed: 'primary education should without delay be applied to every child in the kingdom and that in addition to this a good technical education should be open to every person engaged in connection with the industry of the country' (ibid., 1871).

The 1874 Congress urged further independent action appropriate to their needs:

> ... the time has come when it would be well for the *workingmen's organisations to actively take up the question of technical education, with a view to developing skill* and that with this object, schools for technical instruction ought to be established in every centre of industry, supported by grants from the Education Department. (Ibid., 1874; my emphasis)

The term 'further independent action' highlighted the fact that a number of working-class initiatives in this direction had been attempted in 1867–9.

This was a new concept of technical education, embodying a recognition of its relation to the acquisition of 'skill', as the 1874 resolution testifies in its reference to 'technical education' and 'technical instruction'. The TUC clearly acknowledged their members' need for technical education based on universal primary education. There was also a recognition that such provision would require government support and could not be overdependent upon voluntary provision.

Thus union thinking on technical education throughout this period was premised upon the idea of the inseparability of a structured craft training system and some form of technical education. In 1880 it was resolved that 'a regular system of *indentured apprenticeship* extending over a stipulated period is *the best means of furthering the development of technical knowledge and increasing the skill of workmen* in the United Kingdom' (ibid., 1880 (Congress at Dublin); my emphasis). Such a proposition appears far-sighted, but revealed a misreading of the prevailing industrial situation. Neither sustaining the apprenticeship in its historic form nor supporting a national technical-education system figured in the employers' industrial policies. It was also plain that from 1852, skilled workers were being drawn inexorably into a struggle against the pressures of a 'market-led' economy and the effects of an ideology of short-termism, held by both State and employers. Pervading this ideology was the conviction that British industry was well adapted to current needs and demands. Encouraged by the strength of their belief in the free-market, employers adhered to essentially short-term measures.

'Short termism' in this context referred to a conception of planning for skilled-labour reproduction based on meeting current industrial and commercial demands, not projecting future skilled-labour requirements – a view still held, as one modern employer recently reiterated: 'We have to train for today's jobs and today's requirements ... we should have to train for those jobs which already exist and not worry that these jobs may not exist in 10 years time ... ' (Smith, of the Sturmey-Archer Company, quoted by Carroll (1979).

The first critical factor that artisans failed to acknowledge was the extent to which technical education had become tied to market forces. They were unable to foresee that, for all practical purposes, its development was being relegated to a series of ad hoc strategies within which they were to have an increasingly diminished role.

Problems underlying the TUC case for retention of the apprenticeship system as a base for technical education

The unions perceived the employers' increasing use of unskilled labour through machine technology as a direct threat destined to weaken their workshop autonomy. Employer control over the labour process thus had significant implications for the attitudes and policies on technical education the artisans were attempting to put forward as part of the general aim to preserve the apprenticeship system.

It was central to the union argument that it was only through systematic training that the craftsman could effectively resist skill dequalification and decline to a 'mere appendage of the machine'. In 1885 it was argued therefore that through the apprenticeship system '[the] workman would become the controller of the mechanical forces; [and] instead of being part of a machine he would supply the knowledge, the skill, and the artistic taste' (TUC Minutes, 1885). TUC proposals for technical education, apparently unambiguous in their intent, however obscured a second factor, the social and technical significance of a fundamental principle in union policies: their assumed craft and social exclusivity. The historical pattern of trade practices rigidly excluded non-apprenticed workers, especially in negotiations with employers. In presenting a case for some form of technical education, artisans repeatedly sought to distance themselves from unskilled workers. In this they were prepared to align themselves with the employers over certain issues, for example, improving 'industrial efficiency', in order to secure their skilled status vis-à-vis the unskilled. This had little effect on the employers' position regarding craft training and education, for they were implementing new technologies which relied less on skilled workers and made substitution viable and more profitable. Hence any basis for skilled employee–employer cooperation was undermined, weakening the case for a technical education system based on the apprenticeship form of trade training. The question of artisan status and privilege became one of the central issues in the 1897–8 conflict.

Employer domination of production processes correlated directly with the force of their control over innovative technologies and in inverse relation to the strength of the craft-apprenticeship system. If the unions claimed the apprenticeship system to be central to technical education, it followed that employer control over the apprenticeship was construed as also control over incipient technical education. A link may be established between two apparently unconnected events: the debates on technical education from the 1860s and the engineering strike and lockout nearly 40 years later. Given the increasing structural strength of the employers, what initiatives regarding technical education were open to artisans?

Despite incongruities, the craft unions had made a significant contribution to technical education thinking at the time. In formulating their challenge to employer tactics on new technological implementation, artisans turned to alternative propositions on technical-education provision, through which they attempted to strengthen their claims to skilled status and exclusivity. Over the years from the end of the previous century they had put forward a number of educational initiatives which were out of the mainstream of educational thinking and have been frequently underestimated in recent historiography.

Accounts of trade union attitudes to technical education

Nineteenth-century craft unions are often portrayed as apathetic, indifferent and even hostile to technical education. The unionised workers, that is, the skilled workers, are said to have been concerned only with their own sectional interests. This perception serves to justify an acceptance of the inevitable separation of technical education from work and, in particular, the apprenticeship system. It also serves to reinforce the argument that technical education was an evolutionary development arising out of the existing school structure.

The Webbs (1920b), despite their advocacy of workers' education, provide an illustration of this perspective: 'Notwithstanding their almost infinite variety of technical detail, trade union regulations may be reduced to economic devices: Restriction of numbers and the Common Rule' (p. 704). The narrow interest of trade unionism was said to have embodied little notion of technical education. Trade exclusivity was their hallmark; they were intent on restricting access to jobs traditionally done by artisans: 'For a whole generation, from the fifties to the eighties, the A.S.E. (the Amalgamated Society of Engineers), had tried without effect to exclude unapprenticed men. After that the attempt was abandoned' (Clapham 1938: 326). A more limited perspective maintained that workers were skilled or unskilled, 'according to whether or not entry to the occupations is deliberately restricted and not according to the nature of the occupation itself' (Clegg et al. 1964: 84; Flanders 1964: 184). Flanders (1964), arguing that the apprenticeship controlled not standards, but numbers, said: 'For craft unions the main purpose of an apprenticeship was to regulate entry into the trades they organised. It was one of the buttresses of their basic device ... the restriction of numbers' (p. 184). Trade unions, according to these versions, were 'never wholeheartedly in favour of technical education' (Musgrave 1967: 106); being overconcerned with the supply of labour, they neglected the educational aspects of the traditional apprenticeship system. He said: 'The influence working against technical education was the attitude of the trade unions towards the apprenticeship ... to the unions the apprenticeship carried few educational implications' (p. 71).

But artisan opinions on technical education had been moulded by the outcome of the many industrial disputes from 1850, and most specifically after the 1897–8 conflict. After the defeat in this confrontation they were increasingly concerned with the effects of increasing mechanisation on their artisan status. Unquestionably, their attempts to restrict the number of entrants to the trade had become a source of irritation to employers, who strongly resisted union attempts to retain historic controls over the proportion of apprentices to tradesmen. Such control was a union strategy aimed at subverting the effects of substitution, and was highly contentious during the strike and in the ratification of the Terms of Settlement after the 1897–8 strike and lockout.

Progressive mechanisation of production made any educational element in the traditional apprenticeship redundant. The consolidation of labour controls principally deriving from technological advances, such as the metrological innovations of Whitworth in the 1850s and 1860s, and the discovery of high-speed steel at the turn of the century by F. W. Taylor, continued in the face of union opposition.

The origin of 19th-century technical education, the decline of the apprenticeship system and union apprenticeship policy have been conventionally analysed against a background of reluctant unions opposed to technical education and overconcerned with protectionism.

Another interpretation is clearly possible. The unions were not indifferent to technical education but were actively debating it as part of the general issue of apprenticeship, particularly the ramifications of its decline, as early as 1868 (TUC, 1868 Reports). Throughout most of the 19th century the unions were on the defensive, engaging in a series of struggles over the employers' expanding labour-control strategies, particularly the substitution question. A major part of the union case was a concept of technical education conceived as an extension of the apprenticeship and not abstracted from it.

Arguments relating to union opposition to technical education rest upon a main supposition that technical education was logically an extension of general schooling. The inevitability of a part-time, evening-class pattern of technical education from the 1880s was thus commonly accepted. In view of its separation from the workplace and its location in the school system, for example in the 'continuation' school, it was clear that technical education, on this basis, would develop on a part-time, evening pattern.

It has not often been registered that the skilled workers had had an enduring interest in some form of technical education and were prepared to submit their ideas for consideration. In the main, their perception of what was considered technical education differed from the prevailing dogma.

The roots of working-class influence on technical education

Throughout most of the 19th century a key factor in government attitudes to mass education was the idea that work was the dominant feature in working-class lives. Ironically, certain sections of the working class, the artisans, seemed to concur in this and accepted, for example, a model of secondary education which was based on the principle of evening classes. A motion put by an artisan representative at a Society of Arts Conference (1868) read:

> That as the demands of labour make it impossible that children of the working classes shall be retained at day schools until their education is complete, and as their attendance at evening classes is essential to the completion of their education ... provision should be made ... [for] support for systematic instruction in evening classes. (*JSoA*, 31 Jan. 1868, pp. 185–6)

This resolution, which was passed, portrayed children of the working classes in a certain light: they required education which would facilitate their adaptability and accommodation to the demands of the prevailing labour system.

But as in a previous militant phase, Chartism, workers were also engaged in a more or less constant struggle to improve their working environment. In his analysis of 19th-century skilled workers, E. P. Thompson (1977) argued that the first half of the century must be seen as a period of chronic underemployment, in which the skilled trades 'are like islands threatened on every side by technological innovation and by the inrush of unskilled or juvenile labour' (p. 269). Therefore in the articulation of education and work, the principle of part-time evening classes as the 'means of secondary education' for the masses had a critical bearing on working-class ideas of 'technical education'. The de facto situation did not radically alter throughout the century. After the Cockerton Judgement of 1900, School Boards could only conduct, out of the rates, elementary schools, and in these schools, whether day or evening, only elementary education could be given. This clearly implied that the upper age limit was 14 years. The situation was legalised in 1901 (Memorandum on the new scheme of Regulations for Evening School and Classes under the Board of Education, Statistics and Returns, 1894–1901, PRO Document ED24/83). But evidence from earlier in the period demonstrates that working-class attitudes to education had not always been necessarily normative.

The influence of the Sunday Schools on 19th-century ideas of technical education

The concept of non-state educational provision has had a relatively long working-class history, going back at least to the 1780s. At that time it was an activity engaged in by a fairly broad stratum of the working class; sometimes at considerable cost. Thompson (1977) refers to an 'intellectual culture' of the working class, in which the 'articulate consciousness of the self-taught was above all a political consciousness' (p. 781). Working-class institutions, according to this view, generated a toughness and resilience, in which class acquired significance: 'everything, from their schools to their shops, their chapels to their amusements, was turned into a battleground of class' (ibid., p. 914)

Laqueur (1976) also argued that the years 1780–1850 were formative for education, perceived as part of a working-class culture. Education, he maintained, linked with the ideology of Protestantism, providing the language of radicalism, which found expression in later conflicts between the trade unions and employers. Applegarth, a leading trade unionist, and a member of the Junta, retained some of his evangelical zeal in his work with the carpenters' union in the 1860s. He insisted, for example, on union meetings being conducted in temperance halls rather than public houses. Working-class ideology was also an integrative force in England, particularly through the working of the Sunday Schools (ibid., p. 24 ff). Laqueur maintained that these schools mirrored 'the comparative strength of cohesive over disintegrative forces in society, an aspect of working class culture not often registered' (ibid.).

Nineteenth-century pleas by working-class groups for provision of general and technical education reflected the seriousness and persistence of the workers' earlier educational thinking. This is not to argue that the later ideas on technical education were similarly autonomous or independent. TUC resolutions from 1868 recognised the necessity for some kind of state or employer funding for technical as well as general education. There was plainly a change in technology in use from the 1860s as social and technical relations came to be characterised by the increasing dominance and aggression of industrial employers and the artisans' resistance to work reorganisation. The changing relations of production still embodied some sense of continuity regarding artisan solidarity and education in subsequent developments of the 1860s and 1870s.

Working-class attitudes to education thus remained positive but had been radicalised. Their claims to education, framed by a transformed industrial, social and ideological structure, making greater demands on their time and energy, would not be so readily served as they had been by a self-serving system such as the Sunday School System. After the mid-19th century the educational self-sufficiency engendered by and within the Sunday School movement and beyond was perceived by some workers as less appropriate within the changing relations of production. The Artisans' Reports, produced in 1868 and based on their observations at the Paris Exhibition of 1867, provide a case in point. Contemplating the change from a religious to a more defined secular ideology, institutionalised religion was viewed with scepticism, but not entirely rejected, by artisans. One artisan argued, for example: 'Government in effect now says Education is all-important, it is essential to your welfare ... if you are to have education you must take my dogmas with it ... ' (Randall 1868: 297). This view was reiterated in the following year at an international workingmen's congress by Applegarth, anxious to separate education and religion: 'We are in want of education and the State must give it free from religion' (Applegarth 1869).

The voluntary Sunday School system had been concerned with basic literacy and numeracy in addition to religious studies. Expectations from a universal primary education system, as a preliminary to technical education, of necessity presupposed a more general, 'provided' system. The Sunday Schools had been staffed predominantly by working-class people and funds came from working-class communities.

The amalgamation of skilled working-class ideas of the Protestant ethic and demands for secular education, resulted in agitation for technical education. The more generalised force of the earlier religious ideals was partially reaffirmed in educational thinking in the 1860s. As Laqueur said, 'a highly developed culture of self-help, self-improvement and respectability, which nurtured many of the political and trade union leaders of the working class, emerged from the ... Sunday School' (1977: 155). (Marx was to note, not without cynicism, the same tendency: 'Odger and Applegarth[1] are both possessed with a mania for compromise and a thirst for respectability' (1869: 278).)

The earlier evangelical Christian idealism was therefore evident in some of the later working-class educational developments in the period between the 1860s and 1880s. The alignment with organisations previously sponsored or organised by religious denominations illustrates the point.

The working men's educational union

The Working Men's Educational Union, founded in 1852, was a descendant of the Sunday School Movement. The combination of the religious and the secular may be recognised in its aims: 'the leading feature of this ... organisation was the attempt to unite Christian men ... [and] furnish them at the cheapest possible rate with the material requisites for popular, entertaining and instructive learning' (WMEU 1853: 24).

There were other institutions of a non-religious kind, such as the Co-operative movement, which put forward plans to provide and encourage, through education, 'partnerships in industry' (Ludlow & Jones 1867: 24).

One of the clearest illustrations of 19th-century Evangelism at work in working-class politics was the Working Men's Club and Institute Union (WMC & IU). This organisation was founded ('sponsored') by a Unitarian minister, Henry Solly, in 1862. Solly maintained that the 'integrity' of the working man should be constantly upheld, and asserted that the WMC & IU should be an autonomous institution: 'No working man will go near a club if it is not their own' (Solly 1866). However, later he seems to have lost confidence in the abilities of workmen to organise their own affairs: 'any committee of working men or a committee chosen by the members would be fatal to the movement' (ibid., 12 May, 1868). In the mid-1870s Solly's attitude to working men was thus condemned as patronising and authoritarian: 'Mr. Solly's attempts [at authoritarian control] have not recommended him to the working man. He has never worked unless allowed the entire lead as well as good pay. And he has never been over-scrupulous in obtaining his ends' (Weiler 1875: 131).

It was to the Working Men's Club and Institute Union that certain artisans in London first turned in order to stimulate the development of some kind of technical-education system. As one metal-working artisan expressed it:

> I should like to see a number of institutions, they might be called colleges, or any other name, I would have them fitted up with a number of workshops for different trades, and one large room to be used as a lecture room, ... There should be schools attached ... Working men in large towns have a great difficulty in finding convenience to do anything for themselves by way of improvement. (Winstanley 1867: 165)

Another illustration from a worker in the carriage trade, the nearest equivalent to modern motor-body building, argued:

> It is one of the greatest importance to the workmen that they should possess an intimate knowledge of drawing and mechanical appliances. And I regret to say ... in the great City of London there are no classes or instruction ... I must confess that our French fellow workmen have greater facilities for obtaining [a] more scientific knowledge ... (McGrath, in Reports of Artisans 1867: 169)

These views expressed an artisan perception of the relation between technical education and 'economic' and 'technical efficiency'. They contrast with the scepticism displayed in the employers' journal, *Engineering*:

> We are not aware that any student of our technical schools, and we have several of them, has yet given us a valuable invention ... who would otherwise be *valueless members of the industrial community* ... (*Engineering*, 4, 2 Aug. 1867; my emphasis)

Technical education lacked universal appeal, according to another contemporary journal. It noted:

> We entertain the greatest doubt ... as to the wisdom, in any sense of trumpeting those very generally weak and jejune productions of half educated men, seeing in a country where most of them were ignorant of a word of the language spoken round them, things necessarily understood but imperfectly ... and attempting to make the world believe that the Society had elicited and discovered superhuman talent in their workmen ... ' (*Practical Mechanics Magazine*, Apr. 1868, p. 19)

The views on education and work of at least a fraction of the working class, were treated with an undisguised reserve. Certain artisan groups persevered and for a time developed models for consideration as technical education programmes.

The formation of the workmen's technical education committee

There were more favourable responses to artisan initiatives than the criticisms imply. One of the outcomes of artisan approaches made in the Artisan Exhibition Reports, and to the WMC & IU was the organisation of a conference, sponsored by the Society of Arts, held in March 1868. From this came a proposal to form a Workmen's Technical Education Committee. Its terms of reference included a brief to promote technical instruction in workshops and 'manufactories', to relate the instruction to existing educational provision in accordance with artisans' perceived needs. In particular it was to ascertain how far existing institutions, in London particularly, could be made available for the instruction of 'apprentices and artisans in the principles and practices of their trade' (Report, WTEC 1868).

The committee's inquiries in London found that there was no provision in the metropolis adequate to the wants of workmen, that is at such hours and at such terms that would place such provision within their reach (ibid. p. 6). This confirmed the criticism made by the various contributors to the artisan reports on the 1867 Exhibition. Its recommendations, drawing upon Continental experience, included a plea for the provision of technical schools for instruction in the details of the various handicrafts similar to the 'écoles d'apprentissage in Paris' and a 'Great Central School for foremen like the École des Arts et Métiers in France' (ibid).

Further innovatory ideas emerged from this meeting. There was a proposal for the establishment of suitable training schools for technical teachers. Another, in the final clause of the proceedings, recommended that the law should empower employers to release apprentices 'for a certain portion of their time in obtaining technical and scientific instruction relating to their calling' (ibid., p. 8).

Two significant factors may thus be distinguished: a recognition of a need for specialised training for technical teachers and one of the first proposals for part-time day release. A similar proposition was put in the following year by Scott-Russell in his Systematic Technical Education (1869), who also made reference to an 'F.E.' concept on a part-time day basis.

The WTEC anticipated by some 12 years one of the principal provisions under the City and Guilds system. After 1878, the Central Institute at South Kensington, for example, provided academic technical courses, and also introduced systematic training for technical teachers.

In addition to the more radical proposals for day-release, the WTEC recommended an extension of existing science and art classes. The Jermyn Street classes (School of Mines) were not accessible to artisans during the day, and the evening classes at Kings' and University Colleges were too expensive (ibid). Apart from the issue of time, the question of funding was a critical and recurring factor whenever working-class educational issues such as this were discussed. The legislation which followed the 1889 Technical Instruction Act was also preoccupied with funding for technical education. Thus 20 year after this recommendation by the Workmen's Technical Education Committee it was being argued in the House of Commons: 'there was a want of funds and the fees are so high that the working classes cannot avail themselves as much as is desirable ... very few boys from the elementary schools are able to attend, consequently very little good is done ... ' (Hansard 1869a, Col. 1252).

Money was eventually found from an unexpected source, within the aegis of the Customs and Excise Act of 1890. But in 1869, the first annual meeting of the Workmen's Technical Education Society (WTES) was held in the theatre of the Royal School of Mines in Jermyn Street. Under the chairmanship of Lord Elcho (Earl of Wemyss), it was resolved that a permanent organisation be established with the name 'Workmen's Technical School Union' (*The Times*, 25 June 1869). It was further resolved that 'trade societies be recommended to establish schools, classes, and museums for the children and apprentices of their members ... ' (ibid.). The *Educational Times* noted the significance of the recommendation that large companies ('manufactories') be requested to open schools for technical education in their respective establishments (19 July 1869). Again this deliberation anticipated provisions through the City Livery Companies in 1879.

Skilled workers showed considerable acumen in advocating a form of technical-education provision at least ten years before the establishment of the City and Guilds of London Institute in 1878. The beginnings looked promising. During the first year of the WTEC's existence, in addition to the research into technical-education facilities, nine lectures on engineering-related topics were arranged and delivered between 26 May and 23 June 1869 (*Report of the Proceedings* 1868). But this particular initiative was, in fact, short-lived; the committee disbanded in 1869.

In political terms the Workmen's Technical Education Committee was relatively ineffectual. In the event, it was too late to submit its views and recommendations to a government Committee of Inquiry under Samuelson (S.C. on Scientific Instruction 1868; Chairman, Sir Bernhard Samuelson).

There are a number of possible explanations for the demise of the Workmen's Technical School Union after only one year. There was clearly the question of funding, which was a problem at both local and national level. Further explanations lie within the political and ideological framework of these artisan proposals. The artisans were, in effect, isolated from most of the working class. Their insistence on striving to maintain exclusivity and status had its downside, particularly alienating the unskilled. The employers, intent on breaking the artisan monopoly in the workplace, were unenthusiastic about any development that gave more purchase to the skilled over the development of technical education or technological developments. One compelling explanation of the failure of the artisan initiatives therefore concerned the ambiguous position of the skilled workers relative to the employers and the unskilled. Another was their misguided association with non-working-class figures, such as Lord Elcho and Henry Solly.

The alignment of skilled workers with non-working-class people such as Lord Elcho and Solly compromised skilled workers whenever employers' and artisans' views were incompatible or irreconcilable. It is not entirely clear why Elcho, an ardent anti-socialist, was invited to chair the inaugural meeting of the WTEU. The association with Solly was later to prove misguided also.

The Trades Guild of Learning and the Artisans' Institute

Solly's interest in working-class education was continuing. In 1873 he proposed the formation of a Trades Guild of Learning. His intention was that the guild should promote 'the delivery of lectures and the formation of classes, to assist members of Trade Societies and other skilled workmen in acquiring a knowledge of history, political economy, and technical education ... ' (Solly 1873). This also formed part of a paper read by Solly to the London Trades Council in an effort to encourage their ideological and material support. The response from the Council was to affirm the principle 'without pledging delegates to anything further' (London Trades Council, Minute Book, 8 April 1873).

This cautious response seems to have been justified in the light of subsequent events, as the development of the Artisans' Institute reveals. This Institute was an important off-shoot of the Trades Guild of Learning. It was formed under Solly's direction in 1874. Initially it appeared a substitute for the defunct Workmen's Technical Educational Union in the promotion of technical education, in terms of a 'demand from below'. At its inaugural meeting there were representatives from at least twelve skilled trades, including two from engineering branches.

The Artisans' Institute was innovatory in the sense that through Solly it was proposed to conduct classes staffed by teachers who were themselves tradesmen: 'we regard as a fundamental axiom for any real improvement in Technical teaching ... that we must look among skilled workmen for Technical teachers ... we must give them the means of instructing their fellows' (Solly 1873; Solly 1878: 11). These perceptive ideas on technical education were overlaid by his ambiguous and patronising attitude towards workers. On the one hand was his advocacy of having workers conducting classes. On the other was the prescription for a change in the workers' social attitudes and beliefs: 'A change in the habits and an improvement in the tastes of some workmen, with a willingness on the part of the steadier and more educated shop-mates to help them "onwards and upwards" (Solly 1873). There was also a missionary or reformist ideology behind his proposals. He argued for 'the substitution of Trades Halls and Clubs for public houses as places of business, social intercourse and recreation' (ibid.).

Like the Workman's Technical Education Committee, Solly's initiative was also short-lived. Within three years it was in financial difficulties. The Science and Art Department refused a request for a grant in 1876 (*The Globe*, 30 May 1876). This action reinforces the belief that government was reluctant to commit public funds to this form of technical education at this time. The 'amateur' status of Solly's movements clearly made no appeal to government regarding funding.

But at least one journal considered the Artisans' Institute an important factor in the promotion of trade and technical education of the period. *The*

Globe wrote that 'at the present moment this institute ... contain[s] probably ... whatever germ there is of hope for the survival of English trade' (*The Globe*, 30 May 1876). The Trade Societies, composed mainly of local skilled workers' representatives, were approached again for help by the executive of the Artisans' Institute in 1877 (London Trades Council, *Minute Book*, 11–12, 1877). The Secretary Hodgson Pratt, and an executive member, MP Samuel Morley, after an initial appeal made a further approach in the following year. They proposed that the 'trades should take over and conduct in their own way the Artisans' and Mechanics' Institute in St Martins Lane' (ibid., 12 Feb. 1878). This proposal was considered at length, and finally rejected in June 1878 (ibid., 15 June 1878). In the following year Solly resigned (Solly 1878).

Ambiguities in skilled workers' educational initiatives

A dilemma facing skilled working-class groups in this period seeking sponsorship for educational strategies was tied in with the issue of funding and the attitude of their employers, and the political and ideological position of prominent political figures they chose to associate with over these issues. The ambivalence regarding working-class initiatives in relation to Solly's work with the WMC & IU illustrates the point. In the case of the WTEU the connection with Lord Elcho warrants further consideration.

It is possible that Lord Elcho could have been anti-socialist and even strongly biased against working-class ideas and still embody a positive attitude towards technical education. It is clear, however, that his distrust of workers' combinations makes such an interpretation highly speculative. It was his evident distaste for socialism that highlights the ambiguity of his former association with the Workmen's Technical Education Union and working-class groups generally. '"State socialism", he argued, 'saps the qualities of self-reliance and originality which have been pre-eminently the characteristics of our race' (Elcho 1885).

Later he was associated with employers in an aggressive counter to unionism. In this context he was active in the National Free Labour Association of 1893, an organisation founded by an ex-trade unionist, William Collison. Its avowed aim was to cripple the power of the unions and provide a reserve of 'blackleg' union for employers. In action it took two forms: systematic importation of 'blackleg' labour and legal action against what was considered 'intimidating' picketing. Both elements were involved in the protracted engineering strike and lockout in 1897 (Kynaston 1976: 153; Roberts 1958: 153).

In the light of Elcho's views on trade unions generally, it appears to have been questionable to invite an aristocrat to chair the inaugural meeting of the WTEU. It is again speculative to suggest that it was intended to add respectability and credibility of the venture.

That Elcho had a very circumspect view of trade unions is clear. At best he seems to have been ambivalent: 'trade unions are doing great good, as benefit societies ... [they] are the means of keeping men off the poor rates' (Elcho 1867: 12). In 1866 he had written of his mistrust of trade unions. He was arguing the case for an inquiry into the trade union movement, maintaining that it would 'show the danger of trusting these men with the uncontrolled power which they are seeking ... the tyranny of the unions is such that I see an anti-union union is being formed in Derbyshire ... ' (Elcho to Walpole 1866). Coupled with his views on the ideology of socialism was his belief in the unequivocal 'laws' of laissez-faire economics. He made this plain in his speeches and writing in the period from the 1860s through the 1880s.

At the time of the Workmen's Technical Education Union initiative he was arguing '*the laws of political economy are ... clear and defined ...* as those of nature herself' (Elcho 1867: 10; my emphasis).

Elcho's relation with the workers was clearly tenuous. His response to an invitation by Solly to chair a meeting evoked this reply: 'Is it wise to keep at these working men's clubs a staff of Dukes, Lords and authors ready to take the chair, lecture and speak in the way now proposed ... ' (Elcho to Solly 1865).

The contradictory nature of Elcho's association with workingmen's movements notwithstanding, the assumed need for sponsorship on the part of a fraction of the skilled working class was maintained. In 1870 Elcho was approached to attend a public meeting on technical education to be held in July: 'We can only hope to stimulate the latent energies of the artisan population by continued endeavour and there is no doubt that one way of moving them is by showing that noblemen like yourself and gentlemen ... take an interest in their permanent well-being' (G. Murphy 1870).

The London Trades Council had had different ideas and earlier expressed a clearly opposed view: 'The general conduct of Lord Elcho was such that the Council had no confidence whatever in him' (London Trades Council, *Minute Book* 1868). Elcho, however, exerted influence over working-class affairs through Parliamentary activities, particularly sitting on Select Committees. He was a prominent member of the 1868 Commission of Inquiry into Trade Unions.

Artisans and the concept of technical culture

It seems clear that there was a 19th-century working-class definition of technical education which acknowledged a distinction between science and technology. A metal worker expressed the concept in this way:

> A knowledge of geometric forces would be invaluable to the artisan, and lift him from often only being an imitator of others, doing so and so because it has been the custom to do so; but measuring on principles would make him in the highest sense of the word a master of arts ...
> (Bramhall 1867: 164)

This concept of technical education was reiterated at the 1874 TU Congress. In the debate on technical education, workingmen's organisations were urged to 'actively take up the question of technical education with a view to furthering skill, and ... schools for technical instruction ought to be established ... supplied by grants from the Education Department' (TUC Minutes, 1874). The idea of 'technical knowledge' was linked to the central notion of craft apprenticeship, a combination which was later argued to be ' ... the best means of furthering the development of technical knowledge and increasing the skill of workmen ... ' (TUC Minutes, 1880).

This suggests the existence of an alternative to the prèvailing notion of technology as an extension of science, conveyed by Huxley, Playfair, Randall and other established public scientific figures.

Artisan educational initiatives represented the only attempt of substance to promote a concept of technical education as part of a 'technical culture' in the 19th century. It put forward a model of technical education which rejected an emphasis on wholly manual craft practices, and yet avoided the abstractness and esotericism of the purely theoretical.

Influential and education-minded scientists in the period assumed a deterministic model of science, in which science was perceived as promoting 'technical and productive efficiency; through its incorporation into manufacturing processes: the notion of technology as 'applied science'. But at the time the apprenticeship, the basis of skilled craft production, was clearly in decline, its demise accelerating with the transformation of work organisation and increasing employers' control over the labour process. For the 'science establishment', the social relations of production in which science and technology were assumed to be given, unalterable and an essential precondition of modern production. The relation between work and technology was regarded deterministically, and was therefore unquestioned. The events in the engineering industry, particularly the numerous strikes following the major confrontation of 1852, were not perceived by figures such as Playfair, Huxley and others as significant factors in their deliberations about technical education, despite the fact that engineering employers and their employees were principal target groups for technical education.

Artisan attempts to initiate independent sources of technical education through their own organisations such as the Artisans' Institute and the Workman's Technical Education Committee failed in two respects. First, they were unable to convince a cautious and vacillating government of the viability of their proposals; funding therefore remained a stumbling block. Second, the artisans' ambiguous relations with the employers and unskilled workers continued to subvert their ideas for a national technical-education system. The gradual erosion of the dependence of employers upon highly skilled labour was plainly a critical factor here as new technologies were established as indispensable conditions for profit-seeking. Skilled workers, seeking to preserve the apprenticeship and thus their workshop autonomy supported by a newly-formed technical-education system, failed to perceive the inherent contradictions associated with their place in these developments.

The employers, confident in their ability to counter any challenge from the unions, were content to oversee the dismemberment of the apprenticeship system. They had convinced themselves that they could manage without it, unaware that the protected markets of the Empire would eventually dry up, exposing critical skill shortages. Committed to short-term profit-seeking, they showed a marked disinclination to sponsor technical education on terms other than their own. The problem was not simply omission on the part of the employers; it was worsened by government's reluctance and lack of direction over a national policy for technical education. The first technical Instruction Act in 1889 was to come 20 years after the artisan initiatives faltered, and its repercussions were to last well into the next century. The employers' ideology of production and technical education corresponded with the ill-judged aspirations of the state, adhering to laissez-faire economics and half-heartedly seeking the introduction of a national system of technical education based on long-term projections for skilled labour.

These ambiguities had a profound influence on the development of technical education in the last decades of the century. They became more pronounced due to the effects of the Great Strike and Lockout of 1897, a connection often unrecorded in accounts of the origin and development of technical education, with their stress on the contribution of a dubious technical education 'movement'.

Concern over the chaotic state of technical training and education and the demise of the apprenticeship system had been expressed earlier, in the 1860s and 1870s, well before the conflict of 1897. In 1878 certain Livery Companies set up an inquiry out of which developed one of the most enduring institutions of the period: the City and Guilds of London Institute. Was this foundation perceived by concerned groups as part of a technical educational 'movement' and a panacea envisaged by an indecisive government?

Notes

1. Odger and Appelgarth were prominent members of the Junta.

CHAPTER SEVEN

Employers, the foundation of the City and Guilds of London Institute and Government legislation

Nineteenth-century employers are often portrayed in histories of technical education as making 'demands' form skilled labour which were met by on-the-job training supported by some for of technical education. Argles (1964) quotes with approval an assertion by Playfair that the 1851 Commission gave 'an enormous impetus to the movement in favour of the reform of our industrial methods ... [which] has revolutionized our system of technical instruction' (p. 14). Playfair stressed the value of a technical education movement but was evidently unsure about the nature of reform and the reorganisation of work. He misjudged the influence of the growing militancy of employers, effectively challenging the skilled workers over work control.

The particular structural characteristics of the CGLI reflected the ideology of engineering management. The views of the prominent engineer-employer, Lord Armstrong, exemplified this ideology. If warranted, the venue for a general technical education programme was the evening class: 'at our factory we have night classes specially for the young ... ' (ibid.). This view, given in evidence to a Select Committee in 1872 (RC on SI 1872: Q. 9238), altered little with time, and embodied a notion of technical education as secondary to the market function of the company. He further maintained that technical education was the preserve of minority: 'Those who would be benefited by scientific education of a technical education ... constitute a very small proportion of the population' (W. G. Armstrong 1888: 50). His philosophy may be illustrated in two views in an 1888 journal article: 'Cheapness and superiority of quality will decide the victory in the race of competition ... [and] *I am inclined to look upon colleges ... as luxuries rather than necessaries*' (ibid., p. 51; my emphasis). This evoked a response from Playfair who argued, 'the capitalist with his large factories worked by machinery, has neither the time nor the inclination to bring up young men with a trained knowledge of his industry ... ' (Playfair 1888: 332).

Different production ideologies correspond to different production relations and authority structures. Thus the 1897 Strike and Lockout was such a crucial event, acting as a catalyst between production ideologies ('technical' issues: length of the working day, machine manning, use of new technologies) and production relations, 'educational' questions (technical training, apprenticeship; general, elementary and technical education).

Despite Playfair's criticism of the capitalists' disinclination to train the young effectively, his own perspective encompassed the prevailing narrow vision and hinged on the issue of 'technical efficiency' and the quality of science teaching. In practice this meant efficiency in terms of worker adaptability and conformity to factory discipline. Sustaining company profits and control within the factory system, not so much competence in the individual craftsman, was the overriding consideration.

He did, however, highlight the more specific issue of the employers' resistance to technical education and training, and rebutted Armstrong, who clearly perceived the company as a source of profit, and not a locus for systematic training (a philosophy ardently pursued by F. W. Taylor in his American workshops). Armstrong's reputation as an engineer and the pre-eminence of his company ensured a strong representation in the newly-formed EEF. A main submission on behalf of employers to the 1892 Royal Commission on Labour came from the Vice-Chairman of the same company, Captain Andrew Noble. During the 1897 conflict the leading representative of the EEF was Col. Dyer, also a director of the Sir W. G. Armstrong Whitworth & Co Ltd.

This is not to imply a conspiracy thesis or a necessary consensus of opinion among engineering employers, but there was an often unrecognised relationship between increasing control over the labour process, particularly by strong, federated employers such as Armstrong, Dyer, and Noble, and their arguments relating to the issue of technical education and training. These found an outlet in a number of ways: official inquiries, reports to Select Committees, responses to TUC demands, EEF Minutes, engineering institutes deliberations published in 'Proceedings', and in the crucial deliberations of the 1897–8 dispute. The principal concerns in these deliberations were pragmatic questions of length of working day, conditions of service, overtime issues and wages. Embedded in these economic issues were quite critical concerns regarding technical education.

In the context of the 1897–8 conflict, the key questions regarding technical education were subsumed under the specifics of machine manning, apprenticeship and labour substitution. That is, technical education *per se* was not a negotiable agenda item in the 1897 dispute, but it clearly formed a critical part of the unions' arguments concerning machine manning and the apprenticeship question. For the union side, the apprenticeship system was conceived as central to any technical-education system. The employers' case was represented by figures such as Dyer, whose decisive views on these issues, reflecting employer dominance over technology, emerged during the dispute. There was a high correlation between control over expanding technologies and pro-active participation in the lockout.

The Terms of Settlement, concluding the 1897 strike and lockout, demonstrated among other things the cautious reserve by employers regarding technical education. They contained the following in the ratified agreement of 1907: 'An apprentice shall be afforded facilities for acquiring a knowledge of the branch of the trade he adopts, and shall be encouraged to obtain a theoretical knowledge thereof *as far as circumstances permit*' (EEF–ASE Agreement (1907), para. 6; my emphasis). This suggests a correspondence with Armstrong's view that colleges were 'luxuries rather than necessities'. It also vindicated Donnelly's earlier criticism of employers, arguing in the 1881–4 Inquiry that 'I do not think there is any strong general feeling on their [employers'] part with regard to the value of such instruction' (RC on TI 1884b: Q. 2572). The clause in the ratification of the 1907 Terms of Settlement relating to the acquisition of technical knowledge by apprentices was a qualified 'concession' to the unions and apprentices; but it plainly implied that technical education was contingent upon the needs of the employer and the company. This concession to trade training did not appear in the two previous Agreements between the ASE and EEF. Both the 1898 and 1901 Agreements avoided reference to apprentices acquiring 'theoretical knowledge' (EEF–ASE Agreements 1898: 90).

The attitude of the employers clearly affected the skilled workers' response both to labour substitution and projections for a technical-education system. The issue of 19th-century technical education was related to a central problem facing a significant part of the skilled working class of the period. This was its relatively disadvantaged social position, and the corresponding difficulties in obtaining benefit from the kind of general and technical education available, from any source. The situation was not perceptibly helped either by the formation of the City and Guilds of London Institute (CGLI) in 1878, or by the enactment of various pieces of legislation from the late 1880s.

By the late 1870s the CGLI's formalisation of two kinds of technical education had been acknowledged by the unions: 'The whole modern organisation of labour in its advanced form rests on a fundamental fact ... the definite separation between the functions of the capitalist and the workman ... each between the direction of industrial operations and the execution in detail' (TUC 1880, Dublin). Artisans were not at all secure in their position regarding technical education. On the one hand they sought to improve their access to such technical education as existed, through public funding. On the other hand, earlier in the century they had attempted alternative strategies through the Workmen's Technical Education Union and similar bodies. They also exercised a lobby through their association with the Society of Arts. Despite the presence of contradictions underlying these educational initiatives, there were practical but limited benefits deriving from these contacts, exemplified in the Society of Arts' organisation of the technological examination system in 1873.

Concerns expressed by skilled workers over the decline of the apprenticeship system were articulated as part of the argument that employers were content, in the main, to allow the system to fall into decay. Employers resorted to increasing use of boy labour as opposed to apprentice labour.

In 1909 R. H. Tawney concluded that progress of invention in mechanical engineering had had the effect of multiplying the number of posts held by boys working automatic machines. There was an increase in the proportion of boys under 15 employed in the trade among toolmakers, and erectors, fitters and turners, 'in fact in that very engineering trade which was once supposed to be a stronghold of the apprenticeship system' (Tawney 1909: 555).

As far as machine tools and foreign competition were concerned, mechanical engineering was probably the most influential of British engineering manufactures, and heavily dependent upon skilled labour, but according to Hobsbawm, 'nowhere did foreign countries leap ahead more decisively than in this field ... ' (1974: 180). In 1878, specific concern over the changing conditions of skill acquisition and the chaotic state of the apprenticeship system in general stimulated certain livery companies in London to consider ways of applying some of their bequeathed funds to encourage some form of technical education. Their immediate interests were the trades with which they were individually associated. The Clothworkers Livery Company especially believed the lack of 'proper' craft training and technical instruction were impediments to trades and manufacturers in England (RC on TI, 7 May 1884b, Minutes of Evidence).

The structure and organisation of the institution which emerged from the livery companies' deliberations strongly reflected the employers' views on training and education, and reinforced the separation of craft practices and the apprenticeship pattern of training from technical education. The formation of the City and Guilds of London Institute, institutionalised a part-time model of technical education for workers, and also put in train the notion of 'evening classes as a means of secondary education for the masses'. These developments were clearly influenced both by the state's reluctance to accept more than minimal responsibility for technical education, and by the power of employers significantly to affect the pattern of trade training and technical education.

The directory and science provision in the 1860s and 1870s

From the 1860s and 1870s the official attitude towards technical education was narrow and based exclusively on existing school science provision. Practical work had been virtually abandoned, due mainly to economic considerations earlier in the century; the Hadow Report of 1926 noted that in the mid-19th century 'it was soon discovered that any effective practical instruction cost much more than the three "R's"' (Board of Education [Hadow Report] 1926: 10). The policy meant that any extension of science provision had to be met either from existing resources under the Directory's science scheme or from voluntary contributions.

The main emphasis was on a theoretical approach to science, a bias which was reflected in the range of science subjects taught in schools, and which was to remain unchanged until 1898. This invites the question of what ideology sustained these provisions and whether they were adequate and relevant to the working classes of the period.

Such provision was plainly fragmentary, particularly in the 1860s. There were elementary classes in science subjects, generally held in connection with mechanics' or literary institutes. They were confined chiefly to London, Lancashire, the West Riding of Yorkshire, Cornwall, Birmingham, Glasgow and Edinburgh. Elsewhere classes scarcely existed, with no classes in the north-east, eastern and west Midlands, or southern counties (RC on SI 1865: pp. iii, iv).

The object of the Science and Art Department was to aid instruction in science in the following 23 subjects: (1) practical, plane and solid geometry; (2) machine construction and drawing; (3) building construction, or naval architecture and drawing; (4) elementary mathematics; (5) higher mathematics; (6) theoretical mechanics; (7) applied mechanics; (8) acoustics, light and heat; (9) magnetism and electricity; (10) inorganic chemistry; (11) organic chemistry; (12) geology; (13) mineralogy; (14) animal physiology; (15) zoology; (16) vegetable physiology and economic botany; (17) systematic botany; (18) mining; (19) metallurgy; (20) navigation; (21) nautical astronomy; (22) steam; (23) physical geography (Privy Council on Education 1867b: 1–3). The administration was based on a payment-by-results system, under the control of the chief executive at the Directory at South Kensington, Donnelly. Direct payments were to be made to teachers only on behalf of adult artisans or the children of artisans (ibid., p. 18).

The avowed aim of government was therefore the encouragement of the teaching of science in elementary schools through grants, and elsewhere through a scholarship scheme. Neither differentiation according to specific skills nor direct applications to industrial practices was made: 'The object is to promote instruction in Science especially among the industrial classes' (ibid., Appendix D).

Government control over science teaching

Limiting the scope of science teaching in institutions under its financial and ideological control, the government also monitored other educational developments. Of these, technical education was a key issue from the 1880s. The pressure from government to make technical education provision self-financing, that is, other than that available under the Science Scheme, may be seen as part of the state's rigid adherence to free-market policies and its reticence regarding this branch of education. Governmental oversight of developments through the payment-by-results system was an ideological as well as an economic strategy, for even within its own terms of equating scientific with technical education, actual state support was limited (see above, Table 6.1): 'the treasury's parsimonious approach ... did not prevent it from censuring any "unnecessary" expenditure which might occur within the stringent limits laid down ... ' (Horn 1982: 22). The Treasury attempted to keep down expenditure on science subjects by placing constraints on the amounts which teachers and pupils could earn in science (Sylvester 1974: 35).

Moreover, supervision of the Science Directory's annual examinations was in the hands of part-time inspectors. These were officers recruited from the Corps of Royal Engineers 'who could be fobbed off with a fee of £1 a day ... as temporary appointees ... ' (C. A. and P. L. R. Horn 1981: 33). Thus despite its non-committal and calculative approach to technical education, government maintained a monitoring role over both state and non-state developments in the area.

Government control was further extended through the use of cross-appointments. This policy provided for a government official sitting on a number of Boards and Committees reviewing science and technical-education provision. Donnelly, who was on the Board of the Society of Arts and later the City and Guilds of London Institute, personified this situation. But the ad hoc administration and the payment-by-results system compounded to make science teaching as a profession unattractive (SC on SI 1868, p. v).

Commenting on a relative decline in the percentage of children taking science subjects as compared with non-scientific subjects between 1882–3 and 1887–8, the *Journal of the Society of Arts* 1889–90) attributed a 13 per cent drop to the negative effects of payment by results: 'other non-scientific subjects were more remunerative on the day of the examination'. Throughout most of the century there was a manifest shortage of science teachers.

Technical education, ill-defined and fragmentary in the 1860s and 1870s, thus engendered cautious government interest, tempered by prevailing financial constraints. Legislation followed in the 1880s which reasserted the government's intention to leave technical-education funding to market forces and to put the onus of financing it on the consumer. This policy had been carried over from the 1860s. In 1869 Playfair alluded to this laissez-faire doctrine, asserting that government sought to foster a 'self-help' attitude in the technical education. For example, referring to Manchester, he argued in the Commons: 'if Manchester desires technical education she ought to provide it solely at her own expense' (Hansard 1869b, Col. 205).

The typical Victorian self-help attitude was reiterated throughout most of the period for example, in a paper delivered by a prominent scientist and lecturer of the next decade, S. P. Thompson, who became the first principal of the Technical College at Finsbury under the City and Guilds of London Institute. Speaking on technical education, he said: 'When they began to specialise instruction, it ought to be paid for by the parents, or by an endowment; it was not the part of the State to provide that kind of education' (S. P. Thompson 1879: 43).

Attempts to modify the Directory's scheme originated as early as 1867 (after the Paris Exhibition) and came from different factions, such as the artisans through the TUC and Society of Arts proceedings. The Society of Arts evaluated provision according to external examination results of Institutes in union with the Society.

W. E. Forster, responsible for the first legislation in compulsory education in 1870, argued in the House that the government's obligation towards technical education was merely advisory and not a practical commitment: 'government's duty was guiding and stimulating those who were engaged in that branch of instruction' (Hansard 1869b, Col. 213). What this 'stimulation' comprised is a matter of conjecture in the light of the government's own vacillating attitude to technical education. The government's free-market policy found favour in the establishment Press of the day. *The Times* reported on 6 February 1868:

> We agree in the conclusion that the interference of the Government in technical education would be an act entirely beyond its proper province. No necessity exists to justify it ... *if technical schools be not established we must conclude that the alleged necessity for them does not exist. We may safely leave such a matter to the ordinary laws of supply and demand.* (My emphasis)

In contrast, throughout the second half of the century the ASE had focused on the decline of the apprenticeship and had made clear its position regarding its place in technical education, provoking many disputes, culminating in the Great Strike in 1897. The historic craft guilds were also clearly affected by the social and technical transformation affecting the traditional craft-apprenticeship system.

The City livery companies and the beginnings of the City and Guilds of London Institute

A committee set up by the livery companies in 1877 to inquire into the state of technical education provision reported in 1878.[1] This report was the first unofficial but comprehensive survey of the extent of technical education in England. It revealed that there were 40 establishments engaged in some form

Table 7.1 Extent and distribution of institutes of technical education in Britain, 1878

The Artisan Institute, St. Martin's Lane, W.C.
South London Workmen's College
Workmen's College, Great Ormond Street
College for Working Women, Fitzroy Square
Middle Class Schools, Cowper Street
Birkbeck Institute, Chancery Lane
St. Margaret's Technical Schools, Westminster (just opened)
The Royal Polytechnic Institute, Regent Street
Islington School of Science and Art, Essex Road, N.
Telegraphist School, General Post Office, E.C.
King's College, London
London Institute, Finsbury Circus
Gresham College
University College, London
Crystal Palace School of Practical Engineering
The Royal School of Mines
The Huddersfield Mechanical Institute and Trades School
Yorkshire College of Science, Leeds
Owens College, Manchester
Keighley Trade School
Oldham Science and Art School
Leeds Mechanical Institute
Strand Mechanical Institute
The Royal Indian Engineering College, Coopers Hill
Trade and Mining School, Bristol
Building Trades Institute, Manchester
Dockyard Schools
Royal Marine Schools
Chemists and Druggists Schools, Bradford
Colliery Schools
Railway Schools
Co-operative Societies Schools, Rochdale
Cookery Schools
Glasgow Technical College
Anderson Institute, Glasgow
The Agricultural College, Cirencester
North of Scotland School of Chemistry and Agriculture, Aberdeen
Royal Naval College, Greenwich
Hull Navigation School
Plymouth Navigation School

Also Whitworth Scholarships, formed in 1868 with an endowment of £3,000.

Source: Livery Companies Committee, Report on Technical Education (London, 1878).

of technical education in England (see Table 7.1). Of these 16 were in London; the remaining 24 covered the rest of the century (Livery Companies Report 1878).

The committee drafted an outline scheme for a national system of technical education. It proposed the foundation in London of a Central Institute for 'higher technical instruction' (a similar proposal had been made by the Workmen's Technical Education Committee in 1868). It also recommended the establishment of trade schools; the organising and administering of technical examinations; and subsidising other institutions in London or in the provinces having technical-education objectives. The City and Guilds of London Institute developed from these proposals in 1879.

Magnus, the first Director and Secretary of the CGLI, was to argue later that the CGLI fulfilled a state function, undertaking work that would have been done by a Department of State in other countries (Magnus 1910: 107). The CGLI established a 'trade school', Finsbury Technical College, and a Central College at South Kensington comparable, it was argued, to the great polytechnic schools of Germany, Switzerland and Italy, and corresponding to the École Centrale of Paris (RC on TI 1884a, sec. vii).

The City and Guilds of London Institute: structure and organisation

The governors of the Institute emphasised that it was not concerned with changing existing social and technical relations. This was recognised early in the life of the Institute and noted by the 1884 Royal Commission:

> ... [the Council of the Institute] ... have no intention of interfering with any existing social institution, such as apprenticeship, or any other relationship between employer and employee, but aim only at supplying the want of *further instruction which is everywhere felt to exist*, by supplementing, and preparing pupils more thoroughly to profit by workshop training. (RC on TI 1884a, 2nd Report, p. 401; my emphasis)

The assumption that workshop training was being systematically carried out, complementing theoretical studies, was plainly evident.

There were four branches to the Institute:

1. The Central Technical College, South Kensington: a college for higher instruction of a 'university character', in mechanics and mathematics; civil, mechanical, and electrical engineering; chemistry.
2. The Technical College: 'An intermediate College' with day courses in mechanical and electrical engineering and chemistry and evening classes in the same subjects; and in applied art.
3. The South London Technical Art School: courses in modelling, drawing and painting; and house decoration.

4. The Technological Examinations Department: for the registration and inspection of classes in technology and manual training, and the holding of annual examinations in the subjects taught in those classes. (CGLI Calendar 1887-8)

The Central Institute had courses arranged to suit specific students: (i) trainee technical teachers; (ii) professional engineers and architects; (iii) persons intending to take the management of industrial works, 'whether sons of employers or managers or superintendents' (ibid., p. 4). Prospective students were required to matriculate, that is, pass an entrance examination, and be prepared to take a complete course of instruction in one of the chosen branches of technology. The vice-president and treasurer, Sydney Waterlow, in his evidence to the 1884 Royal Commission on Technical Instruction, held that the students of the 'Central' would be of high calibre. They were the type of students who previously would have gone for their technological training to Germany or Switzerland. Also included would be students from Finsbury Technical College who entered by free or partially free scholarships. It was envisaged that the Central Institute should therefore be 'a college for the most advanced scientific and technical instruction' (RC on TI 1884a: 518, 519). A complete course lasted three years and the instruction included work in all four departments with a common first year, followed by specialisation in a chosen technology. The matriculation examination for entrance included mathematics and mechanics, mechanical drawing, physics, chemistry, French or German.

Engineering students took a common first year of mathematics, physics and chemistry, plus workshop and drawing office work. The second year included the kinematics of machines, the dynamics of machines, the strength of materials, hydraulics and hydraulic motors. The third year, in addition to 'discipline engineering' such as water supply and bridge construction, included the following: the strength and stability of structures, more advanced parts of the theory of the resistance of materials, theory of the steam engine and gas engines (CGLI Calendar 1887-88). Clearly this kind of course demanded students with a sound basic education capable of coping with three years of full-time instruction – and able to pay fees of £75 per annum.

The courses offered at the Finsbury College were mainly directed at a different type of student.

Finsbury Technical College

From the outset the professed aim of the Finsbury branch of the CGLI was a general provision: 'training on broad, practical and scientific principles, in those subjects which experience has shown best to fit a student to enter one of the many careers connected with Civil, Mechanical, Electrical or Chemical industries' (CGLI Finsbury Programme 1923–4, p. vii). The operation of this college was divided into two distinct sections: day classes for those who were able to devote one, two or three years to systematic technical education; and evening classes for those engaged in industry during the day and willing to take supplementary instruction in the evening.

There were six elements: mechanical engineering and applied mechanics, electrical engineering and applied physics, industrial and technical chemistry, applied art, the building trades, French or German so far as it related to the reading of technical literature (CGLI Calendar 1887–8: 49).

For day students the college prepared courses suitable for intermediate post in industry, and as preparatory to enter to the Central Institute. Admission to the day courses involved an examination in arithmetic, algebra and geometry. For illustration, the test for 1886 included the following:

(i) Simplify
$$\frac{1\ 4/17 \times 6\ 4/5}{3\ 3/5 - 1\ 2/25} + 2/11 \text{ of } (2\ 2/5 - 3/4) - \frac{1\ 3/5}{12}$$

(ii) Show that
$$1 + \frac{a^2 + b^2 - c^2}{2ab} = \frac{(a+b+c)(a+b-c)}{2ab}$$

(iii) Describe a parallelogram equal to a given rectilineal figure, and having an angle equal to a given rectilineal angle. Ibid. (pp. 78, 79, 80)

In the light of the evidence concerning general levels of education put forward by critics such as Playfair, Huxley, Solly and artisans in the Society of Arts conference, the nature and form of these types of questions suggest that few pupils from the elementary schools would qualify for day entrance to Finsbury. Plainly artisans would need further general education or have recourse to the evening classes at Finsbury. This would seem to have been the case.

Evening classes at Finsbury technical college

The evening classes were conducted under the same discipline division as the day courses, with 'practical' additions. These included the art industries, including cabinet-making and decoration in colour and relief. Courses were designed for 'apprentices, workmen, and foremen, engaged in the various trades ... ' (CGLI Calendar 1887–88: 81). There was flexibility in the organisation of course, for no course was compulsory for evening students. Selection of classes was on an ad hoc basis to suit the individual requirements of the students. This represented a student-oriented rather than a structured programme. The mathematics and mechanical engineering department provided practical mechanics, mathematics, mechanical drawing, practical geometry.

The day classes in 1886 attracted about 155 students, mostly from 15 to 19 years of age, in the main studying for the full course of three years, leading to the Certificate of the College. Evening classes in the same year had 900 students, the great majority of them workers, 14 to 40 years of age, employed during the day in the workshop or factory (ibid.).

Data relating to both colleges show the number of evening students far exceeded day students. In the case of the Central there were two and one half times as many evening students, and at Finsbury four times as many (CGLI 1896: 6–7). The preponderance of part-time evening students reinforces the argument that evening classes represented a form of 'secondary school for the masses'. This pattern was consolidated by the 'distance-learning' characteristics of the CGLI examination structure. The predominance of the part-time evening-class model in England may be contrasted with comparable institutions abroad at the turn of the century (see Table 7.2).

Table 7.2 Numbers of day and evening-class students in selected German and English towns in 1900

| | Students | | | Students | |
German towns	Day	Evening	English towns	Day	Evening
Berlin	20	250	Bolton	40	2 500
Chemnitz	60	—	Leicester	18	1 000
Crefeld	200	—	Derby	100	1 000
Mülhausen	150	—	Salford	60	1 500
Reutlingen	150	—	St Helens	—	1 000

Source: Shadwell (1906): 423.

Some provision was made for day-time study and this was provided at the Central Institute at South Kensington and at Finsbury. The relevance of the Central Institute was itself a centre of debate. It was held, for example, that its location was likely to prove 'not readily accessible to workmen' (Magnus 1910: 98). Its structure and organisation were premised on the separation of work and education. In this it reflected aspects of prevailing educational ideas which similarly separated mental and practical activities. In this respect Johnson (1969) has argued that English education from the mid-1860s was conceived as a source of work-discipline or rational economic behaviour. At the same time the industrial economy rested on a base of child, female and adolescent labour, placing school and work in competition.

The CGLI pattern of technical education portrayed it as separate from its historical form, the craft apprenticeship, and institutionalised the separation. A recent analysis states: 'the decline (of the apprenticeship) ... called for a system of technical education which did not demarcate between the "principles" and the "technicalities" of technology ... ' (Beecham 1982: 64). But this is the very pattern that originated with the CGLI. Beecham assumes that the dichotomy only arises 'whenever the technical education ... came under the control of the State ... ' (ibid, p. 62).

The directors of the new system of technical education and training, mainly City livery companies, assuming effective practical training was being carried out in industry, believed in the need for a separation of the exercise of craft skills, and the organisation, direction and control of those skills in industry. The structure of the CGLI replicated this belief.

The technological examinations department at the CGLI

The technological examinations department was responsible for the organisation and administration of the 'distance learning' students, that is, those who studied in their own provincial and metropolitan institutes and were entered for the Institute examinations. These were set and marked in London.

Such was the prestige of the department that towards the end of the century the Institute directorate in technology came to regard the CGLI as 'a powerful agency in encouraging the establishment of technical schools and classes throughout the country' (CGLI 1896: 8). The figures of attendance and papers worked by students seem to support this claim. There was an increase in the number of candidates' papers from 202 in 1879 (the year the Institute took over responsibility from the Society of Arts) to 10,293 candidates in 1895 (CGLI 1901, Department of Technology, Report 1900–1901).

Given that there had been only very limited experience in distance-learning under the Society of Arts from the late 18th century, it was significant that the director of the Department, Magnus, perceived its function in terms of a national educational context. Technology examinations, he claimed, acted not merely as benchmarks against which various trades' knowledge could be compared but also as 'fixing the standard of technological instruction for artisans throughout the country' (CGLI 1896: 10). Magnus's well-publicised view failed to take into account the political and ideological background to the rapidly declining apprenticeship system. He too believed that the work of the CGLI examinations department was being complemented by necessary practical training in the workshops. This was highly questionable.

It is difficult, therefore, to see how Magnus could have justified this assertion, in the light of criticisms concerning the quality and lack of technical teachers, the chaotic state of the apprenticeship system, and the overall lack of technical education provision. As Foden (1982) has argued, 'There is little direct evidence of any kind that the examinations had much demonstrable social and industrial impact at all. Industrialists, trade unions, and the main educational establishment ... remained on the whole quite indifferent to what the Institute was doing ... ' (p. 79). Notwithstanding these reservations, the examination department had an impact on the inchoate structure of technical education development.

The CGLI examination structure

In 1879, the Institute assumed complete responsibility for all technical-related examinations originally organised and administered by the Society of Arts. Technological examinations had been introduced by the Society of Arts in 1873, the first of their kind. By 1877 the examination structure involved six separate examinable areas: (a) commercial knowledge, (b) domestic economy, (c) fine arts applied to industry, (d) music, (e) technology of arts and manufacturers, (f) elementary (Society of Arts 1878: 85). The inclusion of both music and technology in the programme of examinations indicates the wide range of subjects covered by the Society and the difficulties associated with definitions of 'technology'. The number of candidates at this early stage was never great: six entered in 1870, 68 in 1873, and 184 in 1878. There was a graded system of elementary, advanced, and honours in the examination. The specific subjects for examination were: cotton manufacture; paper, silk, steel making; carriage building; pottery and porcelain manufacturing, gas, cloth, silk-dyeing, calico-bleaching, dyeing and printing; alkali manufacturing; blow-pipe analysis (ibid.).

The CGLI thus inherited, in 1879, a system of technological examinations originating with and sustained by the Society of Arts. These were based on local preparation of candidates for examinations set and examined in London. It also subsidised existing educational establishments, exercising a function the government had been unwilling to take up. The Samuelson Commission, the first public inquiry into technical-education provision, noted in 1884 that without this kind of assistance institutions providing technical instruction would probably have languished (RC on TI 1884b: 814).

Donnelly, at the Directory, was responsible for the initiation and administration of the payment-by-results system organised from there. He was also a member of the executive committee of the CGLI. In this capacity he objected strongly to the CGLI assuming the examining role of the Society of Arts, with which he was also associated as an executive member. In a letter to *The Times* he complained that the scientific basis of the Science and Art Department examination system was being eroded by the scheme proposed under the CGLI (Lang 1978: 23). A Secretary of the Institute replied that the value of the examination scheme could be measured by the number of candidates taking the Institute's paper. His evaluation was substantiated: in 1882 there were 1,961 candidates sitting for examination (ibid.).

The examination scheme of the Institute was perceived as an alternative to the Directory's science-based technical education, which was the basis of Donnelly's criticism.

Differentiation of knowledge in the CGLI

A critical structural characteristic of the CGLI was the formation of two distinct foundations, the 'Central' and Finsbury Technical College, principally for evening classes. The vast majority of the Institute's students attended the latter. Central students, exposed to certain forms of technical knowledge, were destined for supervisory roles in industry. Finsbury College evening students were prepared by the Institute to become more 'competent workers'.

The Central College concentrated mainly on the theoretical principles of industrial practices, geared towards 'professional' people (not exclusively engineers); 'Centralians' were to organise and direct the activities of the workers. The Evening Class department at Finsbury held courses directed at subordinate workers, who were presented with a different conception of what was meant by 'technical knowledge'. As the *Calendar* explained, 'The object of the Central Institute is to give ... advanced instruction ... in those kinds of knowledge which bear upon the different branches of industry, whether Manufacture or Arts' (CGLI Calendar 1887–8: 4). The Finsbury College provided 'education of a thoroughly practical kind for apprentices ... ' (ibid., p. 48).

Clearly the Central was directed towards more theoretical aspects. Students taking other courses not directly organised by the Central, free to choose the form and duration of their courses, were advised that classes at this level could be restricted to trades that were relevant.

But students outside the Central Institute seem to have been handicapped. Lacking preparation, they were, as one Institute teacher noted, 'totally unprepared by previous training for taking notes, and having little aptitude for dealing with formulae, were unable to assimilate the technical food placed before them ... ' (H. Adams 1883, Preface).

Despite such reservations, expectations of the evening-class student were uncompromising. In 1901 students taking the ordinary grade examination, part I, in mechanical engineering would be expected to answer questions of this kind:

> The difference of tensions on the tight and slack side of a belt which drives a 30 in. pulley being 750 lbs., what H.P. is being transmitted to

the shaft on which this pulley runs if it makes 120 revolutions a minute? (30 marks). (CGLI 1901 Report, p. 219; one of nine questions to be answered)

Under the section dealing with fitter's work the following questions is found in the part II examination:

Sketch turning tools for the following purposes, showing clearly the cutting angles in each case:
a) Roughing out mild steel; b) roughing out gun-metal; c) finishing mild steel; d) parting mild steel; e) knifing mild steel; f) cutting a square thread of 1 in. pitch. (20 marks) (Ibid., p. 223; one of the four questions to be answered)

These illustrations represent workshop knowledge an artisan or apprentice would be expected to draw upon in the CGLI examination in mechanical engineering. (In 1900 there were 955 candidates for this examination with 498 passes; ibid., p. 7).

The CGLI was differentiated along class and occupational lines, structured to accommodate prevailing work norms. At the smaller Institute, Finsbury Technical College, in 1892 the day school had 78 students from grammar and other endowed schools; 64 students from middle-class schools; 57 from private schools, and 14 students from Board schools. This put the representation of students from manual-working backgrounds at 6½ per cent. Attendance at evening classes at the same institute showed over 50 per cent artisan adults and young workers, mostly in the engineering trades (CGLI Finsbury Programme (1893–4).

The foundation and development of the CGLI has long been regarded as the cornerstone of English technical education from the late 1870s. It is questionable whether such a development would have taken place uninfluenced by radical changes in industry, and by the political effects of numerous localised strikes and a national industrial strike. Perceived as a national system, technical education clearly would not operate in isolation from the political and legislative structure. The origin and development of the CGLI has to be seen against the background of relevant legislation of the period. The most important in the 1880s was the first Royal Commission to inquire into technical education provision, which was published in 1884. But the origins of this Royal Commission itself reveal the prevailing ambivalence in government thinking about technical education.

The Royal Commission on Technical Instruction 1881–1884

The Royal Commission on Technical Instruction (RC on TI) 1884 was the first 'official' attempt to determine the prevailing situation regarding technical education and training in England and Wales.

The first formal investigation had been undertaken by the City livery companies in 1878; the 1881–4 Royal Commission arose out of this livery company inquiry. Under Samuelson it was originally conceived as an unofficial inquiry, that is, not directly initiated or funded by the government. It was proposed by an MP, Anderson, in a House of Commons debate in 1881 (Hansard 1881a, Col. 251). Mundella, the vice-president of the Council, was unenthusiastic, and suggested that members might instigate their own research, 'at their own expense' (ibid). Eventually, four members of the Commons particularly concerned with the issue of technical education formed an ad hoc committee in 1881. (Table 7.3 shows the composition of this committee, with brief biographical notes.)

Table 7.3 Membership of the Royal Commission on Technical Instruction, 1881–1884

Bernhard Samuelson (Chairman) (Liberal MP for Banbury and North Oxfordshire for over 30 years)

H. E. Roscoe (Liberal MP for South Manchester after 1885)

Philip Magnus (the only member to live well into modern times, dying in 1933 at the age of 91; he was appointed Director and Secretary of the new City and Guilds of London Institute in 1880; after 1888 he was Superintendent of the Institute's Department of Technology)

John Slagg (Liberal and Free Trade MP for Manchester from 1880)

Swire Smith (became a Liberal MP in 1915)

William Woodall (Liberal MP for two pottery towns from 1880 to 1900; he studied developments in technical education in Germany in 1897)

Source: Argles (1959).

The Commission was especially significant in highlighting for the first time and in a systematic way the employers' views on technical education during the course of its inquiries between 1881 and its publication in 1884. The Commission asked employers to comment on 'the influence, on the industry in which you are engaged of the Science and Art classes, and other sources of technical and general instruction, which are available to the workmen, foremen and employers of your district ... ' (RC on TI 1884c, Appendix G).

The Inquiry provided firm evidence of employer resistance to technical education. Donnelly, during his evidence, in reply to the question 'Can you suggest ... the best means of promoting technical training ... ? prefaced his reply by suggesting first: The operative classes were much more convinced of the value of technical instruction than employers; second, an essential condition for a technical education programme was the need to engage the support of employers: 'The Commission, or some other body, should get the employers of labour of this country to see and fully appreciate the value of such instruction' (RC on TI 1884b, Q. 12871).

Industrial employers were reluctant to commit themselves, or they simply did not consider technical education a high priority. The Commission's research was first directed at the two sources of relevant education: the Directory's science scheme, and 'other sources', the CGLI and the Society of Arts. The 'more important' replies (published as Appendix C in the Report) showed that more than 50 per cent of employers responding had a negative view of the effects of technical eduction (ibid., pp. 642–53).

Government concern over employer attitudes to technical education

The attitude of the employers, revealed in the Inquiry, clearly concerned Donnelly. Neither the Commission nor Donnelly fully grasped that problems of technical education implementation and organisation were compounded by the free-market policy of the government and its misplaced faith in the employers as sponsors of a national system. The economic implication of this policy was the need to attract funding from the market, prime targets being influential employers.

Donnelly attempted to persuade employers to accept more responsibility for technical education: '[the employers] might ... at once do for science and art and industrial education, what the recent Education Act did for Elementary education' (RC on TI 1884b: Q. 25721). A prominent engineer-employer, Siemens, rationalised the employers' attitudes to technical education by suggesting that there was a bias against technical matters and a 'prejudice against innovation' on the part of the English employers (1884b: ibid., Q. 1486). Tradesmen were frustrated by employer resistance, one said: 'I do not know what we should have to do to get [employers] to take an active interest in it [technical education]' (ibid., Q. 3818). And on the issue of apprenticeship the workers' representative raised the issue of systematic training: 'Employers should ... afford facilities for youths to be systematically taught for a given or fixed term, say of 5 years ... ' (ibid., p. 2854).

After it had begun its work the Commission was granted Royal Commission status (i.e. it was no longer an amateur, unofficial enquiry, self-funding and self-motivating). Following an injunction that the basis of a sound technical-education system was a unified system of elementary and secondary education, its main recommendations came down to this: existing arrangements for technical education were inadequate. Replicating Continental models of technical education was rejected; it was considered inappropriate to introduce the practice of foreign countries into England. This guarded attitude led the President of the Institution of Mechanical Engineers to suggest much later that there was nothing comparable to the German Technische Hochschule due, he argued, to the fact that Britain never understood the significance of secondary education while 'in Germany the whole educational fabric rested on it' (Institution of Mechanical Engineers, *Proceedings*, 89 (1915), 309). It is evident that in philosophy and projection the Royal Commission's main propositions supported the prevailing model of technical education exemplified by the City and Guilds.

Regarding technical education for management of industrial enterprises, the Commission distinguished 'capitalists' who 'will take the general, as distinguished from the technical direction of large establishments; and those at the head of small undertakings, or the persons more especially charged with the technical details of either ... ' (RC on TI 1884a: 555), and those with a 'technical' function educated in an institution where 'sound knowledge of scientific principles has to be combined with the practical training of the factory ... ' (ibid.). There was a reaffirmation of the basic educational philosophy which assumed working-class education to be secondary to work: 'For the great mass of *our working population ... must necessarily begin to earn their livelihood at an early age* ... ' (ibid., p. 517; my emphasis). Skilled workers concurred in his view. They perceived educational institutions as paralleling the ineluctable hierarchical structure of industrial work organisation, under which a minority administered ('manage'), the majority laboured (TUC Minutes 1880).

The Commission's specific recommendations for workers' technical education were undramatic and bland, emphasising the inclusion of practical subjects in elementary schools with more science instruction:

1. Elementary schools should be encouraged to include drawing, metalwork and woodwork.
2. Science and art classes should be part of the school boards' curricula. Science should be 'more practical'.
3. Teacher training should include more provision for science.
4. Endowed schools should include technical and scientific instruction in the curriculum.

Even these modest recommendations made little impact. Government was under no obligation to implement or subsidise any element of the Report's recommendations. Five years after the Report, major deficiencies in provision were still evident. A subsequent Inquiry thus referred to 'disastrous gaps' (in provision) (National Association for the Promotion of Technical and Secondary Education 1889: 133). By the turn of the century the effects of a lack of central directive and coordination were also manifestly clear (Committee on the Co-ordination of Technological Education 1900).

There were wider implications of the state's non-interference in technical education developments, some aspects of which had been misconstrued by the Dean and Professor of Mechanical Engineering of the Central Institute, W. C. Unwin. Recent developments, he maintained, had confirmed the positive factors of the prevailing 'self-help' policy. He argued later that from the 1880s science and engineering had largely been developed by individual initiative and voluntary effort, emerging as part of a 'marked jealousy of state interference' (Unwin 1904). But the evidence is clear: the Inquiries of 1884 (and reaffirmed in 1889) highlighted the state's narrow vision and the employers' continuing resistance to technical education.

Neither the state nor the employers was prepared to make a full commitment to a national system of technical education. The government was prevaricating, with no national policy for the training and supply of technical teachers; no overall strategy for higher education; inadequate funding, and lack of preparation to administer a national scheme.

As to the employers, a single domestic example from later in the century points up their position: in a comprehensive report for a Special Committee on Technical Education for the London County Council in 1892, it was stated that in respect of part-time release for technical education, London in particular was singularly lacking: 'London is not only very far behind Germany and France in quantity and quality, but also far behind our chief provincial towns' (Llewellyn Smith 1892: 4). To be on a par with Manchester in the numbers of students in technical classes, London could have had, pro rata, 148,000 entries: the report showed 24,000 registered (ibid.). By 1895 it was evident again that in London many employers were unable to make concessions to boys for an allowance for part-time classes, although some encouraged attendance at evening classes (*London Technical Education Gazette* 1895).

There was pressure from a variety of sources on the employers to assume at least partial responsibility for technical education. But their inflexibility had hardened throughout the century. They approved the Establishment policy of non-interference in technical education, favouring, if anything at all, a part-time pattern. The combination of indecisiveness on the part of government and the employers' stance ensured that the technical education of young workers was relegated to an inferior, part-time system which made few demands on either employers or the State.

Continuing reluctance of employers: legislation from the 1880s

Pleas for more positive action by the National Association for the Promotion of Technical and Secondary Education (NAPTSE), the TUC, the Trades

Councils, and other artisan sources, such as the Workingmen's Technical Education Union, added weight to the general concern over technical education, for a number of legislative reforms relating to technical education followed. They were attempts to focus the aims and objectives of both secondary and technical education. Subsequent legislation, however, still embodied an unjustified confidence in bodies like the newly-constituted CGLI, and on the capacity for cooperation on the part of employers.

Technical-education legislation instituted in the 1880s, by and large, was in line with the recommendations of the 1884 commission. Roscoe was prominent in this, particularly in his work in the House of Commons (NAPTSE 1901: 5). But these efforts were handicapped by the continuing problem of the locus of administration of technical education. A turning point came with the passing of the Local Government Act of 1888, which made possible the local organisation of post-elementary education on a systematic basis.

The Local Government Act of 1888

This Act brought into being the County Councils, which replaced the School Boards, a product of the 1870 Act. Under this new provision wide areas of local administration, of which education was to be part, were formed. With respect to education, for the first time the whole country was placed under the jurisdiction of local authorities, which were also to be responsible for raising a levy of a penny rate for technical or manual instruction. Any Council was able to appoint a Technical Instruction Committee. In addition, representatives of these Committees were to be incorporated into the governing bodies of all schools, colleges and institutions giving technical instruction (RC on SE 1895: 12–13).

The Act finally removed what hitherto had been considered a serious impediment to educational administration, that is, the absence of a representative and locally elected county authority (ibid.). This was an earlier major criticism raised in the School Enquiry Commission of 1868. The 1888 Act was one of two specific Acts, the other being the Technical Instruction Act of 1889, which were innovatory in bringing non-elementary education under the aegis of rate-aid financing, ensuring that a form of technical education henceforth could be locally administered. This accorded with the frequently reiterated precepts of 'self-help' favoured by the government.

The Technical Instruction Act of 1889

The government's central position regarding technical education remained unequivocal: existing science provision would constitute the core of state technical-education provision. During the course of a debate in the House which preceded the 1889 Technical Instruction Act, government's policy of non-interference in technical education was reasserted. W. Hart-Dyke, Vice-President of the Council, argued the government case: The Bill 'proposes to do no more and no less than extend the curriculum now existing in the Science and Art Department at South Kensington, throughout the country' (Hansard 1889b, Col. 509). The responsibility for technical education innovation and expansion fell to local authorities, not central government. This later prompted Magnus (1910), principal of the Central Institute, to observe:

> ... the pedantic refusal on the part of the State to give trade teaching was one of the causes of our belated efforts to organize for this country a system of technical education ... the direction of technical instruction remains very largely in the hand of a body receiving no direct help from the State ... ' (pp. 107–8).

It was also clear that the Technical Instruction Act would have little to do with elementary school, for it did not apply to scholars receiving instruction in the obligatory or standard subjects. Technical instruction according to the Act meant 'instruction in the application of science and art applicable to industries ... it shall not include teaching the practice of any trade, or industry, or employment' (TI Act (189), Section 8). The separation of work and education was reaffirmed.

The 1889 Technical Instruction Bill was introduced in the Commons in March by Henry Roscoe. With H. D. Acland he was one of the first secretaries of a new association, the National Association for the Promotion of Secondary and Technical Education (NAPTSE). Together they had served on the executive committee of the Association, which they had initiated in July 1887, under the Presidency of the Duke of Devonshire. There were twenty-four members on the executive (NAPTSE 1907: 2).

The executive had a generous representation from the earlier 1884 Samuelson Commission (Roscoe, Magnus, Swire Smith). The Association was a strong lobby for a model of technical education as conceived by the 1884 Commission. It has also been cited as evidence of the technical education 'movement': 'This was the first formalization of the existence of the *"technical education" movement and its work continued until 1907 ...* ' (Bailey 1983: 47).

Its principal aim was the promotion of legislation on technical education. The Association was critical of the 'general state of chaos' represented by the elementary education system, particularly the 'baneful' overlapping of the work of educational authorities. The uneven spread of educational provision and the fragmented nature of the administration compounded the associated problems of funding. The structure of the Education, the Science and Arts Departments and the diversified work of the Charity Commission made administration unwieldy, confirming Playfair's criticism of 1871. The payment-by-results system was denounced and there was criticism concerning the lack of technical teachers, manifesting 'disastrous gaps in the educational system ... chiefly in large centres of population ... ' (NAPTSE 1889: 22).

The problems of the supply of technical teachers

Apart from the difficulties of administering a technical-education system without a coordinated policy of administration, there were inadequacies in the grant system covering elements in the Science and Art Scheme, particularly in making grants contingent upon examinations. The Association's criticism of the system for training technical teachers indirectly added substance to the skilled workers' case for retention of the apprenticeship system as central to a technical-education system. A technical-education system institutionalised as separate from workshop activities represented a crucial abstraction of work from education.

This highlighted the problem of teachers who were generally ill-prepared for teaching technical subjects (ibid., p. 63). Analysis of the type of qualifying test for tradesmen and technical teachers illustrates the problem, first, the Ordinary grade, Part I mechanical engineering paper, for tradesmen; and second, the First Year Final Examination for Teacher's Certificate in metalwork:
Ordinary grade, Part I, Mechanical Engineering:

> Q. Given the effective pressure on the piston in a direct-acting steam engine at any instant (corrected for effect on inertia of reciprocating parts), show how it is possible by a simple graphical construction to determine the tangential turning force at that instant acting on the crank. Prove the correctness of any construction you give. (One of nine questions)

First Year examination for Teacher's Certificate:

> Q. Name and briefly describe the kinds of metal you have used in workshop practice, stating their characteristic properties. (One of four questions) (CGLI 1901: 220, 301)

There was a marked difference in expectation of fitters and turners and similar artisans, who sat the first kind of paper, and prospective teachers who would attempt the second. The knowledge content is also plainly different, with an assumed understanding of thermodynamics and graphical drawing in the fitters paper. The teachers' paper had an elementary, even superficial, knowledge content, compared with the knowledge expected of a general fitter or machinist in carrying out skilled workshop operations.

Another illustration from the Teacher's Certificate paper serves to emphasise differences of expectations:

> Q. What is meant by 'Case hardening' and why is it adopted? Explain how to case-harden some small article. (One of four questions)

This kind of knowledge and application would be part of the fitter and turner's daily routine.

This adds weight to the NAPTSE criticism regarding inadequate preparation of teachers of technical subjects. The knowledge content of the examination questions and expectations of fitters taking CGLI engineering papers presupposed a greater understanding of the relation between engineering craft practice and theory. Teachers, unless competent craftsmen, by virtue of their specialism would be unfamiliar with the structure or reproduction of workshop culture. However, opportunities for capable workers to attempt the technical teachers' paper were very restricted, as they rarely obtained release from work. The report concurred in the existing policy of government and the Commissioners on technical instruction that the 'true place for the teaching of trades was the workshop'. Despite evidence that this was not happening in any systematic way, the NAPTSE report thus argued, 'the object is not to interfere with the teaching of trades in workshops, or with the industrial and commercial training in the manufactory and in the warehouse' (NAPTSE Report 1901: 2).

Thus the limited recommendations of the 1881–4 Royal Commission on craft training continued into the next century. A subsequent Board of Education report argued, 'It is a mistake to assume that training in school laboratories and workshops could in large part ... replace the workshop experience gained in works ... ' (Board of Education 1908–9: 90). The issue of what constituted technical education was still unresolved. The Bryce Commission was to note in 1895 that the government had been 'liberal rather than strict in interpretation of technical instruction' (RC on SE 1895: 28). At this time the eclectic nature of the technical curriculum was revealed; it included 'banking and financial science, principles of commerce: singing and musical notation, instrumental and orchestral music ... veterinary sciences ... ' (ibid.).

A number of contradictory factors thus characterised the situation from the 1880s:

1. An ad hoc administration of the state education system, with organisation and financing fragmented and uncoordinated.
2. A policy for the provision of 'science' in schools and evening classes, inadequately serviced and weakened by a system of payment by results.
3. A prevailing assumption that the structure and level of trade training in

industry was adequate, justifying a policy of non-interference on the part of the State.

The Bryce Commission of 1895 focused upon 'a rich variety of [our] educational life ... [and] the usual results of dispersed and unconnected forces, needless competition ... and frequent overlapping of effort, with much consequent waste of money, of time, and of labour' (Ibid., pt. 1, pp. 17, 18).

Pervasive laissez-faire doctrines and the philosophy of self-help, particularly in technical educational affairs, was maintained and came to be embodied in further legislation.

The Local Taxation (Customs and Excise) Act, 1890

The Local Taxation (Customs and Excise) Act of 1890 afforded further opportunity for self-help on the part of local authorities. Through this, financial support for the new technical-instruction legislation came from an unexpected source, unconnected with normal educational funding procedures. Technical instruction was mentioned in this 1890 Act as one of the purposes to which a residue of the money directed to be paid to local authorities from the Exchequer in respect of beer and spirit duties might be applied. This residue grant, known as the 'whisky money', was a windfall for a government intent on curbing excesses in alcohol consumption. In a move designed to scrap redundant public houses, considerable sums were generated which were not appropriated, in accordance with the intentions of the Act. Surplus funds were thus available. Acland, Vice-President of the Privy Council Committee on Education, proposed that in England the money should be reallocated to technical education. This proposition was accepted and the Science and Art Department administered the allocation of the money, which in 1892–3 amounted to £472,000; by 1901–2 had reached £859,000 (Brennan 1959: 88).

The provisions of these Acts were extended by an amending Act in 1891 (Technical Instruction Act, 1891), under which a local authority could aid educational institutions outside its own district. Scholarships also became available through this provision, enabling students to pursue courses of study, as existing, outside their residential district (TI Act, 1891, Sec. 8).

The significance of these various Acts for the development of technical education on a national basis has more relevance if they are examined together. The impetus provided by the 'whisky money' which arose out of the Customs and Excise Act extended provision for local technical instruction. This interconnection was possible because the funds under the 1888 Act could not have been diverted to technical education but for the existence of the 1889 Technical Instruction Act. But the appropriation of money and the rating powers granted under the 1888 local Government Act were not exercised on a national basis. A number of the newly-formed authorities were evidently not taking up the option of providing assistance to technical instruction in their areas.

The slow rate of uptake of available funds for technical education may be explained by local authorities diverting funds to other sectors. London, for example, applied its first allocation of 'whisky money' to relief of rates in the metropolis (Brennan 1959). In 1890–2 no money was spent on technical education, out of an allocation of £342,000. In 1892 the council spent £29,000 of its allocation in this way; this sum increased to £180,000 by 1902–3 (Argles 1964: footnote p. 31; Brennan 1959: 89).

It was clear that the special funds were being reallocated to secondary as well as technical education. A memorial delivered on behalf of Trades and Labour Councils, and Co-operative Societies, to the Bryce Commission in 1895 focused on this situation. Arguing that the secondary education of the working classes must to a large extent be technical and manual, the memorial pleaded for a permanent allocation of funds for technical and manual instruction:

> We conceive that the very words of the Act which limits the application of this money, if used for educational purposes, to technical and manual instruction show that it should be chiefly applied ... to those who will be engaged through their life in manual work, and whose work requires, for its highest excellence, technical knowledge and skill. (RC on SE 1895)

Acts of 1902 and 1903: school boards made redundant

Efforts were made to rationalise the generally ad hoc arrangements for the administration of secondary and scientific education, by the establishment of a Board of Education in 1899. This took the place of the Education Department (including the Department of Science and Art). The Board was charged with the 'superintendence of matters relating to education in England and Wales ... '

Two subsequent Acts of 1902 and 1903, the Education Act and the Education (London) Act, respectively, finally eradicated the old School Boards. They removed restrictions placed upon the kind of higher education which county council, boroughs and urban district could aid. These Acts of 1902 and 1903 obligated local authorities to 'consider the educational needs of their area ... ' (Royal Colleges 1906: 6). For the first time funds were to be allocated for the purpose of technical education as a part of higher education provision. The Acts of 1902 and 1903 called for (a) the definite appropriation to purposes of 'education other than elementary' of the grant available under the Customs and Excise Act; (b) The extension of the rating limit for post-elementary education to two pence in the pound (it had previously been limited to a penny rate).

This legislation provided the administrative framework against which the development of the CGLI was continuing. The context is important, for a number of issues arose. The various pieces of legislation attempted to resolve initial legal and administrative difficulties, which constrained the allocation of funds for education purposes other than elementary. The time scale is significant: It was not until 1899 that for the first time the government was committed to legislation for technical education. The enactment came 30 years after the tentative proposals of the Workmen's Technical Education Committee, and 20 years after the foundation of the CGLI. Government response was both circumscribed and slow.

The 1889 Act once again made it plain that it did not cover the teaching of trades, but restricted 'technical instruction' to 'instruction in the principles of science and art applicable to industries, and in the application of special branches of science and art to specific industries and employments. It shall not include teaching the practice of any trade or industry or employment '(TI Act, 1889, Sec. 8). This was a crucial reaffirmation of a long-standing policy, and begged a number of questions, particularly relating to the attitudes of employers to technical education and the status of the apprenticeship system. Neither the CGLI, nor the State, had jurisdiction over factory-based training, but employers clearly did. The CGLI structure did, however, meet with the approval of most employers because of the part-time evening pattern of courses.

The short-term effects of the extension of employer influence beyond the confines of the factory into technical education developments were not readily apparent. The critical impact of the employers', and government's, attitudes towards technical education needs to be assessed in the longer term.

19th-century problems of educational provision and access carried over into the 20th century

As with the recommendations of the 1884 Royal Commission, the 1889 Technical Instruction Act had only a marginal effect on technical education development. The employers still remained to be convinced of the need of their support for technical education.

In 1889 one-tenth of the total number of students in science and art were being taught under school Boards (Hansard 1889b, Aug. Co. 509). Some groups later found the situation unexceptional; in the year of the Great Strike one leading newspaper noted: 'technical education is not needed for the masses of people. Indeed they are better without it ... [it] only teaches the workman to think that he is as good as his master or overseer ... ' (*The Times*, 20 Jan. 1897).

But by 1902 the effects of years of ad hoc, torpid administration and the lack of a definite policy for higher education surfaced. Representatives at a higher education conference concluded that after the 1902 Act, technical education was in serious danger of being neglected. Under this Act, the provision covering special funds (referred to above) reserved for its use was altered (Higher Education Conference 1903: 18).

In 1903 it was once more feared that the level of technical and secondary education was in a low state compared with countries such as Germany and Denmark (ibid.). Figures showed that cities such as Liverpool and Birmingham, with populations of 685,000 and 600,000, had fewer than 7,000 and 5,000 pupils respectively in secondary schools. This compared unfavourably with places with similar populations like Hamburg (700,000) and Copenhagen (400,000) which had 22,000 and 12,600 pupils respectively in secondary schools (ibid., p. 26).

In 1904 no institutes in England offered specialised instruction on steam locomotive work vis-à-vis Boston, Cornell, Zurich, and Berlin (I.Mech.E. *Proceedings* vol. 67: 304).

The influence of the employers was again highlighted in the early part of the century. A Board of Education memorandum in 1905 expressed concern over the employers' response to renewed appeals for technical-education provision. An inspectors' inquiry found their response 'disappointing': 'unless this co-operation exists in some way or another neither employers nor employed will derive full advantage from the expenditure of national and local funds upon technical instruction' (Board of Education Memo 1905). Two further factors emerged in this inquiry: the attitude of foremen to technical education, and the issue of part-time release for study at institute classes. Both also figured in an inquiry by the Association of Technical Institutes (ATI) which reported that the

> ... older race of works managers and foremen [who] have not been technically educated themselves ... do not appear to like the idea of the younger generation knowing more than they do ... evening trade students [say] that their foremen will not set them free from working overtime on their class nights ... (ATI 1905: 30).

The 1905 ATI survey revealed that of 59 firms, 19 allowed some kind of day-release for young workers to study, i.e. 30 per cent. Of these, 12 firms paid the necessary fees, and four paid for books. Twenty firms did not recognise the technical institute certificate; and 13 firms filled vacancies with students from technical institutes, while 27 did not.

The Institution of Mechanical Engineers pointed to such weaknesses in the technical-education system in 1903, highlighting in particular the lack of coordination between workshops and colleges and commenting on prejudices found in the factories: where many employers were suspicious of college-education youths (I.Mech.E. Proceedings 1903).

Firms appeared more inclined to support the younger workers when attending evening classes. Forty-three out of the 59 encouraged students to attend, suggesting engineering employers were more favourably disposed to a technical-education system that had minimal impact on workshop schedules. Employers were conscious of the disadvantages of day-release: factors such as a fall in production; release of 'good' workers from valuable workshop time; the difficulty of replacement, particularly when apprentices were working jointly with tradesmen. Of the 59 firms covered by the survey, 26 were engaged in engineering, of which 42 per cent allowed some form of part-time release (ATI 1905). The attitude of foremen was critical here also, for it was within their province to allow young workers to forgo overtime in the works on evenings when classes were held. Frequently evening-class students found that foremen would not free them from overtime working on class nights, or even on the evenings of the annual examinations (ibid.). In one town foremen were reported as 'very obstructive' (ibid., p. 30).

The foremen's traditional supervisory functions had been extended in a number of ways in the course of technological and labour management changes. First and foremost were their critical abilities as competent craftsmen in workshops increasingly manned by unskilled labour. Second, they were crucial intermediaries between management and workers on the workshop floor with respect to the operation of management strategies such as the piecework system and the deployment of boy labour. Third, and a relatively new function, they closely monitored young workers' access to technical education.

Their standing with management had been previously reaffirmed in the 1884 Inquiry. A large engineering employer (Anderson of Easton and Anderson Iron Works) stated of foremen: 'We promote those (skilled workers) who, we fancy, have got the knack of organisation'. (Royal Commission on Technical Instruction 1884b, Q. 1792).

The evening-class system, subject to further criticism from educationalists, also became the focus of further inquiries into the 'release' system of technical education. Other bodies, concerned principally with engineering, were critical of the emphasis on the part-time, evening structure. For the first time the professional engineering institutes were among these.

The professional engineering institutions' first inquiry into technical education

The first major inquiry undertaken by the professional engineering institutions reported in 1906. The instigation for this came from the president of the

Institution of Mechanical Engineers, J. Hartley Wicksteed, who broached the subject with the president of the 'leading' institute of the time, the Institute of Civil Engineers in 1903 (ICE 1906). This inquiry was significant, being a cooperative investigation covering the whole range of educational provision relating to technical education. The following major engineering institutes were represented: Civil, Mechanical, Naval Architects, Iron and Steel, Electrical, Gas, Engineering and Shipbuilding in Scotland, Mining, N.E. Coast Institute of Engineers and Shipbuilders.

The inquiry was comprehensive, covering preparatory education in schools; training in offices, workshops, factories, or in works; training in universities and higher technical institutes; and post-graduate work. The largest survey of is kind, having no official sanction from the government or government representatives on the committee, it targeted 676 engineering firms, of which 39.5 per cent (267) replied on the questions of technical education.

The committee was strongly critical of the prevailing tendency in engineering firms to encourage study by the evening-class system and argued: 'Nothing should be done in the form of evening study which would impose undue strain ... the Committee think it is most important that all boys should at least maintain their scholastic acquirements during the introductory workshop course ... ' (ICE 1906: 13). The committee censured the employers' negative attitudes to technical education, maintaining, 'The sympathetic assistance of employers is essential to improvement in engineering education and training' (Ibid., p. 17). The survey also revealed that of the mechanical-engineering employers approached (200), of whom 41 per cent (82) replied, only 7 per cent stated they were willing to grant facilities for training (ibid. p. 26). The other largest single engineering group approached was Naval Architects and Shipbuilders (119 firms, of which 26.8% (32) replied).

The engineering employers' 19th-century attitudes to technical education had been carried over to the next century: They remained suspicious and cautious, if not hostile, particularly regarding any alternative to the evening-class model, for example day-time release of workers for study.

The findings of the Engineering Institutes' specific study confirmed a more general study carried out by Sadler in 1904. M. E. Sadler, later to become secretary of the Board of Education, maintained the evening-class system was difficult for students to follow, due to work commitments. It was also inefficient as a means of technical education (Sadler 1904: 121 ff.). He focused on the inadequacies of the elementary school system as an explanation for this, arguing as did the Engineering Institutions, that much of the work done in evening classes was remedial in an attempt to compensate for shortfalls in the school system. Poor attendance due to long working hours and incidence of illness on the part of workers was reflected in examination performance. This aspect of workers' education was further constrained by the rigidity of the external examination syllabus, for example the CGLI.

The bulk of workers and young people seeking education had recourse to the evening school as the only source of secondary or technical education. Some workers, whilst acknowledging the importance of economic efficiency at a national level, sensed that laissez-faire doctrines were not necessarily conducive to their needs. In a document to the Board of Education outlining their recommendations for Educational Reconstruction, they argued that 'in order to serve the needs of the community, technical education should as far as possible be divorced from the prevalent atmosphere of commercialism ... ' (Workers Educational Association, Recommendations ... 1916, PRO ED/24/1474). The Board's reply was not encouraging: 'they do not show any consciousness either of the enormous cost of the reforms proposed, or of the fact that in putting them forward the Association cannot claim to be ... representative of the great mass of working-class sentiment ... ' (ibid.).

Sadler's inquiries: the employers' position in 1906 and 1907

Another survey, under Sadler, into the extent of facilities granted to young workers was published in Manchester in 1907 (Sadler 1907). This limited inquiry addressed 16 railway companies and 195 firms, representing some of the chief trades and industries; of these 67 firms replied. The questions focused upon technical-education facilities and the nature of assistance granted by firms.

The results showed that 52 per cent of engineering firms (18 of 34) allowed some kind of release for attending technical classes. Ten of 34 granted special facilities for attendance at evening classes. This tended to take the form of (a) release from overtime on the night of the class; (b) permission to leave work early on class nights; (c) permission to come late one morning in the week if a certain, minimum number of classes were attended. On the matter of fees, 24 of the 34 firms offered some kind of inducement. These covered fees for classes, fees refunded (generally on condition of satisfactory attendance and examination), increase of wages, prizes and so on.

Sadler's inquiry suggested that individual firms exercised social and educational control beyond the workshop, even where there was no company-run school. Company conditions usually took the form of inducements of the kind referred to above regarding fees and attendance. A common condition of employment for young workers was compulsory attendance at evening classes (Daimler Motor Co., Coventry; Dobson and Barlow, Bolton; Mather and Platt, Oldham; Hans Renold Ltd).

Some employers insisted that apprentices be given no choice in this connection. As one prominent employer uncompromisingly expressed it: 'During his apprenticeship attendance at evening classes should be one of the conditions which the boy must comply with, for two or three nights a week, the neglect of which would render him liable to be discharged' (Mather 1909: 346). Some employers granted part-time day-release and practical assistance with fees. But, for the engineering industry as a whole, it was a relatively small sample involving only 34 firms. It included some of the larger companies of the time: W. G. Armstrong and Co.; Cadbury Bros.; Vickers, Sons and Maxims; the United Alkali Co. The largest companies were also in a position to exercise considerable local control through the use of their own company school. The ideology of workshop control, although limited, could be projected into a localised form of social and technical education. At Armstrong's at Elswick:

> ... classes not only develop thought and intelligence, but they also foster studious and steady habits and to raise the tone of the students ... students who are most regular ... and most earnest in their endeavours ... turn out to be the most efficient workmen ... ' (W. G. Armstrong & Co. Response to RC Circular, p. 647)

Clearly, institutional arrangements in a company-run school enabled employers to oversee the occupational socialization of their young workers.

It would be unrealistic to conclude from such a restricted sample that there had been a discernible change in the attitudes of a generality of engineering employers.

This research was published at the time of the EEF/ASE Agreement signed in 1907. Regarding technical training, the circumscribed nature of clause 6, in which facilities for training were contingent upon the demands of the factory, has been noted above. Clause 7 spelled out the ideology of the workplace and employers' attitudes to issues such as the day-time release of workers: 'Employers in view of the necessity of obtaining the *most economical production whether by skilled or unskilled workmen,* have free discretion to appoint the men they consider suitable ... ' (EEF Minutes 1907; my emphasis). This clause unequivocally laid down the principles upon which engineering production was organised. This applied to Federated members, and would not necessarily include all mechanical-engineering concerns. The central point remained: the ASE had conceded the principle of workshop autonomy, and acknowledged their dependence upon employers with regard to access to any form of technical training and education. It had important implications for the form and organisation of the apprenticeship system as the practical component of technical education, interacting with the training outside the factory, in the technical institute: 'There shall be no recognised proportion of apprentices to journeymen ... ' (EEF/ASE Agreement, clause 6).

A London County Council inquiry into employers' attitudes to technical education in the metropolis

Concern over the effectiveness of evening classes as a means of providing for the technical education of young workers prompted a London County Council inquiry in 1906 (LCC 1906). A memorandum was sent to principals of polytechnics and other technical institutes through whom employers in the skilled mechanical trades were contacted. The object was to determine, with reference to part-time classes, the extent and nature of the cooperation which might be established between the employers in London and the Council 'in the matter of technical education' (letter from Clerk of the Council, Mar. 1906).

The subsequent Report showed local employers to be ignorant of the facilities that existed at the time: 'it is very doubtful whether the majority of employers fully realise what is being done, or avail themselves ... of the advantages offered to their employees' (ibid., p. 6). The LCC later offered £5 bursaries for use by apprentices in order that they might be able to attend classes in the daytime. This was again offered through technical institute principals who contacted locally related firms (LCC 1909b: 419).

Of the 27 replies received by the LCC, only two 'indicated a willingness to allow apprentices time off during the day under this scheme' (ibid). The LCC concluded that 'at present [the results of the inquiries] do not afford much prospect of the introduction of "part-time" classes on any scale at all commensurate with the need' (ibid., p. 422).

Another LCC sub-committee, the Skilled Employment Committee, instituted a similar inquiry; it recommended that a limited extension to existing provisions be introduced, an early evening class starting at 5.15, at Shoreditch Technical Institute. This was the concept of the 'twilight class'. It also met with little success (LCC 1909b).

The general conclusion reached by the LCC inquiries over the period 1892–1909 was that employer response was of 'the most meagre dimensions'. The employers had again demonstrated negative attitudes to technical education and confirmed their unwillingness to make concessions regarding a part-time day-release pattern. The Council concluded, 'there appears no prospect of inducing employers on any large scale to co-operate with us in the establishment of a satisfactory system ... ' (ibid., p. 422). This suggested to the Council that a more authoritarian approach might be necessary: 'It would seem desirable for Parliament to give the education authority power to compel employers to allow their apprentices and learners "time off" during the day to attend classes ... ' (ibid., p. 423).

The frustration of the council is evident in the proposal to use compulsory powers in local administration of technical education. The influence of Sidney Webb, who was Chairman of the LCC Technical Education Committee, the first of its kind, may be detected in this political manoeuvre. He argued, in particular, for local government control over its financing and administration. It was Webb who had earlier suggested that the City livery companies should devote some of their accumulated bequests to the cause of technical education in the metropolis (Brennan 1959).

Significant for the time, the impetus given to higher education by legislation such as the Royal Commission of 1884 and the 1889 and 1902 Acts, in the event, was largely counteracted in practice by other social forces creating priorities which local authorities felt compelled to meet. The LCC had experienced this, as the allocation of funds granted under the new Acts of 1890 and 1901 had shown. This issue had caused concern to trade unionists in 1895, and was expressed in a memorial to the Bryce Commission of that year.

The results of early 20th-century inquiries such as the ATI's 1905 survey, Sadler's 1904 and 1907 studies, and the LCC 1906 and 1909 research confirmed the State's grindingly slow response, and the historical prejudice of employers against certain forms of technical education. It is plain that it was not only a question of employer ideology; national and local government political and economic priorities also intruded.

A Board of Education Report for 1908–9 admitted that these kinds of political and economic considerations significantly affected the extension of technical education provision (Board of Education 1908–9: 68). The report recommended that one of the duties of managers of technical schools was to establish and maintain the closest possible relations with those under whom their students were employed. Under existing conditions, 'great importance attaches to any action taken by employers' (ibid., p. 85). Its inquiries in 1907–8 had shown that the increase in the number of students who were attending technical classes, particularly during the day, was 'lamentably small' (ibid., p. 89). The Board further advised an extension of the opportunities for part-time day study. Such an increase would not, it was suggested, be costly (ibid., p. 86).

The Board's reports confirmed that one of the main reasons for the lack of growth of technical institutions was a bias amongst the generality of employers against the so-called 'college-trained' man, and the employers' belief that the technical institute would replace workshop experience gained in the works (ibid., p. 90). This was a reassertion of the commonly held but mistaken view that employers were actively engaged in systematic training of young workers. The evidence relating to technological developments from the 1850s and the major disputes such as the 1852 and the 1897–8 Engineering Strike points to another rationalisation. It was not that employers expressed fear about the decline or transfer of the training function, as the Board later implied. On the contrary, the engineers' dispute showed, if anything, that employers were concerned to consolidate their control of the labour process and extend the application of the principles of substitution. From the 1850s they continually sought ways to replace skilled workers by unskilled operatives requiring little or no training. The origin and development of technical education therefore took place against the background of this overall employer strategy.

Mainly concerned with general educational issues, the Board of Education was nevertheless anxious to involve employers in technical education, despite clear evidence of their disinclination, over 20 years, to make more than a minimal commitment. The Board did not recognise the nature of the employers' influence over technical education, not appreciating that it had been their tactic to extend the limits of control over the labour process beyond the workshops.

Under the 1889 Act the Board, however, was responsible for sanctioning instruction in technical subjects in addition to administering the Victoria and Albert Museum, the Royal College of Music, and overseeing the Whitworth Scholarship scheme. It is significant that 'technology' was not defined until 1900, by a committee appointed to examine the function of the Board. In other words, there had been no modus vivendi governing technical education in the 20 years following the foundation of the CGLI and the 11 years after the 1889 Technical Instruction Act.

In 1900 'technology' was defined as

> ... the application of different and specialised kinds of knowledge to practical occupations, including a) arts and manufactures, b) agriculture, c) commerce ... *It may be considered as a division of technical education ... superimposed on primary and secondary education* ... (Committee on the Co-ordination of Technological Education 1900; my emphasis)

A subsequent Board Report of 1908–9 provided another restatement of the need to relate technology to both the wider educational and industrial systems. This again inferred employers were a crucial mediating group. But as in the case of the LCC, at a local or metropolitan level, the Board was unable to judge the extent to which employers could resist demands on both levels for more active cooperation. The analysis of the 1897 dispute has pointed to the central issues here. A combination of the new technologies and the defeat of the leading artisan union in the 1897–8 conflict strengthened the grip of employers on the total labour process. There was much to be gained by widening that control into areas concerned with the reproduction of labour power, that is, schools and institutes concerned with aspects of technical education.

A more easily funded, part-time evening class pattern, administratively diversified, became the dominant feature of English technical education from 1879. Throughout the whole of the period from 1879, well into the next century, neither government nor employers modified their fundamentally cautious and calculating attitudes towards technical education. It was recognised later that 'no formulated technical education policies exist ... and in some trades the subject has not even been considered ... ' (Committee of Inquiry, the 'Emmott Report', 1927, ED/24/1869). Thus the effect of the 1897-8 conflict was first, to cement in place a particular management and production ideology, informed by the principles of the free market, that had been maturing since the onset of modern engineering practices, based on substitution, in the 1850s.

Second, subsequent legislation left untouched the penetrating effects of the strike and lockout of 1897-8 and the ratification of the Terms of Settlement in 1907. It confirmed that engineering employers in particular were primarily concerned, not with future skilled labour requirements, but with current production needs. As Noble, the spokesman for the EEF, expressed it in 1906, 'In the engineering industry the epoch of change dates from the agreement effected between the Federated Engineering Employers and certain allied trade unions in January 1898 ... ' (RC on TC and TC 1906: 161). The evidence supports this claim: during the 1897 dispute, his company had 10,000 men at work at a time when nearly all the works in Newcastle were closed (Noble was director of the Armstrong works in Newcastle). His company had introduced at that time hundreds of milling machines (these machines were discussed above and used as a major production tool and in order to overcome the problem of rotating work which often required skilled turners). Not one turner or high-class machineman was employed on these machines, *'as it was not at all necessary'* (ibid., Q. 2415, p. 163; my emphasis).

Noble's reference here to machine manning focuses upon a form of technical development relating to the skilled/unskilled issue. It was a development that reached back to 1854, when Nasmyth made a similar proposition about meeting current labour requirements rather than projecting future skilled labour needs: 'if we took the right means we do not require to depend upon what are reputed to be regularly-bred mechanics in the particular line, or what we call tradesmen' (Nasmyth 1854: 108). By 'right means' he clearly implied right for the employer to pursue profits by employing cheap labour: 'The great result of employing proper machines is, that you do not depend on dexterity. All you want is intellect and the faculty of managing machinery. You do not require manual dexterity' (ibid.). It was Nasmyth who later dismissed the apprenticeship system as the 'fag-end of the old feudal system' (RC on TU 1867-8: Q. 19201).

Two of the major strikes of the 19th century both involved engineers, in 1852 and 1897. Wider economic consideration, particularly in the latter dispute, tended to overshadow an equally crucial factor: the employers' powerful mediating influence on the form and course taken by technical education development after mid-century. Engineer-entrepreneurs such as Nasmyth,

Whitworth, Armstrong, Dyer and Noble had no definitive view on technical education, but they had a strong influence on the way technical education was perceived. Whitworth instituted valuable scholarships for artisans in 1868, but these were limited and their original function changed considerably over time.

Control of the labour process entailed dominance over new technologies, and extended control of labour power, including its reproduction in a technical education system (Clause 6, Terms of Settlement). The consolidation of corporate employer power, especially in the mechanical-engineering industry, was reasserted in 1898. Complete control over practical training and access to technical education outside industry was predominantly vested in the engineering employers (Clauses 5, 6, 7 of the Terms of Settlement).

Technical education, from its beginning, even under the aegis of the CGLI, always had a central component controlled by employers – practical training. Despite allowing the apprenticeship to decline throughout the century and their calculative approach to the broad concept of technical education, the employers never relinquished that control. Neither the local authorities, the CGLI, nor the Board of Education from 1890 had any jurisdiction over this element of technical education.

Nineteenth-century employers in the engineering industry, like other employers, were primarily concerned with short-term profit-seeking, organising and controlling 'technology in use' in order to satisfy current production needs. It is clear that they were not engaged in long-term projections of skilled-labour requirements or promoting technical education, towards which, at best, they had always been ambivalent. From the 1880s the federated employers in particular vigorously pursued their aim to render impotent the ASE. The Royal Commission of 1884, the Technical Instruction Act of 1889, and the subsequent Acts failed to induce any radical alteration in employer attitudes.

After 1898, as members of a corporate body such as the EEF, many engineering employers recognised that they had greatly increased their capacity to impose virtually any conditions of work and concomitantly to control access to technical education for workers in the industry. The shift in the balance of power in favour of employers made it very difficult, if not impossible, for workers to defend their position regarding technical education. Thus the only realistic alternative concept of technical education, based on a close integration of craft practice and theory, was made redundant.

Note

1. The following were members of the Committee: Thomas Huxley, Sir Douglas Galton (scientist and soldier in Royal Engineers), Sir Henry Trueman Wood

(Assistant Secretary of the Society of Arts), Lord Armstrong (leading engineering employer and industrialists), and Major General Sir John Donnelly (Secretary of the Department of Science and Arts).

CHAPTER EIGHT

Industrial conflict and 19th-century technical and educational change

The stress throughout this book has been on the social and technological changes accompanying conflicts within the mechanical-engineering industry and their particular significance in understanding the distinctiveness of English technical and educational developments from 1850.

Scholarship addressing the origin and development of 19th-century technical education is, in the main, more narrow in focus. Set predominantly within a consensualist framework, there is an emphasis on the opinions and prescriptions of concerned 19th-century personalities such as Playfair, Huxley, Roscoe, Scott-Russell and other public figures, usually outside industry. The attribution of the label 'movement' to an ad hoc 19th-century structure of technical education, perceived as an evolutionary growth out of the general-education system, is misjudged and gives an unmerited approbation to an underfinanced and basically unstructured system of the period.

The struggles over the reorganisation of industrial work and technological innovations underpinned the events which led to the faltering development of a national system of technical education from 1870. Analysis of these events offers new insights into unravelling some of the significant forces at work other than those directly concerned with education.

Powerful employers, managing many skilled and unskilled workers, exercised an often unrecognised influence beyond the immediate concerns of the factory. Their influence extended over much of the lives of young workers for whom technical education was ostensibly being drafted.

Focusing on the issues of labour control and the conflicts which resulted from work reorganisation, changing definitions of skill and the implementation of new technologies, two main ideas have been put forward. First, the relation between the social and technical relations of production and ideologies concerned with technical education was essentially conflictual. Second, the forces underlying the development and implementation of new technologies were also those at work in the demise of the apprenticeship system and in the origin of a particular pattern of technical educational development. Embedded in many of the employer–employee disputes over changing definitions of skill and the apprenticeship system were fundamental but often obscured ideas about technical education.

The Great Strike and Lockout of 1897–8 entailed crucial negotiations over factors of technical change which had accelerated after the many disputes and the earlier major engineering strike of 1852. The 1897 strike highlighted in the interrelation between issues of machine manning and innovation and transformed power relations. These issues had ramifications outside the industry, as in the course taken by technical education developments.

The context of the 1897–8 conflict also provided a previously unexplored framework within which to analyse the significance for technical education development of the predominance of the prevailing laissez-faire economic policy. The outcome of the strike was twofold: an outright consolidation of engineering employer power, and confirmation that underpinning the employers' inflexible attitudes to work reorganisation and technical education developments was a determination to subdue the craft unions and debase engineering craft skills. The objective was to maximise profits with an unqualified reliance upon short-termism.

Encouraged by the state's singular adherence to the workings of the free market with respect to economics and technical education, federated engineering employers introduced a series of strategies for labour control and technology management which inevitably fostered a narrow vision of technical education. The formation of the City and Guilds of London Institute and educational legislation from the 1880s did little to counteract the baneful effects on technical education of the employers' overriding commitment to control over the total labour process and profit maximisation accompanied by the apparent irrational demise of the artisan class. The employers' unfailing belief in a part-time, evening-class structure rendered inoperative consideration of any development of technical education on a more sympathetic and rational basis. Contradictions emerging from this and state policies both in economics and education obscured one of the more direct consequences of the 1897 dispute: the cementing in place of an essentially short-term ideology of production and a corresponding set of negative attitudes towards technical education which were to last well into the next century.

Problems of artisan elitism

Technical-education provision, particularly from the 1870s, was plainly part of wider social developments embodying political and ideological issues beyond those frequently considered strictly relevant and germane to an analysis of technical education developments. The ideology and practices of engineering artisans were especially significant because of their primacy in the leading manufacturing industries of the 19th century. Data from their conference resolutions and union proceedings revealed their attitudes and beliefs about technical education. These were crucially linked to their hostile reaction to the widening power of the employers over the reorganisation of work. Nineteenth-century engineering employers had clear strategies for maximising their control over the details of work operations. Significant changes in production relations in the workplace were evident as artisans attempted to align themselves with the employers over the apprenticeship issue vis-à-vis the unskilled workers. This does not imply a reductionism, as suggested by writers such as P. K. Edwards (1990). The artisans offered the only articulated response, outside the limited mainstream of educational thinking, to any prevailing notions of technical education.

Declarations of artisan elitism, bound up with the skilled workers' concerns regarding technical education and their assumed exclusivity, therefore took on special significance, characterised by the work of such groups as the 'Junta'. Their status-seeking class consciousness was not without its problems. As an elite group of union representatives of the leading crafts, the Junta did not display hostility to the notion of profit-seeking, nor did they, to paraphrase Briefs (1937), show expressions of class solidarity or prove a 'gathering point for anti-capitalist, proletarian feelings' (p. 209). On the contrary, engineering tradesmen, throughout the period from 1852 through to 1897, despite many industrial disputes, attempted an uneasy alignment with employers, as the details of the events leading to the Great Strike and Lockout of 1897 show. But as long as it served the artisans' sectional interests it continued. In 1869, for example, they appeared to share common capitalist objectives with the employers: '*if we are to keep pace with our foreign rivals*, in the artistic and scientific departments of industry, we must be afforded greater facilities for acquiring a larger amount of artistic and scientific instruction ... ' (*Journal of Society of Arts*, 21 May, 1869); my emphasis).

In pursuing their own concerns, seeking accommodation with employers on some aspects of technical education, engineering artisans failed to perceive the contradictions in their position with respect to the employers and the unskilled workers in the industry. They underestimated the political and ideological implications of such an alignment for the implementation of broader principles of technical education. Control of the technologies at the site of production was inseparable from control of both the technical and social relations of production. As P. Thompson (1983) put it, 'the battle over craft skills was part of a general struggle by employers ... to rationalise production throughout the U.K. ... ' (p. 94). The deployment of new technologies, particularly metrology and automatic machines of the 19th century and the introduction of management strategies such as the piecework system, replaced artisan control of production by management-dominated technology. A revolution in metal-cutting transformed engineering manufacture. For the first time in the history of metal-machining, the tool was effectively removed from the artisans' hands and located on a machine capable of producing work of greater accuracy and finish, with a minimum of skill input. By 1868 it was possible for an employer such as Nasmyth to argue: 'The day will come in which *steam engines will be made by girls*. There is as much skill required in superintending a power loom or a spinning Jenny with its thousand spindles, as a steam engine ... ' (RC on TU 1868c, Qs. 19190, 19194).

Contradictions on the artisans' side in their conflicts with the employers took different forms; clearly evident was their attempt to strengthen their status relative to the labourers, primarily through retention of the apprenticeship, and relative to the employers through the pursuance of the claim that they were historically repositories of skill. Major engineering employers, gradually building a more comprehensive federation, were determined to eliminate the basis upon which artisans justified their negotiating status: access to generalised craft knowledge. Thus a series of conflicts was generated throughout the second half of the century.

The artisans' reluctance to make concessions to unskilled engineering workers, reaffirming their status as 'aristocrats' of labour, hardened the attitude of the employers and alienated the labourers. The implementation of new classes of machines and workshop reorganisation was premised upon widespread use of untrained labour. The prospect of manning machines presented the labourers with an incentive to collaborate more closely with employers rather than maintain their traditional, subordinate roles in artisan-dominated workshops. Cole's (1937) thesis that employers constantly sought to break down skilled–unskilled divisions in the factory is supported by the evidence.

Control over technology and management of labour: the issue of interchangeability of parts and labour

A key characteristic of the skilled 19th-century engineering craftsman was the ability to produce high-quality finish and accuracy of dimension. Measurement (skilled use of relatively fine instruments) defined engineering craftsmanship as distinct from 'gauging' (simple comparison with pre-made templates). Early in the century the manufacturing limits on component sizes were quite arbitrary and owed much to the discretion of the individual workman. The pivotal work of Whitworth in metrology, particularly his development and deployment of predefined limits and use of guages was highly significant for employers seeking to extend areas of control in the workshops. He focused brilliantly on the essence of engineering skill: the ability to control accuracy in production work. He had recognised early on the great difficulty of profitably using unskilled labour without standardisation based on high levels of accuracy: 'there was ... [without them] ... endless trouble, hopeless confusion, and enormous expense ... ' (analysis above based on Smiles 1876). The use of gauges and templates in place of measuring and the increasing prevalence of automatic machines revolutionised engineering workshops: 'All the mechanic has to do now ... is to sharpen his tool, place it on the machine in connection with the work, and set it on the self-acting motion ... nine-tenths of his time is spent watching the delicate and beautiful functions of the machine ... ' (Nasmyth, RC on TU 1868b).

For capital the massive contribution to economic production of Whitworth and Nasmyth (and F. W. Taylor in America from the 1880s) cannot be overestimated: they judged the relation between control over technology and precision measurement to be fundamental to both machine and labour control. Technology-management and man-management coalesced, overall dominance being more firmly vested in the employer. Employer access to alternative methods of reproducing precision work systematically eroded the crucial distinction between the skilled and unskilled in engineering workshops: 'Interaction with machine technologies necessitates standardized behaviour on the part of the workers ... ' (Rosen and Baroudi (1992: 215). Nineteenth-century factory management and organisation was thus radically restructured by employers intent on the increased employment of 'boy labour' and 'girl labour', as opposed to the traditional indentured apprentices.

A significant element of engineering trade training, the acquisition of the vital skills of precision working, was thus effectively removed from the artisan. Interchangeability of parts (based on newly established standards) entailed interchangeability of labour. Burawoy (1985) expressed this in terms of 'market despotism', characterising a labour process subject to fragmentation and mechanisation, in which 'skill and specialised knowledge can no longer be a basis of power' (p. 123). With a history of negotiation from industrial strength, the artisans were prepared to challenge the employers over the diminution of their historical status and traditional controls over workshop procedures. They struck often in attempts to subvert workshop reorganisation; integral to their case were pleas for a retention of the traditional craft apprenticeship as the core of a technical-education system. Metal machinists were central to artisan resistance.

Metal-machining innovations: the significance for employer power

Technical innovations underpinned the employers' systematic subdivision of technical knowledge and craft skills, formerly conceived as part of the repertoire of engineering tradesmen. Technical knowledge became increasingly mystified and became accessible only on a need-to-know basis: operators no longer required a knowledge of cutting speeds and feeds, tool characteristics, cutting times, tool angles. Machining data and work schedules became a product of the toolroom. The leading American exponent of skill transfer was F. W. Taylor, who installed a toolroom as an essential feature of the restructured workshops at Bethlehem Steel.

Taylor's revolutionary work in the sphere of metallurgy and tool-cutting made him a key figure in American and European engineering. Undoubtedly, his major contribution was to bring into contemporary engineering practice his rigorous studies on metallurgy and cutting-tool technology, similar to Whitworth's metrology in England. He combined the innovative principles of 'standards' and interchangeability with his own metallurgical discoveries, particularly his development of High-Speed Steel, from the 1880s.

Accounts of 19th-century technological development, and labour process theories of management control of labour, accentuate the ideological component of Taylor's work, 'scientific management'. They underrate metallurgical and metrological innovations, which revolutionised the machining of metals. Whitworth and Taylor established as a management principle the inseparability of the ideology of control, machine-tool design and the metallurgical processes of metal-cutting. Both made the reconstruction of labour control a high priority in order to eliminate dependence upon skilled labour, and to cut costs.

Consolidation of control over technical knowledge and the labour process by employers was vigorously pursued throughout the century and, as events of the Great Strike of 1897–8 showed, was unambiguously confirmed by the defeat of the Amalgamated Society of Engineers (ASE) in 1898. Ratification of the employers' power came through the ASE–EEF Agreements of 1901 and 1907. There was no need for a 'creative engagement' of the workforce (Pollert 1991: 21). Even at this relatively early stage in rapid industrial change it is possible to anticipate later developments which reinforced the effects of widening employer dominance and the downturn in viability of skilled artisan labour. As Pollert (1991) further argues in a modern commentary, 'In the car industry, taken as the paradigmatic case of change, only 5 per cent (of the workforce) ... were of the skilled category, almost 90 per cent were semi-skilled and unskilled manual workers, and 50 per cent required no training ... ' (1991: p. 21).

The struggle over power relations: the breaking of union autonomy

The reorganisation of engineering industrial practice was characterised by increasing antagonism as the radicalising of engineering skills continued throughout the century. The conflict of interests and the struggle over power relations re-emerged after the 1907 Agreement; in fact the issues of machine manning and the apprenticeship question were repeatedly in contention from 1898. The redefinition of skill accompanied the engineering employers' recurrent interpretation and assertion of the 'right to manage'. There was also intensified pressure for integrating the General Workers' Union, a union of unskilled workers, within employer–union discussions. Reiterating the Terms of Settlement of 1907, the EEF argued: 'In making ... appointments the employers shall have regard to the nature of the work to be done on ... machine tools, and the degree of ability required from the workman ... ' (Engineering and Allied Employers Federation 1927: 23). The ASE was forced to expand its craft interests 'downwards' in order to retain control over the lower-grade processes that accompanied the new technologies, a process referred to as skilled workers 'following the machines'. Unskilled workers, encouraged by the employers, increased their demands for machine-operating opportunities. They claimed they were 'entitled to progress according to their ability ... and the opportunities that occur ... ' (ibid., p. 24).

The interaction between expanding forms of technology and an ideology of production based on widespread use of unskilled labour intensified. It was also evident that employers were not prepared to moderate their qualified attitude over access to trade training and education. At a local level some employers had introduced company-specific training based on the acquisition of limited skills, using up-graded unskilled labour. This element of work reorganisation continued to be a source of conflict between skilled workers and employers. The employers' threat to skill marketability and exclusivity had remained undiminished from the early period. This strongly suggests that the forces underlying the development and implementation of new technologies were also those at work in the demise of the apprenticeship system and thus the development of a particular form of technical education.

Labour-process theories have been influential in their contribution to the debate over the conflicts associated with the nature of changes in the definition and use of skilled labour. The increasing domination and extension of managerial control and the transformation of work has been central and focuses largely on the critical contribution of Braverman (1974). Data from America and the UK indicate how it was possible for employers effectively to decompose craft skills through the design and implementation of new technologies, the explicit details of which were assumed in Braverman. It should be added that Braverman was concerned with an overview of capitalist production trends and not a detailed exegesis of changes in manufacturing processes. More contentious, however, are the broader extrapolations drawn from his work. The criticism of labour-process theories is that despite their more or less universal critique of aspects of Braverman's thesis they are constrained by historicist notions of technology and do not extend the analysis beyond taken-for-granted assumptions regarding the productive process and machine technology.

Nineteenth-century employer-employee conflicts first revolved around practical issues such as skill reproduction, machine manning and economic efficiency. On a political dimension they significantly promoted the growth of the Engineering Employers' Federation. EEF representation at Inquiries and on Royal Commissions revealed the ideology of production and, if only tacitly, underlying attitudes to technical education not previously recorded. Typical among employers were Sir W. G. Armstrong Whitworth, Mather Platt's of Oldham, Atlas Engineering, and Vickers Maxim, whose submissions pointed to the emergence of a philosophy of technical education other than that projected in strictly educational sources. It became clear that they had limited regard for technical education; buttressed by the captive markets of the Empire, they believed they had managed quite well without it, and reasoned that its benefits were outweighed by the costs. They favoured the part-time evening class as a venue for technical education.

Employers, technology and early influences in technical education

The employers' influence on technical education and related issues may be traced back to mid-century, in Inquiries and Commissions from the 1850s. Whitworth's deliberations on the advantages of standardisation and the use of unskilled labour, for example, were revealed as early as 1854 in his submission to the Royal Commission on Small Arms of that year. Further official sources, such as the Royal Commission of 1884, the Technical Instruction Act of 1889, and subsequent research by the Association of Technical Institutes (1905), Sadler (1907), the Engineering Institutes, and the CGLI all highlight the struggle for control over the organisation of work and the development of technical education. From the 1880s especially there was an increasingly close connection between powerful employers, such as engineers, implementing new technologies, and extension of their control of the labour process beyond the workshops.

The Great Strike and Lockout of 1897 is especially relevant as it put into sharper relief the ideological position of employers and workers regarding technical education. Engineering employers perceived by government, at local and national levels, as highly significant were consistent in the level of support they were prepared to provide young workers: it was guarded and remained largely peripheral to the espoused needs of workers. The overriding consideration was maintaining manning levels at minimum cost, i.e. using raw labour.

It is difficult to extrapolate from evidence relating to a small number of large, influential employers to a generality of employers. There is little evidence, for example, regarding the attitudes and beliefs about technical education of the smaller firms; 19th-century engineering was essentially a small-firm industry. Analysis of firms in the British economy today reveals a similar profile with 97 per cent of all business enterprises employing fewer than 25 people (*Skills and Enterprise Briefing* 1995). There is also a critical problem in explaining an assumed relation between an abstraction, 'employers', and judgments concerning local employers of labour engaged in the production process. However, it seems reasonable to conclude that they were not concerned with projecting future skilled manpower commitments, but satisfying current production needs. Engineering employers were at best equivocal about technical education, often openly hostile to schemes other than those based on the evening-class principle. A pattern of technical education based on the separation of work and education located predominantly in evening classes was a development clearly suited to employer ideology.

The Association of Technical Institutes' research of 1905 reaffirmed that the evening-class system was favoured by most employers because it suited their ideology of work and it was cheap. Evening classes under the auspices of the City and Guilds of London Institute were free for young workers on a pick-and-mix system at Finsbury College. No production time was lost through workers being released for part-time day classes. But a Board of Education Report of 1908, substantially supported by Sadler's survey of the same year, unambiguously argued that the prevailing pattern of technical education based on the evening-class pattern 'retarded ... and disheartened the student before he has obtained even such knowledge as he requires if he is to be an intelligent hand-worker ... ' (Board of Education 1908–9: 86). Nevertheless, it is clear that the pattern of technical education, for all practical purposes, had been affected by the collapse of union resistance to work reorganisation and skill redefinition, particularly after the strike of 1897–8. Throughout much of the 19th century the craft-apprenticeship mode of training was the only form of technical education; it was perceived as such by the unions. For artisans the craft apprenticeship was therefore central to any technical-education system. The transfer of control from artisan-dominated production processes to a model of employer-dominated technology, as part of the reorganisation of work, ensured that control over technical education was also displaced.

Other forces were at work in formulating ideas of technical education. From mid-century, the artisans' perception of technical education in some respects was consonant with the prevailing views of scientists such as Huxley, Lyon Playfair and Scott-Russell, who were among the leading public figures expressing concern about the development of technical education. Tradesmen also concurred in a more generalised view that technical education made the skilled workers more competent and 'technically efficient'. But the reality of the economic and political situation, misconstrued by skilled workers, was that technical-education provision was inordinately influenced by employers and subordinated to the working of the free market. This combination clearly undermined the artisans' case for a retention of the apprenticeship as a basis for technical education. It also deflected attention from a consideration of an alternative model of technical education as suggested by the unions.

The State, employers and labour

The 1897–8 conflict was the culmination of a series of conflicts between skilled engineering workers and their employers throughout the second half of the century. The strike and its outcome proved decisive in the transformation of union power and set firmly in place a set of ideas concerning the apprenticeship system and the issue of technical education.

In the aftermath of the strike, employer power was further strengthened, consolidating the link between the reorganisation of work and control of the labour process and the maximisation of profits. The subordination of artisan unions, such as the ASE, was an imperative for 19th-century employers. This fitted the wider liberal economic policies of Victorian Britain, characterised by industrial expansion and entrepreneurialism.

Often unrecognised are the implications of the State's perception of technical education as subject to the dictates of the free market. The distinguishing characteristic of this policy was that it was essentially short-term. Short-termism is crucial to the argument here. Within the context of 19th-century manufacturing, the focus was on technical change, which entailed movement of the workforce. Some trades diminished and skilled workers in particular were displaced by unskilled labour, often young workers. When this happened, there was a need for a sound technical-education system flexible enough to help retrain them for new skills.

At the levels of the individual employer, profit-seeking constituted rational economic behaviour. But the expectation of the State regarding a national policy for technical education was directed at long-term projections for skilled labour. Thus the downturn in the supply of skilled labour, responding to short-term profit maximisation, appeared to manifest irrational economic behaviour. The Terms of Settlement concluding the dispute of 1897–8 regularised this position, for no concessions to long-term training had been considered or formulated. Rational decisions at the level of the individual employer proved counterproductive at the level of national policy.

The legacy of the Great Strike and the role of the State

The Great Strike confirmed the economic short-termism of employers, supported by the state. Subsequent legislation on technical education was clearly influenced by this prevailing doctrine. Official Reports of 1902, 1903, 1905, 1910 and government reports on trade training and education after the First World War showed that the predominantly laissez-faire policies inherited from the 19th century fostered a neglect of technical education.

The contradictions inherent in these developments have been misunderstood, partly because the behaviour of employers was, on the one hand, perceived as rational, but on the other it was incongruent with putative national policies on technical education. These contradictions permeated policies for technical education from this period on; they also characterise consensualist accounts of the development of technical education.

The technological and parallel technical-educational developments in the late 19th century were more than late Victorian phenomena; the critical influence of employers was sustained beyond the period under review. But do subsequent events beyond this period serve to validate this finding? Did government, persisting with its free-market policies, continue to perceive technical education on all ill-formulated tripartite model, involving the State, local authorities, and employers?

A brief examination of some of the inquiries relevant to the State, local authorities and the employers in the first decades of the 20th century serves to illuminate these issues.

The government, from the outset ambivalent about its role in technical education, rationally assumed that the principal beneficiaries of technical education would be employers and young workers. The latter group, for all practical purposes, despite their politicisation, were powerless with respect to work organisation and labour control. The government's belief was that employers, with support from local authorities, could be realistically expected to assume at least partial responsibility for technical education development. Was there any justification for this view?

The Acts of 1902 and 1903 which empowered local authorities to administer technical education in their areas were evidently failing by the end of the First World War. A large number of authorities had no Technical Instruction Committees, and a still larger number had no Advisory Committees composing employers and workmen, as laid down in the Acts (Board of Education 1919).

It was also acknowledged at this time that the system of indentured apprenticeship had 'almost died out'. Few employers allowed some form of part-time day-release for classes, and it was admitted 'It cannot be expected that the majority ... will do so voluntarily ... ' (ibid.).

Despite reliance upon the workings of the free market, there was a marked tendency to shift responsibility for the perceived inadequacies in technical education away from the government, particularly after the war.

An uneasy alliance: the state, employers and local authorities

The reluctance of local authorities to provide for the administration of technical education was attributed by the President of the Board of Education, Fisher, to the influence of employers. He argued there was a 'small and feeble response ... from the industries which the Education Authorities tried to serve ... '

(Board of Education 1919). Employers, in general, were still said to be ignorant of the provision made in schools and colleges: 'The industries know nothing of the technical schools; they know nothing of the use which they might make of these schools; they do not believe in them ... ' (ibid., p. 31).

Fisher's strictures notwithstanding, government's long-held conviction remained: a key factor in the resolution of the problem of technical-education provision was a positive contribution from the employers. They should formulate their needs, and be prepared to provide at least partial funding and further organisational support: 'It is almost imperative that [industries] should make financial contributions towards the work which is carried on for their benefit by local Education Authorities ... ' (ibid., p. 2). This reveals that government had yet to understand the political implications of the anomalies created by economic short-termism coupled with long-term expectations for skilled labour. There appeared to be no recognition of the significance for technical change of power relations in industry or of the ideological position held by employers regarding the organisation of work and control of labour, which had remained basically unaltered since before 1898. The general education system was ill-prepared, disparate and underfunded. It was not in a position to provide, over the long term, education for people being forced to change jobs. If there was any such recognition it was not revealed in government thinking whenever technical training and education were under discussion.

Through the last decades of the 19th century the employers had unfailingly demonstrated their unwillingness to support technical education on terms other than their own, and which did not correspond with the prevailing ideology of production. Central to this ideology was the implementation of sophisticated technologies premised upon the decomposition of craft skills. The demise of the craft apprenticeship was part of the employers' more generalised and highly circumspect attitude towards institutionalised technical education.

The government, adhering to a questionable belief in 'gifted amateurism' regarding the administration and delivery of technical education, was determined to maintain a distance from the day-to-day problems associated with its structure and organisation. The well-publicized ineffectiveness of the employers' responses deflected attention from the State's own very cautious attitude to technical education on a national scale. Early in the century, for example, government had rejected the recommendations of a Committee on Technology and Technical Education which reported in 1901. The committee's submission to the president of the Board of Education, Lord Devonshire, stated: 'technology (a division of technical education) requires for the purposes of administration a somewhat special organization as a division of the Office (Committee on the Coordination of Technological Education 1901). Regarding the local authorities, Fisher later criticised the lack of plan or method and the ad hoc development of technical education. Local authorities, he argued, were 'not well adjusted to the needs of technical education ... ' (letter to Board of Trade 1919).

Thus government attributed the relatively poor state of technical education to insufficient support from employers, and the inability of local authorities to provide adequate administrative servicing. This highlights the contradiction originating in the disjointed structure of technical education which emerged from the 19th century: the State's insistence on tripartism in technical education, whilst acknowledging the failure of the employers and the local authorities to make adequate provisions.

Tripartism in technical education: Emmott and Dugald Clerk

The government continued to perceive technical education as structured on a tripartite model: State, local authorities and employers. But up to 1927 *there had been no systematic contact between industry, local authorities and education.* The Emmott Report of that year was the first in the history of education to consider the collective opinions of education authorities, learned societies and institutions such as the Federation of British Industries (FBI) and the General Federation of Trade Unions. Its significance is further heightened by the fact that it was only the second full inquiry into technical education in England and Wales, the first being the Royal Commission over 40 years earlier in 1884.

As with the 1884 Inquiry, the Emmott Committee had only semi-official status, having been instigated by the Association of Technical Institutes (ATI), and was not government-sponsored. Its main finding was that technical education was 'patchy and disorganized' rather than an organic whole. Given evidence from the various official and unofficial inquiries, and the generally acknowledged effects on apprenticeship and technical education of the 1897–8 strike, a coherent pattern of development seemed unlikely. One journal noted that the report showed how 'ill-coordinated were the parts of the educational machinery ... ' (*Journal of Education and School World* 1928: 10).

The Emmott report was quickly followed by an inquiry into engineering education (Clerk Advisory Committee 1930). Under Dugald Clerk, this revealed the disturbing finding that systematic organisation of works *training was comparatively rare in the United Kingdom.* Its main conclusion was that very large numbers of engineering firms '*have little or no acquaintance with, or influence on, the provision made in technical schools*' (p. 28; my emphasis).

Both Emmott and Dugald Clerk therefore confirmed the underlying inadequacies of the prevailing technical-education system, inherited from the previous century, without penetrating either the philosophy of education or the ideology of production which legitimised them. But a minority report in Dugald Clerk (H. E. Berriman), did allude to the power of the employers:

> ... no material advance is likely to be made in the technical education of the ordinary apprentices in the engineering trades until this subject is a recognised and established part of the Association[1] sphere of interest, and therefore regarded as coming within the administration of labour ... ' (Clerk Advisory Committee 1930: 30).

Responding to a deputation from the Emmott Committee, Lord Eustace Percy, President of the Board of Education, emphasised the need to convert the evening-class system, which dominated the part-time pattern of technical education, into part-time day education. But the failure of government to recognise the power of the employers over this issue was again evident. Resolute in its adherence to laissez-faire economic behaviour, it was not prepared to challenge the employers' position regarding short-term profit-seeking or their intransigence over day-release of young workers. The government's ideological position makes logistic sense if the state of the apprenticeship is considered: by 1925, less than 8 per cent of apprentices to the machinist trade were under indentures or written agreements, and over 40 per cent of general engineering firms employed no apprentices at all (HMSO 1928b).

Percy repeated the theme which had run since the 1870s: 'it will probably be found that the degree to which part-time education can supplement workshop practice ... will depend largely on the willingness of employers to cooperate ... in increasing the number and range of part-time classes ... ' (Board of Education, General Information Memo, No. 8 (1928), p. 14).

The issue of a part-time day-release structure reappeared in the Balfour Report of 1929, which similarly reiterated the case for enlisting the support of employers. It maintained, 'the allowance for time off does not appear to be nearly so widely adopted as one thinks it deserves to be ... ' (Balfour Report 1929: 208). A weak education system notwithstanding, Balfour referred to the concept of 'education as a factor in efficiency'. This conceptualisation, with its emphasis on economic forces and the fear of foreign competition, featured largely in the ideas of thinkers on technical education such as Huxley, Lyon Playfair, Scott-Russell; it permeates justifications for present technical-education structures.

The decomposition of craft skills, was well advanced even as the structure of the first formal technical-education system was being debated by these scientists. The decline of systematic craft training had reached the stage in the late 1920s when this aspect of technical training, referred to by Balfour, was moribund; but still government expectations of the employers persisted.

By the 1930s the pattern established in the 19th century had become stabilised. Successive governments' inability or unwillingness to seek ways of moderating the employers' dominance and control over access to technical education served to reinforce the structure. Subsequent developments, disrupted by the Second World War and punctuated by post-war education legislation, produced few innovations, and the pattern continued well into the Robbins era and beyond.

The contemporary situation: dependence on employers reasserted

Research from the 1970s reaffirmed the problems attendant upon over reliance on industrialists' support. A major study of the education of engineers for the manufacturing industry by the British Association for the Advancement of Science (BAAS) (1977) examined the place of employers in craft training. It concluded that 'Good training places are scarce and much of industry does not appear to recognize its role in the development ... of the engineer ... it has been evident for some time that the traditional providers (of training places) ... can no longer be expected to meet ... the demand' (BAAS 1977: 32).

A Commons Select Committee on Science and Technology, in the previous year, identified a basic lack of collaboration between the medium and small companies and technical-education institutions. The report also recognised the recurring problem of funding carried over from the 19th century. This was an issue taken up by the Conservative Political Centre (CPC). The CPC set up an inquiry under Professor Thornton in 1977, publishing its report in 1978. One of the main proposals was the creation of an 'integrated education-training programme' (paras. 3.4–3.7). But it could not fail to see a critical dependence upon the employers for the success of this kind of structure: 'integrated courses will involve close collaboration between educational institutions and engineering organizations ... ' (para. 3.39). The resistance of the employers to the release of staff to attend courses was noted (para 3.12). The recommended solution was novel in its attempt to stimulate employer interest through proposed tax subsidies as an incentive to support technical education: 'the cost ... of up-dating courses ... together with any associated costs of retaining should be directly allowable for tax purposes ... ' (ibid., p. 29).

Education versus labour control

Criticisms of the employers' response to appeals for technical-education support continued up to the 1980s. The persistence of these criticisms has had important implications for the way the current EEF perceives its position on technical education and it also marks the consistency with which employers have maintained their guarded attitude regarding its provision.

Since the last century the EEF has rationalised the problems of technical education in terms of its interrelation with employer control over the total labour process. Recent Select Committees, the BAAS, and other institutions focused on the problems of inadequacies of training within the industry; the EEF deflected criticism by arguing that the needs of 'industry' were different from those of the 'individual company'. The focus has remained on training for the internal labour market: 'the employer is best suited to identify the training needs of ... young people ... ' (EEF 1976: 23).

The position has changed little in the past 25 years. The decline in apprenticeships has been directly attributed to the continued practice of training for limited 'in-company' skills: '[there is] ... an increasing reliance by employers on "growing their own" trained workforce with specific skills through internal market arrangements ... ' (*Employment Gazette*, Feb. 1995, p. 70). This is an echo from the past. The Terms of Settlement of the 1897 strike acknowledged that employers then were similarly concerned with 'identifying needs of young workers': 'Employers have the right to select, train and employ whom they consider best adapted to the various operations carried on in their workshops ... ' (Terms of Settlement 1898, clause 6). The influential 1976 manpower study by the EEF had itself been condemnatory in this respect: 'the fact that many ... young people receive little or no training is a matter of serious concern. It warrants attention by both employers and the Engineering Training Board ... ' (EEF 1976, Appendix D, para. 9).

Since 1898 engineering employers have consolidated both their control over access to technical education and their hegemonic control over production processes. A concept of trade training as a basis for technical education closely tied, as it was, to the dogmatism of the employers' 'rights to manage' was as illusory in the 1870s as it appears to be in the 1970s, 1980s and 1990s. Engineering employers still perceive the training issue predominantly in terms of the individual companies' 'need' for increasing control of labour, and the use of technology as a means of improving productivity rather than in terms of complementing a long-term, flexible national system of technical education. Hence the employers' rationalisation of the problem as 'a conflict of interests': 'there is an inherent conflict, as yet unresolved, between the interests of the industry as a whole and those of the individual ... ' (ibid., p. 21).

Manufacturing investment levels in the UK have been part of a process of de-industrialisation, one effect of which has been to weaken the local infrastructure. This has led firms to switch their focus to a narrow range of specific skills to meet their immediate needs, precipitating a skilled-labour crisis. This, despite sustained levels of spending, much of which is directed to 'in-house' needs, ' ... not necessarily giving employees the flexibility and range of skills needed for adaptability' (Kitson and Michie, 'Incredible Shrinking Britain', *Observer*, 29 Jan. 1996).

Modern management thinking rests on four assumptions, which manifest a singular familiarity: 'First, the need to give a greater attention to the management of manpower ... secondly, the need to improve greatly our use of existing manpower, so as to improve productivity ... ' (EEF 1976: 12). With regard to new recruits, a third assumption states, 'there is a particular need to keep the age of recruitment low ...' , while the fourth speaks simply of the need 'to improve the image of the industry' (ibid.).

Many factors concerning the problem of training and the issues of technical education remain partly obscured in current employers' thinking, as they did with their counterparts in the previous century. In the contemporary situation, skilled artisans, no longer considered high in an order of demonology or as threatening, have been substituted by another assumed potential block on total control of the labour process, professional engineering groups.

Two specific EEF papers, Manpower in Industry (1976) and the submission to the Finniston Inquiry of 1980, support the contention here.

Employers and the question of professional autonomy

The Federation clearly holds a circumscribed view of the professional-engineering institutions, in effect relegating their function to the provision of a forum for their members (EEF Submission to Finniston 1979). The academic function of the institutes, according to the employers, is overvalued: 'they should reduce or cut out their quasi-academic role and carefully consider offering membership independent of academic qualification ... (ibid.). This strongly reflects the employers' historic perspective on technical education: a system of technical education will be 'tolerated' if it is calculated not to intrude in control of the production process, that is, not to interfere with the deployment of men and machines, but to support the demands of current production. This serves to underline the point that some powerful engineering employers have harboured a long-standing suspicion of groups capable of autonomy legitimised outside the workplace. Such groups were perceived as inimical to total control in the 19th century in the case of the artisans. The Institution of Mechanical Engineers was founded in 1847, but it never represented a buffer to employer control of the labour process; accreditation by the Institute came much later in the century, and the managerial–technical function bifurcation was to become a 20th-century phenomenon.

The post-war period in relation to 'professional' engineers is analogous to the artisans' in the 19th century. Just as the ASE conferred skilled status on certain workers, 'artisans', the professional institutes confer professional status. Such a system of credentialism contradicts a conception of control held by certain employers: 'Membership of one of the professional institutions puts little added value on a person ... ' (EEF Submission 1979: 4). The

EEF concluded that there was no case for 'licensing of engineers to practise their profession ... it would not be a practical proposition' (ibid.).

Engineering employers seemed to believe that the existence of an accrediting, professional body outside the industry would diminish their overall control of the labour process. Institutions, anxious to promote the interests of their particular engineering specialisms, were critical of the employers' poor response to appeals for technical-training provision.

Professional-engineering institutions, the Institute of Electrical Engineers especially, expressed dissatisfaction with the general level of trade training. In 1979 it argued that the failure of the engineering industry 'to attract recruits was due 'to the poor and in many cases a total lack of training (in the industry itself) ...' (*New Scientist*, 25 Oct. 1979, p. 283).

For ten years the IEE had advocated a restructuring of education for engineers, and was instrumental in the setting up of the most significant inquiry into education for engineering in recent times, the Finniston Inquiry of 1980.

The Finniston Inquiry

Finniston (1980) held a specific view of professional-engineering institutions, arguing, 'We believe that the Institutions are uniquely placed to promote awareness of development in engineering practice and new technology ... [and] the quality of assessment [of competence] by the best of them is extremely thorough and rigorous ... ' (paras. 5.39, 5.43). The question of funding and the provision and level of training provided by industry was raised again and regarded as inadequate, contrasting unfavourably with the practice on the Continent, USA and Japan: 'it is generally agreed that the provision of training was inadequate both in quantity and quality ... [and] there were few proposals as to [how suggestions for training] were to be financed ... ' (p. 187). It concluded that industry should be 'responsible' for training (ibid.). Reference was also made to the ill-defined nature of local authority support, and implied that legislative provisions were still relatively unclear, 'apart from oblique references to inadequate training grants ... ' (para. 5, p. 187).

Continental practice and British industrial culture

Finniston's comparative assessment points up the effect of the critical influence of engineering employers over the labour process in England, and also the singular development of industrial managerial practice as opposed to foreign countries. Of the Continental countries it was argued: 'working practices were systematized, formalized and written down ... the companies concerned placed great importance on these systems ... ' (ibid., p. 40). It further suggests that this approach did not correspond with the individualism characterising a liberal, free-market philosophy. Work organisation, it said, 'may not accord with the British industrial culture which has traditionally emphasized personal freedom' (ibid.).

This statement begs a number of crucial questions concerning the nature of freedom within British industry. Of particular concern are the processes whereby access to technical education and training has been systematically channelled by employers concerned more with depressing costs and widening control than education.

The Finniston Report was again critical of the attitude of British employers, expressing particular dissatisfaction over the nature and degree of links between the various branches of the education system and industry. It highlighted the lack of interest shown by them in each stage of the education-industry process: 'the employers of engineers have been insufficiently involved in each stage, although they are the ones who inherit the product others have produced ... ' (ibid, para. 6.5).

This book has indicated how it is possible for such a statement to be made 60 years after Fisher, President of the Board of Education, said: 'Up to the present time technical instruction has been organized from outside the industries whose full interest and cooperation it has never succeeding in securing ... ' (Board of Education 1919: 1).

A pattern for the future: lessons unlearned?

In August 1989 the Secretary of State for Employment, Fowler, argued that the new technologies, more advanced computers and robots change the nature of jobs and the demand for skills. More, not less, skilled workers are needed and the new technology is 'increasing demand ... for people with higher level skills ... ' (*Employment Gazette*, Aug. 1989, p. 408).

The reproduction of this skilled labour is to be the responsibility of the familiar triumvirate of government, education authorities and employers. Of the latter Fowler, restating the established view, said, '[They] should invest in re-training their own employees ... ' (p. 408). In this capacity they are expected to be part of the main agencies for change in technical education and training, supporting the Training and Enterprise Councils (TECs), 'potentially the biggest revolution in training in our history ... ' (ibid.).

Throughout the country 90 TECs were envisaged, of which 82 had been approved by 1996. The model is a highly decentralised structure, serving local areas. Training and Enterprise Councils coordinate local organisations, becoming 'a focal point for improving the integration of vocational education, training and economic development ... ' (ibid, p. 399).

In 1993 the Confederation of British Industries (CBI) focused upon the long-standing ambiguities in technical-training provision. It pointed up the confused and conflicting messages and different sets of priorities from various government departments and made a plea for clear-sightedness on the part of government. It called for: 'a long-term and unified mission and an accompanying strategy and business plan ... within which TECs are asked to operate ... ' (CBI 1993: p 28, para. 60).

The TECs and the LECs, local Enterprise Companies, established in Scotland, were set up as a network throughout Britain. By 1994 36 per cent of employers had made links with TECs/LECs. The TECs provided 23 per cent to the training process, implying a large proportion were seeking training elsewhere. However, of the small firms (25-49 employees) only 14 per cent had their own training facilities. The type of training carried out by all employers is significant. Thirteen per cent only carried out training for apprentices, while 50-60 per cent focused on Health and Safety and induction training, clearly an important priority (*Skills and Enterprise Briefing*, 16, Nov. 1994).

The response from government has been slow and not altogether focused. A recent report has argued that much of the government's training effort was 'a huge waste of money' (quoted in Business Monitor, *Daily Telegraph*, 20 Nov. 1995). Market failure has been acknowledged to be 'endemic in the small-firm sector ...' (DTI Funded TEC Services (1995: 5). Furthermore, the free market '... has not provided a range of customised services to address that failure ...' (Ibid. para.1. p. 1).

It is not clear, with these latest initiatives, how employers are to be persuaded to embark on this development. As Sir Bryan Nicholson, Chairman of the CBI in 1993, said, 'the key factor which will determine the degree of success of the TECs ... is the willingness of the employers to get involved in all aspects of their work ... ' (CBI 1993: 5). Some employers have maintained their suspicion regarding technical education and training; two-fifths surveyed in 1995 expressed concern at being involved in transferable skill training, fearing the loss of workers to other companies ('Training in Britain', Sec. 1, HMSO 1995). Thus in 1999, less than 15 per cent of all establishments had used a TEC service in the previous 12 months (Weller, P 1999: 1). Of those employers who are aware of the TECs in their area 67 per cent were reported to be uninterested in becoming involved at Board level (Ibid. p. 2).

Many TECs and employers also remain sceptical about accelerated Modern Apprenticeships (reducing the training to two–three years), believing funding to be insufficient and the time scale too short (L. Ward, *TES* 19 Nov. 1995). A funding crisis has led to the collapse of one of the country's longest-established training agencies, LASER, serving London and the south-east (Training in Britain, sec 6, HMSO 1995).

The CBI contends that companies have sustained levels of spending on training; it is increasingly apparent that it goes on limited company-specific skills. It is not being used to give flexibility and range in skills (I. Nash and A. Nicholls, 1 Dec. 1995)

It would seem old contradictions remain. On the one hand, the CBI argued in 1989 (*Employment Gazette*, Aug. 1989), 'Britain's workforce is undereducated, undertrained and underqualified ... ' ('Vocational Education and Training Task Force', p. 402). On the other hand, the Secretary of State maintained 'it is a far cry from the black days of the collapse of the apprenticeship system at the end of the 1970s to where we are at present. There are over 386 000 young people in training ... ' (p. 408).

Most evidence points to the collapse of the apprenticeship system in the last century; the Secretary of State's reference appears a gloss on a long-term decline, the origins of which may be traced back to the mid-19th century. In terms of the proportion of workers under training, the figures from the *Gazette* show that in 1989, the percentage of employees who were apprenticed in mechanical engineering trades was 1.9; other trainees account for 0.7 percent (ibid., table 1.14, 'Apprentices and Trainees by Industry: Manufacturing Industries'). For the manufacturing industry as a whole, only 11.5 per cent of employees are receiving some job-related training. For craft and related trades, 4.8 per cent and 3.3 per cent of employees are receiving off-the-job and on-the-job training respectively (Education and Training Statistics 2000, tables 3.18, 3.19: 61, 62).

It is ironic that one of the reasons for the long-term decline of the apprenticeship system put forward recently has been the waning influence of the trade unions. The unions have until recent times provided strong institutional support to training for skills and particularly the apprenticeship system, and its decline clearly reflects the diminution of union power and influence (*Employment Gazette*, Feb. 1995: 70).

More recent findings reaffirm government's continued uncertainty concerning technical education. Throughout the period under discussion, it has seemed plausible for the State to assume that employers would assist in its funding and organisation. But it is clear that lack of direction bedevils government initiatives, compounding the problems associated with long-standing employer reticence; political considerations are overriding pragmatic attempts to develop a wider skill base. It has been suggested that the TECs have been deflected from their economic purpose of focusing on a skilled workforce to the social problem of targeting the unemployed. As one critic put it, the Councils (TECs) have become the 'dumping grounds' for government problems (P. Bassett, 'Is the political clock ticking away for the TECs?', *The Times*, 10 Jan. 1994). The problem for government is worsened by the effects of a lack of clear direction, creating damaging competition between training agencies. One of the latest initiatives, based on new National Targets for Education and Training, outlines three objectives, including an injunction to employers to 'invest in employee development ... and ensuring all individuals have access to education and training opportunities leading to recognized qualifications ... ' (HMSO, Competitiveness: Forging Ahead, Cmnd. 2867, 1995: 80).

Today only a minority of apprenticeships have a formal, written agreement. In order to recapture the more recognisable concept of apprenticeship, the government-inspired Modern Apprenticeship, beginning in 1994, reinstated formal training agreements between employers and trainees (*Employment Gazette*, Feb. 1995).

But the new concept of the apprenticeships, part of the initiative launched in 1994–5, has run into difficulties, with the apprenticeship scheme battling with colleges for the best qualified young people (L. Ward, 'Fight is on for 'A'-Teens', *TES*, 5 Jan. 1996). Furthermore, the government '*still faces the problem of attracting new employers*' (ibid.). Skill needs will continue rising whether there are short-term difficulties or not; growth in demand is predicted beyond the year 2000. Significantly, there is a longer lead-time in developing the required skills (*Skills and Enterprise Network Briefing* 16, Nov. 1994).

The National Vocational Qualification (NVQ) has been criticised for trying to teach administrative and managerial skills which industry is not seeking: 'What the businesses really need is skill ... at the basic level of mechanical competence' (CBI Response to Mrs Shephard, Secretary of State, after her conference speech, quoted in Business Monitor, *Daily Telegraph*, 20 Nov. 1995). This again is an echo from the past.

If the issue of technical education is considered solely at the company level, as an element of Research and Development, one of the key effects of short-term profit-maximisation has been to depress consistently the amounts invested by companies in training. Firms which switch their focus to a narrow range of specific skills to meet their immediate needs are faced with the problem of finding skilled labour when they want to expand (Kitson and Michie, 'Incredible shrinking Britain', *Observer*, 20 Jan. 1996). The imperative to distribute bigger dividends to shareholders has been a characteristic of British firms anxious to fend off hostile takeovers, dampening the flow of funds available for education and training. R and D investment has subsequently lagged behind other countries (W. Hutton, 'Short changed by short-termism', *Guardian*, 21 June 1990).

More recent moves by government have included the introduction of a strategy for education and training from 14 to 19 (Learning to Compete: Education and Training for 14–19 Year Olds, DFEE HMSO Dec. 1996). Recognising the need to raise skill levels (p. 13), it proposed to extend the payment-by-results system to schools as well as colleges. In September 1997 it introduced Learning Credits for young people aged 14–21, providing training suitable to their needs, up to level 2 (GVNQ).

Sir Ron Dearing, principal curriculum adviser to the government, focused upon the critical group on whom the success of the initiative depends, 'the support of the employers [is] crucial to its future success' (ibid., p. 17). The government, even at this stage, remains unsure whether this support is forthcoming. Affirming the vital role to be played by employers, its scepticism is transparent: '[employers] need to be convinced that involvement is in their own interests' (ibid., p. 22). If necessary, government will challenge and 'encourage a wider range of employers to become involved' (ibid., p. 25), stressing, once again, that employers are key beneficiaries of 14–19 learning: 'They have a corresponding responsibility to contribute to its improvement and success' (p. 50).

Further research is required to deepen understanding of the rationale underlying the state's apparent inability to perceive the implications of the employers' highly circumspect view of technical education. This book has shown that part of such analysis is the need to unravel the complexities involved in basing long-term projections for a national system of technical education, and clearly it has to be long-term, while locking it into a system maintaining rigid adherence to short-term economic policies, based on free-market principles.

Government's failure to recognise the interrelationship between the implementation of new technologies and social and technical developments beyond industry is underestimated in existing scholarship on the origin and development of technical education. Much of this work embodies the belief that an explanation of the rise of technical education in 19th-century England is principally a question of how it contributed to economic efficiency, and its place as part of educational policy and reform. The ambiguities inherent in economic short-termism, so powerful in Victorian Britain, and its long-term implications are also underestimated.

The engineering employers' transformation of work and critical redefinitions of skill accompanying the implementation of new technologies in the 19th century have not been considered by successive governments as significant beyond the immediate, instrumental impact on industrial production. Since the late 19th century, there has been a failure to perceive the wider social and technical implications of transformed technologies. The reorganisation of work was not merely a change of hardware and production techniques. It involved a transformation of the control of labour, and the introduction of a radical ideology of production, so ably demonstrated by F. W. Taylor at the beginning of the century. The essence of this ideology was the decomposition of skilled labour and the deployment of new technologies premised on widespread use of cheap, unskilled labour schooled in a narrow range of low-level, company-specific skills. The decline of the traditional apprenticeship makes logistic sense against this background. If the traditional apprenticeship represented a form of technical education for much of the 19th century, its decline symbolised for employers the irrelevance of a formal, institutionalised system of technical education.

Radical technological innovations developed by employers from the late 18th century had a profound effect on the way technical education was perceived by them. The conflicts generated by ensuing work reorganisation critically influenced the structure and form of technical education from the last decades of the 19th century.

Note

1. The reference to 'Association' here is the Engineering Employers' Association (EEA), a body which assumed the role of the old EEF, and which was later to revert to the Engineering Employers Federation (EEF) later in the century.

References and Bibliography

Acherkan, N. (ed.) (1967), *Metal Cutting Machine Tools* (Moscow: MIR Publishers).

Ackers, Peter, and Black, John (1992), 'Watching the Detectives', in Sturdy, Knights and Willmott (1992).

Ackrill, M. (1987), *Manufacturing Industry since 1870* (Oxford: Philip Allan).

Adams, E. W. (1911), 'Time and Motion Study in the Link-Belt Company', *American Machinist*, **34**.

Adams, Henry (1883), Notes in Mechanical Engineering (London: E. and F. N. Spon). (Adams was a 'Registered' CGLI Institute Teacher.)

Adamson, J. (1964), *English Education 1789–1902* (Cambridge: Cambridge University Press).

Addison, F. (1979), 'The Social Imagery of the Skilled Engineer', Ph.D. thesis, University of London.

Aldcroft, D. H. (ed.) (1968), *The Development of British Industry and Foreign Competition, 1875–1914: Studies in Industrial Enterprise* (London: Allen & Unwin).

Amalgamated Society of Engineers (ASE) (various dates), Annual Reports (later Amalgamated Union of Engineering Workers).

—— (1872), Resolution (extract) passed at Manchester Conference of the ASE, 24 July, in Reports from Commissioners (1875).

—— (1897), ASE Reply to Col. Dyer, LSE Library R (Coll EB XLIX.9.MIII).

—— (1898), Notes on the Engineering Trades Dispute, London, ASE. LSE Library (HD 5/39 P2669).

American Society of Mechanical Engineers (ASME) (1893), *Transactions*, **15**.

—— (1903), *Transactions*, **24**.

—— (1906), *Transactions*, **28**.

—— (1912), Majority Report of Sub-Committee on Administration of ASME, in C. B. Thompson (ed.) (1914).

Amos, Ewart C. (1898–9), *The Engineering Times*, **1** (Dec. 1898–June 1899). (Member, I. Mech. E.)

Anderson, J. (1854), Evidence to Select Committee on Small Arms (1854), Parliamentary Papers, Vol. XVIII, Qs. 371, 794. (Chief Engineer of Royal Arsenal Woolwich.)

—— (1867), Reports on the Paris Universal Exhibition, Pt. 2, 1867–8. Report on Machine Tools, Parliamentary Papers, Vol. XXX.

—— (1877), Philadelphia International Exhibition. Report on Machine Tools for Working Metal, Wood and Stone, *Reports from the Commissioners*, 34.

—— (1880), *Paris Universal Exhibition of 1878*, Vols. 1 and 2 (Introduction to General Machines), Parliamentary Papers, Vol. XXXII, *Reports from the Commissioners*, 32.

Appelgarth, R. (1869), Report on the International Working Men's Congress at Basle, Sept. 1869, in *The Times*, 15 Sept. 1869.

Argles, M. (1959), 'The Royal Commission on Technical Instruction, 1881–4, its Inception and Composition', *Vocational Aspects*, **11** (23).

—— (1964), *South Kensington to Robbins: an Account of English Technical and Scientific Education since 1851* (London: Longmans).

Armstrong, P. (1984), 'Management Control Strategies and Inter-Professional Competition', in Thompson (1984), pp. 97–120.

Armstrong, W. G. (1872), Address to British Association for the Advancement of Science (London: BAAS).

—— (1888), 'The Vague Cry for Technical Education', *Nineteenth Century*, **24** (July), London.

Armytage, W. (1970), *A Social History of Engineering* (London: Faber & Faber).

Armytage, W. H. G. (1964), *Four Hundred Years of English Education* (Cambridge: Cambridge University Press).

Artizan Club (1869), *The Artizan* (A Monthly Journal) (July/Aug.).

Ashby, Sir Eric (1965), 'Education for an Age of Technology', in Singer *et al.* (1965), pp. 776–99.

Ashworth, William (1963), *An Economic History of England, 1870–1939* (London: Methuen).

Association of Technical Institutes (1905), *Report of an Inquiry as to the Co-operation of Employers over Technical Education* (London).

Baernreither, J. M. (1889), *English Associations of Working Men* (London: Swan Sonnenschein).

Bailey, Bill (1983), 'Policies of Government: Influence of Pressure Groups 1850–1900, the Technical Education Movement', *Journal of Further and Higher Education*, **7** (3), pp. 55–68.

Balfour Report: Committee on Industry and Trade, Pt. 4: Survey of Metal Industries, Board of Trade (1928), 3 vols. (1930–31).

Barnard, H. C. (1963), *A History of English Education* (London: University of London Press).

Barth, C. G. (1914), 'Slide Rules for the Machine Shop as a Part of the Taylor System of Management', in C. B. Thompson (ed.) (1914).

Becker, D. M., and Brown, W. (1905), 'High Speed Steel in the Factory', *The Engineering Magazine*, **29** (Sept.).

Beecham, B. J. (1982), 'The Universities and Technical Education in England and Wales', *Journal of Further and Higher Education*, **6** (1).

Bell, D. (1973), *The Coming of Post Industrial Society* (New York: Basic Books).

REFERENCES AND BIBLIOGRAPHY

Bement, Mills & Co. (1893), *Illustrated Catalogue of Metal-Working Tools* (Philadelphia).

Benjamin, C. H. (1906), *Modern American Machine Tools* (London: Constable). (Professor of Mechanical Engineering at the Case School of Applied Science, Cleveland, Ohio.)

Berg, Maxine (1982), *The Machinery Question and the Making of Political Economy* (Cambridge: Cambridge University Press).

—— (1985), *The Age of Manufactures* (London: Fontana Press).

—— (ed.) (1979), *Technology and Toil in 19th-Century Britain* (London: CSE Books).

Bingham, J. H. (1949), *The Period of the Sheffield School Board, 1870–1903* (Sheffield: Northand).

Blanchet, J. (1953), 'Public Opinion and Technical Education in England 1867–1906: A Study of the Awakening of Public Opinion to the Importance of Scientific Research and Technical Education as Factors of Economic and Military Power', D.Phil. thesis, University of Oxford.

Blauner, R. C. (1973), *Alienation and Freedom* (Chicago: University of Chicago Press).

Board of Education (1905), *Memorandum of Board of Education, 1905* (London: HMSO).

—— (1908–9), Report from Commissioners, Vol. 22 (1910), Col. 5130.

—— (1919), Proposals for Developing the National System of Technical and Commercial Instruction. PRO document 3 Dec.

—— (1926), *Survey of Technical Education* (London: HMSO).

—— (1928), *General Information Memo*, No. 8 (London: HMSO).

Board of Education, Statistics (1894–1901), Memorandum on the New Scheme of Regulations for Evening Schools and Classes under the Board of Education, Statistics and Returns, PRO Document ED24/83.

Board of Trade (1915), *Inquiry into the Conditions of Apprenticeship and Industrial Training* (London: HMSO).

Bonazzi, Giuseppe (1994), 'A Gentler Way to Total Quality? The Case of the Integrated Factory at Fiat Auto', in Elger and Smith (eds) (1994).

Bowles, S., and Gintis, H. (1977), *Schooling in Capitalist America* (London: Routledge & Kegan Paul).

Brackenbury, H. L. (1910), 'High Speed Tools', *Proceedings of the Institution of Mechanical Engineers*, **79**.

Bramhall, W. (1867), in Reports of Artisans, *Journal Society of Arts*.

Braverman, H. (1974), *Labor and Monopoly Capital* (New York and London: Monthly Review Press).

Brecher, J., et al. (1978), 'Uncovering the Hidden History of the American Workshop', *The Review of Radical Political Economies*, **10** (4).

Brennan, Edward (1959), 'Sidney Webb and the Technical Education Board', *Vocational Aspect*, **23** (Autumn) (also Apr. 1960).

―― (1975), *Education for National Efficiency: The Contribution of S. and B. Webb* (London: Athlone Press).
Briefs, Goetz A. (1937), *The Proletariat: a Challenge to Western Civilization* (New York, McGraw Hill).
Briggs, Asa (1970), *The Nineteenth Century: Contradictions of Progress* (London: Thames & Hudson).
―― and Saville, J. (1967), *Essays in Labour History* (London: Macmillan).
British Association for the Advancement of Science (1879), 49th Annual Report, London.
―― (1977), Report (London: BAAS).
British Labour Statistics (1978), *Historical Abstracts (1886–1968)*, Department of Employment and Productivity) (London: HMSO).
Brown, A. B. (ed.) (1868), *Engineering Facts and Figures for 1868* (London: Spon).
Brown & Sharpe Manufacturing Company (1891), *Treatise on the Construction and Use of Universal and Plain Grinding Machines* (Providence, RI).
Buchanan, G. & Co. (1864, 1884), *Descriptive List of General Machinery* (London).
Buchanan, R. (1841), *Practical Essays on Mill Work and Other Machinery*, 3rd edn, rev. G. Rennie (London: John Weale).
Buchanan, R. A. (1985), 'Institutional Proliferation in the British Engineering Profession, 1847–1914', *Economic History Review*, **38** (1), pp. 42–60.
Buckingham, Earle (1920), *Principles of Interchangeable Manufacture* (2nd edn, New York: Industrial Press, 1941). (Member, American Society of Mechanical Engineers, ASME.)
Burawoy, Michael (1978), 'Towards a Marxist Theory of the Labor Process: Braverman and Beyond', *Politics and Society*, **8** (3–4).
―― (1979), *Manufacturing Consent: Changes in the Labor Process under Monopoly Capitalism* (Chicago: University of Chicago Press).
―― (1985), *The Politics of Production* (London: Verso).
Burgess, K. (1969), 'Technological Change and the 1852 Lockout in the British Engineering Industry', *International Journal of Social History*, **14** (Pt. 2).
―― (1972), 'Trade Union Policy and the 1852 Lockout in the British Engineering Industry', *International Review of Social History*, **17** (Pt. 3).
―― (1975), *The Origins of British Industrial Relations* (London: Croom Helm).
―― (1986), 'Authority Relations in the Division of Labour in British Industry with Specific Reference to Clydeside, c1860–1930', *Social History*, **7** (May).
Burn, D. L. (1931), 'The Genesis of American Engineering Competition, 1850–1870', *Economic History*, **2** (Jan.), pp. 292–311.
Burnett, J. (1881), 30th Annual Report, ASE.

—— (1886), 'Trade Unions as a Means of Improving the Conditions of Labour', in Oliphant (ed.) (1886).
Burns, T. (1962), 'The Sociology of Industry', in Welford (ed.) (1962).
Burris, Val (1980), 'Capital Accumulation and the Rise of the New Middle Class', *The Review of Radical Political Economics*, **12** (Spring).
Burton, F. G. (1905), *Commercial Management of Engineering Works* (Manchester: Scientific Publishing Co.).
Butler, J. & Co., Victoria Iron Works, Halifax, General Catalogue.
Calder, J. (1910), 'Rapid Production in Machine Work', *Proceedings of the Institution of Mechanical Engineers*, **79**. (Calder was a member of ASME.)
Calvert, M. A. (1967), *The Mechanical Engineer in America, 1830–1910* (Baltimore: Johns Hopkins Press).
Cantrell, J. A. (1984), *James Nasmyth and the Bridgewater Foundry: a Study of Entrepreneurship in the Early Engineering Industry* (Printed for the Chetham Society).
Cardwell, D. S. L. (1972a), *The Organisation of Science in England* (London: Heinemann).
—— (1972b), *Technology, Science and History* (London: Heinemann).
Carpenters' Company's Technical School (1964), *The Story of the Carpenters' Company's Technical School, 1891–1905* (London: Old Carpentarians Association).
Carroll, C. (1979), 'Craft Education and Training for the Engineering Industry', *Coombe Lodge Report*, **12** (3).
Chadwick, R. (1965), 'The Working of Metals', in Singer *et al.* (1965), pp. 605 ff.
Chapman, W. A. J. (1943), *Workshop Technology, Pt. 1* (London: Arnold).
Checkland, S. G. (1972), *The Rise of Industrial Society in England, 1815–1885* (London: Longmans Green).
Children's Employment Commission (CEC) (1864), 3rd Report, Appendix and Evidence, Parliamentary Papers, Vol. XXII.
 1. Evidence of F. N. Cotterill of Cotterill's Screw Bolt Works.
 2. Evidence of J. Hetherington.
 3. Evidence of G. Norton, Manager, Horton's Screw Bolt Manufactory, Darlaston.
 4. Evidence of W. Elkington, Manager, The Crown Nail Co., Wolverhampton.
 5. Evidence of foreman at Messrs Walker and Hackney, Bury.
 6. Evidence of Nathaniel Shaw of John Hetherington & Sons, Machine-Makers, Manchester.
 7. Evidence of Mr Walker of Walker & Hackney, Bury.
 8. Evidence of W. Madeley, partner in Messrs Parr, Curtis & Madeley.
 9. Evidence of Mr Palmer, partner in Messrs Platt Brothers & Co., Oldham.

10. Evidence submitted by Messrs Iver & Hall, Bury.
11. Evidence of Johnson of the Ashbury Railway Carriage and Iron Company, Openshaw, Lancs.
12. Evidence of John McEwen, submitted to Government investigator H. W. Lord.

City and Guilds of London Institute (CGLI) (1880), Technological Examinations for 1879, London.

—— (1882, 1883), Report to Governors.

—— (1887–8), Calendar for the Session 1887–8.

—— (1896), *A Short History of the City and Guilds of London Institute for the Advancement of Technical Education* (London: CGLI).

—— (1901), Department of Technology, Report 1900–1901, London.

—— Finsbury Technical College Programme (1893–4); also Programme for 1923–4 (1924).

—— (various dates), *The Central* (Journal of the Central Institute of the CGLI, ed. E. Frankland Armstrong.)

Clapham, J. H. (1938), *An Economic History of Modern Britain*, Vol. 3 (Cambridge: Cambridge University Press).

Clark, J., McLoughlin, I., Rose, H., and King, R. (1988), *The Process of Technological Change* (Cambridge: Cambridge University Press).

Clarke, R. O. (1957), 'The Dispute in the British Engineering Industry, 1897–1898: an Evaluation', *Economica*, **94** (May), pp. 128–37.

Clegg, H. A., Fox, A., and Thompson, A. F. (1964), *A History of British Trade Unions since 1889* (Oxford: Clarendon Press).

Clegg, S., and Dunkerley, D. (1980), *Organisation, Class and Control* (London: Routledge & Kegan Paul).

Clements, R. V. (1961), 'Trade Unions and Popular Political Economy 1850–1875', *Economic History Review*, 2nd ser. **14** (1).

Clerk Advisory Committee (1930), Committee on Education for the Engineering Industry Board of Education Report, July 1930 (Dugald Clerk).

Cole, G. D. H. (1937), 'Some Notes on British Trade Unionism in the Third Quarter of the Nineteenth Century', *International Review of Social History*, **2**.

Collier, Wm., & Co. (1863), *Price List of Machines and Tools* (Manchester).

Collins, H., and Abramsky, C. (1965), *Karl Marx and the British Labour Movement* (London: Macmillan).

Colt, R. (1854), Evidence to Select Committee on Small Arms. Parliamentary Papers, Reports from Committees, Vol. XVIII, pp. 84–99. (Leading arms manufacturer and employer.)

Coltham, S. (1965), 'George Potter, the Junta, and the *Bee-Hive*', *International Review of Social History*, **10**.

Committee on the Co-ordination of Technological Education (CCTE) (1900),

Minutes 1900–1901, Report to President of Board of Education, the Duke of Devonshire, PRO ED 24/36.
Committee on Education and Industry: Second Part. Ministry of Labour (Malcolm Report).
Confederation of British Industry (CBI) (1993), *Making Labour Markets Work*, London.
Conference on Technical Education, Conference Report (1868), *Journal of Society of Arts*, 31 Jan. 1868.
Conservative Political Centre (CPC) (1978), *The Engineering Profession, a National Investment*. Report of the Working Party under Prof. John Thornton.
Coombs, Rod (1978), 'Labour and Monopoly Capital', *New Left Review*, **107**.
The Correspondence of Marx and Engels, 1846–1895, ed. Dona Torr (1934), (London: Martin Lawrence).
Cotgrove, S. (1958), *Technical Education and Social Change* (London: Unwin).
—— (1968), *The Sociology of Science and Technology* (Bath: Bath University Press).
—— and Box, S. (1970), *Science, Industry and Society* (London: Allen & Unwin).
Couch, V. J. (1955), 'A Sociological Interpretation of the Development of Technological Education in England, France and Germany during the 20th Century', Ph.D. thesis, University of London.
Cowan, I. R. (1969), 'Sir William Mather and Education', *The Vocational Aspect of Education*, **21** (48) (Spring), pp. 39–46.
Crocker, F. B. (1901), 'The Electric Distribution of Power in Worshops', quoted in Du Boff (1967).
Cronin, James (1979), *Industrial Conflict in Modern Britain*, London: Croom Helm.
—— (1987), 'Strikes and Power in Britain, 1870–1920', *International Review of Social History*, **32** (2).
Crowley, D. W. (1956), 'The Origin of the Revolt of the British Labour Movement from Liberalism, 1875–1906', Ph.D. thesis, University of London.
Curtis, S. J. (1963), *The History of Education in Great Britain* (London: University Tutorial Press).
Cutler, Tony (1978), 'The Romance of Labour', review article, *Economy and Society*, **7** (1), p. 80.
Davies, M., and Broadhead, F. (1975), 'Labor and Monopoly Capital: A Review', *Radical America*, **9**.
Department for Education and Employment (DFEE) (1996), *Learning to Compete: Education and Training for 14–19 Year Olds*, Cm 3486 (London: Stationery Office).

Department of Trade and Industry (1995), Evaluation of DTI Funded TEC Services (London: HMSO).

Derry, T. K., and Williams, T. I. (1960), *A Short History of Technology* (Oxford: Clarendon Press).

Dickinson, H., and Erben, M. (1982), 'Technical Culture and Technical Education in France', *British Journal of Sociology of Education*, 3 (2).

Dictionary of National Biography (1965), ed. S. Leder and S. Lee (London).

Dictionary of Scientific Biography (1976), ed. C. C. Gillespie, Vol. 13 (New York: Charles Scribner's Sons).

Digest of Statistical Information (1971), The Mechanical Engineering Industry, National Economic Development Office (NEDO), Sept., table 4.1.

Directory of Science (1895): *A Directory of Science, Art and Technical Colleges in the U.K.* (London: Institute of Civil Engineers).

Dobbs, A. E. (1919), *Education and Social Movements 1700–1850* (London: Longman, Green & Co.).

Donajgrodski, A. P. (ed.) (1977), *Social Control in Nineteenth-Century Britain* (London: Croom Helm Totowar).

Donnelly, C. (1868), Evidence to Royal Commission on Trade Unions.

—— (1884), Evidence to Royal Commission on Trade Instruction.

Douglas, P. H. (1921), 'American Apprenticeship and Industrial Education', Ph.D. diss., Faculty of Political Science, Columbia University, New York.

Du Boff, R. (1967), 'The Introduction of Electric Power in American Manufacture', *Economic History Review*, 20 (3).

Dubin, R. (1959), *Working Union–Management Relations: The Sociology of Industrial Relations* (New York: Prentice Hall).

Dunlop, J. T., and Galenson, W. (eds) (1978), *Labor in the Twentieth Century* (New York: Academic Press).

Dunlop, O. J. (1912), *English Apprenticeship and Child Labour* (London: T. Fisher Unwin).

Education and Training Statistics 2000 (London: HMSO).

Edwards, P. K. (1990), 'Understanding Conflict in the Labour Process: the Logic and Autonomy of Struggle', in Knights and Wilmott (eds) (1990), *Labour Process Theory* (Basingstoke: Macmillan), pp. 125–52.

Edwards, R. (1979), *Contested Terrain* (London: Basic Books).

Elbaum, B. (1979), 'The Labour Process, Marxist Structures, and Marxist Theory', *Cambridge Journal of Economics*, 3.

Elcho, Lord (1856), Letters to Walpole, 2 Nov. 1856 and Dec. 1866, Wemyss MSS (RH4-40/8). (Elcho was the eldest son of the 8th Earl of Wemyss; National Archives of Scotland (NAS) (microfilm), RH4-40/9.)

—— (1865), Letter to Solly, May 1865, Wemyss MSS (RH4-40/8).

—— (1867), Address by the Executive Committee representing the operative classes of the United Kingdom, to Lord Elcho, Glasgow (RH4-40/8).

—— (1885), Speech in House of Lords, Socialism at St Stephens, 1864–

1885, Liberty and Property Defence League (London). (Elcho was President of the League.).

Eldridge, J. E. T. (1971), *Sociology and Industrial Life* (London: Nelson).

Elger, A. (1979), 'Valorization and Deskilling: A Critique of Braverman', *Capital and Class*, no. 7.

—— (1982), 'Braverman, Capital and Accumulation and Deskilling', in Woods (ed.) (1982).

—— and Smith, C. (eds) (1994), *Global Japanization?* (London: Routledge).

Emmott Report (1927), Report of Committee set up by the Association of Teachers in Technical Institutions, the Association of Technical Institutions, and the Association of Principals of Technical Institutions (under Lord Emmott).

Engels, F. (1882), Letter to Kautsky; (1883), Letter to Bebel; (1889), Letter to Sorge, in Torr (ed.) (1934).

Engineering Employers Federation (EEF) Minute Book, no. 1, 1895–1899 (London).

—— (1895–1906), Case Register, Minutes.

—— (1896a), Conditions of Federation, LSE Lib. R(Coll), E.B. xlvi, 4.

—— (1896b), Minute Book, Minutes of Executive Board of the Engineering Employers' Federation, 13 Aug. 1896; 19 Dec. 1896.

—— (1897), Minute Book, Minutes of a Meeting of the Whole of the Members of the Federated Association, London, Feb. 1897.

—— (1898), 'Federated List', List of Federated Engineers and Shipbuilding Employers who Resisted the Demand for a 48-Hour Working Week, Glasgow: EEF, Preface.

—— (1898, 1901), EEF–ASE Agreements.

—— (1903), Index Nos. 1–2, Minute dated 10 Nov. 1903.

—— (1903–4), Case Register, Minutes 28 Dec. 1903, Jan. 1904, 5 Feb. 1904.

—— (1904a), Case Register (b), Minutes 9, 10 and 12 Aug. 1904.

—— (1904b), Article 7 of Agreement between Engineering Employers Federation and Amalgamated Society of Engineers, made on 22 Mar. 1897, minuted as complete document in EEF Minute Book No. 3 (1904).

—— (1904–7), Minute Book No. 3.

—— (1906), Circular Letters to Local Associations, Jan. 1901–Dec. 1906, Index nos. 1–294, 13 Mar. 1906.

—— (1907), Minutes, Agreement between EEF and ASE, 22 Mar. 1907. See above, Appendix to Chapter 5.

—— (1926), Decisions of Central Conference, 1898–1925, LSE Lib. Rx20.972.

—— (1976), Manpower in Industry (EEF 1976).

—— (1979), Submission to Finniston Inquiry (EEF).

Engineering and Allied Employers Federation (1927), *Thirty Years of Industrial Conciliation* (London).

Evans, Austin (1890), *The Law Relating to Apprentices* (London: Reeves and Turner).
Evans, Francis (1986), 'Masters of the Machine', *The Times Higher Education Supplement*, 19 (9).
Eyre, J. V. (1958), *Henry Edward Armstrong* (London: Butterworth).
Fairbairn, W. (1864), *Treatise on Mills and Millwork*, 2nd edn, 2 vols. (London: Longmans).
Faunce, W. A., and Form, W. H. (eds) (1969), *Comparative Perspectives on Industrial Society* (Boston: Little Brown).
Feldman, A. S., and Moore, W. E. (1969), 'Industrialisation and Industrialism', in Faunce and Form (1969).
Ferguson, E. S. (1968), *Bibliography of the History of Technology* (Cambridge, Mass.: MIT Press).
Finniston, M. (1980), *Engineering our Future. Report of the Committee of Inquiry into the Engineering Profession.* G. B. Committee of Inquiry into the Engineering Profession (London: HMSO Cd. 7796)
Fisher, H. A. L. (1919), Proposals for Developing the National System of Technical and Commercial Instruction; letter to the Board of Trade: Reply to Prime Minister's Inquiry regarding Technical Education, PRO Document, 3 Dec.
Flanders, Allan (1964), *The Fawley Productivity Agreements: a Case Study of Management and Collective Bargaining* (London: Faber & Faber).
—— (1970a), *Management and Unions* (London: Faber & Faber).
—— (1970b), 'Trade Unions and the Force of Tradition', in Flanders (1970a).
Fleck, Sir A. (1965), 'Technology and its Social Consequences', in Singer *et al.* (1965).
Fleming, A. P. M., and Brocklehurst, H. J. S. (1925), *A History of Engineering* (London: A. & C. Black).
—— and Pearce, J. G. (1916), *Principles of Apprentice Training* (London: Longmans).
Floud, Roderick (1976), *The British Machine Tool Industry, 1850–1914* (Cambridge: Cambridge University Press).
—— (1985), 'Technical Education, 1850–1914: Speculations on Human Capital Formation', in Joberg and Rosenberg (1985).
Foden, F. (1982), 'The Technological Examinations of the City and Guilds of London Institute', in McLeod (ed.) (1982).
Ford, H. (1922), *My Life and Work* (London: William Heinemann).
Form of Indenture (1904), Tyneside Engineering Company.
Foster, John (1977), *Class Struggle and the Industrial Revolution* (London: Methuen).
Foster, W. E. (1870), in Hansard (1870), Vol. 199, Cols. 438–66.
Friedman, A. (1977), *Industry and Labour: Class Struggle at Work and Monopoly Capitalism* (London: Macmillan).

—— (1990), 'Managerial Strategies, Activities, Techniques, and Technology', in Knights and Willmott (1992), 177–208.
Galloway, D. F. (1958), 'Machine Tools', in Singer et al. (1958), pt. 7, ch. 26. (Director of Research Association, G.B.)
Garner, A. D. (1985), 'The Society of Arts and the Mechanics' Institutes (1851–1854)', *History of Education*, **14** (4 Dec.).
Garnsey, Elizabeth (1981), 'Rediscovery of the Division of Labor', *Theory and Society*, **10** (3 May).
Gibbons, M., and Johnston, C. (1970), 'Relationship between Science and Technology', *Nature*, **227**.
Gledhill, J. M. (1904), 'The Development and Use of High Speed Tool Steel', in *Iron Age*, 10 Nov.
Goldthorpe, J. H. (1964), 'Social Stratification in Industrial Society', *Sociological Review Monograph* No. 8.
Gordon, D. M. (1976), 'Capitalist Efficiency and Socialist Efficiency', in Baxendale et al. (1976).
Gorz, André (1976), *The Division of Labour* (Brighton: Harvester Press).
Gospel, H. F., and Littler, C. (eds) (1983), *Managerial Strategies and Industrial Relations* (London: Heinemann).
Goss, D. (1988), 'Diversity, Complexity and Technological Change: an Empirical Study of General Printing', *Sociology*, **22** (3), pp. 417–43.
Gowing, Margaret (1978), 'Science, Technology and Education: England in 1870', *Oxford Review of Education*, **4**, pp. 3–17.
Gramsci, A. (1971), *Selections from the Prison Notebooks*, ed. Q. Hoare and G. Newell Smith (1971) (London: Lawrence & Wishart).
Granovetter, M., and Tilly, C. (1988), 'Inequality and Labor Process', in Smelser (ed.) (1988).
Gray, R. Q. (1973), 'Styles of Life: the Labour Aristocracy and Class Relations in Later Nineteenth-Century Edinburgh', *International Review of Social History*, **18**, pp. 428–52.
—— (1976), *The Aristocracy of Labour in 19th-Century Britain, c 1850–1914* (London: Macmillan).
Groh, Dieter (1978), 'The Intensification of Work and Industrial Conflict in Germany, 1896–1914', *Politics and Society*, **8** (3–4).
Grossick, G. (1976), 'The Labour Aristocracy', *Journal of Victorian Studies*, **14** (3).
Gulowsen, Jon (1988), 'Skills, Options and Unions: United and Strong or Divided and Weak', in Hyman and Streeck (eds) (1988).
Habakkuk, H. J. (1962), *American and British Technology in the Nineteenth Century* (Cambridge: Cambridge University Press).
Hackwood, F. (1889), *Wednesbury Workshops; or Some Account of the Industries of a Black Country Town* (Wednesbury: Horton Brothers).

Hadow Report (1926), *Report of the Consultative Committee on Education of the Adolescent* (London: Board of Education).

Haines, George (1958), 'German Influence upon Scientific Instruction in England 1867–1858', *Journal of Victorian Studies*, 1 (Mar.), pp. 215–44.

Hall, B. T. (1912), *Our Fifty Years: the Story of the Working Men's Club and Institute* (London: Working Men's Club and Institute Union).

Hansard (1869a), Col. 160. Report to House by B. Samuelson (Chairman of Samuelson Report on Technical Education 1868).

—— (1869b), 3rd Ser., Vol. 198 (July–Aug. 1869).

—— (1881a), 3rd Ser., Vol. 260 (Mar.–May 1881), Col. 546 (speech by Broadhurst, MP for Stoke).

—— (1881b), Cols. 527, 537, 538 (on the decline of the apprenticeship).

—— (1889a), 3rd Ser., Vol. 339 (Aug. 1889), Col. 1252. (Mather, MP.)

—— (1889b), 3rd Ser., Vol. 340.

—— (1892), 4th Ser., vol. 1.1.

Harrison, J. F.C. (ed.) (1974), *George Howell, Eminently Victorian* (London: BBC).

Harrison, Royden (ed.) (1971), *The English Defence of the Commune 1871* (London: Merlin Press).

—— and Zeitlin, J. (eds) (1985), *Divisions of Labour: Skilled Workers and Technological Change in 19th-Century England* (Brighton: Harvester Press).

Hartwell, R. M. (1971), *The Industrial Revolution and Economic Growth* (London: Methuen).

Hathaway, H. K. (1914), 'Elementary Time Study as a Part of the Taylor System of Management', in C. B. Thompson (ed.) (1914).

Hearn, Francis (1978), *Domination, Legitimation and Resistance: The Incorporation of the Nineteenth-Century English Working Class* (Westport, Conn.: Greenwood Press).

Heward, Christine (1980), 'Industry, Cleanliness and Godliness: Sources in the History of Science and Technical Education and the Working Classes, 1850–1910', *Studies in Science Education*, 7.

Higher Education Conference (1903), Report of Proceedings of the Conference on Higher Education between NAPTSE (National Association for the Promotion of Technical and Secondary Education) and Representatives of the County and County Borough Councils and Other Educational Bodies, Held at the I.Mech.E., 17 March 1903 [Chairman Lord Avelney], in *Tracts on Education, 1850–1903*, London (1904).

Hill, C. P. (1973), *British Economic and Social History 1700–1964* (London: Arnold).

Hirszowicz, M. (1981), *Industrial Sociology: An Introduction* (Oxford: Robertson).

HMSO (1915), *Inquiry by Board of Trade into the Conditions of Apprentice-*

ship and Industrial Training in Various Trades and Occupations in the U.K., London. [Engineering, Shipbuilding and Allied Trades, p. 57]

—— (1928a), *Legal Status of Apprentices at Common Law*, in Ministry of Labour (1928c), para. 5, pp. 18–20 (London).

—— (1928b), *Ministry of Labour. Report of an Inquiry into Apprenticeship and Training. History of Apprenticeship, Pre-War Apprenticeship, 1814–1914* (London).

—— (1928c), *Ministry of Labour. A Report of an Inquiry into Apprenticeship and Training for Skilled Occupations in Great Britain and Northern Ireland 1925–6* (London: HMSO).

—— (1995), 'Training in Britain' (London: HMSO).

—— (2000), 'Education and Training, Statistics for the United Kingdom' (London: HMSO)

Hobsbawm, E. J. (1951), 'The Tramping Artisan', *Economic History Review*, 2nd ser., **3** (1950–51).

—— (1954), 'Labour Aristocracy in Nineteenth-Century Britain', in Saville (ed.) (1954).

—— (1961), 'General Labour Unions in Britain 1889–1914', *Economic History Review*, 2nd ser., nos. 1, 2, 3 (1960–61), pp. 123–42.

—— (1968), *Labouring Men* (London: Weidenfeld & Nicholson).

—— (1974), *Industry and Empire* (London: Penguin).

—— (1984), 'Labour Aristocracy', *Economic History Review*, **37** (3).

Hoffman, Ross J. (1933), *Great Britain and the German Trade Rivalry 1875–1914* (Philadelphia: University of Pennsylvania Press).

Hollingum, Jack (1976), 'America's Contribution to "Rough-and Ready" Labour Saving Tools', *The Engineer*, **242**.

Horn, C. A., and Horn, P. L. R. (1981), 'Payment by Results and Technical Education', *Journal of Further and Higher Education*, **5** (1), pp. 30–39.

—— —— (1983), 'The ATTI and its Policies, 1904–1914', *Journal of Further and Higher Education*, **7** (1), pp. 8–22.

—— —— (1984), 'The CGLI and Technical Education in Victorian England', *JFHE*, **8** (1), pp. 75–89.

Horn, Pamela (1982), 'The Corps of Royal Engineers and the Growth of British Technical Education', *Journal of Educational Administration and History*, **14** (1).

Horner, J. G. (1900), *English and American Lathes* (London: Whittaker & Co.). (Member, I.Mech.Eng.)

Hounshell, David A. (1985), *From the American System to Mass Production 1800–1932* (Baltimore: The Johns Hopkins University Press).

Howell, George (1877), 'Trade Unions and Apprentices', *Contemporary Review*, **30**.

—— (1878), *Conflicts of Capital and Labour Historically and Economically*

Considered, Being a History of the Trade Unions of Great Britain (London: Macmillan).
Hoxie, R. F. (1914), *Objections to Scientific Management* (New York: Appleton).
—— (1918), *Scientific Management and Labor* (New York: Appleton). (This publication, based on the 1915 investigation into 'scientific management' on behalf of the US Commission on Industrial Relations, includes, in addition to an analysis of Taylorism, an examination of the principal variants of the system which were the Gant and Emerson models, insofar as these differed significantly from the main tenets of F. W. Taylor's model.)
Hughes, T. P. (1985), 'Edison and Electric Light', in MacKenzie and Wajcman (eds) (1985).
Hutton, F. R. (1883), Miscellaneous Documents of the House of Representatives, 42nd Congress, 2nd Session, Report on Machine Tools and Woodworking Machinery, in *Report on Power and Machinery Employed in Manufactures* (Washington).
Huxley, T. H. (1868), Paper on Technical Education at Conference on Technical Education, *Journal Society of Arts*, **15** (31 Jan.).
—— (1887), Address on Behalf of the National Association for the Promotion of Technical Education, in T. H. Huxley, *Collected Essays*, Vol. 3 (London, 1893).
Hyman, R., and Streeck, W. (eds) (1988), *New Technology and Industrial Relations* (Oxford: Basil Blackwell).
Imperial College of Science and Technology (1967), List of Papers and Correspondence of Lyon Playfair.
Inglis, John (1894), 'The Apprentice Question': paper read before the Economics Section, Philosophical Society of Glasgow, Glasgow.
Institute of Civil Engineers (ICE) (1891), *Engineering Education in the British Dominions* (London).
—— (1906), *Report of the Committee, Appointed 24th Nov. 1903, and Report to the Council upon the Subject of the Best Methods of Education and Training for all Classes of Engineers* (London).
Institution of Mechanical Engineers (I.Mech.E.) (1901), *Proceedings* (London).
—— (1903) *Proceedings*, 64; Discussion Paper on Technical Education, Vol. 67 (London, 1904), pp. 281–349.
—— (1923), *Abstract of Selected Papers, 1841–1921* (London).
Iron Trades Employers' Association (ITEA) (1876a), *The Piece Work Question and its Results in Engineering and Other Shops in the Iron Trades of the Country*, Manchester. (The ITEA was the forerunner of the EEF.)
Isherwood, N. S., and Senker, P. S. (1978), 'Technical and Organizational Change in the Machine Shop' (EITB mimeograph).
Jacoby, R. (1976), 'Harry Braverman, Labour and Capital', *Telos*, **29** (Fall).

Jalee, Pierre (1977), *How Capitalism Works* (New York: Monthly Review Press).
Jefferys, J. B. (1945), *The Story of the Engineers, 1800–1945* (London: Lawrence & Wishart).
—— (1948), *Labour's Formative Years 1849–1879* (London: Lawrence & Wishart).
Jefferys, M. (1947), 'The Skilled Engineer in 1861', *Economic History Review*, **18**.
—— and Jefferys, J. B. (1947), 'The Wages, Hours and Trade Customs of the Skills Engineer in 1861', *Economic History Review*, **17** (1).
Jevons, W. S. (1910), *The State in Relation to Capital* (London: Macmillan).
Joberg, L., and Rosenberg, N. (eds) (1985), *Technological Changes, Employment and Investment*. 8th International History Congress, Budapest, 1982 (Lund: Lund University, Department of Economic History, 1985).
Johnson, R. (1969), *The Blue Books and Education, 1816–1896* (Birmingham: Centre for Contemporary Cultural Studies).
—— (1977), 'Educating the Educators: Experts and the State, 1833–9', in Donajgradski (1977).
Johnston, R. D. (1972), 'The Internal Structure of Technology', *Sociological Review Monograph*, **18**.
Jones, Gareth Steadman (1974), 'Working Class Culture and Working Class Politics in London, 1870–1950', *Social History*, **7** (Summer), pp. 450–508.
Jones, Bryn, and Wood, Stephen (1985), 'Tacit Skills' (Division of Labour and New Technology, mimeo).
Joyce, P. (1980), *Work, Society and Politics: the Culture of the Factory in Later Victorian England* (London: Methuen).
—— (1984), 'Labour, Capital and Compromise: a Response to Richard Price', *Social History*, **9**.
Keane, P. (1970), 'The Evolution of Technical Education in 19th Century England', Ph.D. thesis, University of Bath.
Kerr, C., Dunlop, J. T., et al. (1973), *Industrialism and Industrial Man* (London: Penguin).
Knights, D., and Willmott, H. (eds) (1990), *Labour Process Theory* (Basingstoke: Macmillan).
—— —— and Collinson, D. (eds) (1985), *Job Redesign: Critical Perspectives in the Labour Process* (Aldershot: Gower Press).
Knowles, L. C. A. (1966), *The Industrial and Commercial Revolutions in Great Britain during the 19th Century* (London: Routledge & Kegan Paul).
Knox, W. (1986), 'Apprenticeship and De-skilling in Britain 1850–1914', *International Review of Social History*, **31**, pt. 2, pp. 166–84.
Koenigsberger, F. (1962), 'Metal Cutting Tools', in Wright Baker (ed.) (1962).
Koss, S. E. (1970), *Sir John Brunner, Radical Plutocrat, 1842–1919* (Cambridge: Cambridge University Press).

Kransberger, M. (1962), 'Milling', in Wright Baker (ed.) (1962).
Kranzberg, M., and Pursell, C. W. (1967), *Technology and Western Civilization*, Vol. 1 (Oxford: Oxford University Press).
Kynaston, D. (1976), *King Labour: the British Working Class 1850–1914* (London: Allen & Unwin).
Landes, D. (1969), *The Unbound Prometheus* (Cambridge: Cambridge University Press).
Lang, J. (1978), *City and Guilds of London Institute, Centenary 1878–1978* (London: CGLI).
Laqueur, T. W. (1977), *Religion and Respectability: Sunday Schools and Working Class Culture, 1780–1850* (London and New Haven: Yale University Press, 1977).
Larson, Margali Sarfatti (1980), 'Proletarianisation and Educated Labour', *Theory and Society*, **9**.
Law, J. (1987), review of MacKenzie and Wajcman (eds) (1985), *The Sociological Review*, **35** (2).
Lazonick, William (1977), 'Appropriation and Reproduction of Labor', *Socialist Review*, **38**.
Layton, E. T. (ed.) (1974), 'Technology as Knowledge', in *Technology and Culture*, 15 Jan.
Lee, D. J. (1979), 'Craft Unions and the Force of Tradition: the Case of Apprenticeship', *British Journal of Industrial Relations*, **17** (1).
—— (1981), 'Skill, Craft and Class: a Theoretical Critique and a Critical Case', *Sociology*, **15** (1), pp. 56–78.
Le Guillou, M. (1981), 'Technical Education 1860–1914', in Roderick and Stephens (eds) (1981).
Levine, A. L. (1954), 'Industrial Change and its Effects upon Labour, 1900–1914', Ph.D. thesis, University of London.
—— (1967), *Industrial Retardation in Britain, 1880–1914* (London: Weidenfeld & Nicholson).
Liepmann, Kate (1960), *Apprenticeship: an Enquiry into its Adequacy under Modern Conditions* (London: Routledge & Kegan Paul).
Lineham, R. S. (1895), *A Directory of Science, Art, and Technical Colleges, Schools and Teachers in the UK* (London: Chapman & Hall).
Littler, Craig R. (1978), 'Understanding Taylorism', *British Journal of Sociology*, **29** (2).
—— (1980), 'The Bureaucratisation of the Shop Floor. The Development of the Modern Work System', Ph.D. thesis, London (LSE).
—— (1982), *The Development of the Labour Process in Capitalist Societies* (London: Heinemann.
—— and Salaman, Graeme (1982), 'Braverman and Beyond: Recent Theories of the Labour Process', *Sociology*, **16** (2).

—— (1990), 'The Labour Process Debate: A Theoretical Review 1974–1988', in Knights and Willmott (eds) (1990), pp. 46–94.

—— (ed.) (1985), *TheExperience of Work* (Aldershot: Gower Pub. Co.).

Livery Companies Report (1878), Report on Technical Education (London: W. Trounce).

Llewellyn Smith, H. (1892), London County Council, Report to the Special Committee on Technical Education.

London County Council (LCC) (1893), Resolution of London County Council, Appendix A35, Feb.

—— (1906), London County Council, Education Committee, Report of the Section appointed to consider the Question of Apprenticeships, London, Jan. 1906.

—— (1909a), Higher Education Report, on return of occupations to which children who left school during the educational year 1906–7 were sent, Feb. 1909.

—— (1909b), London County Council Higher Education sub-committee Report, Minutes of Proceedings, Feb. 1909.

London Trades Council (1869), Minute Books, 19 May 1868; 8 Apr. 1873; Feb. 1878.

Ludlow, J. M., and Jones, Ll. (1867), *Progress of the Working Class, 1832–1867* (London: Strahan).

MacKenzie, D., and Wajcman, J. (eds) (1985), *The Social Shaping of Technology* (Milton Keynes: Open University Press).

Magnus, P. (1910), *Educational Aims and Efforts, 1880–1910* (London: Longmans).

Maier, C. S. (1970), 'Between Taylorism and Technocracy: European Ideologies and the Vision of Industrial Productivity in the 1920s', *Journal of Contemporary History*, **5** (2), pp. 27–61.

Malcolm Report (1928), Committee on Education and Industry. Second Part, 23 April (London: Ministry of Labour).

Manchester Association of Engineers (1922), Report of the Lathe Tools Committee.

Manchester College of Science and Technology (1896–7), Syllabus for Session, Manchester Technical School.

Mann, Tom (1897), *Monthly Journal*, June 1897.

Manwaring, T., and Wood, S. (1984), 'The Ghost in the Machine: Tacit Skills in the Labour Process', *Socialist Review*, **74** (Mar.–Apr.), pp. 55–85.

—— —— (1985), 'The Ghost in the Labour Process', in Knights, Willmott, and Collinson (1985).

Marchington, Mike (1992), 'Managing Labour Relations in a Competitive Environment', in Sturdy, Knights, and Willmotts (1992).

Marglin, Stephen (1974), 'What Do Bosses Do?', *Review of Radical Political Economy*, **6** (Summer).

Marx, K. (1867), *Capital*, Vol. 1 (Moscow, Foreign Language Publishing House, 1961).
—— (1869), Letter to Engels, 5 Apr., in *Correspondence of Marx and Engels*, ed. Torr. (1934)
—— (1878), Letter to W. Liebknecht, Feb. 1878, in *Correspondence of Marx and Engels*, ed. Torr (1934), p. 355.
—— (1976), *Wage, Labour and Capital* (Moscow: Progress Publishers).
—— (1977a), *Capital*, Vol. 1 (London: Lawrence & Wishart).
—— (1977b), *Grundrisse* (Harmondsworth: Penguin Books).
Mather, William (1909), Evidence of Sir William Mather (of Mather & Platt, Engineers of Oldham), the Commission on Poor Laws and Relief of Distress, Parliamentary Papers, Vol. XXXVI, pt. 6.
McCann, W. P. (1970), 'Trade Unionists, Artisans, and the 1870 Act', *British Journal of Educational Studies*, **18** (2), pp. 134–50.
McConnell, J. (1867), *Engineering*, 19 July. (Juror in Machine Section, Paris Exhibition.)
McCormick, Kevin (1988), 'Engineering Education in Britain and Japan: Some Reflections on the Use of the "Best Practice" Models in International Comparison', *Sociology*, **22** (4), pp. 583–605.
McCullock, Gary (1987), 'School Science and Technology in 19th and 20th Century England: a Guide to Published Sources', *Studies in Science Education*, **14,** pp. 1–32.
McGuffie, C. (1986), *Working in Metal: Management and Labour in the Metal Industries of Europe, 1850–1914* (London: Merlin Press).
McIvor, A. J. (1984), 'Employers, Organizations, and Strike Breaking in Britain, 1880–1914', *International Review of Social History*, **29** (1), pp. 1–33.
McKinlay, A. (1986), 'From Industrial Serf to Wage-Labourer: the 1937 Apprentices Revolt in Britain', *International Review of Social History*, **21** (1), pp. 1–18.
McLelland, D. (1973), *Marx's Grundrisse* (St Albans: Palladin Books).
McLeod, R. (ed.) (1982), *Days of Judgement: Science, Examinations and the Organization of Knowledge in Late Victorian England* (Nafferton: Driffield).
McLoughlin, Ian, and Clark, Jon (188), *Technological Change at Work* (Milton Keynes: Open University Press).
McLure, J. S. (1973), *Educational Documents, 1816 to the Present Day* (London: Methuen).
Melling, J. (1980), 'Non-commissioned Officers: British Employers and their Supervisory Workers, 1880–1920', *Social History*, **5,** pp. 183–221.
—— (1983), 'Employers, Industrial Welfare and the Struggle for Work-Place Control in British Industry, 1880–1920', in Gospel and Littler (eds) (1983).
Mill, J. S. (1848), *Principles of Political Economy* (Milton Keynes: Open University Press, 1994).

Ministry of Supply (1950), *Engineering Industries Division, Standard Classification of Machine Tool Types, Pt. 1: Metalworking Machines* (London: HMSO).

Montgomery, D. (1976), 'Workers' Control of Machine Production in the 19th Century', *Labor History*, **17** (Fall), pp. 485–509.

Moore, R. (1987), 'Education and the Ideology of Production', *British Journal of Sociology of Education*, **8** (2), pp. 227–42.

Moorhouse, H. F. (1973), 'The Political Incorporation of the British Working Class: an Interpretation', *Sociology*, **7**.

—— (1978), 'The Marxist Theory of the Labour Aristocracy', *Social History*, **3** (1), p. 70.

More, Charles (1980), *Skill and the English Working Class* (London: Croom Helm).

—— (1982), 'Skill and the Survival of Apprenticeship', in Wood (ed.) (1982).

Morris, R. J. (1981), review of More (1980), in *British Book News* (1981).

Mosely Industrial Commission to the United States of America (1903), Reports of the Delegates; Report by ASE secretary Barnes (Manchester).

Murphy, G. (1870), Letter of 14 July to Lord Elcho regarding a meeting to be held on 22 July at Lambeth Baths, Wemyss MSS, RH4-40/8.

Murphy, P. J. (1978), 'The Origins of the 1852 Lockout in the British Engineering Industry Reconsidered', *International Review of Social History*, **32** (2).

Musgrave, P. W. (1964), 'The Definition of Technical Education', *Vocational Aspect* (Summer).

—— (1966), 'Constant Factors in the Demand for Technical Education, 1860–1969', *British Journal of Education Studies*, **14** (Nov. 1965–May 1966).

—— (1967) *Technical Change, the Labour Force, and Education: a Study of the British and German Iron and Steel Industries* (Oxford: Pergamon Press).

Musson, A. E. (1957), 'James Nasmyth and the Early Growth of Mechanical Engineers', *Economic History Review*, 2nd ser., **10**.

—— (1966), *Joseph Whitworth (1803–1887)*, Exhibition, I.Mech.E.

—— (1976), 'Class Struggle and the Labour Aristocracy, 1830–1860', *Social History*, **3**.

—— and Robinson, E. (1969), *Science and Technology in the Industrial Revolution* (Manchester: Manchester University Press).

Nadworny, Milton (1957), 'Frederick Taylor and Frank Gilbreth: Competition in Scientific Management', *Business History Review*, **31** (Spring).

Nash, Ian and Nichols, Anne (1995), 'Britain wide of training mark', *Times Educational Supplement*, FE Focus, 1 Dec, p. 22.

Nasmyth, J. (1841), 'Remarks on the Introduction of the Slide Principle', in Buchanan (1841), Appendix B.

—— (1854), Evidence to the Select Committee on Small Arms, Reports from Committees, Parliamentary Papers, Vol. XVIII.

—— (1868a), Reports from Commissioners, Royal Commission on Trades Unions, 10th Report. Parliamentary Papers, Vol. XXXIV, Minutes of Evidence.

—— (1868b), Evidence to Royal Commission on Trades Unions, July 1868.

—— (1883), *James Nasmyth, Engineer – An Autobiography*, ed. S. Smiles (London: John Murray).

National Association for the Promotion of Secondary and Technical Education (NAPTSE) (1889), *Technical Education in England and Wales, 1st and 2nd Annual Reports* (London: Cooperative Printing Society).

—— (1890), *Guide to Evening Classes in London* (London: Cassell & Co.).

—— (1901), *The Development of Technical and Secondary Education in England* (see *Record*, **10** (44), pp. 468–73 (Sir Henry Roscoe).

Neale, R. S. (1969), 'Class and Class Consciousness in Early Nineteenth-Century England: Three Classes or Five?', *Victorian Studies*, **12**.

Nichols, T. (1980), *Capital and Labour* (London: Fontana).

Nicholson, J. S. (1878), *The Effects of Machinery on Wages* (London: Swann Sohnenschein, rev. 1892).

Niles Tool Works (1891), Catalogue (Hamilton, Ohio).

Noble, A. (1893), RC on Labour, 3rd Report.

Noble, D. F. (1977), *America by Design: Technology and the Rise of Corporate Capitalism* (New York: Knopf).

Nuttall, T. (1956), *Higher National Certificate Workshop Technology* (London English Universities Press Ltd in the City of London).

Oliphant, J. (ed.), (1886), *The Claims of Labour* (Edinburgh: Cooperative Printing Co.).

Orcutt, H. F. L. (1902), 'Modern Machine Methods', *Proceedings of the Institution of Mechanical Engineers*, **62**.

Oxhey, D. (1981), *The Development of Craftsmen and Limited Workers*, Coombe Lodge Report, 13, 14.

Palmer, Bryan (1975), 'Class, Conception and Conflict: the Thrust for Efficiency, Managerial Views of Labor and the Working Class Rebellion, 1903–1922', *Review of Radical Political Economy*, **7** (2).

Pansieri, Raniero (1980), 'The Capitalist Use of Machinery: Marx versus the Objectivists', in Slater (1980).

Parker, S. R. (1975), 'Industry and Education', in Parker *et al.* (1975).

—— Brown, R. K., Child, J., and Smith, M. A. (1975), *The Sociology of Industry* (London: George Allen & Unwin).

Parliamentary Papers (PP) (1867–8), Vol. XXX: Report of the Royal Commissioners on the Paris Exhibition of 1867. Report on Machine Tools.

—— (1873), Vol. LXXIV: Technical Reports on the Vienna Exhibition of 1873.

—— (1875), Employers and Workmen Act (1875), 38 & 39, Vic. Cap. 90, para 10.

—— (1880), Vol. XXXII: Report of the British Commissioners on the Paris Exhibition of 1878.

—— (1882), Vol. XVIII: Report of the Commissioners on the Melbourne Exhibition of 1880.

—— (1889), Technical Instruction Act (TI Act).

—— (1901), Vol. XXXI: Report of the Royal Commission to the Paris Exhibition of 1900, Report on Machine Tools.

—— (1906), Vol. LIV: Report of the British Commission to the Exhibition of St Louis, 1904.

—— Census of Production (1906), Cd 5005 and Cd 6320 (1912–13), Final Report of Returns under the Census of Production Act 1906, table 21.

Payne, C. L. (1967), 'The Emergence of the Large Scale Company in Great Britain, 1876–1914', in *Economic History Review*, **20** (3 Dec.)..

Penn, Roger (1982), 'Skilled Manual Workers in the Labour Process, 1856–1964', in Wood (ed.) (1982).

—— (1983), 'Trade Union Organization and Skill in the Cotton and Engineering Industries in Britain, 1850–1960', *Social History*, **8** (1 Jan.).

—— (1984), *Skilled Workers in the Class Structure* (Cambridge: Cambridge University Press).

—— (1986), 'Where Have All the Craftsmen Gone?', *British Journal of Sociology*, **37**, pp. 569–80.

—— and Scattergood, J. (1985), 'De-skilling or En-skilling', *BJS*, **36** (4).

—— —— (1988), 'Continuities and Change in Skilled Work', *BJS*, **39** (1).

Perrucci, Robert, and Gerstl, J. E. (1969), *The Engineers and the Social System* (New York: John Wiley).

Piore, M. J., and Sabel, C. (1984), *The Second Industrial Divide* (New York: Basic Books).

Playfair, Lyon (1864), in Hansard (1869b).

—— (1867), Letter to Rt. Hon. Lord Taunton, cited in *Journal of Society of Arts*, **15** (1867), pp. 477–8.

—— (1871), Address at the Transactions of the National Association for the Promotion of Social Science, London.

—— (1888), Reply to Armstrong (1888), *Ninteenth Century*, **24** (London).

Pollard, S. (1981), *Labour in Great Britain*, Cambridge Economic History of Europe, Vol. 8, pt. 1 (Cambridge: Cambridge University Press).

Pollert, Anna (ed.) (1991), *Farewell to Flexibility?* (Oxford: Basil Blackwell).

Polyani, M. (1964), *Personal Knowledge* (New York: Harper Textbooks).

Porter, C. T. (1908), *Engineering Reminiscences* (New York: John Wiley).

Poulantzas, N. (1975), *Classes in Contemporary Capitalism* (London: New Left Books).

Price, R. N. (1971), 'The Working Men's Club Movement and Victorian Social Reform Ideology', *Victorian Studies*, **15** (2).

Price, Richard (1983), 'The Labour Process and Labour History', *Social History*, **8**, pp. 57–77.

Privy Council Committee on Education (1867a), Minute of the Lords of the Committee of Council of Education relating to Scientific Instruction, London, Dec., PRO.

―― (1867b); (1868) Memorandum Relating to the Business of the Privy Council, London, PRO, ED 24/55.

Public Record Office (PRO), Document ED 23/71 (1889), Actual Expenditure as per Appropriation Accounts, for Education in Great Britain, Appendix A, London.

―― PRO Files (1897), The System of Apprenticeships with Special Reference to Apprentice Charities, Assistant Commissioners' Report, Dec. Also Files for 1919.

Rainbird, H. (1988), 'New Technology, Training and Union Strategies', in Hyman and Streeck (eds.) (1988).

Randall, J. (1868), 'Journal', Paper on Technical Education, Conference at Society of Arts, 31 Jan. 1868. (Randall was one of the authors of 'Artisan' Reports, 1868.)

Rankine, W. J. McQ. (1878), *A Manual of Machinery and Millwork* (London: Charles Griffen).

'Record' (Journal of the Iron Trades Employers' Association (1872–1900) (London: ITEA).

Record of Technical and Secondary Education (1901), **10** (42, 44) (London: Cooperative Printing Society).

Reeder, D. A. (ed.) (1977), *Urban Education in the Nineteenth Century* (London: Taylor & Francis).

Reinfelder, Monika (1980), 'Breaking the Spell of Technicism', in Slater (ed.) (1980).

Report of the Committee on the Machinery of the United States of America (1855), Presented to the House of Commons in Pursuance of this Address, 10 July 1855. Parliamentary Papers, Vol. L. Accounts and Papers 1854–55,Vol. XXI (London: Harrison & Son).

Report of the Proceedings of the Workmen's Technical Education Committee (WTEC) (1868) from the Date of Appointment, 14 March.

Reports from Commissioners (1867–8), Vol. 31, 10th Report of the Royal Commission Appointed to Inquire into the Organisation and Rules of Trades Unions and Other Organisations.

―― (1875), Vol. 30, Second and Final Report of the Commission Appointed to Inquire into the Working of the Master and Servant Act, 1867, and the Criminal Law Amendment Act, 34 & 35 Vic. Cap. 32, p. 115.

—— (1893), Report of the Royal Commission on Labour, Minutes of Evidence, Vol. 3.
Reports of Artisans (1867), Papers of Artisans Selected to Visit the Paris Universal Exhibition of 1867, in *The Journal* (official organ of the Society of Arts).
Rezneck, S. (1932), 'The Rise of Industrial Consciousness in the U.S. 1760–1830', *Journal of Economic and Business History*, **4** (4).
Roberts, B. C. (1958), *The Trades Union Congress, 1868–1921* (London: Allen & Unwin).
Robertson, P. L. (1974), 'Technical Education in the British Shipbuilding and Marine Engineering Industry 1863–1914', *Economic History Review*, 2nd ser., **27**, pp. 222–5.
Robinson, J. (1868), Evidence to the Royal Commission on Trade Unions [RC on TU 1867–8]. (Director of Atlas Engineering Co., Manchester.)
Roderick, G. W., and Stephens, M. D. (1970), 'Approaches to Technical Education in Nineteenth-Century England', *The Vocational Aspects of Education*, **22** (52), June.
—— —— (1978), *Education and Industry in the Nineteenth Century* (London: Longmans).
—— —— (1981), 'Where Did We Go Wrong?', in *Industry, Education and the Economy in Victorian Britain* (Lewes: Falmer Press).
Roe, J. W. (1916a), *English and American Tool Builders* (New Haven: Yale University Press).
—— (1916b), *Interchangeable Manufacture*, Transactions of the Newcomen Society, Vol. 18.
Rose, J. (1895), *Complete Practical Machinist* (Philadelphia: Baird & Co.).
Rosen, M., and Baroudi, J. (1992), 'Computer-Based Technology and the Emergence of New Forms of Managerial Control', in Sturdy, Knights, and Willmott (1992).
Rosenberg, N. (1963), 'Technological Change in the Machine Tool Industry, 1840–1910', *Journal of Economic History*, **23** (Dec.).
Rosenbloom, R. S. (1964), 'Some 19th Century Analyses of Mechanization', *Technology and Culture*, **5** (Fall).
Rowan, F. J. (1887), 'On Electro-Magnetic Tools', *Proceedings of the Institution of Mechanical Engineers*, **38**.
—— (1901), 'Economical Manufacture of Marine Engines', *Proceedings of the Institution of Mechanical Engineers*, **61**.
—— (1903), 'Premium System', *Proceedings of the Institution of Mechanical Engineers*, **66**.
Rowe, J. W. F. (1928), *Wages in Theory and Practice* (London: Routledge & Kegan Paul).
Royal Colleges (1906), Final Report of Departmental Committee on the Royal College of Sciences (Historical Survey) (London: HMSO).

Royal Commission on Depression of Trade (1885–6), Parliamentary Papers, Reports from Commissioners (1885–6), Royal Commission appointed to inquire into the Depression of Trade and Industry. Evidence submitted by practising tradesmen, 1885. Q. 1218.

Royal Commission on Depression of Trade and Industry (RC on DT and I) (1886a), Final Report, Minutes of Evidence and Appendices, pp. 1–77 (i–lxxvii in Report).

—— (1886b), Recommendations and Final Report.

Royal Commission on Labour (1893a), 3rd Report, Evidence of A. F. Hills, Managing Director, Thames Iron Works Shipbuilding Co. Ltd., Blackwall, London.

—— (1893b), 3rd Report (Evidence of Wigram, member of the firm of John Fowler & Co. Ltd., Engineers, Leeds), Q. 25767.

—— (1893c), Minutes of Evidence, Vol. 3 (Evidence of J. Inglis, Partners in Messrs A. & J. Inglis, Engineer, Glasgow), Q. 26149.

—— (1893d), Minutes of Evidence, Vol. 3, Qs. 25212, 25217, 25218, 25220, 25323, 25248 (Evidence of Captain Noble).

—— (1893e), Qs. 23235, 325212 (ASE evidence from S. Glennies, ASE).

—— (1893f), Third Report, Minutes of Evidence, Vol. 3 (Whittaker of the ASE).

—— (1893–4), Parliamentary Papers, Reports from Commissioners, Vol. XXXV, pt. 20. Royal Commission on Labour, Summary, p. 115.

—— (1894), Summary, Gp. A: Pt. II, Iron, Engineering, Hardware, Shipbuilding and Cognate Trades.

Royal Commission on Poor Laws and Relief of Distress (1909a), Parliamentary Papers, Reports from Commissioners.

—— (1909b), Reports from Commissioners, Vol. 36, Pt. 6, Ch. 1.

—— (1909c), Evidence to Minority Report, The Misuse of Boy Labour.

—— (1909d), Qs. 93031 and 93035, Evidence of Sydney Webb.

Royal Commission on Scientific Instruction (RC on SI) (1865), Vol. 15. Council on Education (1867–8), copy of Minute of the Lords of the Committee of Council on Education Relating to Scientific Instruction; and Explanatory Memorandum thereon. Accounts and Papers, Vol. 54.

—— (1867), Memorandum relating to the Business of the Privy Council Office, PRO Document 24/55.

—— (1872), Parliamentary Papers, Vol. II, London.

Royal Commission on Secondary Education (1895), Vol. 1, Historical Sketch, Pt. 1 [The Bryce Commission].

Royal Commission on Technical Instruction (RC on TI) (1884a), Parliamentary Papers, Vol. XXIX, 2nd Report, Vol. 3.

—— (1884b), Parliamentary Papers, Vol. XXXI, 2nd Report, Vol. 3, Minutes of Evidence (Shipton, Secretary of Amalgamated Society of House Decorators and Painters: Member of London Trades Council).

―― (1884c), Parliamentary Papers, Vol. XXXI, pt. 2, Appendices C and G.
Royal Commission on Trade Disputes and Trade Combinations (RC on TD and TC) (1906), Reports from Commmissioners, Vol. 56, Q. 2410, 2415.
Royal Commission on Trades Unions (RC on TU) (1867a), 1st Report, Minutes of Evidence, Qs. 631, 641, 644.
―― (1867b), 1st Report, Qs. 674, 675, 698, 841, 846, 895, 998, Evidence of W. Allen.
―― (1867–8a), Parliamentary Papers. Report from Commissioners (1868), Vol. XXXI. Report of Royal Commission appointed to Inquiry into the Organisation and Rules of Trades Unions and Other Associations, 1867–69.
―― (1867–8b), Reports from Commissioners, Vol. 39.
―― (1868a), 10th Report, Minutes of Evidence.
―― (1868b), Q. 985, Evidence of ASE Secretary W. Allen.
―― (1868c), Qs. 18878–19201.
―― (1868d), 11th Report, Minutes of Evidence. (J. Paterson Smith, Secretary, Clyde Shipbuilders' and Engineers' Association)
―― (1868–9), Appendix to XIth and Final Report, Vol. 21, 1868–9, p. 246.
―― (1869a), XIth and Final Report.
―― (1869b), Minority Report, Dissent III pt. VIII (signed 6 Mar. 1869).
―― (1869c), rules 13, 15 of ASE revised, Eleventh and Final Report, Appendix in Parliamentary Papers, Vol. XXI, pp. 246, 252, 253.
Rubery, J. (1978), 'Structural Labour Markets, Worker Organisation and Low Pay', *Cambridge Journal of Economics*, **2**, pp. 17–36.
Ryrie, A. C. (1976), 'Employers and Apprenticeship, Research Note', *British Journal of Industrial Relations*, **14** (1), pp. 89–91.
Sable, C., and Zeitlin, J. (1985), 'Historical Alternatives to Mass Production: Politics, Markets and Technology in 19th-Century Industrialization', *Past and Present*, **108**, pp. 133–76.
Sadler, M. E. (1904), Report on Secondary Education in Liverpool, Liverpool Education Committee.
―― (ed.) (1907), *Continuation Schools in England and Elsewhere* (Manchester: Victoria University Press).
Sakolsky, Ron (1992), 'Disciplinary Power and the Labour Process', in Sturdy, Knights, and Willmott (eds) (1992).
Samuel, Raphael (1977), 'The Workshop of the World: Steam Power and Hand Technology in Mid-Victorian Britain', *History Workshop*, no. 3 (Spring).
Sanderson, M. (1983), *Education, Economic Change and Society in England, 1780–1870* (London: Faber & Faber).
Saul, S. B. (1967), 'The Market and Development of the Mechanical Engineering Industries, 1860–1914', *Economic History Review*, 3rd ser., **20**, p. 106 (London).

—— (1968a), 'Engineering', in Aldcroft (ed.) (1968).

—— (1968b), 'The Machine Tool Industry in Britain to 1914', *Business History*, **10**.

—— (ed.) (1970), *Technological Change: The United States and Britain in the Nineteenth Century* (London: Methuen).

Saville, J. (1954), 'The Christian Socialists of 1848', in Saville (ed.) (1954).

—— (ed.) (1954), *Democracy and the Labour Movement* (London: Lawrence & Wishart).

Schuler, T., and Megarry, J. (eds) (1979), *Recurrent Education and Lifelong Education* (London: Kogan Page).

Schultz, Theodore (1961), 'Investment in Human Capital', *American Economic Review*, **51** (Mar.).

Schwarz, B. (1977), 'On the Monopoly Capitalist Degradation of Work', *Dialectal Anthropology*, **2** (2).

Scott-Russell, J. (1869), *Systematic Technical Education* (London: Bradbury Evan).

Select Committee on Small Arms (1854), Reports from Commissioners, Parliamentary Papers, Vol. XVIII.

Select Committee on Scientific Instruction (1868), Parliamentary Papers, Vol. XV.

Select Committee on Science and Technology (1975–6), House of Commons Papers, Report 3, HC 680.

Sellers, Wm. (1884), *A Treatise on Machine Tools as Made by Wm. Sellers & Co.* (Philadelphia). (This 'treatise' is in fact a sales catalogue.)

Shadwell, A. (1906), *Industrial Efficiency: A Comparative Study of Industrial Life in England, Germany, and America* (London: Longmans).

Sharp, P. R. (1971), 'Whisky Money and the Development of Technical and Scientific Education in the 1890's', *Journal of Education Administration and History*, **4** (Dec.).

Shepherd, Michael (1978), 'The Origin and Incidence of the Term "Labour Aristocracy"', *Society for a Study of Labour History*, **37** (Autumn).

Silver, H. (1983), 'Ideology and the Factory Child: Attitudes to Half-Time Education', in idem, *Education as History: Interpreting Nineteenth- and Twentieth-Century Education* (London: Methuen).

Simon, B. (1965), *Education and the Labour Movement, 1870–1920* (London: Lawrence & Wishart).

—— (1969), *Studies in the History of Education, 1780–1870* (London: Lawrence & Wishart).

Sims, G. (1981), 'Engineering', in Roderick and Stephens (eds) (1981).

Singer, Charles, *et al.* (eds) (1965), *A History of Technology*, Vol. 5 (Oxford: Clarendon Press).

Singh, B. R. (1974), 'The Development of Technical and Vocational Education in Britain and America, 1870–1940: a Comparative Study', Ph.D. thesis, University of London.

Skills and Enterprise Briefing, issue 16 (1994), issue 3 (1995) (Sheffield: DfEE).

Slater, Phil (ed.) (1980), *Outlines of a Critique of Technology* (London: Ink Links).

Smelser, Neil (ed.) (1988), *Handbook of Sociology* (London: Sage Publications).

Smiles, Samuel (1876), *Industrial Biography, Iron Worker and Tool Makers* (London: John Murray).

—— (1879), *Self Help* (London: John Murray).

—— (1904), *The Lives of the Engineers* (London: John Murray).

Smith, C. S. (1967), 'Metallurgy: Science and Practice before 1900', in Kranzberg and Pursell (1967).

Smith, Merrit Roe (1977), *Harpers Ferry Armory and the New Technology*, (Ithaca, NY: Cornell University Press).

Society of Arts (SOA) (1868), Report on Conference on Technical Education, held on 23 Jan. 1868, *Journal of Society of Arts*, 16 (793), pp. 183–209.

—— (1869), A Petition from the Society of Arts to House of Commons for a Systematic Education Provision and a Competent Technical Education Service, 21 May (Journal).

—— (1878), Programme of Examinations, 1859–1877 (London).

Sohn-Rethel, A. (1972), 'Mental and Manual Labour in Marx', in Walton and Hall (eds) (1972).

—— (1976), 'The Dual Economics of Transition', in *Bulletin of the Conference of Socialist Economists*, **2** (2).

—— (1978), *Intellectual and Manual Labour: a Critique of Epistemology*, Critical Social Studies (Basingstoke and London: Macmillan).

Solly, H. (1866), Letter to Lord Lyttleton, in *Occasional Papers of the W.M.C. & I.U. Tracts 1863–1883* (London: Working Men's Club and Institute Union).

—— (1868), 'Facts and Fallacies connected with the Working Men's Club and Institute' (paper read before the Social Science Association at Sheffield, Oct. 1865).

—— (1873), 'Trades Guild of Learning', in *Workman's Magazine*, nos. 1 and 5, published under Literacy and Critical Tracts, London.

—— (1878), 'Technical Education: a Few thoughts and Facts about it', address to the Trustees of the Artisans Institute, London.

—— (1833–93), Miscellaneous papers, LSE Collection, 154.

Sorge, A., and Streeck, W. (1988), 'Industrial Relations and Technical Change: the Case for an Extended Perspective', in Hyman and Streeck (eds) (1988).

Spon, E. (1885), *Mechanics' Own Book* (London: E. & F. N. Spon).

—— and Spon, F. N. (1882), *Papers on Mechanical Subjects*, Pt. 1 (London: E. & F. N. Spon).

Spon's Dictionary of Engineering (1873), Division VII (London: E. & F. N. Spon).

—— (1874), Vol. 3, ed. O. Byrne and E. Spon (London: E. & f. N. Spon).

Stanley-Stone, A. C. (1925), *The Worshipful Company of Turners* (London: Lindley Jones).

Stark, D. (1980), 'Class Struggle and the Transformation of the Labor Process', *Theory and Society*, **9** (1), pp. 89–130.

Steeds, W. (1969), *A History of Machine Tools, 1700–1910* (Oxford: Clarendon Press).

Stephens, M. D., and Roderick, G. W. (1973), 'Changing Attitudes to Education in England and Wales, 1833–1902', *Annals of Science*, 3 June.

—— —— (1983), 'The Role of Scientific and Technical Education in Early Industrialization in America and England', *Vocational Aspects of Education*, **35** (90), Apl. 1983, **35** (90), pp. 17–22.

Stewart, C. P. (1861), 'Description of Seller's Screwing Machine', *Proceedings of the Institution of Mechanical Engineers*, **12.**

—— (1974), 'National Attitudes towards Scientific Education in Early 19th-Century England', *Vocational Aspects of Education*, **26** (65).

Stonier, T. (1979), 'Changes in Western Society: Educational Implications', in Schuler and Megarry (eds) (1979).

Sturdy, A., Knights, D., and Willmott, H. (eds) (1992), *Skill and Consent: Contemporary Studies in the Labour Process* (London: Routledge).

Sweezy, P. (1942), *The Theory of Capitalist Development* (New York: Monthly Review).

Sylvester, D. W. (1974), *Robert Lowe and Education* (Cambridge: Cambridge University Press).

Tawney, R. H. (1909), 'The Economics of Boy Labour', *The Economic Journal*, **19,** pp. 517–37.

Taylor, F. W. (1894–5), *Transactions of the American Society of Mechanical Engineers (ASME)*, **16.**

—— (1895), 'A Piece Rate System, Being a Step Toward a Partial Solution of the Labor Problem', *Transactions of the American Society of Mechanical Engineers*, **16** (1894–5), repr. in C. B. Thompson (ed.), (1914), pp. 636–83.

—— (1906), 'On the Art of Cutting Metals', *Transactions of the American Society of Mechanical Engineers* (1906) and in C. B. Thompson (ed.) (1914).

—— (1910), Contribution to a meeting of the Institution of Mechanical Engineers (England), 10 July 1910, in *Proceedings of the Institution of Mechanical Engineers*, 79.

—— (1911a), *The Principles of Scientific Management* (New York. Special Edition for confidential circulation among ASME members).

—— (1911b), *Shop Management* (New York: Harper & Row) (first read as a paper at a meeting of the American Society of Mechanical Engineers, Saratoga, 1903).

—— (1911c), Testimony before the Special House Committee, in F. W. Taylor, *Scientific Management* (1964).

—— (1912a), Testimony before the Special House Committee, June 1912, in F. W. Taylor, *Scientific Management* (1964).

—— (1912b), Hearings before the Special Committee of the House of Representatives to Investigate the Taylor and Other Systems of Shop Management (Washington: Government Printing Office).

—— (1964), *Scientific Management* (London: Harper & Row).

Taylor, P. W. (1975), 'The Development of Higher Technological Education in Britain', *Journal of Educational Administration and History*, **8** (2).

Technical Instruction Act (1892), Parliamentary Papers, Vol. IV, pp. 226–8.

Tholfsen, Trygvie (1961), 'Transition and Democracy in England', *International Review of Social History*, **6** (2), pp. 226–48.

—— (1971), 'The Intellectual Origins of Mid-Victorian Stability', *Political Science Quarterly*, **80** (Mar.).

—— (1976), *Working Class Radicalism in Mid-Victorian England* (London: Croom Helm).

Thomas, D. H. (1940), 'The Development of Technical Education in England, 1851–1889, with Special Reference to Economic Factors', Ph.D. thesis, University of London.

Thompson, C. B. (ed.) (1914), *Scientific Management: a Collection of the More Significant Articles Describing the Taylor System of Management* (Cambridge, Mass.; Harvard University Press).

Thompson, E. P. (1977), *The Making of the English Working Class* (Harmondsworth: Penguin).

Thompson, K. (1984), *Work, Employment and Unemployment* (Milton Keynes: Open University Press).

Thompson, P. (1983), *The Nature of Work: An Introduction to Debates on the Labour Process* (London: Macmillan).

—— and Bannon, F. (1985), *Working the System: the Shop Floor and New Technology* (London: Pluto Press).

Thompson, S. P. (1879), *Apprenticeship, Scientific and Unscientific* (Lecture given before Society of Arts), *The Journal*, **28** (34) (London: Hamilton Adams).

Thomson, A. W. J., and Hunter, L. C. (1978), in Dunlop and Galenson (eds) (1978).

Thornton, J. (1978), *see* Conservative Political Centre (CPC) (1978).

Tomlinson, Jim (1982), *The Unequal Struggle: British Socialism and the Capitalist Enterprise* (London: Methuen).
Tracts on Education, 1850–1903 (1904) (London).
TUC Congress Minutes (1868), TUC microfilm. Also Minutes for 1871, 1874, 1880, 1882, 1885, 1889, TUC Library.
Turner, H. A. (1962), *Trade Union Growth, Structure and Policy* (London: Allen & Unwin).
Unwin, C. W. (1904), article in *Central*, 2, London. (Official journal of the Central Institute of the City and Guilds of London Institute.)
Urwick, L., and Brech, E. F. L. (1946), *The Making of Scientific Management* (London: Management Publication Trust).
US Commission on Labor (1904), Eleventh Special Report, Regulations and Restriction of Output, US Congressional Hearings, 41st–73rd Congresses, 1869–1934, Washington.
US Committee on Labor (1911), evidence to Hearings before the Committee on Labor of the House of Representatives, 62nd Congress, 1st Session on House Resolution 90. *Investigation of the Taylor System of Shop Management*, April Congressional Hearings, 41st–73rd Congresses, 1869–1934, Vol. 41 (1908–11), p. 254. (Evidence of Samuel Gompers, President of the American Federation of Labor, AFL, quoting Harrap.)
US Congressional Hearings (1913–15), The Stop Watch and Bonus System in Government Work, Evidence of Congressman Tavener, Vol. 103.
Usher, J. T. (1895), *The Modern Machinist* (London: E. & F. N. Spon).
Veblen, T. (1921), *The Engineer and the Price System* (New York: B. W. Huebsch).
Venables, Ethel (1967), *The Young Worker at College: a Study of a Local Tech* (London: Faber & Faber).
Vincenti, Walter G. (1990), *What Engineers Know and how they Know it: Analytical Studies from Aeronautical History* (Baltimore: The Johns Hopkins Press).
Walker, Jill (1981), 'Markets, Industrial Processes and Class Struggle: the Evolution of the Labour Process in the U.K. Engineering Industry', *The Review of Radical Political Economics*, **12** (4).
Walker, Pat (ed.) (1978), *Between Labour and Capital* (Montreal: Black Rose Books).
Walton, P., and Hall, S. (eds) (1972), *Situating Marx* (London: Human Context Books).
Ward, James (1865), *Workmen and Wages at Home and Abroad* (London: W. S. Orr).
Ward, L. O. (1973), 'Technical Education and the Politicians (1870–1918)', *British Journal of Educational Studies*, **21** (1).
Warde, Alan (1992), 'Industrial Discipline: Factory Regime and Politics in Lancaster', in Sturdy, Knights, and Willmott (eds) (1992).

Warren, Kenneth (1989), *Armstrong of Elswick: Growth in Engineering and Armaments to the Merger with Vickers* (Basingstoke: Macmillan in association with the Business History Unit, University of London).

Waterhouse, Rachel (1957), *A Hundred Years of Engineering Craftsmanship: A short History of the Adventurous Development of Tangyes Limited, Smethwick 1857–1957* (Smethwick: Tangyes Ltd).

Watson, Hamish Brocket (1976), 'Organisational Bases of Professional Status: a Comparative Study of the Engineering Profession', Ph.D. thesis, University of London (LSE).

Wearmouth, R. F. (1937), *Methodism and Working Class Movements* (London: Epworth Press).

Webb, H. L. (1898), 'English and American Methods in the Engineering and Iron Trades', *Engineer*, 21 Jan.

Webb, S. (1904), *London Education* (London: Longmans).

—— and Webb, B. (1907), *The History of Trade Unionism* (London: Longman Green & Co.).

—— (1911), *Industrial Democracy* (London: Longmans).

—— —— (1919), *The History of Trade Unionism* (London: Longmans).

—— —— (1920), *Industrial Democracy* (London: Longmans).

Weekes, B. M. (1970), 'The Amalgamated Society of Engineers, 1880–1914', Ph.D. thesis, University of Warwick.

Weiler, A. (1875), Letter to Sir Thomas Brassey, quoted in R. N. Price (1971).

Weissenborn, G. (1861), *American Engineering* (New York: Charles Scribner's Sons).

Welford, A. T. (ed.) (1962), *Society: Problems and Method of Study* (London: Routledge).

Weller, Peter (1999), Employers' Views of TECs and their Services (GB: DfEE).

Wemyss Manuscripts, National Archive of Scotland (NAS), Edinburgh (RH 4/40/9, microfilm). (Lord Elcho, references to whom appear above, was the eldest son of the 8th Earl of Wemyss (1841–1908).)

Whalley, Peter (1986), *The Social Production of Technical Work* (London: Macmillan).

Whitworth, J. (1840), 'On Plane Metallic Surfaces', address to British Association, Glasgow, 1840, in E. and F. N. Spon (1882), p. 8.

—— (1841), 'On a Uniform System of Screw Threads', paper read to the Institute of Civil Engineers, in E. and F. N. Spon (1882), p. 19.

—— (1854a), Special Report on the New York Industrial Exhibition presented to House of Commons, 6 Feb. (London: Harrison).

—— (1854b), Evidence to Select Committee on Small Arms, Parliamentary Papers, Vol. XXXI.

—— (1855), Report of the Committee on the Machinery of the United States of America, London.

—— (1856), Presidential Address, Institute of Mechanical Engineers, Glasgow, in *Proceedings of the Institution of Mechanical Engineers,* **8.**

—— (1857), 'On a Standard Decimal Measure of Length', *Proceedings of the Institution of Mechanical Engineers,* **8,** pp. 131–48.

—— (1870), 'On Machinery', observations at a dinner of the Foremen Engineers, London, Feb. 1870, in E. and F. N. Spon (1882), p. 60.

—— (1876), 'On Measurement', paper read at the Conference of the Exhibition of Scientific Instruments, May 1876, in E. and F. N. Spon (1882).

—— (1882a), *Papers on Mechnical Subjects,* Pt. I: *True Plane, Screw Threads, and Standard Measure* (London: E. & F. N. Spon).

—— (1882b), *Illustrated Catalogue of Engineers' Tools Manufactured by Sir Joseph Whitworth and Company, Manchester,* July 1882.

Wigham, E. (1973a), *The Power to Manage: a History of the Engineering Employers Federation* (London: Macmillan).

—— (1973b), 'The Terms of Settlement (1898): General Principle of Freedom to Employers in the Management of their Works', quoted in Wigham (1973a), Appendix D.

Wigram, J. (1893), Evidence to RC on Labour (1893b).

Williams, T. I. (ed.) (1969), *A Biographical Dictionary of Science* (New York: Charles Scribner's Sons).

Winstanley, T. (1867), report on Exhibition of 1867 in *Journal of the Society of Arts,* **16.**

Wood, S. (1988), 'Between Fordism and Flexibility? The U.S. Car Industry', in Hyman and Streeck (eds) (1988).

—— (ed.) (1982), *The Degradation of Work?* (London: Hutchinson).

—— and Kelly, J. (1982), 'Taylorism, Responsible Autonomy and Management Strategy', in Wood (ed.) (1982).

Woodbury, R. S. (1967), 'Machines and Tools', in Kranzberg and Pursell (eds) (1967).

—— (1969), 'Machine Tools', in Williams (ed.) (1969).

—— (1972), *Studies in the History of Machine Tools* (Cambridge, Mass.: M.I.T. Press).

Woodward, J. (1965), *Industrial Organization: Theory and Practice* (Oxford: Oxford University Press).

Wordworth, J. V. (1905), *American Tool Making and Interchangeable Manufacture* (London: E. & F. N. Spon).

Working Men's Club and Institute Union (WC & IU), Tracts 1863–1883, London (1886).

Working Men's College, 12th Annual Report (1880).

Working Men's Educational Union (WMEU) (1853), First Annual Report, London.

Workmen's Technical Education Committee (1869), Report of Proceedings from 14 Mar. 1868 to date (London, 1869).

Wright, Thomas (1871), 'The Journeyman Engineer', *Fraser's Magazine*, **4** (19), pp. 62–8.

—— (1873), *Our New Masters* (London: Strahan).

Wright Baker, H. (ed.) (1962), *Modern Workshop Technology* (London: Macmillan).

Young, Nigel (1967), '"Prometheus or Troglodyte?" The English Working Class and the Dialectics of Incorporation', *Berkley Journal of Sociology*, **12**.

—— (1974), 'Technical Education: A Local or National Responsibility?', *Education and Training*, **16** (7).

Zeitlin, J. (1979), 'Craft Control and the Division of Labour: Engineers and Compositors', *Cambridge Journal of Economics*, **3**, pp. 263–74.

—— (1983), 'The Labour Strategies of British Engineering Employers, 1890–1922', in Gospel and Littler (eds) (1983).

—— (1985), *see* Harrison and Zeitlin (eds) (1985).

—— (1987). 'From Labour History to the History of Industrial Relations', *Economic History Review*, 2nd ser., **40** (2), pp. 129–84.

—— and Harrison, Royden (eds) (1985), *Divisions of Labour* (Brighton: Harvester Press).

—— and Tolliday, S. (eds) (1985), *Shop Floor Bargaining and the State: Historical and Comparative Perspectives* (Cambridge: Cambridge University Press).

Zimbalist, Andrew (ed.), (1979), *Case Studies on the Labour Process* (New York: Monthly Review Press).

Index

Abortive Machine Conference, The 132
accreditation 250
accuracy 107, 112, 236
Acland, H. D. 216, 219
Advisory Committees 243
Agreement between EEF and ASE 1907 158–61, 226, 238
Allen, W. 79, 80, 88, 95, 96, 108, 109, 117
Allis Chalmers Company of Chicago 10
Amalgamated Society of Engineers (ASE) 7, 10, 34, 77, 79, 80, 88, 89, 91, 92, 95, 97, 98, 100, 107, 106, 109, 111, 112, 113, 117, 121, 122, 126, 128, 129, 130, 132, 133, 134, 135, 137, 139, 144, 149, 155, 182, 197, 201, 226, 231, 238, 239, 242, 250
  black list 98
  contingency funds 147
  exclusivity 127
  Glasgow 130
  qualifying time for membership 108
  membership 128
  rules 98
  shop steward interference 127
  status 139, 145
Amalgamated Society of Railway Servants 147
American Federation of Labour (AFL) 59, 63
American Locomotive Company 10
American Society of Mechanical Engineers (ASME) 46
Anderson 29–30, 31–3
Anderson M.P. 211
Anderson of Easton and Anderson Iron Works 223
Applegarth 79, 109, 184, 185
apprentices 104, 113, 117, 118, 141, 225, 246
  bound 104, 117, 155
  indentured 237
  politicisation 118
  ratio to journeymen 111, 115, 117, 121, 143, 144, 149–50, 182
  restriction in numbers 128
  training 252
apprenticeship 56, 76, 129, 179, 195
  craft system 3, 4, 5, 65, 72, 75, 77, 97, 98–123, 124, 150, 154, 156, 167, 168, 175, 177, 180–81, 194, 196, 208, 212, 217, 221, 226, 230, 231, 236, 238, 241, 242, 245, 246, 253, 254
  decline of 11, 197, 201, 207, 248, 256
  demise of 233, 239, 244
  Elizabethan Statute of 1563 103
  employer attitude to 33, 38, 58, 121–22
  forms of 104–5
  free contract 117–18
  grants from charities 119, 167
  indentured 111, 119, 243
  law 115
  legal sanctions on employers 115, 116
  oral agreement 103, 104–5
  premium 117, 119
  written agreement 103, 104, 246, 254
aristocracy of labour 75–7, 106, 108, 236
Armor School of Technology 10
Armstrong & Co., Sir Wm. 90, 112, 114, 128, 129, 226
Armstrong, Lord 122, 195, 196, 197, 231
Armstrong Ordnance Works, 130
Armstrong Whitworth & Co. Ltd., Sir W.G. 9, 53, 82, 137, 148, 196, 240
Armstrong workshops in Newcastle 91
Arnold, Matthew 165
artisan 75, 106, 107, 110 see also skilled worker
  demise of 234
  elitism 234–6
  exclusivity 111, 113, 124, 180, 235
  monopoly 125
  resistance to work reorganisation 60–63, 66, 72, 102, 105, 123, 127, 148, 178, 185
  status 181, 182, 235, 236, 250
Artisans' Institute 8, 179, 190, 191, 193
ASE see Amalgamated Society of Engineers

Ashbury Railway Carriage & Iron
    Company 95
assemblers 102
assembly 99, 101, 102
Association of Teachers in Technical
    Institutes (ATTI) 7
Association of Technical Institutes (ATI)
    222, 240, 245
    1905 survey 222, 228, 241
Atlas Engineering 112, 117, 240
autonomy
    of skilled workers 110, 125–7
    professional 249–50
    workshop 180, 226

BAAS *see* British Association for the
    Advancement of Science
Balfour Report 246, 247
bargaining 77, 141, 142, 143
Barnes, George 10, 109, 131, 132, 134,
    135, 139, 140, 141, 142, 144, 151
Barrow 129, 130, 131, 132
Barth, Carl 59
Bedaux System 68
Bee-Hive 78, 79
Belfast Employers Association 129, 130,
    131
Berriman, H. E. 246
Bertram Company, J. 148
Bethlehem Steel Company 18, 44, 50,
    89, 237
Beyer of Beyer, Peacock & Co. 112, 151
bicycles 18, 38, 74, 81
Biggar 144, 145
Birmingham Trades Journal 137
Board of Education 163, 177, 218, 220,
    222, 224, 225, 229, 231, 244, 245,
    246, 251
    Report for 1908–09 228, 229, 241
Board of Trade 134, 136, 138
Boiler Firemen's Society of Great
    Britain 147
Boilermakers Society 132, 133, 140
bonus payments 86, 91
Boyle, Sir Courtenay 136
boys
    census of occupations 119–20
    concessions for class attendance 214
    employment of 36, 65, 92–7, 100,
        113, 114, 117, 119, 124, 149,
        153, 198, 223, 237

Braverman, H. 40, 43, 63, 64, 65, 66,
    68, 69, 70, 105, 239
British Association for the Advancement
    of Science (BAAS) 247, 248
British Smelters' Association 147
British Standard Whitworth system
    (B.S.W.) 28, 55
Brooklyn Naval Yard 62
Brown & Sharp 17, 18, 37
Browne, Sir Benjamin 9
Browne & Co., John 53
Bryce Commission 163, 168, 218, 219,
    228
Buchanan, G. 23
Buckley, Samuel 53
Burnett, John 79, 108, 109, 117, 142
Burns, John 135, 138, 142
bursaries 227
Butty System 90, 91–92, 96, 176

Cadbury Bros. 226
Capital 33
Card Machine Tenders' Society 147
CBI *see* Confederation of British
    Industry
census of production, first 6
Central College, South Kensington 203
Central Institute 166, 188, 204, 205,
    206, 209, 214, 216
CGLI *see* City and Guilds of London
    Institute
chargehand 56
Charity Commission 217
Charity Commissioners 121, 167
Chartism 76, 183
child labour 12, 39, 65, 66, 73–97, 111,
    115, 116, 120
Children's Employment Commission 4,
    91, 92, 111, 117, 121
Cigarmakers' Society 147
City and Guilds of London Institute
    (CGLI) 3, 166, 177, 188, 189, 194,
    195, 197, 198, 200, 201, 203–4,
    212, 213, 215, 221, 224, 231, 234,
    240, 241
    examination structure 208–9
    Technological Examinations Depart-
        ment 204, 207–8
Clerk Advisory Committee 246
Clerk, Dugald 246
Clothmakers Livery Company 198

INDEX

Clyde employers 129
Clyde Mitchell 148
Cockerton Judgement 184
Cole, Henry 168
Collison, William 191
Colt, Colonel 33, 107
Colt factory 32
combination
  by employers 6, 127, 129, 132, 136, 148, 154
  by workers 191
Committee on Technology and Technical Education 245
Confederation of British Industry (CBI) 252, 253
Conference of Amalgamated Trades 79
conflict
  inter-worker 67, 72, 77–8
  horizontal forms 68
Conservative Political Centre (CPC) 247
control
  centralisation of 102
  direct 107
  of labour 133, 137, 151, 233, 237, 244, 248, 255
  of the production process 249
  of technology 235, 237
  of work 87, 151, 195
  over the labour process 118, 121, 150, 154, 178, 180, 193, 196, 228, 229, 231, 234, 242, 248, 250
  quality 102, 113
Co-operative movement 186
Co-operative Societies 220
Corps of Royal Engineers 200
Coulson 79
County Councils 215
CPC *see* Conservative Political Centre
Cramp's Shipbuilding Company 44
Cranbrook, Viscount 163
Customs and Excise Act *see* The Local Taxation (Customs and Excise) Act
Cutting Tools Research Committee, Institution of Mechanical Engineers 46

Daimler Motor Co. 225
Dearing, Sir Ron 255
death of manual workers, average age at 120

demarcation
  between skilled and unskilled 103
  disputes 152
  job 150–52
  of work 129
Denominations of Standard Gauges 30
deskilling 2, 56, 69, 70, 105, 106
Devonshire, Duke of 216
Devonshire, Lord 245
differential pay rates 62
differentiation between skilled and unskilled 109
dilution of craft skills 8, 102
Direct Control 65
distance-learning 206, 207
Dobson and Barlow, Bolton 225
Dobson, Sir Benjamin 137
Donnelly, Major General Sir John 197, 199, 200, 208, 209, 211, 212
Dunsmuir and Jackson's 129
Durham Miners' Association 147
Dyer, Colonel 128, 129, 137, 155, 196, 231

Earle's, Messrs at Hull 129
École Centrale of Paris 203
Écoles d'apprentissage 188
Écoles des Arts et Métiers 171, 188
education
  compulsory 163
  continuing 176
  elementary 196, 212, 216
  English 165
  expenditure 169
  funds 172
  further 175, 176, 177
  general 163, 165, 167–8, 172, 196, 205, 233, 244
  government strategy for 14–19, 254–5,
  legislation 234
  primary 179
  remedial 177
  science 165, 169, 170, 171–76
  secondary 212, 213, 220, 222
  secular 185
  separation of work and 206, 216, 241
  state-provided 175
Education Act 1902 220, 221, 228, 243
Education (London) Act 1903 220, 243
EEF *see* Engineering Employers Federation

eight-hour day 132–3
Elcho, Lord 8, 135, 188, 189, 191–92
electro-magnetic tools 23
Elementary School Department 167
Elswick works 122, 130, 155, 226
embourgeoisement 76
Emmott Committee 163, 245
Emmott Report 230, 245, 246
employers
　attitude to technical education 195–232, 234, 241, 244, 251
　control of access to technical education 231, 239, 247, 251
　control of technology 140, 196
　federation 127, 128–30, 144
　militancy 195
　responsibility for technical education 214, 243
　right to manage 238, 248
　rights 131, 136, 142
Employers and Workmen Act of 1875 103
Endowed School Commissioners 167
Enfield Armoury 17, 29, 31, 82, 91
Engels 75, 76, 110
Engineer, The 17, 18, 38, 142, 143
Engineering 133, 140, 187
Engineering Employers' Association Executive Committee 144
Engineering Employers Federation (EEF) 6, 75, 115, 118, 121, 127, 130, 131, 132, 133, 136, 137, 138, 139, 144, 149, 152, 153, 155, 196, 230, 231, 239, 248, 249
　formal proposals 1897 141–44
　manpower study 1976 248, 249
　membership 153
Engineering Industry Training Board (EITB) 10
engineering output 146
Engineers' Society 147
Engineers' Society in Johannesburg 147
en-skilling 118
evening class/es 7, 176, 177, 183, 195, 198, 205, 209, 210, 223, 224, 227, 229, 234, 240, 241, 246
Exhibitions, Great Industrial 166
　Artisans' Reports 185, 187
　jurors' reports 166
　London, 1851 166, 167, 168
　Paris, 1867 36, 166, 170, 185, 201

Universal Exhibition, Paris, 1900 40, 50
exports, engineering 135

Factory Act 91, 152
Fairbairn 11
Federated Employers 67
Federation of British Industries (FBI) 245
Ferranti, Sebastian de 139, 140
Finniston Inquiry 249, 250–51, 252
Finsbury Technical College 201, 203, 204–7, 209, 210, 241
　class differentiation 210
　day classes 205, 206
　evening classes 205–6, 241
firearm production 30, 32
Fisher 244, 245, 251
fitters 99, 100, 101
fitting 99, 100–102
foreign competition 162, 164, 166, 198, 246
foreman 56, 61, 65, 87, 90, 91, 94, 96, 97
　attitudes to technical education 222, 223
　functional 56, 57–8, 90
　non-union 127
Forster, W.E. 201
Fowler, John, Engineers, Leeds 86
Fowler, Secretary of State for Employment 251
fragmentation 64, 65, 66
Frankland 170, 176
Free Labour Association 145
Free Labour Protection Association 135
free market 201, 212, 230, 234, 241, 242, 243, 244, 251, 255
funding for technical education 185, 188, 190, 191, 193, 197, 212, 214, 217, 244, 247, 250, 253

gang 87, 91, 93
Gasworkers and General Labourers' Union 147
gauges 87, 140, 236
　plug 29, 30
　ring 29, 30
　standard 28
　workshop 29
gauging 236

INDEX

General Electric Company 148
General Federation of Trade Unions 245
General Workers Union 238–9
Gilbreth 22
girls, employment of 99–100, 237
Gladstone government 198
Glennies, W. 153
Globe, The 190–91
Gompers, Samuel 63
grants 168, 199, 217, 250
Great Strike and Lockout of 1897–98, 7, 41, 56, 67, 68, 72, 80, 96, 115, 118, 122, 124–61, 178, 181, 191, 194, 195, 196, 197, 201, 228, 230, 233, 234, 235, 238, 240, 241, 242, 243, 245
  financial aspects 135–6
  implications 149–50
  Press reaction 136–7
Greenwood & Batley 10
Guile 79

Hadow Report 199
handymen 149
Hans Renold Ltd. 225
Hardy, Keir 134, 136, 138, 140, 144
Harpers Ferry 74, 75
Harrap 62
Hart-Dyke, W. 216
helpers 117
Herbert of Coventry 10, 54
High Speed Steel (HSS) 39, 47, 50, 51, 63, 69, 238
horizontal boring machine 20–21
  work sequence 21
House of Commons 116, 172, 188, 200, 201, 211, 215, 216
House of Lords 163
Howell, George 109
human capital theory 107, 108–9
Huxley, Thomas H. 3, 8, 76, 165, 174, 176, 177, 193, 205, 233, 241, 247

ideology
  missionary or reformist 190
  of control 150, 238
  of production 42, 57, 124–5, 144, 163, 194, 195, 230, 239, 240, 244, 246, 255
  of Protestantism 184
  idling time 34–5

indenture 103, 104, 115, 246
Independent Labour Party 156
individual negotiation 141, 142
Inquiry
  of 1868 154
  1881–84 197, 214, 223
Inquiry Note 128
Institute of Civil Engineers 224
Institute of Electrical Engineers (IEE) 250
Institution of Mechanical Engineers 213, 222, 223, 250
  Inquiry and report 223, 224, 240
integrated work processes 93, 96
intensification of labour 34, 63
interchangeability
  of labour 236–7
  of parts 11, 27, 29, 55, 58, 74, 81, 99, 101, 107, 236–7
inter-union rivalries 152
Iron Trades Employers' Association (ITEA) 128–9, 133, 135, 144, 150
Ironfounders' Society of Great Britain and Ireland 147
ITEA *see* Iron Trades Employers' Association
Iver & Hall, Messrs 94

Japanization of work practices 68
job time comparisons 87
Joint Committee of Trades 132, 133, 134, 144
Joint Committee of the Allied Unions 144
journeymen 104, 107
Junta, the 78, 79, 184, 235

Kelly's Directory of Merchants, Manufacturers and Trades 9

labour
  blackleg 135, 191
  control over 44, 57, 58, 70, 73, 74, 80, 82, 83, 96
  division of 57, 107, 114, 125, 139
  hierarchy of 78
  pool 141
  power 7, 150, 231
  projections 164
  skilled *see under* skilled workers
  surplus 124

undifferentiated 127
unionised 78
Labor Committee of Congress 59
Labour Leader 134
labour-process theories 239
laissez-faire 163, 200, 219, 225, 234, 243, 246
LASER 253
lathe
  capstan 17, 149
  centre 17, 25
  turret 17, 31, 36–9, 41, 124, 148, 149, 152
  vertical 20
  workers 100
LCC *see* London County Council
leading hand 90
leadscrews 25
Learning Credits 255
Leicester Iron Trades Employers' Association 133
length
  of working day 195, 196
  of working life 153
Liberal Party 76, 110, 165, 168
limitation of hours 129
Link-Belt Engineering Company 18, 53, 63
Livery Companies 189, 194, 198, 201–203, 207, 228
  survey of technical education provision 201–203, 211
local authorities 243, 244, 245, 250
Local Enterprise Companies (LECs) 252
Local Government Act of 1888 215, 219, 220
Local Taxation (Customs and Excise) Act, 1890 188, 219–20, 221, 228
lockout 98, 131, 133, 135, 138
locomotive
  frame plates 23
  tyres 20
London and Provincial Society of Coppersmiths 132
London Carpenters 78
London County Council 229
  Technical Education Committee 118, 214, 227; inquiry and report 1906 119, 227–31; research 1909 228; Skilled Employment Committee 227

London Society of Compositors 147
London Society of Drillers 132
London Workingmen's Association 79

MacDonald 146
Macdonald, Ramsay 152
machine
  boys 152
  manning 67, 77, 96, 107, 124, 132, 133, 148–9, 152, 195, 196, 230, 234, 236, 238, 239
  men 95, 152
  minder 34, 62, 65, 95, 98
  minding 34, 149
  Question 56
  tenders 117
  tending 41, 94
  typology of functions 41
machine tools 198
  causes of failure 46
  classification 16–18
  cutting speeds 50–51
  cutting variables 59
  design 238
  industry composition 9
  manual control 24
  object of 42
  operation sequence 13–16
  performance 50, 51
  variables in cutting process 42, 44
machines
  automatic 31, 38, 41, 56, 65, 73, 81, 119, 149, 235, 236
  self-acting 96, 111, 115
Magnus, Philip 203, 207, 211, 216
Manchester District Engineering Employers Association 131
Manchester District Engineering Trades Association 139
manifesto, engineering employers' 136, 137–41
Mann 132
Marx, Karl 33, 41, 68, 156, 175
mass-produced products 26
mass production 30, 74, 81
materials in engineering production 12–13
Mather and Platt, Oldham 225, 240
Mather, William 163
Maudslay, Henry 1, 11, 18, 20, 24, 25, 26, 28, 31, 39, 50, 69, 106

mechanical engineering industry 6–7, 9–10
  England 64
  range of machines 1860–1910 22–3
  workers employed in 6
Mechanics' Institute 174
metrology 11, 26, 65, 69, 99, 113, 235, 236, 238
micrometer wheel 28
middle-class values 76
Midvale Steel Company 43, 44, 48, 58, 60, 63, 66
militancy
  of skilled workers 67
  trade union 79
  untrained workers 114
Mill, John Stuart 163–4
Mill Sawyers' Association 147
Modern Apprenticeships 253, 254
Morley 191
Muir 11
Muir, Wm. 149
multi-tool cutting 38
Mundella 76, 211
Mushet, Robert 46, 47, 48
Mushet steel 53

Nasmyth 1, 11, 25, 31, 33, 36, 39, 61, 69, 74, 103, 107, 111, 112, 117, 118, 230, 236, 237
National Association for the Promotion of Technical and Secondary Education (NAPTSE) 214, 216, 218
National Free Labour Association 191
National Targets for Education and Training 252, 254
National Vocational Qualification (NVQ) 254
Naval Construction and Armaments Company, Barrow 130
Nicholson, Sir Bryan 252
night school 93
Niles-Bement-Pond Co. 20
Niles Tool Works 19
Noble, Captain Andrew 8, 9, 112, 113, 114, 117, 122, 151, 152, 153, 196, 230, 231
non-union labour 98, 128, 129
non-unionised workers 80, 111, 117, 118, 125, 126

North-East Coast Association 129, 130, 131
North Western Association 130
Northampton Institute in Clerkenwell 38
Novo steel 52–3

Odger 79
Operative Bricklayers Society 109, 147
overtime 94, 126, 129, 141, 196

part-time technical education 7–8, 12, 82, 94, 96, 97, 148, 165, 175, 176, 198, 227, 246
  day study 228, 241, 243, 246
  evening-class 234, 240
Pattern Makers 133, 140
payment-by-results system 199, 200, 208, 217, 255
Penrhyn quarrymen 147
Percy, Lord Eustace 162–3, 246
piecemaster system 81, 90, 91–92, 96
piece-rate system 60
piece-rate differential 61, 88
piecework 141, 142
  system 38, 81–92, 96, 97, 175, 223, 235
  unions and 89–92
Platt Bros of Oldham, Messrs 111
Platt Works 94
Playfair, Lyon 3, 8, 76, 165, 168, 170, 171, 172, 174, 175, 176, 193, 195, 200, 205, 217, 233, 241, 247
Poor Law Commission 1909 151, 152
Potter, George 78, 79
Pratt, Hodgson 191
Pratt & Whitney 37
precision measurement 65, 69, 70, 102, 106, 237
premium system of wage payment 116
Protestant ethic 185

railway
  engineering 23
  workshops 91
Randall 193
rate fixing, in piece work 87–8
religion 185
respectability 109, 110
Responsible Autonomy 65
Reynolds Newspaper 141
Robinson 112, 117, 144, 151

Robbins 247
Robbins & Lawrence of Vermont 17
Rock Island Arsenal 62, 63
Roscoe, H. E. 165, 211, 215, 216, 233
Rowan Company 82
Rowan, R. J. 83, 84
Royal Arsenal at Woolwich 30
Royal Commission of Inquiry
　1851 195
　1868 154, 164
　1893 113
　into the Depression of Trade, 1886 4, 121
　on craft training 1881-84 218
　on Labour 1892 196
　on Small Arms 1854 107, 164, 240
　on Technical Instruction 1884 3, 164, 203, 204, 210-14, 215, 221, 228, 231, 240, 245
　on the Poor Laws 1893 120, 121
　on the provision of technical education in England 1881-84 121, 166
　on Trade Disputes 152
　on Trade Unions 1867 79, 80, 98, 109, 111, 121, 192

Sadler, M. E. 224, 225, 226
　1907 enquiry 225, 240, 241
Samuelson Commission of 1868 174
Samuelson Commission 1884 208, 216
Samuelson Inquiry 1881 163
Samuelson, Sir Bernhard 163, 165, 189, 211
scholarships 199, 219, 231
School Boards 215, 220
School Enquiry Commission 1868 215
School of Mines 168, 174, 188
schools
　continuation 177, 183
　elementary 180, 184, 199, 205, 216, 224
　endowed 168
　factory and industrial 168
　military and regimental 168
　naval and ship 168
　pupils in 222
　science 169, 174
　secondary 171, 222
　technical 188, 228, 244
　trade 203

union 168
workhouse 168
Science and Art Department 199, 208, 217, 219
science teaching 196, 199, 200
　government control 199-201
　state support 200
'scientific management' 3, 40, 44, 63, 68, 74, 107, 238
Scott-Russell, John 3, 170, 171, 172, 174, 175, 176, 188, 233, 241, 247
screw-thread 27-8
　English system 19
　production 18-20
　standardised system, US 19
Select Committee
　1854 31, 36
　1868 175
　1872 195
　of Inquiry 172, 189
　on Science and Technology 1976 247
　on Science Instruction 170-71
self-acting mechanisms 36
self-help 78, 200, 201, 214, 215, 219
Sellers Company, William, of Philadelphia 18, 19, 44
Sellicks 141
Senate Commission 1911 59
sewing machines 81
Shipbuilders Association 133
shipbuilding 23, 145
Shoreditch Technical Institute 227
short-termism 164, 180, 234, 242, 243, 244, 255
Siemens 137, 212
Singer Sewing Machine Company 81
skill 2, 12, 24, 32, 34, 65, 70, 72, 99, 118, 175, 179, 233, 234, 236
　boundaries 151
　concept of 105-8, 113
　credentials 107
　dequalification 180
　differentials 95, 154
　redefinition of 75, 238, 241, 255
　specialisation 116
　transference 42
　transmission 104
skilled workers 31, 32, 34, 42, 50, 55, 56, 62, 63, 65, 69, 70, 72, 76, 81, 102, 110, 112, 251
　dequalification 124

INDEX

downgrading 11
supply 242, 249, 254
skills
    company-specific 107, 139, 150, 178, 248, 253, 256
    craft 75, 100
    decomposition of 56, 141, 148, 163, 244, 247
    deconstruction of 43
    marketability 239
    tacit 106
    transferable 252
Slagg, John 211
slide rest 20, 24–6, 37, 99
Slide Rules 56, 58–60
small arms industry 81
small firm 6, 9, 10, 240
    attitude to technical education 240
    training provision and facilities 242, 252
Smiles, Samuel 25
Smith, Daniel, & Co. 126
Smith, Llewellyn 118
Smith, Swire 211, 216
Social Democratic Federation 135
socialism 139, 191, 192
Society of Arts 172, 183, 197, 200, 201, 205, 207, 208, 212
    Journal 175, 200
soldiering 61
solidarity 146–8
Solly, Henry 186, 189, 190, 191, 192, 205
South Kensington
    Department of Science and Art 166, 167, 168–70, 190, 220
    Directory 169, 172, 199, 208; examination structure 172; examination supervision 200; science scheme 172, 200, 212
South London Technical Art School 203
Spon's 23
Springfield Armory 29
standards 11, 12, 30, 43, 55, 58, 65, 101, 107, 237, 238
standardisation 26, 29, 55, 81, 99, 107, 113, 236, 240
status
    differences 106
    loss of 112
    occupational 108

Statute of Apprentices of 1557 103, 118
Steam Engine Makers 132
stockpiling 38
stopwatch 62, 63
strike
    first major engineering strike, 1852 6, 8, 72, 110, 124, 127, 128, 230, 234, 235
    longest, Sunderland 1883 128–9
    pay 135, 139
strike-breaking, employers' tactics 98, 135
strikes 72, 107, 113, 130, 135, 152, 193, 210
substitution 42, 229
    of juveniles for adults 94
    of labour 126, 132, 138, 141, 153, 164, 176, 181, 183, 195, 196, 197
    of untrained workers for skilled 4, 5, 8, 11, 31, 42, 55, 56, 64, 66, 67, 74–5, 96, 125, 127, 129, 134
    skill 124, 148, 154
Sunday school 8, 184–6
Sunderland Forge and Engineering Company 130, 131, 132

Taunton, Lord 170, 171
Tawney, R. H. 198
Taylor, F. W. 3, 18, 20, 22, 39, 40–70, 73, 74, 88, 90, 102, 182, 196, 237, 238, 255
'Taylor system' 59, 63
Taylorism 66, 68, 69
teachers
    science 172, 174, 200
    technical 188, 207–8, 214, 217–9
teaching profession 167
TECs *see* Training and Enterprise Councils
technical colleges 176, 197
technical education 76, 77, 79, 80, 82, 93, 94, 96, 97, 105, 111, 116, 121, 124, 155, 176–7, 184, 196, 220, 222, 233–56
    administration 215
    and government 201, 243, 251
    and science 171–76, 198–9
    day-release 176, 188, 222, 223, 224, 226
    definition 162

employer philosophy 241
evolutionary model 165
facilities and assistance offered by firms 225, 226
incentives to employers 247
inducements by company 225
legislation 197, 200
management 213
market principles 164
national system 162–94, 203, 214, 233, 242
separate from the workplace 177–8, 181, 183
state responsibility 198
tripartism 245–7
working-class initiatives 178–80
Technical Instruction Act 1889 3, 116, 157, 163, 165, 168, 188, 194, 215, 216–17, 219, 221, 228, 229, 231, 240
Technical Instruction Act 1891 219
Technical Instruction Committees 243
Technische Hochschule 213
technology
  as autonomous 73
  definition 208, 229
Terms of Settlement 122, 125, 145, 148, 155, 161, 182, 197, 230, 231, 239, 242, 248
theory, separate from practice 175, 209–10
Thompson, S. P. 201
Thornton, Professor 247
time studies 63
Times, The 136–7, 138, 142, 170, 201, 208
tolerances 12, 27, 100
toolroom 22, 55, 102, 237
tool-setters 37
tool steels
  alloys 47
  composition 46–8
  cutting rate 42
  developments 69
  experiments 48–50
  machining stresses 53
  problems 46
Trades Councils 79, 214, 220
  London 109, 128, 146, 192
Trades' Conference, London, 1867 109
Trades Guild of Learning 179, 189–90

Trades Union Congress (TUC) 7, 108, 110, 115, 116, 185, 196, 201, 214
  1874 179, 193
  and the apprenticeship system 180–81
  first 5, 178
  training 58, 66, 72, 80, 82, 93, 102, 105, 107, 111, 112, 114, 117, 121, 141, 151, 155–6, 171, 212, 237, 242, 246, 247, 250
  company-specific 239
  craft 163
  factory-based 221
  for internal labour market 248
  formal agreements 254
  lack of 56
  of children 119
  of young workers 124, 150
  on-the-job 81
  structured system 179
  trainee system 155
Training and Enterprise Councils (TECs) 252, 253
true plane 26
turners 100
twilight class 227

unemployment 120, 134, 145, 153
unionised labour 6, 39, 110
unions 7, 76, 80, 96, 97, 128–30, 182, 241, 253
  amalgamated 124
  attitude to technical education 181–83
  histories 77
  levies 147, 148
  membership 128
  officials 62
  sanctions 110
United Alkali Co. 226
United Kingdom Coachmakers' Society 147
United Machine Workers Association 132
United Society of Smiths and Hammermen 132
unskilled labour 19, 24, 31, 33, 37, 39, 41, 50, 62, 65, 67, 70, 72, 76, 77, 95, 98, 101, 102, 110, 124, 125, 131, 138, 140, 239
Unwin, W. C. 214
US manufacturing 9

Vickers Maxim 9, 53, 226, 240

wage
  calculations 143
  differentials 32–3, 109
  rates 130, 147
Waterlow, Sydney 204
Watertown Arsenal 59, 62, 68
Webb, Sidney 118–21, 227, 228
Webbs, the 75, 76, 78, 79, 181
Weights and Measures Act 1878 28
Wemyss, Lord 8, 135, 188
Westinghouse Company 10
whisky money 219, 220
White, J. Maunsel 48, 59
Whitworth, Joseph 1, 3, 11, 12, 19, 24, 25, 26–31, 36, 39, 55, 69, 74, 75, 87, 100, 101, 102, 106, 107, 113, 118, 140, 182, 231, 236, 237, 238, 240
  measuring machine 27–8
  scholarships 11, 229, 231
Wicksteed, J. Hartley 224
Wigram 86
wire-feeding 38
Woodall, William 211
Woolwich Arsenal 91
work
  organisation 68, 142
  reorganisation 73, 83, 84, 102, 137, 141, 154, 164, 185, 195, 233, 234, 239, 241, 242, 255
worker
  solidarity 61
  subordination 73

vertical mobility 7
workforce size 9–10
working-class
  children 183
  culture 184
  education 213
  ideology 184
  influence on technical education 183–4
  reaction 66
  values 78
Workingman's Club 8
Working Men's Club and Institute Union (WMC&IU) 8, 186, 187, 191
Working Men's Educational Union 186–7
Workingmen's School Union 179
Workingmen's Technical Education Union 215
Workmen's Technical Education Committee (WTEC) 187–91, 193, 203, 221
Workmen's Technical Education Society (WTES) 188
Workmen's Technical Education Union 190, 191, 192, 197
Workmen's Technical School Union 188–9
workshop
  management 102
  organisation 22, 139, 143
  reorganisation 42, 140, 236, 237
  training 203, 207, 228
Wright 76, 109